THE CAMBRIDGE COMPANION TO

WILLIAM BLAKE

EDITED BY

MORRIS EAVES

Department of English
University of Rochester

CAMBRIDGE
UNIVERSITY PRESS

PUBLISHED BY THE PRESS SYNDICATE OF THE UNIVERSITY OF CAMBRIDGE
The Pitt Building, Trumpington Street, Cambridge CB2 1RP, United Kingdom

CAMBRIDGE UNIVERSITY PRESS
The Edinburgh Building, Cambridge, CB2 2RU, UK
40 West 20th Street, New York, NY 10011-4211, USA
477 Williamstown Road, Port Melbourne, VIC 3207, Australia
Ruiz de Alarcón 13, 28014 Madrid, Spain
Dock House, The Waterfront, Cape Town 8001, South Africa

http://www.cambridge.org

First published 2003

Printed in the United Kingdom at the University Press, Cambridge

Typeface Sabon 10/13 pt   *System* LATEX 2$_\varepsilon$ [TB]

A catalogue record for this book is available from the British Library

Library of Congress Cataloguing in Publication data

The Cambridge companion to William Blake / edited by Morris Eaves.
(Cambridge companions to literature)
Includes bibliographical references and index.
1. Blake, William, 1757–1827 – Criticism and interpretation – Handbooks, manuals, etc.
I. Eaves, Morris II. Series.
PR4147.C36 2002
821'.7 – dc21 2002067068

ISBN 0 521 78147 7 hardback
ISBN 0 521 78677 0 paperback

CONTENTS

CONTENTS

ILLUSTRATIONS

NOTES ON CONTRIBUTORS

DAVID BINDMAN (Durning-Lawrence Professor of the History of Art, University College London) is the author and editor of numerous works on Blake and Hogarth. He curated *The Shadow of the Guillotine* at the British Museum and co-authored *Roubiliac and the Eighteenth-Century Monument.* His latest publication is *Ape to Apollo: Aesthetics and the Idea of Race in the Eighteenth Century.*

MORRIS EAVES (Professor of English, University of Rochester) is author of *William Blake's Theory of Art* and *The Counter-Arts Conspiracy: Art and Industry in the Age of Blake*; and co-editor of *Romanticism and Contemporary Criticism, The Early Illuminated Books* in *Blake's Illuminated Books* (Blake Trust), *Blake/An Illustrated Quarterly*, and the William Blake Archive.

ROBERT N. ESSICK (Professor of English, University of California, Riverside) is the author of several books on Blake, including *William Blake Printmaker, The Separate Plates of William Blake: A Catalogue, William Blake and the Language of Adam*, and *William Blake's Commercial Book Illustrations*; and co-editor of *The Early Illuminated Books* and *Milton* in *Blake's Illuminated Books* (Blake Trust) and of the William Blake Archive.

ALEXANDER GOURLAY (Rhode Island School of Design) studies and writes about Blake and Hogarth, their responses to their times, and their relationship to other literature and art.

NELSON HILTON (Head of the English Department, University of Georgia) is author of *Literal Imagination: Blake's Vision of Words*, editor of *Essential Articles for the Study of William Blake, 1970–1984*, co-editor of *Unnam'd Forms: Blake and Textuality*, review editor for *Blake/An Illustrated Quarterly*, and webitor of the Blake Digital Text Project.

MARY LYNN JOHNSON (formerly Adjunct Professor of English and Special Assistant to the President, University of Iowa) is co-author of Blake's *Four Zoas: The Design of a Dream*. Among her current projects are an interlocking series of articles on the multinational publication history of J. C. Lavater's *Physiognomy* and an update, with her husband John E. Grant, of their Norton Critical Edition, *Blake's Poetry and Designs*.

ANDREW LINCOLN (School of English and Drama, Queen Mary, University of London) is author of *Spiritual History: A Reading of William Blake's Vala, or the Four Zoas*, and editor of *Songs of Innocence and of Experience* in *Blake's Illuminated Books* (Blake Trust).

SAREE MAKDISI (Associate Professor of English and Comparative Literature, University of Chicago) is the author of *Romantic Imperialism* and *William Blake and the Impossible History of the 1790s*.

JON MEE (Margaret Candfield Fellow in English, University College, Oxford) is the author of *Dangerous Enthusiasm: William Blake and the Culture of Radicalism in the 1790s* and a co-editor of the *Oxford Companion to the Romantic Age*. He has written widely on recent Indian fiction in English and on the cultural politics of the Romantic period. He is completing *Enthusiasm, Romanticism, and Regulation: The Policing of Culture in the Romantic Period*.

ROBERT M. RYAN (Professor of English and Director of the Graduate Program in Liberal Studies, Rutgers University, Camden) is the author of *Keats: The Religious Sense* and *The Romantic Reformation: Religious Politics in English Literature, 1789–1824*, and co-editor of *The Persistence of Poetry: Bicentennial Essays on Keats*.

DAVID SIMPSON (Professor of English and G. B. Needham Fellow, University of California, Davis) is the author of books on Blake, Wordsworth, British and German Romanticism, American English, and other subjects. His latest is *Situatedness; or Why We Keep Saying Where We're Coming From*.

JOSEPH VISCOMI (James G. Kenan Professor of English Literature, University of North Carolina at Chapel Hill) is author of *Prints by Blake and His Followers* and *Blake and the Idea of the Book*; and co-editor of *The Early Illuminated Books* and *Milton* in *Blake's Illuminated Books* (Blake Trust) and of the William Blake Archive.

AILEEN WARD (Albert Schweitzer Professor of the Humanities, Emeritus, New York University) is author of *John Keats: The Making of a Poet* and of articles and reviews on British Romantic writers, and editor of selected works by Blake, Keats, and De Quincey. She is currently at work on a biography of Blake.

SUSAN J. WOLFSON (Professor of English, Princeton University) is the author of *Formal Charges: The Shaping of Poetry in British Romanticism*, and co-editor of *The Romantics and Their Contemporaries*, which includes the only letterpress edition of Blake to follow the lineation of his plates. She is the editor of *The Cambridge Companion to John Keats* and a contributor to several other Romantic-era volumes in this series.

ACKNOWLEDGMENTS

A book as various as this Companion to William Blake needs a large injection of editorial consistency. That came first from Kari Kraus and Wayne Ripley at the University of Rochester, who gave their knowledge of Blake, their sharp eyes, and their editorial skills to the project in its late stages when it and I needed their help most. Sarah Jones and Katherine Ekstrom arrived just in time to get the final script over the Cambridge threshold. Linda Bree and her colleagues took it smoothly and expertly from there. All of us together could succeed only because every one of the original contributors were true collaborators – responsive, flexible, and patient. Any collaborative abilities I may have, I learned by imitating my role models: my wife Georgia, my sons Dashiell and Obadiah, and their partners Kimmarie and Karina, whose collaborations inspire, entertain, and instruct. I mean every word.

ABBREVIATIONS

Note: Blake often made several copies of his illuminated books, and those copies often differ from one another in significant ways. Scholars distinguish those copies by assigning letters of the alphabet to them: thus, for example, *The Marriage of Heaven and Hell* copy F. Sometimes the order of the pages (called "plates" because they were printed from engravers' copper plates) differs from copy to copy, and scholars occasionally indicate alternative page ordering in square brackets: thus, for example, *Jerusalem* plate 44 [30].

anno.   Blake's annotations to [Reynolds, etc.]
ARO   *All Religions are One*
BL   *The Book of Los*
BR   G. E. Bentley, Jr., *Blake Records* (Oxford: Clarendon Press, 1969)
Butlin   Martin Butlin, *The Paintings and Drawings of William Blake* (New Haven and London: Yale University Press, 1981), 2 vols. References are to catalogue entry numbers rather than page numbers.
DC   *A Descriptive Catalogue of Pictures*
E   David V. Erdman, ed., *The Complete Poetry and Prose of William Blake* (1965), rev. edn. (Berkeley and Los Angeles: University of California Press, 1988).
EG   *The Everlasting Gospel*
Essick   either Robert N. Essick, *William Blake's Commercial Book Illustrations* (New York: Putnam's; Oxford: Clarendon Press, 1991); or *The Separate Plates of William Blake: A Catalogue* (Princeton: Princeton University Press, 1983); as indicated.
FR   *The French Revolution*
FZ   *The Four Zoas*
J   *Jerusalem*
MHH *The Marriage of Heaven and Hell*
NNR   *There is No Natural Religion*

PA	*Public Address*
PS	*Poetical Sketches*
SE	*Songs of Experience*
SI	*Songs of Innocence*
SIE	*Songs of Innocence and of Experience*
SL	*The Song of Los*
VDA	*Visions of the Daughters of Albion*
VLJ	*A Vision of the Last Judgment*

CHRONOLOGY

AILEEN WARD

1757	Born in London, 28 November, at 28 Broad Street, Westminster
1768	Enters Pars's Drawing School
1772	Apprenticed to James Basire, engraver
1779	Enters Royal Academy Schools; meets Flaxman, Stothard, and Cumberland
1780	Begins engraving for booksellers; takes part in Gordon Riots
1780–85	Exhibits seven watercolors at the Royal Academy
1782	Marries Catherine Boucher
1783	*Poetical Sketches* privately printed
1784	Opens printshop with James Parker; writes *An Island in the Moon* (1783–84)
1787	Death of Robert Blake; meets Henry Fuseli
1788	First works in illuminated printing: three religious tractates; annotates Swedenborg (c. 1788–90)
1789	Attends first General Conference of the New Jerusalem Church; *Tiriel, Songs of Innocence, The Book of Thel*
1790	Moves to Lambeth; *The Marriage of Heaven and Hell* (1790–92?)
1791	*The French Revolution*
1793	*For Children: The Gates of Paradise; Visions of the Daughters of Albion; America: A Prophecy*
1794	*Europe: A Prophecy; The First Book of Urizen; Songs of Experience*
1795	*The Song of Los, The Book of Los, The Book of Ahania;* the Large Color Prints
1795–97	Designs and engraves *Night Thoughts* illustrations for Edwards
1797–1808?	Composes *Vala, or The Four Zoas*

1821	Moves to 3 Fountain Court, the Strand; begins painting final (unfinished) version of *The Last Judgment* (1821?–27)
1822	*The Ghost of Abel*
1823–26	Illustrates the Book of Job in twenty-one plates for Linnell
1824	Illustrates *Pilgrim's Progress;* meets Samuel Palmer and the "Ancients"
1825–27	Illustrates Dante for Linnell
1827	Dies, 12 August

I

MORRIS EAVES

Introduction: to paradise the hard way

I recently heard one poet praise another for achieving "balance between re-straint and revelation." Few would think to offer that praise to Blake. James Joyce's characterization would be more applicable: "Armed with this two-edged sword, the art of Michelangelo and the revelations of Swedenborg, Blake killed the dragon of experience and natural wisdom, and, by minimizing space and time and denying the existence of memory and the senses, he tried to paint his works on the void of the divine bosom."[1] Though wrong in some details, Joyce's characterization conveys well the extravagance, even the impossibility, of Blake's ambitions, which has played a major part in the attraction–repulsion response that has always dogged him. His poetry risks every kind of excess to achieve revelation. It brushes aside elements that might restrain it, including formal poetic conventions that help to shape and contain the drive to revelation. Enveloping the stressful, straining poems are the handsome, odd, bizarre, grotesque, weird, lovely images, which supply no balancing force.

William Blake testified that "a Great Majority of Fellow Mortals... can Elucidate My Visions & Particularly they have been Elucidated by Children..." (E 703). They would have been very exceptional children. Many original artists are hard to understand, but the difficulty of Blake can seem of another order. Hence the many passing references to it in the present volume, which is designed, accordingly, to be a helpmate in your early encounters. The basic strategy behind this Cambridge Companion is to respond to the difficulties with a variety of critical and historical explanations from several perspectives which seem to offer the most hope of catching Blake in the act of meaning something we can understand. The coverage is as broad and various as it can be under the circumstances, limited only by the usual practical constraints.

Simplifications

If the prospect of Blake's difficulty alarms you initially, you should be aware of the many well-trodden ways to sample simpler Blakes. Two techniques, especially, have proven their value for generations of readers. (For reasons that will become apparent, "readers" is a grossly inadequate term for Blake's audience, but I shall use it as convenient shorthand throughout.) One: stick to the shortest and simplest works. Two: parse them into their constituent parts, usually words and images, and keep those segregated. Blake is simplest when the two techniques are combined.

The venturesome newcomer can "read" Blake's two-part collection, *Songs of Innocence and of Experience*, as Blake originally published them: words combined with images in a graphic medium he called "Illuminated Printing" (E 693). But the *Songs* have been most often approached as short poems and appreciated by readers of literary inclination for a rare combination of simplicity with formal variety and lyrical intensity. *The Tyger* (E 24–25) may be the most anthologized poem in English, and several others from the collection are transplanted nearly as often. The *Songs* have that wondrous characteristic that even great poems can only occasionally claim: they are enjoyable at any level of scrutiny. Their concentrated music makes them sound good when read aloud the first time and the fiftieth; most of them make some kind of sense right away, while repeated readings yield new insights. And they read remarkably well as a collection; their multiple interconnections can make them seem a hall of word-mirrors, each refracting at least several of the others.

But it is also possible to appreciate the original pages of any illuminated book simply as a set of small-scale pictures. When the visual design is the main object of attention, the poem is perceived as one visual element among other visual elements organized in the space of the page to satisfy the desires and habits of the eye. This is a very old method of appreciating Blake. Since his contemporaries knew him primarily for his images, they often came upon his work from this angle – not in the search for words in literary forms, as a bookbuyer might, but for images in artistic forms – and purchased them with this in mind. Joseph Viscomi has emphasized that Blake's own treatment of his illuminated books changed between the 1790s, when he tended to favor book-like formats and light coloring, and later years, when he started treating them as portfolios of highly finished images, more picture than book.

Either of these searches for a more accessible Blake, by the verbal or the visual road, can be extended. He left manuscripts of unpublished writings that include (to the surprise of readers who come expecting the pious devotion of a religious poet) big helpings of scurrilous, angry, naughty, and hilarious literary efforts in a heady genre stew of epigrams, jingles, shorter poems, longer ones, prose and verse satires, essays, letters, and marginal comments in books, among others. Likewise, on the visual side it is entirely possible to explore Blake's considerable lifetime output of pictures in several media and relish the creative abundance of powerful and striking ways of picturing physical and mental worlds in two dimensions. His longest illuminated book, *Jerusalem*, comprises 100 plates that can seem, from the verbal standpoint, utterly dominated by the thousands of lines of poetry and prose. But when laid out in full sequence on the walls of an art exhibition, those plates create an array of visual innovations strong enough to stun the eye into the realization that Blake was one of the most inventive artists who ever lived. We can experience this without reading a word of *Jerusalem*. Moreover, he produced many other works that will repay the efforts of the eye through far more conventional and familiar subject matter, such as his many watercolors in illustration of the Bible or of Milton's poems. Many have regarded Blake's late series of line engravings, *Illustrations of the Book of Job* (1825), as his masterpiece. The Job series forms a natural cluster with other late graphic projects, such as the exquisite shadow-world of Blake's miniature Virgil illustrations (1820), his only wood engravings, and the fine drawings and engravings of the extensive Dante project that he was still working on when he died in 1827.

Complications

But no matter which route you take, if you travel far enough, the wide, well-paved roads will dwindle, the going will get rough, and you will arrive at a mountain of difficulty. Traditionally the difficult Blake has been identified with his so-called "prophecies," a term harvested from the titles of two illuminated books (composed, along with most of the others, in the 1790s) but then applied generically to all the more narrative works in illuminated printing through to the most ambitious and extensive ones, *Milton* and *Jerusalem*. From there "prophecies" is easily and naturally broadened further to cover unpublished earlier and later works such as *Tiriel*, *The French Revolution*, and *The Four Zoas*. Having gone this far to make Blake an obscure prophet, it is tempting to throw in other items, such as *The Mental Traveller*, that seem to be in one way or another products of his lifelong effort to concoct an original but universal myth that would retell the story of human existence so as to reveal its fundamental meanings.

I can think of no adequate word to characterize this, the quite extraordinary Blakean world of newly minted characters and places – Oothoon, Urthona, Enitharmon, Urizen, Golgonooza, Udan-Adan, Bowlahoola,

Entuthon-Benython – who appear alongside familiar-sounding ones – Albion, Eden, Jerusalem, London, Jesus, Satan – and real-life entities in partial disguise – Hyle for Blake's erstwhile patron William Hayley, Hand for the Hunt brothers who edited a magazine critical of Blake – and those using their own first names – brothers William and Robert Blake. These furnish an extensive but dense web of plots that unfold in a multidimensional, multimedia space where (ultimately, in the later developments) much attention is given to the symmetrical arrangements of a "fourfold" fictional universe – furnished with four Zoas, four faces, four levels, four stages, four compass points, four gates, etc. – penetrated by vortexes in an elaborate game of Identities and Selfhoods subjected to conversions, redemptions, and cosmic marriages. Here the world we may think we know, the London and Felpham of real people, streets, and houses and the Britain of real mountains, rivers, towns, trees, birds, and cathedrals, are mapped onto and against the Jerusalem and New Jerusalem of the Bible.

Such elaborate and apparently precise symmetries have always tantalized some members of Blake's audience into searching for the system that presumably produced them. Even readers who are usually wary of such aggressive private mythmaking ultimately find it impossible to avoid completely. Yet here again the two techniques of simplification can be effective: stick to the shorter, simpler prophecies (*The Marriage of Heaven and Hell* has been a favorite entry point) and focus attention on either words or images. But, because he had unprecedented capabilities of creating difficulty wherever he went, a few even of Blake's *Songs* display in miniature the puzzling quality that has stumped readers of the "prophecies." *The Tyger* reads hypnotically, but it is tough to explain satisfactorily in any terms other than its own (it has inspired many elaborate commentaries).

Other notable examples of great difficulty in a small space include the pair of poems that introduce *Songs of Experience*: *Introduction* and *Earth's Answer* (E 18–19), which make it apparent that Blake is envisioning even his short lyrics of social criticism, such as *London* or *The Chimney Sweeper*, as well as his psychological fables, such as *A Poison Tree*, as components in an evolving narrative framework of fall and redemption that is applicable on several interpenetrating levels – individual, social, religious, political, artistic, cosmic. Narrative perspectives shift alarmingly as Blake cultivates his extraordinary penchant for telling several stories at once in a system constructed to deliver simultaneously the fall and redemption of a single human life *and* of humankind *and* of a single work of art *and* of Art, etc. But who would know how to read such stories?

Furthermore, the meanings of some of those little poems are quite unstable: *The Sick Rose* is as much riddle as poem; it drives the reader to guess what "rose" and "worm" stand for, but never answers (and readers have kept guessing). *The Chimney Sweeper* and *The Little Black Boy* of *Innocence*, which seem to offer simple religious solace to children in dire situations, may be highly ironic – or not, or they may toggle back and forth in a very Blakean way between contrary perspectives of harsh critique and Christian consolation. *The Little Girl Lost* and *Found* take the form of a brief mythical episode that may or may not be about the family consequences of an adolescent's sexual development; like *Introduction* and *Earth's Answer*, they seem to posit other narratives that are implied but not present.

The pictures could help clarify and stabilize the meanings of the poems – but that, we soon realize, is a drunkard's dream. Instead, the pictures have the maddening habit of multiplying the contested territory of meaning, often of destabilizing it – the little "black" boy can be pictured as white or black depending on the copy. Texts and pictures, despite their presence on the same pretty page, coexist as semi-autonomous strata: rifts and faults in one stratum disrupt the features of the adjacent stratum, making conditions ideal for mental earthquakes. The more closely you scrutinize those little *Songs*, and the further you move out from the words on the page to the designs to other words and other designs in the collection, the larger the contested territory becomes and the higher the level of enigma rises. Such leaks, as it were, around the edges of all simplified approaches are sure indications of their inadequacy: they are critical reductions, and sometimes useful for that, but not critical solutions.

Routines of resistance

Blake's difficulties seem to reside in an impenetrable kernel of meaning at the center of a vast linguistic and pictorial architecture. As the reader circles the core, the architecture of the whole refuses to stand still, appears different from every angle, making orientation a word-by-word, picture-by-picture problem.

The vortex, which Blake grew fond of in his later works, sometimes seems to describe his audience's lot all too well. His reassuring promise to the reader of *Jerusalem* –

> I give you the end of a golden string,
> Only wind it into a ball:
> It will lead you in at Heavens gate,
> Built in Jerusalems wall
>
> (J 77, E 231)

– reminds me of the paradises promised to persuade gullible nineteenth-century travelers to move their lives to the outbacks of Australia or North

America. Blake's pledges to his audience – "Mark well my words! they are of your eternal salvation" (*Milton* 2:25, E 96) – are also claims upon his audience, and such ultimate claims on "your" devotion can leave you feeling hung out to dry, with only yourself to blame for your failures.

His extreme demands have produced a fascinating history of reader resistance and resentment that marks his place in cultural history. These routines of resistance have been remarkably long-lived – they amount to a critical history of encounters with Blake's difficulty – and the repertory of his potential audience and anti-audience remains well stocked with them. A short list of the most revealing begins with the most extreme (but also one of the most common): outright rejection via the accusation of insanity – why else would the works be so far removed in medium, style, and message from the conventional channels through which we make artistic sense? "Perfectly mad," writer Robert Southey's dismissal of *Jerusalem*-in-progress (*BR* 229), was a label applied so often and so painfully that Blake read a book on insanity (E 662), presumably to see if he could locate his own mind somewhere in it.

Other forms of resistance have found in his work the evidence of uneven talents and skills. The closely allied notions that he could conceive but not execute (good ideas, bad technique), or that he could paint but not draw (interesting compositions, awkward figures), have often served as reasons for demotion. Other common criticisms have employed similarly divisive tactics: his poems are better than his images; his images are better than his poems; his early work (more lucid) is better than his later "prophetic" work (obscure, off the rails); or (the most complex assessment), his simple but original early poems are better than the immature and derivative early images, but as the later poems sink into obsessive ranting, his images belatedly shine forth – a chiasmic, or X-shaped, evaluation assembled from the previous two.

These critical formulas have led a double life. They have been offered up as reasons for readers and viewers to restrict attention, but they have also served as useful ways of focusing attention by underwriting the very techniques of simplification with which we began. The process of simplification got well underway during Blake's lifetime, and there are many examples. Anthologists lifted the words of individual poems from the *Songs* from their imagery for reprinting in conventional formats alongside other word-only poems. In the other direction, Blake himself, probably in response to customer requests, separated images from their original texts to make up portfolios of designs. After his death, when his executor Frederick Tatham tried to come up with a way of selling *Jerusalem*, he urged customers to ignore the words and appreciate the sublime images (*BR* 520).

These symptomatic instances became systematic when the principles behind them hardened into editorial procedures. It is one thing to express a preference for poems or images but more consequential to divide, physically, the produce of Blake's imagination into specialized products. The same Victorians who laid the foundations for Blake's successful revival after years of neglect were also the first to see clearly the advantages of isolating the culturally familiar parts of his strange work for delivery to specialized audiences through well-established specialized channels. The most important channel by far was literary. Blake's illuminated works were streamlined for literary transmission by systematically deleting the images and rectifying some unconventional features of the text – Blake's handwriting (transposed into standard type fonts), spelling, grammar, and punctuation – to make his poetry friendlier and more legible. This editorial transformation boosted it out of the twilight zone of painted picture poetry into the cultural daylight of British poetic tradition, and thereby gradually emerged the William Blake who, as a major Romantic poet, earns a place in this Cambridge Companion series.

Editorial simplification also prepared the way for serious study and reflection on a scale previously unthinkable. As W. M. Rossetti wrote in reaction to a nineteenth-century facsimile of *Jerusalem* (1877), "the publication in ordinary book-form, without designs ... of the *Jerusalem* and the other Prophetic Books, is highly to be desired. Difficult under any circumstances, it would be a good deal *less* difficult to read these works in an edition of that kind, with clear print, reasonable division of lines, and the like aids to business-like perusal."[2] Here is the straight road of literacy and legibility. When, after all, did someone first read all the words of *Milton* or *Jerusalem* in sequence – much less read them slowly and thoughtfully? Almost certainly no one in Blake's lifetime ever did, though his wife Catherine may have been exposed to long stretches of recitation. A careful reading probably did not occur until the time of those Victorian rescuers, if then. And no matter how much time they spent with the difficult works, they certainly began to recognize and advertise the *value* of reading them, and hence the value of providing others with readable texts.

Why so difficult?

What do these formulas of resistance, echoed in simplifications, tell us? They depend largely on specialized habits of mind that characterize modern human understanding.

The problem is that Blake is fundamentally resistant to specialization, which puts him at odds with the long list of social routines that it aids and abets: rationalization, scientific thinking, professionalization, industrialization, commercialization, institutionalization, modernization. This is not always strictly speaking Blake's choice: in various ways he participated in his profession, in the marketing and sale of his work, in the spirit of technological innovation. But virtually every attempt he made turned sour for one fundamental reason: he was a synthesizer, and not an encyclopedic one but a mythic or metaphorical one. This involved a rejection of key aspects of modern human life and various "returns" to past states of being, as he imagined them: to religion (from science), to archaic artistic styles (from modern taste), to paradise (from corrupt modern society).

That reductive summary points toward a root cause of Blake's difficulty. His choice, perhaps his destiny, to work as maker of words, maker of images, and crossbreeder of both, amounted to a decision to live in incommensurable neighborhoods of meaning. In doing so he positioned himself facing upstream against the mainstream of modern human understanding, whose bedrock is the principle of specialization as a means of acquiring, organizing, encoding, and transmitting information. He abandoned us in turn to a modern dilemma: can the whole be understood through its parts? Can a simplified, specialized approach ever connect us to the vast and elusive whole that he used his multiple talents to incorporate in one package?

Blake's tangled and troubled relations with the structures of conventional knowledge contributed to his problems and ours. Again, very simply, information as we understand it cannot be efficiently gathered without highly specialized categories that are mirrored in specialized systems of encoding facts, perceptions, and ideas (as images, for instance, and as words). Tongue in cheek, Blake describes how "knowledge is transmitted from generation to generation" when a printing house in hell – his own – is available instead of the usual boringly earthbound ones (MHH 15, E 40). Blake's reader confronts a challenge to the techniques of information management that create familiar circuits of production and reproduction. Blake attempted, ambitiously and perhaps recklessly, to interrupt the ordinary processes of this central dynamic structure by feeding into it complex information that it could only reject or reconfigure. Reactions to Blake often follow from this fundamental incompatibility. His defiance of the institutional structures of knowledge and the technological divisions that correspond to them resulted in unorthodox works that seemed ungainly if not ugly and shocking to his potential audience, who in their aversion have sometimes perceived a mind operating out of control.

The difficulties in taking hold of Blake with conventional categories can be seen in the difficulty of labeling him. You may come to him knowing that he "was" a painter, for instance, or a poet, printmaker, prophet, or visionary. Blake certainly wanted to be taken seriously in all these categories and was distressed whenever others questioned his aspirations to them. He himself put "a Prophecy" in the titles of two works (*Europe: A Prophecy* and *America: A Prophecy*), "Visions" in another (*Visions of the Daughters of Albion*), "a Poem" in a third (*Milton*). And who composes prophetic visions and poems except prophet–visionaries and poets? But then it was not for nothing that he kept having to return to his self-image as John the Baptist, outcast prophet in the wilderness. Blake made a career of being an outsider looking in, an interloper aspiring to legitimate modern vocations (painter, poet) by performing roles of questionable legitimacy (prophet–visionary).

"I know myself both Poet & Painter" (E 730–31), he asserted in response to his sometime patron Hayley's attempts to restrict the range of his activity, as several others including his most powerful allies did as well, no doubt thinking that restriction was in his best interest – as surely it was, from what we might now see as a career perspective. Painter and especially poet were callings for which his credentials were flawed and suspect, leaving him some distance from the center of the contemporary professional action – less poet or painter than one who sought status in both roles on the condition that the dominant definitions of each change to accommodate his aspirations.

But his claims to the title of printmaker were solid. He acquired the credentials of the trade conventionally and he practiced it all his life with varying success. In trying to understand Blake it can be very helpful to come to grips with the proposition that in many respects he thought, acted, and survived economically as a printmaker with a printmaker's social position and alliances. Much of what we today consider his best work was executed as prints in printmaker's media. But he did not thrive economically even in that role, largely because he defied the expectations associated with it. He was unique among his peers for investing so much effort in original prints, often using innovative technical means and homemade-looking styles, even when he was not seeking ways to amalgamate printmaking to painting, poetry, and prophecy. Even as he resisted the role of printmaker as ordinarily defined, his society resisted granting him many of its rewards for being one of its printmakers.

When his contemporary audience, faced with this manifold conglomeration of efforts, asked who he was, it could not answer to its own satisfaction. In its confusion, it applied outlandish labels. This underlying problem of recognition is at the heart of Blake's difficulties then and his difficulty for us now. He was determined to make a creative life for himself by doing some of several different things and – this is important – putting all the particularly Blakean bits together whenever he could, if necessary by methods of his own devising. (Illuminated printing and monotype color printing were of course among those methods.) That is, he was not notably distracted by his multiple talents into multiple pursuits; he did not flit from talent to talent. He was capable of extraordinary focus and persistence, but he was, by nature it seems, a synthesizer whose electrified senses tended to experience, because they desired to experience, everything in terms of everything else, to see all channels of life as the tributaries of one vast waterway. The concept of an isolated episode or accidental occurrence seems to have been anathema to him. Whenever he found a broken connection between A and B, he read it as a defect and attempted a remedy. Early on he learned to make constructive use of those (otherwise dispiriting and potentially tragic) moments of blocked perception as installments in an endlessly extensible, ever more complex and layered narrative of fall and redemption.

You can see the evidence in virtually all he said or did. One of his first works in illuminated printing, the brief tractate *All Religions are One*, makes the classic Blakean move to synthesis when it concludes that "all men are alike (tho' infinitely various)" and "all Religions... have one source... The true Man... the Poetic Genius" (E 1–2). He insists here, as he always will, that variety need not be sacrificed, but he manages to do so only through paradox. The variety, however infinite, is contained within the ultimate unity. Note too – this is again utterly characteristic – how close the sequence "men... Religions... Man... Poetic Genius" comes to pure metaphorical identification: the poetic genius is the true man, the true man is all (true) men, and all true men are the true religion (because they embody it). The language of the previous six "principles" that lead to this final seventh is similarly all-inclusive: "all men are alike in outward form," "all men are alike in the Poetic Genius," "all sects of Philosophy," "The Religions of all Nations," etc.

In one of Blake's last relief-etched works, thirty-odd years later, the urge to synthesis is, if anything, stronger than ever. On a single sheet, around his own reproduction of the famous *Laocoön* statuary group depicting an event from the Trojan wars, Blake has wrapped a cluster of tightly spaced aphorisms that at a glance appear to be on several different subjects: the ancient Greeks and Trojans, the ancient Romans, the ancient Hebrews, Jesus, statements about war, religion, morality, philosophy, science, and art, with the occasional Hebrew and Greek characters mixed in with the roman alphabet and the English language. The mixture seems extraordinarily heterogeneous, bizarre, artistically grotesque, and perhaps insane unless you come to it forearmed with some sense of what to expect from the man who made it, in which case you soon recognize the familiar gestures of thought by which all these different things from different times and places, some mythical (Lilith, Adam and Eve), some actual (Plato, Socrates, Virgil), are all present on the same page because they are all cross-convertible into the same things, into one another. And the primary aim is neither historical, factual, or fictional narrative about Greeks, Trojans, Romans, or Hebrews but present application. Nothing is "neutral" or "historical"; all references to past events are relentlessly applied to this present moment. Everything points to what can be learned from it...now. "Then," in fact, *is* "now." As time is collapsed, so is space: all places are *here*, and talking about Jerusalem "then" is a way of talking about London "now." The fusion of the human and the divine in such a scheme can be no surprise:

> The Eternal Body of Man is THE IMAGINATION.
>   God himself
> that is   [Yeshua] JESUS we are his Members
>   The Divine Body
> (*Laocoön*, E 273)

Once we notice this pattern, the number and extent of pure metaphorical sequences is staggering: Lilith *is* Satan's Wife *is* the Goddess Nature *is* War and Misery; the whole business of man *is* the arts; Christianity *is* art; Jesus and his apostles *were* artists; prayer *is* the study of art; the man or woman who *is* not an artist *is* not a Christian; the Bible *is* the great code of art, etc.

In a sense Blake had the conclusion of his master plot in mind all along. The larger problem was how to get there. In its naked forms the purely metaphorical landscape could be very monotonous, and indeed one of Blake's most difficult assignments as a forger of poems and images was to learn to vary it – a test that prolific Swedenborg had failed miserably as he explored his own prefabricated visionary universe, based similarly in the metaphorical structures he called "correspondences," in book after book. Drama comes from conflict, but where is credible conflict to come from when the drive to unity is so fierce and urgent? At bottom, Blake seems to derive his conflicts from two simple elements: pure negation, the direct opposite of metaphor (A is not B), and what he sometimes calls "hypocrisy," or one thing disguised as another, named for another, pictured as another, taken for another, and so on (X mistaken for Y): "Nor pale religious letchery *call* that virginity, that wishes but acts not" (emphasis added; *MHH* 25, E 45). Negations and hypocrisies are, simply, *illusory* obstacles to the drive for unity. Blake's epic plots depict a complex process of masking and subsequent confusion and misery, followed by equally complex unmasking, the identification of negations posing as metaphors, and the restoration of the true (original) links of identification: paradise regained, with everything back in its rightful place with its true identity under its actual name.

For the reader, the challenge is to appreciate how subtle and sophisticated Blake's dramatic skills became without losing sight of his ultimate holistic

aim, which was to arrive at a point of reunification where the immense variety
of human life can be contained in a single metaphorical sequence, a kind of
artistic genetic code that reveals the simple unity underlying all complex
variation. *Jerusalem* is, to my mind, the definitive illustration of both Blake's
mature dramatic skills and this primary urge to union, which combine to
produce a plot of daunting complication that twists and turns its way to a
magnificent conclusion as powerful as anything in the Bible. The ending of
Jerusalem is solidly founded on the anticipated string of metaphorical identifications, which reach out to support and encircle the redeemed universe
projected by Blake's synthetic imagination:

> Four Living Creatures Chariots of Humanity Divine Incomprehensible...
> are the Four Rivers of Paradise And the Four Faces of Humanity fronting
> the Four Cardinal Points... And they conversed together in Visionary forms
> dramatic... Creating Space, Creating Time... throughout... Childhood,
> Manhood & Old Age... & Death... & every Word & Every Character...
> & they walked To and fro in Eternity as One Man.

This vision – mystical vision indeed – of "All Human Forms identified even
Tree Metal Earth & Stone. all Human Forms identified" (*J* 98–99, E 257–58,
line divisions omitted) is the ultimate expression of Blake's holism. True,
his version of unity labors mightily to incorporate far more opportunities
for diversity than other comparable mystic–mythic constructions known
to me – the biblical New Jerusalem and Christian Heaven are tedious by
comparison – but it leaves no doubt about which, unity or diversity, trumps
which. While orthodox Christians are dividing eternity between good and
evil, Blake is leaving nothing behind in his myth of ultimate integration.

Alexander Gourlay, in the Glossary on p. 276 below, defines "Eternity"
in two deft and reassuring strokes:

> Eternity for Blake was not simply an infinite amount of time but rather the
> absence of the illusion of linear time and its sequentiality. From a truly eternal
> perspective, all events happen simultaneously and all space is the same infinite
> place. Much of the vertigo that attends reading Blake's prophecies diminishes
> when one recognizes that they are in part intended to make something like an
> eternal perspective available to us.

Easier said than done: from the everyday point of view, perhaps the sane
point of view, the simplicity of this "eternal perspective" is very disorienting
and difficult because it wants to eradicate all the distinctions that we depend
upon utterly for daily living and install in its place an all-or-nothing logic, the
dynamics of which run contrary to virtually all the structures of knowledge
with which we operate.

Why bother?

Blake positioned himself as an outcast prophet in the wilderness, but why should we go out there in search of him? The trail of refusal and severely qualified appreciation is by now so long, wide, and well paved that it is virtually impossible to maintain that it leads *nowhere*. If Blake is going to prove impossible to master, why bother making the effort when there are so many satisfying but less taxing artistic experiences available? It is not necessary to commit to the ultimate readability of Blake to find him worth reading. I have only space enough to mention in the most general terms a few of the exceptional rewards for venturing into this wilderness of artistic offerings. Some of these come from personal experience, some from the accumulated experience of several generations of readers.

Blake's many faces conspire to make his works simultaneously among the most resistant and yet available of all artistic accomplishments – something in them will always respond to a particular reader's particular knowledge and experience. Of course there are many examples of critics who have brought Blake into their territory and "understood" him by their lights rather than ventured into his alien worlds. But in the end Blake forces you to read, look, and understand on his terms. That is among the most valuable of all artistic experiences, and Blake offers it in one of its most fundamental if extreme forms. On this I agree entirely with Northrop Frye, who explained what he got from Blake as a "necessary" lesson in reading poetry: "Blake, in fact, gives us so good an introduction to the nature and structure of poetic thought that, if one has any interest in the subject at all, one can hardly avoid exploiting him."[3] Not freakish nor unique, then, but the epitome of reading itself. As extravagant as this sounds, I believe there is something in it, even for those of us who feel less well equipped than Frye to grasp the utterly fundamental.

For those willing to venture, Blake can become a way to think, or call it a lesson in mythical thinking. In this respect he also presents a classic case of modern and postmodern appreciation, as an artist to be valued far more for the questions he raises, and for the contradictions a reader must embrace in digesting him, than for the answers he offers. I am not at all inclined to seek enlightenment through transcendence myself, but those for whom unanswerable questions are a means to enlightenment may find their share in Blake. Those seeking answers should keep their distance.

Blake is not a cornerstone of truth but a giant intersection in a vast network of facts, ideas, and speculations that run in all directions. In this way he may offer the ultimate centrifugal artistic experience. This is surprising, even tricky, because in most respects he seems quite the opposite, a stubbornly centripetal artist who gives us, as he says, strings that lead inward to some central sphere of meaning. But the realization that there may be no such centerpiece at the end of the quest can be liberating. Instead, the connections made possible by the hard questions his hard work raises have been, for me, altogether more valuable than any internal connections that might have led to the gate in the new Jerusalem that he promises at the end of the golden string. His wide-ranging interests, because they fed his art and now feed our wonderment and confusion, have a way of becoming of necessity the audience's interests: painting, printmaking, and poetry are basic, of course, but other leads almost inevitably take a reader much further afield, to history, technology, the organization (especially the division) of labor, the organization of knowledge, and the organization of society. The history of "reception," as scholars call it – the ways in which audiences have regarded, and coped with, an artist's work – is always a potentially interesting subject for any artist, but remarkably so in Blake's case, where, as always, the picture is made so richly complicated by the number of interactive filaments. No matter which approach or combination of approaches you take, Blake always leaves you feeling that you lack some essential knowledge, some key connection that, if only you could make it, would lead you...

A cliché that one would prefer to avoid seems finally inescapable: Blake is an education – one of the best reading teachers available, a radical challenge to the reasoning mind, a training ground for knowledge in as many areas as you are willing to open for yourself. Perhaps all of the greatest creative artists are educations in themselves. Blake is no greater than they, less great by conventional measures, but capable of sustaining even greater interest, partly for being an altogether more demanding case, and to me, for that reason, more consistently, if strenuously, inspiring.

After Blake died, it took the passage of several decades and the emergence of a new artistic culture to provide the new openings that his work required to get its first fair hearing. Clearly, the chief rewards for those who led the Blake revival in the nineteenth century were the thrills reserved for pioneer adventurers. Their words and deeds resonate with the privileged pleasures of those who have ventured far out into the unknown and returned with reports of a new artistic wonder of the world previously buried, now recovered. Victorian explorers had their sea quests and their Africa; adventurous British literati had their Blake. Since then, curiously, Blake's difficulty has done much good work on his behalf. Having to bother a great deal with great difficulties in multiple media has been a key element in his almost magnetic attraction for some readers and viewers. For them – a human breed of extremophiles, those creatures that survive punishing environments – his works can be the intellectual equivalent of extreme sports, and the wisest of Blake's audience have indeed coped with his challenges the way mountain climbers wring their hard pleasures from the toughest ascents and most catastrophic failures. Because the inner reaches of Blake's work remain so impenetrable, it is impossible to venture into its essential strangeness without feeling a bit like an explorer yourself, even now. Furthermore, Blake's works, with their ravenous, unsatisfiable demand for interpretation, benefit most from such adventurous readers.

Travel tips

A few final pointers may help you confront the challenges of Blake's work fully armed. The most helpful techniques and attitudes will not, in the end, require simplifications or other fatal compromises; they will be capable of responding to the whole Blake. Because his metaphorical way of thinking embodies his holism, the most valuable technique, I suggest, is a mastery of metaphor, the building block of his synthetic narratives. Blake's reader must be prepared to trace his metaphorical logic as it saturates language and image in the drive to express cosmic states of fusion.

The corresponding attitude is one that will help to withstand the assertions of firm belief and final resolution that crop up everywhere in Blake. Rather than be fooled by them, a reader will fare better by cultivating the attitudes suggested by Coleridge's "suspension of disbelief" and Keats's "negative capability" – strong openness to new artistic experiences, unbiased by prior commitments. Such positive indifference will increase your flexibility and stamina, help free you from resentment at being dragged into such difficulties, and keep you alert to Blake's surprisingly refined ability to express himself in dramatic terms – that is, not as himself but as any one of his host of characters. It is all too easy to overlook just what a chameleon of a creator he is. The aim, in the long run, is to keep faith with Blake's fundamental unreadability. He does not respond well to targeted searches for meaning – or he responds all too well. The journey is far more important than the destination.

Critics are often suspected of inventing mountains to climb where there are only molehills of difficulty. But Blake's works leave no doubt that these are Himalayas. The pleasure lies in coping with extremes; at the summit there is only Blake's (or Urizen's) haunting question: "Which is the Way / The Right or the Left" (E 673)? The reader must be satisfied with survival and another chance.

Christian now went to the Spring and drank thereof to fresh himself, and then began to go up the Hill; saying,

> *This Hill, though high, I covet to ascend,*
> *The difficulty will not me offend:*
> *For I perceive the way to life lies here;*
> *Come, pluck up, Heart; lets neither faint nor fear....*
> (John Bunyan, *The Pilgrim's Progress*[4])

Notes

1. "William Blake," in *The Critical Writings*, ed. Ellsworth Mason and Richard Ellman (New York: Viking, 1959), p. 222.
2. Quoted in R. W. Peattie, "William Michael Rossetti's Aldine Edition of Blake," *Blake/An Illustrated Quarterly* 12 (1978), p. 7.
3. Frye, "The Keys to the Gates," *Romanticism and Consciousness: Essays in Criticism and Society*, ed. Harold Bloom (Ithaca: Cornell University Press, 1970), pp. 234–35.
4. In *Grace Abounding to the Chief of Sinners and The Pilgrim's Progress*, ed. Roger Sharrock (London: Oxford University Press, 1966), p. 172.

Further reading

Bentley, G. E., Jr., ed. *Blake Records*. Oxford: Clarendon Press, 1969.
  William Blake: The Critical Heritage. London and Boston: Routledge & Kegan Paul, 1975.
Eaves, Morris. "Graphicality: Multimedia Fables for 'Textual' Critics." *Reimagining Textuality: Textual Studies in the Late Age of Print*. Ed. Elizabeth Bergmann Loizeaux and Neil Fraistat. Madison: University of Wisconsin Press, 2002. 99–122.
Frye, Northrop. "The Keys to the Gates." *Romanticism and Consciousness: Essays in Criticism and Society*. Ed. Harold Bloom. Ithaca: Cornell University Press, 1970. 233–54.

I

PERSPECTIVES

2

AILEEN WARD

William Blake and his circle

The life of William Blake became a legend even before he died, and in discussing his life the two must be disentangled as far as possible. This presents several problems. First of all, the essential materials for his biography – letters, journals, memoirs, official records, comments of friends and others – are meager, while the uncertain dates of many of his works complicate the task of a chronology. Only ninety-two of his letters survive, the first a short note from 1791, when he was thirty-four, and most of the others are concentrated in a single decade, 1799–1808, like the few remaining letters written to him. For the most part his letters are concerned either with prosaic business matters or with what Keats called "the life of allegory," only remotely connected to outward events and relationships. There was little external incident in Blake's life, and he lived in obscurity for most of it; except by a small group of admirers his name was largely forgotten within a decade of his death in 1827, as the subtitle of the first full-length biography, Alexander Gilchrist's 1863 *Life of William Blake*, "Pictor Ignotus," suggests. So sparse a record as this is a temptation to biographers to fill out with more or less fictional detail.

The origin of the Blake legend can be traced in several biographical essays preceding Gilchrist's *Life*, which present Blake in a startling variety of lights – the respectable and unjustly neglected engraver portrayed by the schoolmaster Benjamin Heath Malkin, the companionable fellow-painter recalled by John Thomas Smith, the schizophrenic genius conjured up by the literary hack Allan Cunningham, the saintly visionary of the religious fanatic Frederick Tatham, the mild-mannered heretic of the diarist Henry Crabb Robinson (BR 421–549). Gilchrist provided a portrait of Blake the innocent – the "divine child"[1] who grew into the unworldly artist, devoted husband and kindly father-figure to his disciples; Swinburne countered with Blake the anti-moralist and prophet of sexual liberation, while at the end of the century W. B. Yeats and E. J. Ellis presented Blake as an Irish seer out of the Celtic twilight – mystic, symbolist, and occultist.

More significant than the differences in these representations is the thinness of their supporting evidence for the first six decades of Blake's life. Smith knew Blake as a young man but had little contact with him after the death of Blake's brother Robert, whose friend he had been. Malkin's brief account, based on conversations with Blake in 1805, focused on defending him from his growing reputation of madness. Gilchrist, though an indefatigable researcher, located only fourteen of Blake's letters, all but three from his last two years. Nearly all of his informants knew Blake (most rather distantly) only in the last, comparatively serene decade of his life; the friends of his years of struggle and dissent were long since dead. Gilchrist's two chief sources were the painter and engraver John Linnell, who became Blake's closest friend and supporter after meeting him in 1818, and Samuel Palmer, a pious young painter of nineteen who met Blake in 1824 and became the most fervent member of his little band of disciples. Thus Gilchrist's account of Blake's life up to his sixties was based largely on Blake's own recollections of his earlier years as recited to his youthful admirers long afterward, which they recalled in confused fragments thirty years later.[2] His biography, a notable achievement in its time, is still useful in matters of contemporary detail; but as the chief source of the Blake legend today it must be read with awareness of the gaps and errors in its report and the prejudices of its age – sexual, political, religious – coloring its attitude toward its subject.

To turn to the record itself, William Blake was born in London on 28 November 1757, the third son of James and Catherine Blake. His father was a hosier by trade, hailing from Rotherhithe, a shabby district on the south bank of the Thames; his mother was the widow of Thomas Armitage, also a hosier, of 28 Broad Street, Westminster. On their marriage in October 1752, James Blake moved into the Broad Street house, merged the two businesses, and started a family. Six children were born between 1753 and 1764. There is some uncertainty about the birthdate of Robert, Blake's youngest brother (BR 7–8); the likeliest date is 19 June 1762, and the name "Richard" which appears in the baptismal record on that date was evidently a clerical slip.[3] The Broad Street home was a modest house "of the plainest early Georgian type," at the end of a row that had been built over a strip of the Pesthouse Close, where victims of the Great Plague of 1665 had been sequestered and buried.[4] The back of the row looked out on the burial ground for the parish poor, with the parish workhouse and infirmary and the bustling Carnaby Market located nearby. Several blocks to the south was Golden Square, an outpost of gentility, a wilderness of cobblestones with a small garden fenced off by railings at the center;[5] some half dozen blocks to the north lay the escape to open fields and ponds, where a boy could run and swim and play cricket in the cow pastures (E 171–72, 463–64, 850, note on 15:6). So

Blake grew up on a knife-edge of London between poverty and prosperity, identifying with his poorer neighbors while struggling to make his way in the upper-class world of patrons and Academicians. His postal address was Carnaby Market; only in the advertisements to his 1809 Exhibition and his Chaucer engraving did he give it as Golden Square.

Blake's education was evidently haphazard. He was released from formal schooling because, it is said, he "so hated a Blow" (*BR* 510), but he began reading the Bible and Milton at an early age, followed by Shakespeare, Bunyan, and a wide selection of English poets. Noting his skill in drawing, his father enrolled him at ten in Henry Pars's drawing school, where he did well enough to be sent to sketch in the Duke of Richmond's gallery of classical sculpture under the eye of several Fellows of the newly founded Royal Academy. Here he met his first idol, young John Hamilton Mortimer, already a distinguished history painter and an early example of the rebel-artist. And probably it was here that, as he later put it, the spirits came to him and said, "Blake be an artist and nothing else. In this there is felicity" (*BR* 311).

But when at fourteen it was time to decide on a profession, his father chose engraving for him rather than painting as the boy had hoped. The apprenticeship fee was considerably lower, and though engravers were regarded as artisans who reproduced the work of real artists, they could count on a steady if modest income as painters could not. His master James Basire, the old-fashioned but highly respected engraver to the Society of Antiquaries, trained him well in all the current techniques of printmaking, and recognized his talent by sending him to draw the royal tombs in Westminster Abbey for a publication of the Antiquaries. Still Blake persisted in his ambition to become a painter, haunting the galleries and auction rooms and reading widely in British poetry and history as background for the approved mode of historical painting. And at the end of his apprenticeship in 1779 he chose not to enter the Stationers Guild, the preliminary to becoming a master engraver, but to enroll in the Royal Academy Schools to study painting.

Blake is often described as a merely casual student at the Academy, but the evidence shows that he worked hard and profited from the opportunities it offered even while working as a journeyman engraver. Its rigorous training in drawing the human figure as an expressive vehicle was the foundation of all his later work. Furthermore, his record as a student was outstanding: during his six-year term from 1779 to 1785, seven of his paintings were accepted in the annual Academy exhibitions, far more than those of any other man in his class.[6] In spite of this, he won no prizes or scholarships – perhaps because he bluntly spoke his mind to the school director and even to the Academy President Sir Joshua Reynolds, or more likely because he refused to paint in oil, the prescribed medium. Classed as an engraver on his entrance, he must have resented the discrimination against engravers as mere reproductive artists who, along with watercolorists, were for many years denied membership in the Academy, and he bitterly remembered Reynolds's criticizing his drawing as incorrect.[7] Only one of his teachers won his respect: James Barry, an irascible Irish painter noted for his series of heroic murals on *The Progress of Human Culture*.

During his student years he also formed important friendships with three older students – John Flaxman, Thomas Stothard, and George Cumberland. Flaxman, a precocious young sculptor, was later to become Professor of Sculpture at the Academy and famous throughout Europe for his illustrations to the classics. He remained a loyal friend up till Blake's last decade despite occasional estrangements, introducing him to patrons and securing commissions. Stothard became a fashionable painter and illustrator and gave Blake many of his designs to engrave, though years later an acrimonious quarrel was to end their friendship. Cumberland, who remained merely a knowledgeable amateur of engraving, collaborated with Blake on several projects but later withdrew to live on his inheritance in the west of England and grew increasingly distant.

In their student days, however, the four young men were united in their enthusiasm for classical art and their radical stance in politics at a time of growing political and social unrest sparked largely by the American Revolution. Blake's political baptism was his involvement in the Gordon Riots of June 1780. Though most of his biographers have denied that he took an active part, it seems clear that he voluntarily joined the front ranks of the crowd that marched on Newgate at the climax of the Riots to free five of their leaders and ended by sacking and burning the hated prison itself.[8] This event, the formative political experience of his life, resonates throughout his work, from the images of broken chains and liberating flames in *America* to the beatific vision of "dungeons burst & the Prisoners set free" in the last chapter of *Jerusalem* (pl. 77, E 233).

At the end of his six-year term, Blake turned his back on the Academy and did little painting for twelve years after 1785. He had already won a good reputation as a copy engraver and become a family man. On a country holiday in 1781 he had met Catherine Boucher, a pretty and impetuous young woman of twenty, the illiterate daughter of a market-gardener, whom he married in August 1782. Their marriage was a singularly happy one, despite its unexplained childlessness and occasional crises of jealousy. Catherine was perfectly fitted to be the wife of a poor artist, a tireless helpmeet and unquestioning believer in his genius, who later became a skillful assistant in his printing operations. In 1784, after the death of his father, he set up a printselling shop with his friend James Parker and used his inheritance to buy a rolling press. The shop was his chief source of income for the next five years,[9] and the press was to have an important influence on both his art and his writing by liberating him from the standard systems of publication and reproduction.

All during his life Blake read widely in an eclectic array of historians, philosophers, theologians, classical writers, and occult scientists as well as English poets. Since thirteen or fourteen he had been writing poetry, and it was as a poet that he figured in the circle of the Rev. Henry and Mrs. Mathew, prosperous dilettantes to whom Flaxman introduced him in 1782. At their house he not only read his poems but sang them to tunes of his own composing, and they were so much admired that the Mathews paid for the printing of *Poetical Sketches* in 1783. Yet this promising début attracted no attention beyond the Mathews' parlor, and a dozen copies remained unbound and uncut in Blake's hands till his death.

This disappointment, or else what J. T. Smith described as his "unbending deportment" (*BR* 457), caused him to withdraw from the Mathew salon not long afterward. Already his intellectual horizons were widening. Through Basire he had met the leading engravers of the day and perhaps some of the Antiquaries; at Flaxman's he heard Thomas Taylor lecture on the neo-platonists, and through his friend the engraver William Sharp he would have become acquainted with members of the various radical groups of the time, though he seems never to have joined one. Echoes of these and other new contacts are heard in the rollicking satire of *An Island in the Moon* (c. 1784), in which Blake skewered the intellectual pretensions and absur-dities he had encountered in the Mathew drawing room and elsewhere. Already he was working for the hospitable editor and publisher Joseph Johnson, whose bookshop was a center for dissenting intellectuals such as Paine, Priestley, Godwin, Mary Wollstonecraft, and Horne Tooke. In 1787 Johnson introduced him to the Swiss-born painter Henry Fuseli, with whom he formed an enduring friendship based on intellectual rapport and mu-tual artistic respect. Sixteen years older than Blake and already famous for his melodramatic canvases, Fuseli was also an essayist and translator, widely read in literature, philosophy and the history of art, and he had an energizing influence on Blake's style and the range of his thought.

Earlier in 1787 Blake suffered a devastating blow, the death at twenty-four of his beloved younger brother Robert, the one member of his family with whom he felt a bond of sympathy. Though it is unlikely that Robert attended the Royal Academy Schools, as has been suggested (*BR* 20), his surviving drawings reveal a genuine if untutored talent, and it appears that Blake trained him as his assistant in the print shop.[10] Thirteen years after his death, Blake wrote a friend that he conversed with Robert "daily & hourly in the Spirit," saw him in his imagination, heard his advice and wrote from his dictate (E 705). His death was a major turning point in Blake's life. The young mocker who had nicknamed himself "the Cynic" in *An Island in the Moon* was transformed into a steadfast believer in a spiritual world. If he did not actually see Robert's "released spirit" ascending from his body at the moment of death "clapping his hands for joy," as Gilchrist asserted (p. 51), several of his later designs depicting such a scene suggest either a dream image persisting in his memory or a configuration of eidetic images from his highly developed capacity for visual recall[11] – what are usually called, with varying emphases on their relation to reality, his visions. And beginning at this time he developed a deep interest in religion.

The question of Blake's religious beliefs is a vexed one. His parents were Dissenters of no ascertainable denomination and were buried in Bunhill Fields, the Dissenters' cemetery, with all the members of his family; yet Blake and all his siblings were baptized in the parish Church of St. James, Piccadilly. But established religion was anathema to Blake all his life long: "Priest and King" were for him twin symbols of tyranny. It is striking that there are virtually no religious references in the *Poetical Sketches*, and his drawings and paintings before 1787 are based primarily on British history, Shakespeare, and Milton, not on the Bible. Around 1787 he was briefly drawn toward the newly founded Swedenborgian Church, but soon became disillusioned with its increasing conservativism and formalism and rejected its doctrines. The numerous images of Jesus in the *Songs of Innocence* (1789) are supplanted in the *Songs of Experience* (1794) by naturalistic imagery and anti-clerical protests. After 1790, believing that every man may be "a King & Priest in his own house" (E 615), he never attended any church but followed the path of his own religious explorations.

One "vision" of Robert above all was to shape Blake's life decisively. As recounted by J. T. Smith, Robert appeared before him in 1788 and gave him the answer to a question he had been pondering for several years – of how to publish his work on his own press. Blake had toyed with the idea of engraving his poems with separate engraved illustrations (E 465), but this was far too laborious. Robert's revelation was the solution – an ingenious method of relief etching achieved simply by painting his text and designs on the copperplate with a fine brush or pen in acid-resist, and then "biting" the plate in acid to reveal his outlines, printing, and hand-coloring. He first tried the method, which he called "Illuminated Printing" (E 693), in 1788 in three small collections of religious aphorisms whose shaky lettering betrayed their experimental nature; but the *Songs of Innocence* and *The Book of Thel* in 1789 showed a remarkable advance in conception and control. An explosion of creativity followed over the next six years, during which he wrote, illustrated, and published thirteen books of poetry and produced nine original engravings, over eighty commercial engravings, and finally the twelve great color prints of 1795.

The energy that fueled this extraordinary output came not merely from his discovery of a new artistic medium but from the transforming experience of the French Revolution. While anti-monarchical convictions occur in many of his earlier poems and drawings, the concluding poem in *Songs of Innocence*, *The Voice of the Ancient Bard*,[12] is a bold salute to "the rising morn" in France after the sack of the Bastille in July 1789. Not long afterward Blake embarked on an epic poem entitled *The French Revolution*, which he planned in seven books but withdrew after the first was set up in type in 1791. With journalists and publishers being jailed all over the kingdom and radical leaders tried for treason, it was becoming dangerous to speak out in sympathy with the new régime. Blake cloaked himself in anonymity to issue his revolutionary manifesto *The Marriage of Heaven and Hell* (1790–92?) unsigned and undated, and acknowledged himself only as the printer, not the author, of the political prophecies that followed. In these works, perhaps also for fear of prosecution, he abandoned the historical narrative of *The French Revolution* for a new mode of prophetic mythmaking in his new medium of illuminated printing, in which much of the meaning could be carried by the designs themselves. Perhaps in emulation of Barry's *Progress*, he formed an ambitious plan for a survey of the development of revolution in history, reaching from the present back to the beginning of time and encompassing the four continents, which he published in a format twice the size of his previous books. But the exuberant optimism of *America a Prophecy* (1793) soon gave way to doubt and disillusionment in *Europe a Prophecy* (1794) and *The Song of Los* (1795) as bloodshed and terror in France and tightening repression in England overwhelmed his earlier vision of universal freedom. In another group of prophecies Blake's focus shifted from history to the metaphysical determinants of history in a new account of the creation, fall and wanderings of mankind, embodied in a myth of the struggle for power within a pantheon of Eternals. *The [First] Book of Urizen* (1794) recast Genesis in Gnostic terms, depicting the material creation as inherently evil, the result of a splitting of matter from the primal unity of spirit, which produced all the divisions and contradictions of our fallen universe. After two sequels, *The Book of Ahania* and *The Book of Los*, the cycle ended inconclusively; the passage of Pitt's draconian Two Acts against treasonous speech and writing in 1795 finally discouraged Blake from political prophecy, and he gave up illuminated printing for ten years.

The greatest achievement of this period was the series of twelve monumental color prints, mostly dated 1795, in which he abandoned the illustration of a poetic text for freestanding visual expression. Printed from designs painted on millboard (a kind of heavy cardboard used for sketching) with pigments mixed with glue, these monotypes achieved a dramatic effect of deeper color and more varied texture than his earlier watercolors, with which he portrayed a universe of oppression, superstition, disease, and death. Only the print of *Christ Appearing to the Apostles after the Resurrection*, the first large-scale representation of Christ in Blake's art, conveys a ray of hope. Yet the message of this print is equivocal. The six disciples prostrated before Christ, with one other looking up in adoration, may be Blake's comment on the idolatrous nature of Christian orthodoxy; but the figure of Jesus shows the Promethean rebel of *The Marriage of Heaven and Hell* transformed into Christ the Redeemer enshrined in his later work.

In the autumn of 1795 the bookseller Richard Edwards engaged him to illustrate a folio-sized luxury edition of Edward Young's *Night Thoughts*, both the designs and the engravings. *Night Thoughts, or The Complaint and The Consolation* was an immensely popular and long-drawn-out rumination on life, death, and immortality, and whatever Blake thought of the poem he accepted the commission with enthusiasm. Within two years he produced 537 stunning watercolor designs which extend and even subvert the meaning of the lines they illustrate, and transform Young's conventional piety into a dramatic search for religious belief through a world of sense haunted by the fear of death, ending with apocalypse and resurrection. But after he engraved 43 plates for the first volume, Edwards dropped the project because of discouraging sales.

At about this time Blake turned back to his unfinished cosmic history, recreating it as a vast new theogony entitled *Vala* after the sinister goddess of material Nature from whom humanity must struggle to free itself. He worked on the poem intermittently for ten years, changing the title to *The Four Zoas* as his conception of his myth developed. It presents Albion, the Eternal Man, as torn by sexual, psychological, and spiritual conflict personified in his four warring faculties the four Zoas, till he declares an end to the strife and recovers his lost harmony of spirit. Though Blake concluded the poem with a scene of the Last Judgment, he never really finished it. The 139-page manuscript is a tangle of additions, deletions, alternative readings, and bewildering transformations of character, lit up by passages of great poetic power interspersed with erotic drawings depicting the "torments of Love & Jealousy" (E 300). The concluding scene of universal reconciliation at the end of "the war of swords" (E 407) echoes the hopeful mood of the short-lived Peace of Amiens of 1802–3, and probably it was the collapse of this hope that led him to abandon the manuscript, at least for a while.

By 1796 Blake's "genius & invention" were being "much spoken of" among the cognoscenti (*BR* 51–52), though the illuminated books continued to sell few copies. At the request of his old friend the miniature-painter Ozias Humphry, he assembled two selections of his illustrations in *A Large* and *A Small Book of Designs*, all color-printed to demonstrate his latest technique. Humphry evidently showed the books to Joseph Farington, "the dictator of the Royal Academy," who then discussed them several times with fellow RAs.[13] But despite warm praise from Humphry and others, including the president Benjamin West himself, Farington and the fashionable portrait painter John Hoppner disparaged Blake and ridiculed his work as "the conceits of a drunken fellow or a madman" (*BR* 58), and he was never elected to membership. Apparently Blake was attempting a reconciliation with the Academy at this time with a group of "experiment pictures" (E 546) painted in a new medium which he called "fresco," the tempera mixed with glue of his color prints. Two of these canvases, in the eclectic Venetian and Dutch style which he had rejected in his student days, were duly accepted at the Academy Exhibitions in 1799 and 1800.[14]

Yet his fortunes as an engraver were declining during these years. His commercial engravings in 1796 attracted poor notices or none, and when the first part of *Night Thoughts* finally appeared in the summer of 1797 it apparently received no reviews. The country was in the grip of a bank crash, and the war with France was at a dangerously low ebb; the market for art was drying up. Blake received almost no orders for engravings in 1798 and 1799, and a painting ordered by the Rev. Dr. Trusler, a friend of Cumberland's, was returned with a frigid criticism of its fancifulness. Then providentially Blake acquired two patrons who were to rescue him from real failure. Thomas Butts, chief clerk in what came to be known as the War Office and a friend of some years, became Blake's main support for the next decade and a half. In 1799 he commissioned Blake to paint fifty smallish frescos from the Bible at a guinea each; the next year he extended his order to watercolors, of which Blake eventually painted over a hundred. And in 1800 Flaxman's wealthy patron William Hayley persuaded Blake to join him at his home in the seaside village of Felpham, Sussex, to work on engravings for several of Hayley's books.

Poet, connoisseur, and man of letters, Hayley is the only friend of Blake's to appear in his myth, as the equivocal figure of Satan in *Milton*. Hayley was a complex person, generous, enthusiastic, domineering, eccentric. He introduced Blake to his well-born friends, who commissioned miniatures and took drawing lessons from him; he wrote moralistic ballads for children for Blake to illustrate; he set him to decorating his library with portraits of his favorite poets and began teaching him Greek. Yet Hayley had no appreciation of Blake as an artist. He bought none of Blake's original paint-ings or illuminated books, and when Blake loaned him the manuscript of *The Four Zoas* he looked at it "with sufficient contempt to enhance my opinion of it" (E 730). His own mediocre poetry had won him an invitation to the laureateship, which he declined; he saw Blake as merely his well-paid engraver, "an excellent enthusiastic Creature" whom he was training as a miniaturist (*BR* 78).

Inevitably an explosion occurred. Hayley objected to Blake's taking time for anything but "the meer drudgery of business" (E 724), and Blake, kept from his own painting and writing by Hayley's demands, fell into a deep depression and began to lose his mental poise. He was also becoming aware of Hayley's unconscious homosexuality ("His Mother on his Father him begot," E 506) which, along with his drive to domineer, underlies the portrait of Satan in the "Bard's Song" of *Milton* which Blake began writing soon after leaving Felpham. Satan's "soft / Delusory love to Palamabron: admiration join'd with envy" (E 105) allegorized the jealous rivalry Blake sensed in Hayley's patronizing attitude; and after a long inner struggle Blake asserted himself. He resolved to leave the security of Felpham for the uncertainties of London, and precipitated a showdown with Hayley by demanding higher fees for his engravings. Only in London, he now felt, could he "converse with [his] friends in Eternity. See Visions, Dream Dreams, & prophecy & speak Parables unobserv'd & at liberty from the Doubts of other Mortals" (E 728). He confided to Butts that he was "under the direction of Messengers from Heaven" who commanded him "Daily & Nightly" to go on fearlessly with his task (E 724), and he began hatching grandiose plans for publishing with "many very formidable works" he had on hand, from which he expected to reap huge profits (E 726). In July 1803 he announced that he had "perfectly completed into a Grand Poem" a "Sublime Allegory" which was ready to be "Printed & Ornamented with Prints" and published (E 730) – the perpetually incomplete *Four Zoas*.

Reality broke unexpectedly on this scene in the form of an obstreperous soldier intruding into Blake's garden in August. Blake evicted him in a fury, whereupon the soldier went before the magistrate and swore that he had "Damned the King of England" (*BR* 124). Times were tense, with an invasion by the French expected momentarily; Blake risked prison or even hanging for seditious utterance if proved guilty. He was indicted for sedition and tried in January 1804 – and fortunately acquitted. But the experience increased his sense of isolation in a hostile world while also stirring up a sense of mission to oppose its injustices.

In September 1803 Blake and Catherine moved back to London, taking a small second-floor flat in "dingy, gardenless South Molton Street."[15] Orders for engraving were slow in coming, and his plans for publishing withered and died. Then in October 1804 on a visit to the Truchsessian Gallery he had a moment of vision in which he was "again enlightened with the light I enjoyed in my youth" (E 756). Among the 900 paintings on exhibition he found many by the Florentine and Roman artists who had been his original inspiration, along with some Flemish primitives which may have recalled the Gothic subjects of his apprentice work. Suddenly the weight of the academic tradition of Titian and Rubens and Rembrandt under which he had been laboring was lifted, and his path as a true artist became clear before him. Returning to his biblical watercolors for Butts he began working in a new style, less painterly, more hieratic, creating works of a new visionary intensity.

On the same wave of renewed inspiration he returned to illuminated printing with his plan for a new long poem and created a title page announcing *MILTON a Poem in 12 Books To Justify the Ways of God to Men*. Though Milton's poetry had been a guiding star to Blake since his earliest days, in *The Marriage of Heaven and Hell* he had criticized the rationalistic theology of *Paradise Lost* as a betrayal of Milton's prophetic inspiration; now Blake proposed to guide him through a process of redemption for his errors, artistic and sexual as well as religious. He shows Milton in heaven moved by the Bard's Song to recognize Satan's self-righteousness in himself, then descend to earth to oppose the errors of his moralistic religion of "cruel holiness" and the "warlike selfhood" of his classical tradition (E 137, 108), and finally unite with his inspiration, his estranged female counterpart, in an apocalyptic scene of regeneration. In a parallel movement of redemption Blake sees his struggle with the Satanic Hayley as effecting his own union with his inspiration, Los the Zoa of imagination, and thus his identification with Milton in his prophetic role. Four or five years of deepening frustration were to elapse before Blake completed *Milton* in 1808 or 1809, but they did not deflect him from his "mental fight" to denounce the false art and false philosophy and false religion of the false Miltonic heritage (E 142).

In September 1805 Robert Cromek, a former engraver turned publisher, engaged Blake in a new project, to make forty designs with twenty engravings for a luxury edition of Robert Blair's popular and lugubrious poem *The Grave*. Almost at once, however, Cromek began reducing his terms to twenty designs and twelve engravings; he then transferred the commission for engraving Blake's designs to the fashionable and highly paid engraver Louis Schiavonetti after finding the style of the first of Blake's engravings too novel and rugged for his taste. When the volume was finally published in 1808, it was a commercial success and brought Blake to the widest public attention of his lifetime, despite several damning reviews of his designs; but he never forgave Cromek's affront to his abilities as an engraver. He swallowed his pride and accepted the meager fee for his designs but vented his fury in a series of scurrilous epigrams in his Notebook attacking Cromek and other friends who for one reason or another he now believed were betraying him – Hayley, Stothard, Flaxman, and others, sparing only Fuseli ("The only Man that eer I knew / Who did not make me almost spew," E 507).

In his growing estrangement Blake was turning more and more to religion for spiritual support. At about this time he began revising *The Four Zoas*, reinforcing his mythological scheme of Albion's regeneration with a Christian theme of redemption and recasting the apocalyptic conclusion as a Last Judgment. This expectation of an ultimate vindication became a central preoccupation of his later work: he sketched or painted the scene of the Last Judgment at least six times between 1805 and 1810 and in one or more probably two large frescos thereafter.[16] He also described the scene in his prose *Vision of the Last Judgment*, echoing the conclusion of *Milton* in denouncing the perpetrators of naturalistic art and moralistic religion. The Last Judgment will be "an Overwhelming of Bad Art and Science" and of all those "who trouble Religion with Questions concerning Good & Evil"; it is "Necessary because Fools flourish" (E 565, 554, 561).

The crowning injustice he suffered at this time was an egregious example of "Bad Art" painted by his onetime friend Stothard and promoted or even conceived by Cromek as his agent – a large painting of Chaucer's Canterbury Pilgrims starting out on their journey. This became the focus of a bitter controversy, since Blake was convinced that he had made a sketch of the subject himself in 1805 which Cromek had seen and then described to Stothard, whose spectacularly successful painting was exhibited in 1807. It is far more likely that Blake deluded himself about his original sketch and that he made his own work (dated 1808) in response to Cromek's taunt in 1807 that he should "send [him] a better" (*BR* 187) than Stothard's.[17] But when his fresco, painted in an archaic style opposing Stothard's realism, was exhibited in 1809, it was sneeringly dismissed in the one review it received (*BR* 216–17). Undeterred, Blake produced an engraving from his painting in 1810 and composed a "Public Address" (never published, E 571–82) decrying the modern taste represented by Schiavonetti and arguing against Cromek that only the designer of a print can properly execute the engraving. His Chaucer print, however, sold only seven or eight copies out of an edition of thirty during his lifetime.

Ever since 1800 Blake had been sending pictures to the Academy for exhibition and having them turned down, except for two of the Butts watercolors shown in 1808. His mounting anger spilled out in annotations he made to Reynolds's *Discourses on Art* in 1808–9, attacking Reynolds's theory of art as the force behind the rejection of his work since his student days. He then resolved to challenge the academic establishment by holding an exhibition of his own at his boyhood home in Broad Street in 1809. In his *Descriptive Catalogue* for the show Blake summed up his principles of visionary art and vigorously defended his abilities as a painter "against the insolent and envious imputations of unfitness" propagated "by ignorant hirelings" (E 537). His proud assertion of superiority to Titian and Correggio and Rubens and Rembrandt prompted Robert Hunt in the only review of the exhibition to describe him as "an unfortunate lunatic" and his art as "deformity and nonsense" (*BR* 216).

With the failure of his exhibition and the Chaucer engraving, Blake virtually withdrew from the art world for seven or eight years. During this time he painted half a dozen biblical temperas for Butts as well as several sets of watercolor illustrations to Milton's earlier poems which, with a later series for *Paradise Regained*, rounded out the cycle of his illustrations to Milton's major works begun in 1801, and Flaxman gave him his designs for Hesiod to engrave. Otherwise almost his only source of income for these years was hackwork such as outlines of armor and antique gems for the Rees *Cyclopaedia* and teapots and soup tureens for the Wedgwood catalogue. He seems to have become almost totally isolated; among his rare visitors were Robert Southey, who in 1811 called and was shown "a perfectly mad poem called Jerusalem" (*BR* 229), and George Cumberland, who found him "still poor still Dirty" (*BR* 232). It was evidently a time of spiritual struggle, of depression and rage (*BR* 227–28, 241–42) but also exaltation as he worked on his last long poem, *Jerusalem*.

The origins of *Jerusalem* are uncertain. Its strikingly beautiful title page is dated 1804, like that of *Milton*, but may have actually been created years later. It is generally believed that Blake had etched the first sixty of its hundred plates by 1807 (*BR* 187 and n.4); but considering the approximately thirty-two plates referring to events of 1808 or later scattered throughout the text, as well as thirty-seven other plates showing evidence of late composition,[18] this dating seems improbable, and the work was probably composed 1808 to 1820.[19] The poem is a summation of Blake's earlier prophecies, inscribing a triumphant Finis to Albion/England/humanity's long quest for spiritual wholeness. Jerusalem, the allegorical figure of Liberty, is Albion's estranged female counterpart who wanders neglected and degraded through the world and throughout history while Albion lies sick with the spiritual disease of doubt and despair. The various themes of the poem, as announced in the prefaces to the four chapters, are loosely bound together in a series of visions of fallen history, British and biblical, while Los and Vala battle for the souls of the ailing Albion and the exiled Jerusalem. They come to a climax in a vision of the incarnation, where an angry Joseph learns to forgive a sinful Mary and the Spirit of Jesus enters the world as "Continual Forgiveness of Sins" (E 212). So at the end Albion throws himself into the furnaces of affliction and is reconciled with Jerusalem; the entire creation is then transformed into a tremendous living unity, all "the Living Creatures of the Earth" identified or "Humanized" (E 258), in a scene of universal rejoicing.

This apotheosis of forgiveness, so different from the condemnatory tone and self-justification of the conclusion of *Milton*, marks the end of Blake's own struggle toward spiritual wholeness. When in the preface to chapter 1 he could renounce self-righteousness, confess that he was "the most sinful of men" yet claim "to love, to see, to converse...daily, as man with man" with Jesus "the Friend of Sinners" (E 145), he had passed through the ordeal of his failure and could accept the pattern of his life as well as forgive his enemies. In the last decade of his life he was a changed person, remembered by friends and disciples as close to saintliness.

The decade began in June 1818 with his meeting John Linnell, at that time a rising young painter and engraver of twenty-six, who became Blake's closest friend since the death of Robert. Linnell regarded Blake's work with a fresh-eyed admiration that helped Blake recover his mental poise, and brought him out of his isolation by finding him work and introducing him to wealthy patrons and fellow artists such as John Constable. Together they attended exhibitions and occasionally the theater and opera, and Blake became an intimate of Linnell's young family. In 1820 Linnell persuaded his physician Dr. R. J. Thornton to employ Blake to illustrate his school edition of Virgil's *Pastorals*, for which Blake produced seventeen exquisite small wood-block scenes of English rural life that trace a kind of Pilgrim's Progress with intimations of his own spiritual journey. He returned to his own work with renewed energy, reprinting a number of the illuminated books and printing five copies of *Jerusalem*, including one magnificent colored version (never sold), as well as expanding an earlier set of engraved emblems as *For the Sexes: The Gates of Paradise*. He created an illuminated broadside *On Homers Poetry [and] On Virgil* and a two-page drama *The Ghost of Abel* replying to Byron's *Cain*, illustrated Bunyan's *Pilgrim's Progress* and, in the *Visionary Heads* done for the painter and astrologer John Varley, conjured up a number of historical or imaginary figures and produced their portraits.

Yet in all this activity Blake was still close to poverty: he had to sell his precious collection of old prints in 1821 and move into a cramped apartment owned by his wife's brother-in-law in a shabby neighborhood off the Strand. Linnell came to his rescue by commissioning a series of engravings on the Book of Job. Blake had painted or engraved aspects of the story of Job at least half a dozen times since the mid-1780s, coming more and more to identify with him in his afflictions, but his final statement presented a new image of

Job, with a dramatic new depth and complexity of graphic technique. In *The Vision of Christ*, a late design added to his original watercolor series (Butlin 550 17), Blake shows Job recognizing the unity of the Father and the Son: God is no longer seen as an inscrutable Jehovah chastising his presumption and demanding assent to his power (Butlin pl. 538), but as a loving Christ who is one with the Father and with Job himself and teaches neither righteousness nor humility but love of all his creation.

By the time the engravings were published in 1825 Blake was entering an almost Job-like prosperity. The *Job* volume was well received, with one copy going to the King's library. At the prompting of Linnell the Royal Academy awarded him £25 and eventually acquired a set of proofs for its own library. Blake was invited to dine by Lady Blessington and Lady Caroline Lamb as well as by Constable and other artists; at the house of the hospitable collector Charles Aders he met Coleridge, who had admired his *Songs* years before, and Blake's devotee Crabb Robinson, who recorded his unorthodox opinions on philosophy and theology with bemused fascination. He started work on a final statement of the theme of the Last Judgment, a huge fresco which he planned to send to the Academy exhibition of 1828 (Butlin 648). To judge from the drawing which he evidently made in preparation for this work (Butlin 645), Blake's conception of the scene had changed in crucial details from the judgmental tone of his earlier versions to the humane spirit of his conclusion to *Job*.[20]

Perhaps Blake's greatest happiness at this time was his meeting with a little circle of admiring young artists including Samuel Palmer, Frederick Tatham, and George Richmond, who gathered around him in the last three years of his life. Calling themselves the Ancients from their devotion to earlier art, they were profoundly moved by what they understood of his vision, regarding him with the awe due to "one of the Antique patriarchs, or a dying Michael Angelo" (*BR* 291). In various ways they were to follow different aspects of Blake's achievement, and though his influence on their work wore off as the years passed, their memory of him as an exemplar of the true artist, "a man without a mask; his aim single, his path straightforward, and his wants few,"[21] remained with them to the end.

Linnell's last commission was for a series of illustrations to Dante. Although Blake thought Dante an "Atheist" in his belief in "Vengeance for Sin" and his Hell a creation not of God but of Satan (*BR* 325, E 690), he immediately realized the imaginative possibilities of Dante's universe. Starting in 1825 he produced over 100 folio-sized drawings, many in brilliant watercolor, which he postponed engraving till he was finished with *Job* when, beset by illness, he managed to complete only seven. Despite its unfinished state, this group of illustrations is Blake's most drastic act of reinterpretation.

He shows Dante as following a mistaken path toward salvation through Beatrice, the representative of the Church: at the climax of *Purgatory* she is revealed as Vala, who is then transformed into the Whore of Babylon. In *Paradise* Dante is briefly rewarded with a vision of Christ, from which Beatrice is absent; but Blake's final image, a parody of Dante's conclusion, shows the Virgin Mary enthroned on a sunflower, presiding over the Church Triumphant like Vala in *Jerusalem* ruling over the pestilential world of nature.[22]

Blake's last engraving, in the summer of 1827, was in a different spirit and on a very different scale – a tiny design he added at George Cumberland's request to his calling card as a decorative border (E 784, *BR* 347). In a field of wheat a laborer bends over his toil while a boy with a kite runs past; above on the left an angel with a sickle is descending to cut the thread of life held on a spindle by another angel at the right, while souls rise to heaven overhead. Though Cumberland was baffled when he received it, the design is clearly an allegory of life and death, innocence and experience, and Blake's farewell to the friend of his youth.

Blake's health had been declining ever since 1824: he was plagued intermittently with abdominal pains, chills, and fever, increasingly confined to his bed, and occasionally delirious. His symptoms suggest a severe gall bladder infection ("the gall mixing with the blood" was the diagnosis at the time[23]) or perhaps a rare liver disease, sclerosing cholangitis, caused by years of inhaling the fumes of nitric acid while etching his plates.[24] Nevertheless he continued to work till almost the end. On 10 August 1827 Linnell called and found him in a semi-comatose state; "not expected to live," as he noted in his journal (*BR* 341). Two days later Blake died at six in the evening, attended only by his wife and perhaps a neighbor.

Three days afterward George Richmond wrote to Samuel Palmer describing Blake's death: "Just before he died His Countenance became fair – His eyes Brighten'd and He burst out in Singing of the things he Saw in Heaven."[25] Sixty years later Richmond told the Gilchrists' son that he had been present to close Blake's eyes and kiss him in death (*BR* 342): a dubious story, since he did not tell it to Gilchrist to be included in the *Life* twenty-five years earlier (or even to Anne Gilchrist to be added to the 1880 edition), nor did Richmond at eighteen mention being present in his letter to Palmer. The source of the account of Blake's last hours, then, was a witness even more "fervent [and] enthusiastic" than Richmond himself, Catherine Blake.[26] His story immediately passed into circulation, however, to be included and amplified by Smith, Cunningham, Tatham, and Gilchrist in their accounts. Tatham especially waxed eloquent: he described Blake's ecstatic "Hallelujahs & songs of joy & Triumph" making the room peal again and the walls resound "with the beatific Symphony," till at last "his spirit departed like the sighing of a gentle breeze" (*BR* 528). Gilchrist rounded out the account with the words of "a humble female neighbor," that it was "the death, not of a man, but of a blessed angel":[27] a grace note added to the most enduring of the Blake legends.

Such is the power of the story of Blake's life that we find it difficult to give up this culminating detail, which appeals so strongly to our sense of what must have been the drama of his life, no matter what may have been the facts. As he wrote in his last letter to Cumberland, "The Real Man [is] The Imagination which Liveth for Ever" (E 783). The enduring truth of Blake's life is found in the development of his poetry, printmaking, and painting: to this the factual narrative serves at best as introduction.

Notes

1. Alexander Gilchrist, *Life of William Blake*, ed. Ruthven Todd (London: J. M. Dent, 1945), p. 2.
2. Aileen Ward, "William Blake and the Hagiographers," *Biography and Source Studies* 1 (1994), pp. 1–24; Gilchrist, *Life*, p. 301.
3. Aileen Ward, "Who Was Robert Blake?", *Blake/An Illustrated Quarterly* 28 (1994–95), pp. 84–89.
4. *Survey of London*, ed. F. H. W. Shepherd et al., vol. XXXI (University of London: Athlone Press, 1905 et seq.), pp. 196–204.
5. *Survey*, vol. XXXII, pl. 120b.
6. Aileen Ward, " 'Sir Joshua and His Gang': William Blake and the Royal Academy," *Huntington Library Quarterly* 52 (1989), p. 78.
7. Gilchrist, *Life*, p. 275.
8. Aileen Ward, "Romantic Castles and Real Prisons," *The Wordsworth Circle* 9 (1999), pp. 9 and 13 n.15.
9. Ward, "Sir Joshua," p. 92 n.37.
10. Ward, "Robert Blake," pp. 86–87.
11. See Morton D. Paley, *Energy and the Imagination* (Oxford: Oxford University Press, 1970), pp. 201–6.
12. See Geoffrey Keynes on the order of copy G of *Innocence*; in *The Complete Writings of William Blake* (Oxford: Oxford University Press, 1966), pp. 886–87.
13. William T. Whitley, *Artists and their Friends in England 1700–1799*, vol. I (London: Jonathan Cape, 1928), p. 86; Ward, "Sir Joshua," p. 82.
14. Butlin 424, 416; Ward, "Sir Joshua," pp. 83–84.
15. Gilchrist, *Life*, p. 280.
16. *BR* 235–36, 467–68; Ward, "Romantic Castles," pp. 10–12 and nn.18, 19.
17. Aileen Ward, "Canterbury Revisited: The Blake–Cromek Controversy," *Blake/An Illustrated Quarterly* 22 (1988–89), pp. 80–92.
18. G. E. Bentley, Jr., *Blake Books* (Oxford: Clarendon Press, 1977), pp. 225–29.
19. Aileen Ward, "Rebuilding *Jerusalem*: Composition and Chronology," *Blake/An Illustrated Quarterly*, forthcoming.

20. Ward, "Romantic Castles," pp. 12, 14 nn.18, 19.
21. Gilchrist, *Life*, p. 301.
22. Butlin 812 *99* and *J* pl. 53.
23. Gilchrist, *Life*, p. 352.
24. Joseph Viscomi and Lane Robson, "Blake's Death," *Blake/An Illustrated Quarterly* 30 (1996), pp. 36–49.
25. Gilchrist, *Life*, p. 353.
26. Ward, "Hagiographers," pp. 14–15.
27. Gilchrist, *Life*, p. 353.

Further reading

Ackroyd, Peter. *Blake*. London: Sinclair-Stevenson, 1995.
Bentley, G. E., Jr. *Blake Records*. Oxford: Clarendon Press, 1969.
  The Stranger from Paradise: A Biography of William Blake. New Haven and London: Yale University Press, 2001.
Bindman, David. *Blake as an Artist*. Oxford: Phaidon Press, 1977.
Bronowski, Jacob. *William Blake and the Age of Revolution*. New York: Harper & Row, 1965.
Erdman, David V. *Blake: Prophet against Empire*. 3rd edn, rev. Princeton: Princeton University Press, 1977.
King, James. *William Blake: His Life*. New York: St. Martin's Press, 1991.

3

JOSEPH VISCOMI

Illuminated printing

On 12 April 1827, shortly before he died, Blake wrote to George Cumberland thanking him for trying to sell copies of Blake's illuminated books and his recently published engraved illustrations to the Book of Job. Blake had first executed the Job illustrations as watercolor drawings for Thomas Butts around 1805, followed by a duplicate set for John Linnell, who commissioned him to engrave the series in 1823.

Three years later, Blake had twenty-two line engravings that looked very different from the tonal prints then popular. Indeed, they even looked different from engravings, his own included, for they were not executed in the standard "mixed method" technique, in which designs were first etched and then finished as engravings. In this technique, which Blake mastered as an apprentice, the design's outline was traced with a needle through an acid-resistant "ground" covering the copper plate and then etched with acid. The engraver went over these slightly incised lines with burins (metal tools with square or lozenge-shaped tips used to cut lines into the plate) and engraved the plate's entire surface, uniting all parts in a web of crosshatched lines. These advances in technique (Fig. 1) enabled "modern" engravers to represent mass and tone more convincingly than the more linear style of such "ancient " engravers as Blake's heroes, Dürer and Raimondi, whose works were often dismissed as "Hard Stiff & Dry Unfinishd Works of Art" (anno. Reynolds, E 639). The Job engravings were executed entirely with burins and without preliminary etching, with tone subordinate to line and texture and with lines amassed in parallel strokes rather than in the conventional "dot and lozenge" pattern (dots incised in the interstices of cross-hatched lines, the linear system characteristic of bank-note engraving). Blake's emulation of the ancient engravers produced a modern result: original artistic expression in a graphic medium whose materiality and natural language were fully exploited. It was the masterpiece of his lifetime as an engraver, but it would be a tough sell, as Blake and Linnell, who had 315 sets printed in early 1826, must both have realized.[1]

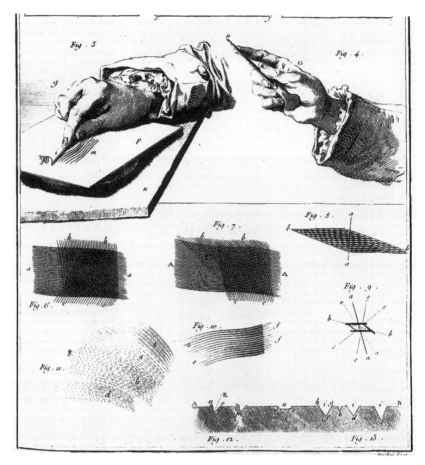

Figure 1 Methods of holding and using the burin (Figs. 4–5); the type of lines and hatching used to delineate and model forms (Figs. 6–11); cross-section of a plate showing types and depths of lines and burrs (Figs. 12–13). *Encyclopédie*, 1767.

Works that Blake had in stock were not selling well. Even if the illuminated books might do better, as Cumberland supposed, the prospect of printing new copies did not excite their maker:

> ... having none remaining of all that I had Printed I cannot Print more Except at a great loss for at the time I printed those things I had a whole House to range in now I am shut up in a Corner therefore am forced to ask a Price for them that I scarce expect to get from a Stranger. I am now Printing a Set of the Songs of Innocence & Experience for a Friend at Ten Guineas which I cannot do under Six Months consistent with my other Work, so that I have little hope of doing any more of such things. the Last Work I produced is a Poem Entitled Jerusalem the Emanation of the Giant Albion, but find that to Print it will Cost

my Time the amount of Twenty Guineas One I have Finishd It contains 100
Plates but it is not likely that I shall get a Customer for it
(letter of 12 April 1827, E 783–84)

Though dubious about their prospects, Blake listed six books he was willing
to reprint – at about twenty times the prices advertised in his 1793 Prospectus
(E 693).

Producing new copies of any illuminated book had become far more labor
intensive, with each illuminated page now printed on one side of the leaf and
elaborately colored, framed with lines, and often touched with gold leaf.
Impressions now looked more like miniature paintings, a far cry from those
produced in the 1790s, when plates were usually printed on both sides of the
paper and lightly colored to look more like pages than prints or paintings.
But six months?

Blake's "Corner" was two fair-sized rooms in the Strand – much less space
than the "eight or ten rooms" (BR 560) in Lambeth, where from 1790 to
1800 he had written, designed, etched, printed, and colored *The Marriage
of Heaven and Hell* (1790), *Visions of the Daughters of Albion, America a
Prophecy, For Children: The Gates of Paradise* (all 1793), *Europe a Prophecy,
Songs of Experience*, the combined *Songs of Innocence and of Experience,
The First Book of Urizen* (all 1794), *The Book of Los, The Song of Los*,
and *The Book of Ahania* (all 1795), and where he also reprinted copies of
his earlier works, *All Religions are One* and *There is No Natural Religion*
(1788), *Songs of Innocence* (1789), and *The Book of Thel* (1789–90). By
1795, Blake had produced over 125 copies of the 168 surviving copies of
illuminated books.[2]

Clearly, six months was a lot of time to devote to an illuminated book. Of
the 111 engravings that Blake had produced between 1789 and 1795, he had
executed 80 between 1790 and 1793, which suggests that he concentrated on
illuminated printing during 1789–90 and 1793–95, intervals that correspond
exactly with the books' dates, and that he underwrote the cost of his original
productions with his commercial work. From one medium-sized engraving,
Blake could earn £15–30 (E 703) or as much as £80 (BR 569). Had he sold
his entire stock of illuminated books at their initial prices, he would have
made less than £50, barely enough to pay for the copper and paper, let alone
his labor.[3] By 1795, with a stock of illuminated books, he began to redirect
his considerable energies toward other projects. These included 12 large
color-print drawings, 537 watercolor illustrations to Edward Young's *Night
Thoughts*, 43 of which he engraved, 117 illustrations to Gray's *Poems*, the
Four Zoas manuscript, and a series of tempera paintings for Butts. The 1790s
were his most successful period financially, not from the sale of illuminated

39

books but from the steady employment by the book and print publishers and his patron. After the intense early periods of illuminated printing, the books never again commanded center stage in his life; even the 150 plates of the major prophecies *Milton* (c. 1811) and *Jerusalem* (c. 1820) were written and etched over many years consistent with his "other Work."

In 1800 the Blakes left London to spend three years in Felpham. On their return they took a first-floor apartment in South Molton Street. Their living quarters became smaller with each move, more suitable for engraving and painting than printing. At Felpham, Blake may have printed a few separate copies of *Innocence* and *Experience*; at South Molton Street, he wrote and printed *Milton* and *Jerusalem*, probably revised *For Children*, and reprinted nine other illuminated books – about twenty-nine copies altogether. These were the years of Blake's 1809 exhibition, illustrations to Blair's *Grave*, illustrations to Milton, most of the Bible illustrations, and the Canterbury Pilgrims engraving. By contrast, when Cumberland wrote him at Fountain Court, he had etched only three illuminated plates, for *On Homers Poetry* (c. 1822) and *The Ghost of Abel* (1822), and had printed only four copies of *Songs* (copies W and Y in 1825, Z and AA in 1826). But, as implied in his letter to Cumberland, he remained as busy as ever.

Blake had been illustrating Dante's *Divine Comedy* for over two years. When he wrote Cumberland, he had 102 designs and was engraving 7 of them. As he told Linnell, "I am too much attachd to Dante to think much of any thing else – I have Proved the Six Plates & reduced the Fighting Devils ready for the Copper I count myself sufficiently Paid If I live as I now do" (letter of 25 April 1827, E 784). The other work was a copy of *Marriage* (I) and one of *Songs* (X), the "Set of the Songs" he was "now Printing." Both were highly finished in gold, watercolors, and pen and ink. His very last book, though, was uncolored copy F of *Jerusalem*, a commission secured by Linnell a few weeks after he wrote Cumberland. Its "100 Plates" did not, however, sell for "Twenty Guineas"; Blake completed it on his deathbed, and its £5 5 shillings sale price helped to pay for his burial.[4]

Three books in six months. Printing illuminated books was still possible, but more difficult than before because they demanded greater artistic attention, disrupted other work, and required more space. The place they occupied in Blake's life had changed. How different things had been with "a whole House to range in," where he could spread out and move through the stages of illuminated printing, from preparing plates and designing pages, to etching and printing designs, to coloring and collating impressions, as though moving through the six days of creation – or the six "chambers" of the "Printing house in Hell" (*MHH* 15, E 40).

In the first chamber was a Dragon-Man, clearing away the rubbish from
a caves mouth; within, a number of Dragons were hollowing the cave

Fifteen of Blake's nineteen illuminated works were executed in a relief-etching technique he had invented in 1788. In his prospectus of 1793 he called it "Illuminated Printing" and announced that he had "invented a method of Printing both Letter-press and Engraving in a style more ornamental, uniform, and grand, than any before discovered, while it produces works at less than one fourth of the expense"; he defined it as "a method of Printing which combines the Painter and the Poet" (Prospectus, E 692–93). Though he never explained the technique, he did describe his "infernal method" as "melting apparent surfaces away, and displaying the infinite which was hid" (*MHH* 14, E 39). In "a Printing house in Hell," he "saw the method in which knowledge is transmitted from generation to generation," and allegorized its major stages as fantastic acts in six "chambers," where a "cave," symbolizing the copper plate, was made "infinite" and "cast" into the "expanse" (*MHH* 15, E 40).

In practice, Blake wrote texts and drew illustrations with pens and brushes on copper plates in acid-resistant ink and, with nitric acid, etched away the unprotected metal to bring the composite design into printable relief. He printed the plates in colored inks on a rolling press and tinted most impressions in watercolors. While the combination of word and image is a prominent feature of illuminated printing, it appears not to have been the impetus for the invention. He credited the method to a vision of his recently deceased brother Robert, and first used it for *The Approach of Doom*,[5] a print in imitation of Robert's wash drawing. The first works to incorporate text were *All Religions are One* and *No Natural Religion*, small philosophical tractates on perception and the "Poetic Genius." The following year he used the technique to publish poetry, beginning with *Innocence* and *Thel*.

Illuminated printing was not mysterious, complex, or difficult. The pens, brushes, and liquid medium enabled Blake to design directly on copper plates as though he were drawing on paper, which in turn encouraged him to integrate text and illustration on the same page. Technically, such integration was possible in conventional (intaglio) etching (as in *Ahania*), but the economics of publishing had long defined etching as image reproduction and letterpress as text reproduction, so that the conventional illustrated book was the product of much divided labor, with illustrations produced and printed in one medium and shop and separately inserted into leaves printed elsewhere in letterpress on a different kind of press. Even when words and images were brought together on the same leaf, divisions in production were maintained.

Whether Blake used relief or intaglio, as author illustrating and printing himself, he would have united the various stages of book production, obtaining control over the production of his illustrated text the same way he did as a graphic artist over his own images. The tools of drawing and sketching, though, freed him to think in new ways, to unite invention and execution in ways defeated by conventional printmaking. Moreover, the idea that an artist's first and spontaneous thoughts are most valuable because they are closest to the original creative spark, often obliterated by high finishing, had become very popular in the late eighteenth century, creating a taste for drawings and sketches and motivating printmakers to invent techniques to reproduce them in facsimile and to simulate their various textures (e.g., chalk, crayon, pen and wash). Such prints, however, were carefully executed with needles, roulettes (a textured wheel used to roughen the plate's surface to produce tonalities), and other metal tools, their spontaneity a crafted illusion. Blake, on the other hand, by actually using the tools and techniques of writing and drawing, had solved the technical problem of reproducing pen and brush marks in metal. He created a multi-media site where poetry, painting, and printmaking came together in ways both original and characteristic of Romanticism's fascination with spontaneity and the idea of the sketch.[6]

No printmaker before Blake had incorporated the tools and techniques of writing, drawing, and painting in a graphic medium, though the materials and tools were commonplace. The varnishes, acid, inks, dabbers, brushes, quills, oils, colors, and paper were in every engraver's workshop – along with the main ingredient, the copper plate. Plates were purchased from coppersmiths, usually cut to size. Because intaglio etchings and engravings had to be printed with pressure great enough to force paper into the incised lines, which resulted in a "platemark" or embossment that revealed the plate's shape, engravers neatly squared the plate and bevelled the sides to prevent them from cutting the paper. For relief etching, Blake cut small plates out of larger sheets himself, cutting them roughly equal size but not uniformly, using either a hammer and chisel or scoring the sheet deeply with a burin and snapping it between boards. Because he printed from raised surfaces rather than incised lines, he used less pressure and avoided pronounced platemarks, and consequently he dispensed with squaring and bevelling. Equally unorthodox, he etched both sides of plates (for example, *Experience*, *Europe*, and *Urizen* were etched on the backs of *Innocence*, *America*, and *Marriage* plates). Cutting the cost of copper, his most expensive material, the "verso" books were the only ones to turn a profit at the time.[7]

Blake prepared plates for relief etching as he did for intaglio etching. He planed plates on an anvil with a hammer (the tools of Los in Blake's mythology), and then, with water, oil, and various grinding stones, polished the surface to a mirror-like finish. Polishing made plates easier to cut with burins or needles and easier to wipe clean of ink, but it deposited a greasy film that had to be removed, otherwise either the etching ground or Blake's "ink" would have adhered to the film rather than metal and could have flaked from the plate in the acid bath. Because relief etchings required a long bite in strong acid, thorough and correct "degreasing" with chalk or breadcrumbs – "clearing away the rubbish" – was of the utmost importance.

In the second chamber was a Viper folding round the rock & the cave,
and others adorning it with gold, silver and precious stones

In intaglio etching, Blake melted a ball of ground consisting of wax and resins and spread it over a warm degreased plate. He smoked the ground to darken and harden it, transferred the design onto it, and cut through the design with a needle (Fig. 2). The metal thus exposed was bitten below the surface with acid. In relief etching, though, he drew the design directly on a clean copper plate with pens and brushes using a liquid medium. Like the etching ground, this medium had to be acid-resistant but it also had to flow easily, adhere when dry, not spread or blot on the plate, and be usable with pens and brushes. In short, it had to behave like writing ink. Linnell identified Blake's "impervious liquid" (*BR* 460 n.1) as being the usual "stop-out" varnish that etchers used to paint over lines sufficiently etched to "stop" the acid from biting them deeper (Fig. 3). By stopping out lines and biting plates in successive stages, etchers varied the depth and width of lines – much as engravers did by cutting them deeper with their diamond-shaped burins. Varying the amount of ink that lines held altered their tone, making possible the modeling of forms and the illusion of aerial perspective.

Blake did not invent his writing medium; he merely adapted one of the brown asphaltum-based stop-out varnishes. With plate, acid-resistant "ink," pens, and brushes, he entered the second chamber and, like "a Viper folding round the rock & the cave," he rewrote his text, first drafted on paper, and illustrated it in a sinuous, calligraphic hand. By cutting into broad areas painted in stop-out, he created fine white and black parallel lines (Fig. 4); by cutting the nib of his quill, he varied the strokes of his letters.

Because the printed image mirrors the plate image, Blake rewrote his text backwards, an "art" his friends acknowledged he "excel[led] in" (*BR* 212 n.1) – and which he pictures himself doing in *Jerusalem* plate 37. He usually started with text and illustrated around it, visually composing the page design while executing it (Fig. 5). How different this was from the way he worked as an etcher and engraver – from all etchers and engravers – even when executing original designs. Their methods and objectives prevented

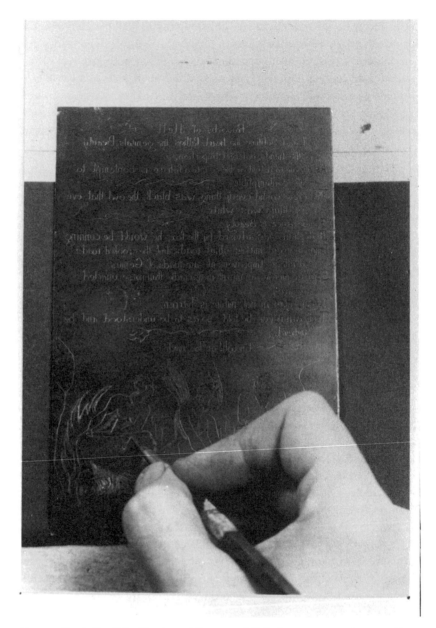

Figure 2 Facsimile of *The Marriage of Heaven and Hell* plate 10, executed as an etching. 15.3 × 10.1 cm; the design cut through the ground with a needle.

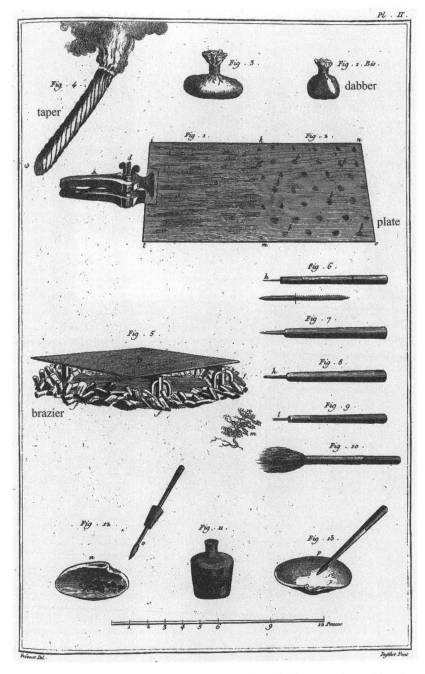

Figure 3 Tools and materials of etching: etching ground and dabber, taper for smoking plates, plate with melted ground, charcoal brazier, various tipped needles, stop-out varnish, brush, and shells. *Encyclopédie*, 1767.

Figure 4 (above) "Title plate," *Songs of Innocence*, 1789. Manchester Etching Workshop facsimiles, line block, printed without borders. 1983. Detail, showing white lines cut into broad brush marks.

Figure 5 (below) Facsimile of *The Marriage of Heaven and Hell* plate 10, executed as a relief etching. 15.2 × 10.1 cm; writing text backwards with a quill with a string as line guide.

designing directly in the metal; the image they reproduced was first worked up on paper and then transferred to the plate as a guide for the needle. Likewise, the engraver needed the lightly etched outline because the burin cuts rather than draws lines, translating them into three-dimensional lines of varying depth and width. But the methods used by engravers to transfer designs did not work in relief etching, and there was no technical need for Blake to transfer the page design or any of its parts, since he was engaged neither in cutting it into the plate nor in translating it into different kinds of lines. The tools and Blake's twenty years of drawing experience enabled him to design his pages as he rewrote his texts on the plates, as though creating an illuminated manuscript.

No illuminated designs that might have been transferred or even redrawn are extant, nor are there any mockups of designs except for two roughly composed, textless pencil sketches for *Thel* plates 6 and 7, and both differ considerably from the printed designs. Blake realized very early that his new medium's autographic nature made the poem the only prerequisite for executing plates, that rewriting texts was also an act of visual invention, and thus that the medium could be used for production rather than reproduction. With no designs to transfer or reproduce, the placement and extent of text, letter size, line spacing, as well as placement and extent of illustration, were invented only during execution.[8] This method of designing meant that Blake did not know which lines or stanzas would go on which plate, or how many plates a poem/book would need. Working without models allowed each illuminated print and book to evolve through its production in ways impossible in conventional book-making. Blake could begin working on a book before it was completely written.[9]

While writing backwards was not difficult, mastering the "ink" and giving small letters the proper slant were, at least initially. Blake could dip brushes directly in the ink, but probably loaded the quill pens used for text with a small brush, a method illuminators used to keep quills from clogging. And like illuminators of manuscripts, he may have slanted his plates to keep his quill as horizontal as possible. Blake could write texts in roman or italic lettering – he used both in *No Natural Religion* – but he quickly favored the latter, which was easier to write and, with fewer letter ends to coordinate, to keep straight and uniform. Italic script also facilitated the next stage: with fewer letter ends exposed to acid, words were better protected against problems caused by the acid pitting and lifting the ground. Tight designs also exemplified Blake's thinking in terms of his medium: to be printable, they do not need to be bitten as deeply as designs with open spaces, and thus require less time in acid. Their dense line systems also facilitated inking by keeping the ink dabber on the surface and clear of the "shallows," the areas bitten below the surface meant to print white.

In the third chamber was an Eagle with wings and feathers of air, he caused the inside of the cave to be infinite, around were numbers of Eagle like men, who built palaces in the immense cliffs

Blake had to etch accurately to retain the autographic quality of his designs. The acid – or "aquafortis" – commonly employed in his day was diluted nitric. Acid is unpredictable, affected by age, temperature, humidity, and the metal's purity – especially in relief etching, because the large amount of exposed metal heats it and makes it bite more viciously. Such "corrosives" may be "salutary and medicinal... in Hell" (*MHH* 14, E 39), but on earth they emit noxious orange fumes and require good ventilation. Blake embedded the plate's edges in strips of wax to create a self-contained tray and poured the acid about a quarter inch deep. He watched it turn blue and gas bubbles form along the design – more bubbles than he had ever seen before, signs of trouble. He passed a feather – the conventional tool to agitate the acid – over the design (Fig. 6), doing so every few minutes as bubbles began to reform, to keep the acid from undercutting or lifting the design: "an Eagle with wings and feathers of air ... caused the inside of the cave to be infinite." Looking down on the flat, dark-brown design on reddish copper in its cloudy blue-tinted bath, he was like Rintrah, shaking "his fires in the burdend air," watching "hungry clouds swag on the deep" (*MHH* 2, E 33). Indeed, he was the Spirit of God that "was upon the face of the deep ... divid[ing] the light from the darkness" (Genesis 1:1–4).

Hours, not days, later, unetched surfaces were divided from shallows and a relief plate was created. Like a god brooding over creation – pictured on *Marriage* plate 14 – Blake was "Melting apparent surfaces away, and displaying the infinite which was hid" (E 39). Displayed, of course, was the composite design now visible in relief, metaphorically materialized as "immense cliffs" large enough to house "palaces" built by "Eagle like men," assistants in the "image" and "likeness" of the Eagle, as signs of their "dominion" (Genesis 1:26). The cliffs and valleys of this small copper plate were indeed a minute particular manifesting creation itself.

Under the watchful eyes of Blake or his trusted "devil," or printer's assistant, his wife Catherine, etching could take much of the day; no doubt a few plates were etched at the same time – but not in one long continuous bite of the acid. In intaglio etching, Blake stopped out selected areas and etched the plate in successive stages to vary line depth and tone. But relief lines are all on the same level and thus receive equal amounts of ink; like woodcuts, they are essentially two-dimensional, boldly contrasting black-and-white forms incapable of producing tonal gradation. Nevertheless, Blake stopped out his plates at least once. (A two-stage etch is indicated by steps around the relief plateaus of Blake's only surviving relief-etched copperplate, a fragment from a rejected *America* plate.) After forty-five to ninety minutes of etching, his design was in slight relief. He poured off the acid, dried the plate, and then carefully painted over words with stop out to protect details from lifting during a longer second bite, which was necessary to deepen the areas around words and lines. Only if the "ink" started to lift would there be additional stopping out. A long day, but at the end, a printable image was created many times more quickly than by engraving, where a square inch of close cross-hatching could take a full day or more.

In the fourth chamber were Lions of flaming fire raging around &
melting the metals into living fluids

After etching the design into printable relief, pouring off the acid, and removing the wax walls, Blake erased the "ink" with turpentine and polished the plate. He was now ready to make printing ink.

Ink for relief and intaglio printing was made by grinding powdered pigment with different grades of burnt walnut or linseed oil. Intaglio ink is tackier and stiffer than relief because it must stay in incised lines when the plate's surface is wiped clean and requires more pressure to transfer evenly. Nevertheless, Blake used it to print relief plates, as is evinced by the slightly reticulated surfaces of his prints, especially noticeable in solid areas. He inked plates on the intaglio printer's conventional charcoal brazier, whose low heat made stiff ink thinner and more fluid and thus easier to manipulate and spread (Fig. 7). Like a "Lion[] of flaming fire raging around & melting the metals into living fluids," he spread glistening, warm ink with a linen dabber, moving its slightly convex bottom across the plate's surface and off the shallows. Plates with wide shallows he inked locally with small dabbers or brushes. Even so, inking relief plates was quicker than intaglio plates, which required a two-step process of rubbing ink into the lines and wiping the surface clean with rags and the palm of the hand.

Blake wiped the ink from any relief surfaces he did not wish to print. He routinely wiped the thin line bordering the plate created by the wax dike used to hold the acid (Fig. 8). The borders formed part of the plate's relief line system and acted as runners for the dabber. Wiping them was similar to wiping the bevelled edges of intaglio plates to prevent them from blemishing the platemark. The result, however, was very different. Platemarks, clean or not, always reveal a plate's shape and hence the image's origin and

Figure 6 Facsimile of *Marriage* plate 10 as relief etching: biting the plate in nitric acid and feathering the gas bubbles away from the design.

Figure 7 Inking an intaglio plate over a brazier with a dabber (Fig. a), and wiping ink off the plate's surface with the palm of the hand (Fig. b); pulling the intaglio plate and paper through the rolling press. *Encyclopédie*, 1767.

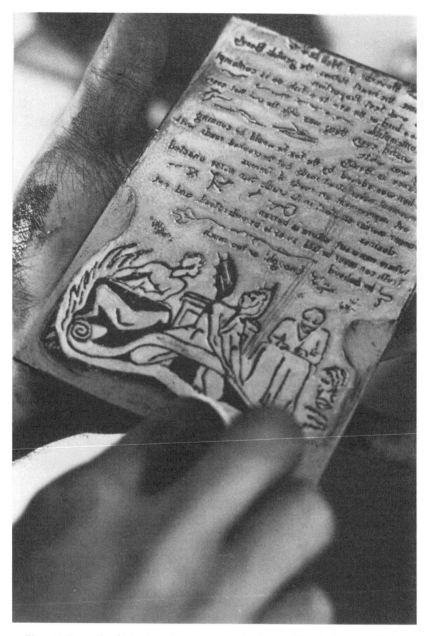

Figure 8 Facsimile of *Marriage* plate 10, as relief etching: wiping the borders of ink.

medium. Because relief etchings produce no pronounced platemark, wiping the borders erased overt signs of the graphic medium. The unframed text and image looked written and drawn rather than printed, a unique rather than a repeatable image, an illusion further enhanced by colored inks and watercolor finishing.

The books were "Printed in Colours" (Prospectus, E 693). The first printing of *Thel*, for example, yielded thirteen (surviving) copies in five different colors. Changing inks during a print run diversified stock but also required more time, but it was not as labor intensive as color printing, in which a few opaque colors were applied to the plate's surfaces and shallows, sometimes heavily, sometimes lightly, and printed with the inked design. Blake had adapted the *à la poupée* technique English printers used for color printing, and used it for nearly everything he printed in 1794–95.[10] In effect, he painted plates with small dabbers (*poupées*) to produce opaque colors and textures resembling oil sketches, which he enriched and finished in watercolors and pen and ink. In 1795, he brilliantly extended color printing more fully into painting, executing "12 Large Prints... Printed in Colours... unaccompanied by any writing." He rarely used the technique for books after that, though in 1796 he created the Large and Small Books of Designs for, appropriately enough, a miniaturist painter, by color printing a "selection" of plates "from the different Books of such as could be Printed without the Writing" (letter of 9 June 1818, E 771).

In the fifth chamber were Unnam'd forms, which cast the metals into the expanse

From the inking station, Blake went to the press, where he again met Mrs. Blake, his printing "devil." Simultaneously the dirtiest and cleanest of arts, involving oily inks and pristine paper, printing was best performed by two people. Printers, though, went unnamed in inscriptions on reproductive prints, which recorded date, title, artist, publisher, and engraver. Blake signed most illuminated works "Author & Printer W. Blake" or "Printed by W. Blake," taking pride in his manual as well as mental labor. The fifth chamber's unpictureable image also puns on "form," which is typeset into pages in a metal frame for printing. "Cast," another printing pun, refers to a stereotype (a solid body of type), as well as to the mold in which molten metals are poured; here, the mold shaping the "living... metals" is the "expanse" of blank sheets of paper, which now embody the relief plate's immense cliffs, valleys, and palaces.

Blake printed on "the most beautiful wove paper that could be procured" (Prospectus, E 693) – the kind used by engravers. And he prepared it as a printmaker rather than a book printer, tearing large sheets of paper into quarters, eights, or twelves, instead of printing the sheet and then folding it into pages. Depending on the size of the sheet and how he cut it, the resulting leaves were basically big, medium, and small, or, according to Blake, "folio," "quarto," and "octavo," because they roughly corresponded with those standard book sizes (he advertised *Songs*, for example, as "octavo"). Like all intaglio and relief printers of the day, he dampened the paper for printing.

Blake had taught his wife how to print, draw, and color, and was especially proud of her printing abilities. She proofed and printed both his relief and intaglio plates (*BR* 459). For relief plates, they decreased the pressure on their rolling press (a machine with two large cylinders between which a board passes when the top cylinder is turned) by slightly raising the roller and probably removing one of three felt blankets placed between plate and roller. Blake laid the inked plate on the bed of the press, face up. Mrs. Blake held top and bottom of a damp sheet of paper and lowered it onto the plate, being careful not to let it sag in the middle and touch the ink, or to move it once it touched the plate, otherwise some lines would print double or slightly out of focus. She covered the leaf registered to the plate with a backing sheet and blankets and turned the press's handle to pull the bed smoothly between two heavy rollers (see Fig. 7). After the "marriage" of inked plate and paper, she removed the printed impression to dry and brought another leaf to the press as Blake brought another plate, returning the printed plate to the brazier to be reinked.

Printing impressions without pronounced platemarks meant Blake could print on both sides of leaves to create facing pages. This conventional book format used less paper, which was Blake's largest expense other than metal, but could present difficulties. Mrs. Blake registered the clean side of the paper just printed onto the newly inked plate, and covered the printed side with a stiff backing sheet or thin metal plate (which she could wipe of offset ink and reuse). Offset was minimal, as in letterpress printing, because the ink was slightly pressed into the paper, and thus below the surface. Alternatively, Blake could print a stack of leaves and then print the versos (kept damp) once the ink was dry to the touch. In 1794, Blake began routinely printing on only one side of the paper, which, though easier, changed the dynamic between book and reader: with no competing image, the solo design dominated the page spread, demanding full attention and, in this format, came to demand more of Blake as it became increasingly more painterly.

By alternating plates, the Blakes kept the press in action and could efficiently print a dozen impressions in an hour. Printing eleven copies of an eleven-plate book like *Visions* (121 impressions) would take less than two full days. Normally, they printed one plate at a time, but for small plates, such as *Songs*, they could print two, each onto a separate leaf, halving their printing time. Registration of paper to plate was sometimes off, resulting in designs hanging low or high, slanted left or right. Blake did not mind; he appears to have rarely discarded impressions, since the quality of inking, printing, and registration varies within copies of books. Creating pages with uniform margins was impossible with plates only roughly equal in size, and given how they were cut, it is not likely that Blake was very exacting about registration. He did not abhor accidents, but saw them as part of the creative process, as revealing the maker's hand and production process.

Hell's "Printing house" has no chamber explicitly designated for coloring impressions. The infernal printmakers, however, incorporated ornamentation and color into the second and fourth chambers: the brushes illustrating text were also "adorning it with gold, silver, and precious stones," and the "living fluids" of colored inks were inherently illuminating. Blake's 1793 prospectus does not explicitly state that impressions were hand colored, only that they were "Printed in Colours." But "illuminated" implies coloring, specifically of manuscripts, and "a method of Printing which combines the Painter and the Poet" implies the same.

As with quills, inks, and varnishes, Blake made his own watercolors. He ground many of the same pigments used to make ink in water and gum arabic instead of oil, and, to make the thicker, more opaque colors, in a thin carpenter's glue, diluting the paste with water to vary the paint layer's consistency. In the early days, when he printed in earth tones (yellow ochre and raw sienna mostly), he applied broad, delicate washes in only a few colors, and usually left texts unwashed. He printed late works in red and orange inks, bright colors that invited a more extensive palette and elaborate coloring. He applied colors in thin washes and translucent layers with detailed brushwork, adding blues, pinks, or yellows behind text and often outlining texts and illustrations in pen and ink (Fig. 9). The result was a beautiful, strongly linear miniature, with legibility sometimes compromised.

He and his wife shared the task of illuminating the prints, at least in the first productions, perhaps adapting the method print publishers used when coloring prints, with each colorist using one or two colors and then passing the impression to the next colorist to add another color or two. For some books, Blake may have finished an impression from each stack of pages as a model, but neither he nor Mrs. Blake copied the other exactly. Making each impression exactly repeatable (as one would expect of books and prints) was not really possible when working by hand with an assistant. While each copy produced was a unique work of art, most impressions printed and colored at the same time do not differ very much; they share

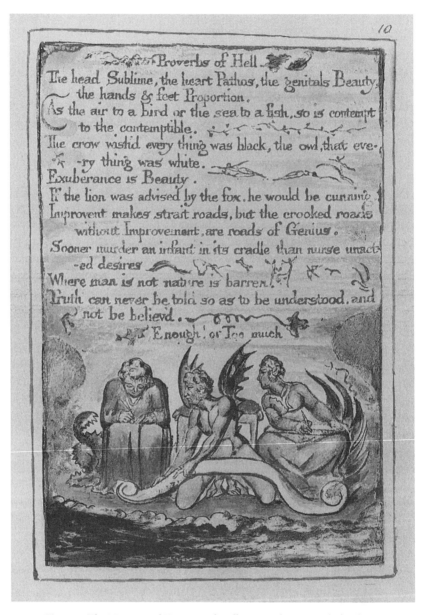

Figure 9 *The Marriage of Heaven and Hell* copy I, plate 10. Relief etching, 1790. 14.9 × 10.2 cm.

printing style, colors, coloring style, and even placement of colors. Making each impression *very* different would have required more labor and time, and, given the objective of producing multiple copies of books "at less than one fourth of the expense," would have been inefficient. Books printed in different periods, though, were also printed and colored in different styles and are visually very different. Overt differences among copies, in other words, usually reveal different periods and styles of production and not revision of the particular work.

There they were reciev'd by Men who occupied the sixth chamber, and took the forms of books & were arranged in libraries

The sixth chamber conflates two actions, collating leaves to form copies of books and distributing them. It also implicitly questions the reception – and perception – of the book.

Like other book publishers of the day, the Blakes knew purchasers would have their books professionally bound. They merely fastened the leaves between two sheets of laid paper by tying string through three or more stab holes. (They varied the plate order for many of the early books, most notably for *Songs* and *Urizen*.) And like the publishers, they warehoused or "arranged" their copies in the printing house. But the "sixth chamber" is also *outside* the printing house, in "the expanse" into which the metals were "cast." The "expanse" is, ironically, the private space defined by the blank paper in the studio, but it is also the public space occupied by that paper as it moves from production to reception. After its gloriously sublime journey, touched by "Dragons," "Vipers," "Eagles," "Lions," "Unnamd forms," and now "Men," the illuminated print shelved in a library seems anticlimactic. But is it? As a "cast" of the original plate, it extends Hell's Printing house to the place of reading. Do the "fires of hell ... look like torment and insanity" or "an immense world of delight"? Is the reader an "Angel ... whose works are only Analytics," or an "Angel, who is now become a Devil," reading in the "infernal or diabolical sense" (*MHH* 6, 7, 20, 24; E 35, 42, 44)? Does the reader participate in or resist the creative process embodied in the book?

In 1795, Blake produced a deluxe set of the books on large paper, possibly to display at the shop of his friend and sometimes employer, the publisher Joseph Johnson. Blake had by this time printed and colored with Mrs. Blake about 125 copies of his illuminated books in small editions very much on his own terms: "No Subscriptions for the numerous great works now in hand are asked, for none are wanted; but the Author will produce his works, and offer them to sale at a fair price" (Prospectus, E 693). Except for *Songs*, most copies of illuminated books executed by 1795 were also printed by 1795: fourteen of the sixteen extant copies of *Thel*; seven of the nine copies of *Marriage*; fourteen of seventeen copies of *Visions*, twelve of fourteen copies of *America*; eight of the nine copies of *Europe*; seven of the eight copies of *Urizen*; unique copies of *The Book of Los* and *Ahania*, and the six copies of *The Song of Los*.

For years he relied on stock, which, for *Songs*, his most popular work, lasted till around 1802, when he reprinted a few copies of *Innocence* and *Experience*, adding a few more in 1804 or 1805. One from the latter printing (Q) he sold to the Rev. Joseph Thomas, who paid "ten guineas" (£10 10 shillings) – the price Blake feared in 1827 he could "scarce expect to get from a Stranger" – as a way of giving this proud artist a monetary gift. This was far more than Blake had ever received for an illuminated book, and "for such a sum" he "could hardly do enough, finishing the plates like miniatures."[11] Indeed, Blake's "fair price" for the *Songs* was originally 6 shillings, 6 pence (Prospectus, E 693). Initially, all his books were sold in shillings, not pounds, priced as poetry rather than as colored prints or small paintings. The following year, in 1806, when Butts requested a copy, Blake's stock of *Songs* was again depleted, so he created copy E by salvaging poorly printed impressions from various 1789, 1794, and 1795 printings of *Innocence* and *Experience* still in the studio, recoloring them and strengthening text and designs in pen and ink. A lot of work but easier than making ink and colors, preparing paper and press, inking plates and printing, which were not worth doing for just one copy of one book – or, at that time, even for a complete set of books.

In December 1808, Cumberland wrote on behalf of a friend who "was so charmed" with Blake's "incomparable etchings...that he requested... a compleat Set of all you have published in the way of *Books* coloured as mine are." If none were "to be had," he was "willing to wait your own time in order to have them as those of mine are" (*BR* 211). Blake refused this generous offer, fearing to disrupt his "present course" of "Designing & Painting":

> I am very much obliged by your kind ardour in my cause & should immediately Engage in reviving my former pursuits of printing if I had not now so long been turned out of the old channel into a new one that it is impossible for me to return to it without destroying my present course New Vanities or rather new pleasures occupy my thoughts New profits seem to arise before me so tempting that I have already involved myself in engagements that preclude all possibility of promising any thing...my time...in future must alone be devoted to Designing & Painting.   (letter of 19 December 1808, E 769–70)

Blake was working on his 1809 exhibition, which netted a scurrilous review but no profits. For the next decade, with his stock of books depleted, Blake continued to work primarily as a painter and engraver, executing temperas (what he called "fresco"), illustrating Milton's major poems, and engraving designs after Flaxman. He finished his *Milton*, printing three copies about 1811, and he continued to etch plates for *Jerusalem* – though, according to Cumberland, he had already etched "60 Plates of a new Prophecy" by summer 1807 (*BR* 187).

Only fourteen copies of four books (*Innocence, Experience, America*, and *Milton*) were produced between c. 1796 and 1818, which means that most illuminated books lay untouched for over twenty years. Blake did not replenish his stock until around 1818, motivated possibly by Linnell, whom he met that summer, and/or an inquiry about the books from Dawson Turner. He sent Turner a list of eight books (*Innocence* and *Experience* were still listed separately) and "12 Large Prints" that he was willing to reprint and their prices, telling him "that any Person wishing to have any or all of them should send me their Order to Print them on the above terms & I will take care that they shall be done at least as well as any I have yet Produced" (letter of 9 June 1818, E 771). For the first time since 1795, he printed copies of *Thel* (N, O), *Marriage* (G), *Visions* (N, O, P), and *Urizen* (G), along with *Milton* (D) and *Songs* (U, T), all in the same orange-red ink, paper, and coloring style. Of these, only *Marriage*, which he did not include in the list for Turner, and *Songs* would he print again.[12] Nor did he list *Jerusalem*, which was still in progress and not printed till c. 1820, in three copies in black ink, one of which Linnell purchased. He did list *America* and *Europe*, but did not print them till 1821, when he produced matching copies (O and K, respectively) for Linnell and began printing and coloring *Jerusalem* copy E in the same style.

The books he offered Cumberland in 1827 were the same as those he had offered Turner (minus *Milton* and with *Innocence* and *Experience* combined), and the prices were £1–2 higher. Though nothing on the list was printed, he was – "consistent with [his] other Work" – printing copies of *Songs* and *Marriage* (again, conspicuously missing from his list), and ended his days printing a copy of *Jerusalem*. When he said he had "none remaining of all that [he] had Printed," he meant it. He had even sold his personal copies: *Songs* copy R (the model for the plate order of the last seven copies), printed c. 1795, to Linnell in 1819, for £1 19sh. 6d. (more than £4 less than he asked Turner for *Songs*) and *Marriage* copy H, printed in 1790, to Linnell in 1821, for £2 2sh. (less than half the then price of *Urizen* – which was etched on its versos). As with *Songs* copy E, he reworked both books before selling them. For *Songs* copy R, he added wide frames around each image and strengthened the coloring. For *Marriage* copy H, initially uncolored but printed in various red, olive, and green inks on both sides of the leaves, Blake elaborately colored the pages, adding gold leaf and, most unusually, going over the texts in various colored inks, word by word.

When he died, Blake had the only complete colored copy of *Jerusalem* (E), which he feared would not find "a Customer," and *Songs* copy W. His wife inherited both but could sell only the *Songs*. All of Blake's illuminated plates, prints, drawings, and manuscripts ended up in the hands of Frederick Tatham, one of the young artists who gathered around Blake in the last years of his life. In the 1830s, Tatham printed uncolored copies of *Songs, America, Europe,* and *Jerusalem* from Blake's plates. The plates disappeared while in Tatham's possession, reputedly sold for scrap metal (*BR* 417 n.3).

From the perspective of book publishing, Blake's illuminated books were produced as fine "limited editions." They were not invented to secure financial independence, and they didn't. And though Blake stated that his method cut production costs (primarily by his not paying for labor, manuscript, or design), it was a labor intensive, and not a cost effective, means of production, mostly underwritten by his commercial work. Printing relief-etched plates was not difficult, but it was slow compared to printing books in the standard way. Considering how few copies Blake could produce during the "run," we can see why he felt that he was "never ... able to produce a Sufficient number for a general Sale by means of a regular Publisher," and why the books proved "unprofitable enough to [him] tho Expensive to the Buyer." But from the perspective of an artist accustomed to producing unique works, illuminated books provided Blake with wider audiences and greater opportunities to make his reputation, as he admitted to Turner: "The Few I have Printed & Sold are sufficient to have gained me great reputation as an Artist which was the chief thing Intended." He also insisted, though, referring to the Large and Small Books of Designs, that printing illuminated plates "without the Writing" was at "the Loss of some of the best things For they when Printed perfect accompany Poetical Personifications & Acts without which Poems they never could have been Executed" (letter of 9 June 1818, E 771).

Looking back from the last year of his life, Blake could see the great contrast between his early and late illuminated books. The first six years of production progressed through a series of three formats: leaves printed on both sides and lightly washed (1789–93), color printing (1794–95), and single-sided printing with borders and richer coloring (c. 1795). After 1795, the format remained the same, though the coloring style continued to become more elaborate. Late practice differed from early in that far fewer copies per book were produced, various titles were produced in the same session,

and printing sessions appear to have been motivated by at least one commission, which made printing other titles viable. Late copies cost far more
than early ones. The dramatic increase in price reflects a change in Blake's
idea of the book – from books of poems to series of hand-colored prints,
from prints as pages to prints as paintings. The latter demanded more from
him and the reader, but, early or late, his books always had the power to
illuminate, to open eyes and convert "angels" into "devils." The apocalyptic
role of his "infernal method" was always clear: "The whole creation will be
consumed, and appear infinite. and holy ... by an improvement of sensual
enjoyment" (*MHH* 14, E 39) – and with that, "the Author is sure of his
reward" (Prospectus, E 692).

Notes

1. Of these, 215 "proof" sets were printed on special papers for connoisseurs and
   sold at £6 6 shillings, and 100 sets were printed on regular paper, at £3 3 shillings.
   For Blake's apprenticeship and lifelong development as a graphic artist, see
   Essick, *William Blake, Printmaker* (Princeton: Princeton University Press, 1983).
2. This total omits the works of one plate, *On Homers Poetry* and *Laocoön*, and
   two plates, *The Ghost of Abel*.
3. See G. E. Bentley, Jr., "What is the Price of Experience: William Blake and the
   Economics of Illuminated Painting," *University of Toronto Quarterly* 68 (1999),
   pp. 628–29.
4. Blake died of liver failure; for a possible connection between that and chronic
   copper intoxication, see Viscomi and Robson, "Blake's Death," *Blake/An Illustrated Quarterly* 30 (1996), pp. 36–49.
5. Robert N. Essick, *The Separate Plates of William Blake: A Catalogue* (Princeton:
   Princeton University Press, 1983), III.
6. For the origins of illuminated printing, see Viscomi, *Blake and the Idea of the
   Book* (Princeton: Princeton University Press, 1993), chs. 4 and 18.
7. Bentley, "Price of Experience," p. 635.
8. After 1800, Blake invented two variations on relief etching (E 694). These required outlines to be transferred on etching grounds and the "whites" scraped
   or scratched through with oval and pointed needles to create images loosely resembling woodcuts or wood engravings (e.g., *J* 14 and 33). Accompanying text
   was still written backwards and the page designed when executed.
9. See Viscomi, "The Evolution of William Blake's *The Marriage of Heaven and
   Hell*," *Huntington Library Quarterly* 58.3&4 (1997), pp. 281–344.
10. French printers favored the multi-plate mode of color printing: a key plate prints
    the outline and separate plates, registered exactly onto the key plate, carry one
    or more colors. For a detailed examination of Blake's color printing method and
    others of his day, see Essick and Viscomi, "Inquiry into Blake's Method of Color
    Printing," *Blake/An Illustrated Quarterly* 35 (winter 2001), pp. 73–102.
11. Alexander Gilchrist, *Life of William Blake*, vol. I (London: Macmillan), p. 124.
12. There are no surviving post-1795 copies of *All Religions*, *No Natural Religion*,
    Book of Los, *Ahania*, or *Song of Los*.

Further reading

Bentley, G. E., Jr. "What is the Price of Experience: William Blake and the Economics of Illuminated Painting [sic Printing]." *University of Toronto Quarterly* 68 (1999): 617–41.

Eaves, Morris. *The Counter-Arts Conspiracy: Art and Industry in the Age of Blake.* Ithaca, NY: Cornell University Press, 1992.

Essick, Robert N. *The Separate Plates of William Blake: A Catalogue.* Princeton: Princeton University Press, 1983.

William Blake, Printmaker. Princeton: Princeton University Press, 1980.

William Blake's Commercial Book Illustrations: A Catalogue and Study of the Plates Engraved by Blake after Designs by Other Artists. Oxford: Clarendon Press, 1991.

Essick, Robert N., and Joseph Viscomi. "Blake's Method of Color Printing: Some Responses and Further Observations." *Blake/An Illustrated Quarterly* 36 (fall 2002): 36–49.

"An Inquiry into Blake's Method of Color Printing." *Blake/An Illustrated Quarterly* 35 (winter 2001): 73–102.

Gilchrist, Alexander. *Life of William Blake.* 2 vols. London: Macmillan, 1863.

Viscomi, Joseph. *Blake and the Idea of the Book.* Princeton: Princeton University Press, 1993.

"The Evolution of William Blake's *The Marriage of Heaven and Hell.*" *Huntington Library Quarterly* 58.3&4 (1997): 281–344.

"William Blake, Illuminated Books, and the Concept of Difference." *Romantic Poetry: Recent Revisionary Criticism.* Ed. Karl Kroeber and Gene Ruoff. New Brunswick: Rutgers University Press, 1993. 63–87.

Viscomi, Joseph, and Lane Robson. "Blake's Death." *Blake/An Illustrated Quarterly* 30 (fall 1996): 36–49.

4

SUSAN J. WOLFSON

Blake's language in poetic form

In the Fifth chamber were Unnam'd forms, which
cast the metals into the expanse.
There they were reciev'd by Men who occupied
the sixth chamber, and took the forms of books &
were arranged in libraries
   ("A Memorable Fancy," *The Marriage of Heaven and Hell*)

From *Unnam'd forms* to *the forms of books*

Is "Blake's language" and "poetic form" an un-Blakean conjunction? In the
wake of eighteenth-century political revolutions, Blake broadcast a revolutionary poetics, seemingly anti-formalist in its determination:

> To cast aside from Poetry, all that is not Inspiration
> That it no longer shall dare to mock with the aspersion of Madness
> Cast on the Inspired, by the tame high finisher of paltry Blots,
> Indefinite, or paltry Rhymes; or paltry Harmonies.

As these inspired lines from *Milton* (pl. 41 [48], E 142) demonstrate, the sneer
at poetic finishing includes not just rhymes but even blank-verse harmonies,
the measure Milton advertised in his note on "The Verse" to *Paradise Lost* as
"ancient liberty" recovered from the "modern bondage" of having to rhyme
heroic verse. But if Milton tropes blank verse as political liberation, Blake
saw him still constrained by the "uniform systems of execution owned by the
culture, or by poetic tradition."[1] His parodically Miltonic note at the front of
Jerusalem – "Of the Measure, in which / the following Poem is written" (pl. 3,
E 145–46) – dismisses "English Blank Verse" as just another "Monotonous
Cadence," which in "the mouth of a true Orator" is not only "awkward,
but as much a bondage as rhyme itself." His poetry is unprescribed, with
"variety in every line, both / of cadences & number of syllables," determined
by inspiration alone. The ringing declaration is "Poetry Fetter'd, Fetters the
Human Race!" and if cultural history shows anything, it is that

Nations are Destroy'd, or Flourish, in proportion as Their
Poetry Painting and Music, are Destroy'd or Flourish!

This is no momentary hyperbole; it is the syntax of Blakean inspiration. Blake's polemics at once announce an epic intention and generate answerable style. In 1791, about halfway between *Songs of Innocence* and *Songs of Innocence and of Experience*, he launched a poetic revolution in *The French Revolution. A Poem in Seven Books* – the sub-title miming divine creation, the poetic one troped in an extravaganza of seven-beat (anapestic septenary) metrical lines. While only the first book got completed, its lines mark a revolutionary path from which Blake would never really retreat. On this preludic occasion he liberates the line, enjambing (running it on past its terminal) at points where an ensuing blank space or pause of suspense can contribute to and participate in the meaning-making power of poetic form. Blake writes these bounding, nearly unbounded lines for "the voice of the people" bound

> Till dawn, till morning, till the breaking of clouds, and swelling of winds,
>   and the universal voice,
> Till man raise his darken'd limbs out of the caves of night, his eyes and
>   his heart
> Expand: where is space! where O sun in thy dwelling! where thy tent,
>   O faint slumb'rous Moon.   (*FR* 11–12: 217–19, E 296)

The repetitions of rhythm, syntax, and sound propel the lines on a locomotion of poetic energy, halting for a heart-beat at "heart" in order to name, with dramatic force at the start of the next line, the poetic imperative: "Expand." Even the seven-beat measure seems only a light prescription.

That Blake means his lines to carry meaning is clear in his next revolution-era fragment, *America a Prophecy* (1793), where the same percussive seven-beat line allies the French Revolution with the inspirational American precedent, now also refreshed as a modern "prophecy": 1793 is the year that monarchal England, to the dismay of political progressives, initiated war against the Republic of France. The Preludium begins with a metrical self-reference:

> The shadowy daughter of Urthona stood before red Orc.
> When fourteen suns had faintly journey'd o'er his dark abode.
>
>   (pl. 1: 1–2, E 51)

"Fourteen suns" (the fraught years of 1762–76, climaxing in America's Revolution) matches the fourteen beats of these opening lines. That Orc is the force of new forms, political and poetic, is an alliance Blake stresses in his interrogation by the enforcer of formal order, "Albions Angel":

> Blasphemous Demon, Antichrist, hater of Dignities;
> Lover of wild rebellion, and transgresser of Gods Law;
> Why dost thou come to Angels eyes in this terrific form?
>
> (pl. 7: 5–7, E 53–54)

The impending terror is Orc's appalling violence, at once revolutionary and rapacious, and the tradition-blaspheming, rebellion-loving, decorum-hating assault on the reader's eyes by the terrific form of a poetic revolution.

Blake's fame today is keyed to this intensely performative antiformalism: his subversive plays against conventions of poetic form, his tradition-defying extravagance with poetic and pictorial forms, his adamant opposition to all forms of enchaining, especially as a constraint on genius. Yet as "performance" and "antiformalism" suggest, even a rebel needs forms against which and through which to articulate a cause. Of the hundreds of words in the Blake *Concordance*, "form" is thirty-fourth in frequency, and words beginning "form-" fill eight pages (not counting the plural, the conjugations, and morphemes such as "deformed," "unformed," "transformed").[2] It is clear that throughout his career, Blake relied on form for self-definition, even if by opposition. His impatience with any "bound or outward circumference of Energy" (*MHH* 4, E 34) never expels his respect for the artistic necessity of form. This allegiance marks even the revolutionary lines of *Jerusalem*, which to John Hollander seem paced to a "traditional modality of meter," a "transformed equivalent of the freest kind of blank verse."[3] Something similar bristles even in the way those revolutionary seven-beat lines allow organization as traditional balladry (4-3-4-3). When, in *Visions of the Daughters of Albion*, Oothoon cries out,

> Infancy, fearless, lustful, happy! nestling for delight
> In laps of pleasure; Innocence! honest, open, seeking
> The vigorous joys of morning light; open to virgin bliss,
>
> (pl. 6:4–6, E 49)

Blake's metrical patterning hints at an invigorating substructure of traditional song (one that might be thus):

> Infancy, fearless, lustful, happy!
> Nestling for delight
> In laps of pleasure; Innocence!
> Honest, open, seeking
> The vigorous joys of morning light;
> Open to virgin bliss

A sensation of a traditional meter underneath the extravagant line is part of the poignancy of Oothoon's hopeless nostalgia, a reference to standard forms that works dialectically into her visionary imaginations. "Nature has no Outline: / but Imagination has," declares Blake's epigraph for *The Ghost of Abel* (E 270), a poem from the early 1820s reflecting a life-long conviction that for "Every Thing . . . its Reality Is its Imaginative Form" (anno. Berkeley, E 663–64).[4]

"Imaginative Form" can take the root "image" literally, sometimes even by the letter, so that not only do pictures and pictorial elements serve as illustration, but so do letters and words, arranged and styled on the page, "the sensuous surface of calligraphic and typographic forms" announcing "symbolic values." On the title page of *The Marriage of Heaven and Hell*, the graceful letters of *MARRIAGE* floating above the austere Roman capitals of *HEAVEN* and *HELL*, suggests W. J. T. Mitchell, evoke "the symbolic marriage that his 'types' prefigure in the text."[5] To Vincent De Luca, the "wall of words" crowding the plates of *Milton* and *Jerusalem* at once presents a text to read and an image to overwhelm perception (and perhaps defy reading) with "sublime effect."[6] Blake's page is a "composite art" (so Mitchell terms it) not just in the interplay of visual image and verbal text but also in its invitation to see the verbal *as* visual.

This invitation may work against, or across, habitual paths of information. Regrettably, most word-text editions of Blake efface what the Santa Cruz Blake Study Group calls "the visual semiotics of Blake's printed page."[7] The Group gives the example of some lines from *The Book of Urizen* chapter III (pl. 5). Letterpress editions (see E 73) print the lines this way:

> 5. But no light from the fires. all was darkness
> In the flames of Eternal fury
>
> 6. In fierce anguish & quenchless flames

Yet this is how Blake placed the words on his page-plate:

> 5. But no light from the fires. all was
> darkness
> In the flames of Eternal fury
>
> 6. In fierce anguish & quenchless
> flames

The words of this violent Urizenic atmosphere are mapped not only for horizontal but also for vertical reading: a downward syntax, and story, of *no light / darkness / flames / fierce anguish / flames*. Blake stresses this vertical forming in chapter VII:

7. He form'd a line & a plummet
To divide the Abyss beneath.
He form'd a dividing rule;

8. He formd scales to weigh;
He formed massy weights;
He formed a brazen quadrant;
He formed golden compasses
(pl. 20: 33–39, E 80–81)

The anaphora (initial repetition) of "He form'd" is a poetry of vertical form, a compelled repetition that tells volumes about Urizen's character, forever caught in its will to formation. The listing seems potentially eternal, remarks Vincent De Luca, even as this eternizing promise yields "an unsettling impression that actual temporal progress is held in suspension."[8]

If, as Blake insists in *Jerusalem*, "Every word and / every letter is studied and put into its fit place" (pl. 3, E 146), what of the syllable? Can design govern in a thing so small? In the double-column text of *Urizen*, at the bottom of the left column in chapter II, appears this verse:

6. Here alone I in books formd of me-
           -tals
Have written the secrets of wisdom

Erdman's text (E 72) straightens out the hyphenated line to read:

6. Here alone I in books formd of metals

Robert Essick is alert to what's been lost, especially in a book whose eponym is "Urizen, so nam'd / That solitary one in Immensity" (pl. 3: 42–43, E 71), and whose visionary scribe has just indulged the heroic declarations of "I alone, even I!" (pl. 4: 20, E 72). Blake etched his texts on metal plates from which he printed his pages. As the etching of the first line of 6 (E 72) neared the center margin, Essick surmises, hyphenation was necessary. Working with the fact that his books "are not just 'formd of me-/-tals'; they are formed *by* the very nature of those metals and the material processes he employed," Blake let his medium "express its own tendencies" with the syllables "me-/-tals" and he discovered thereby new "textual meanings": "An 'accident' resulting from an essential feature of Blake's method of publication has produced a word ('me') with its own associations and contributions to the *Book of Urizen*."[9] As Essick implies, this may not even have been an accident. Blake could have put all the letters of "metals" on the next line (the alignment of the center margin is irregular); or he could have used the customary hyphenation: "met-als." But he sensed a semiotic payoff in springing "me-" from "metals": the way "me-" punningly mirrors the first words of the line, "Here alone I," and so catches a world of Urizenic self-involution in the grain of a chance syllable.

That the liberation of "me-" was more deliberation than accident is suggested by the reappearance of this syllable in the script of *The Marriage of Heaven and Hell* plate 14:

> But first the notion that man has a body
> distinct from his soul, is to be expunged; this
> I shall do by printing in the infernal method, by
> corrosives, which in Hell are salutary and me-
> dicinal, melting apparent surfaces away, and
> displaying the infinite which was hid.

The design (again, erased in Erdman [E 39]) activates "I shall do" by advancing the syllable "me" in "medicinal" – this last word poetically corroded for the effect. The artist's hellfires melt away habitual lexical surfaces to display the artist's sign for himself hid in the medicine he prescribes.

Forming the reader

Blake's infernal method is to make his reader pause over these visual effects, to see the design, as well as process the information of his poetry. His first ventures as a poet, gathered in a volume whose title announces a marriage of the verbal and the visual, *Poetical Sketches*, are so vitally involved with an energetic *forming* of language (even in letterpress) as to seem a polemic for this distinctively Blakean aspect of poem-making. Here, as in the limit-testing propulsions of the lines that carry his later prophecies and unfold those sublime walls of words, the play of poetic form is a meaning-making event. How we are made to read these forms is a critical factor of Blake's practice, and also a critical force in his forming us into the kind of readers he requires. He serves up stanzas that cheerfully violate their paradigms (*An Imitation of Spencer*), or refuse rhyme, or off-rhyme, or play with "eye"-rhymes (where letters but not sounds line up); rhythms that disrupt and defy metrical convention, and line-endings so unorthodox as to strain a practice of enjambment (run-on syntax) already controversial in eighteenth-century poetics. Here's a sample:

> O thou, who passest thro' our vallies in
> Thy strength . . .   (*To Summer*)

> Smile on our loves; and, while thou drawest the
> Blue curtains of the sky . . .
>   (*To the Evening Star*)

> Rouz'd like a huntsman to the chace; and, with
> Thy buskin'd feet, appear upon our hills...
>
> (*To Morning*)

> When the whirlwind of fury comes from the
> Throne of God...
>
> (*Prologue...King Edward the Fourth*)

> "The narrow bud opens her beauties to
> "The sun, and love runs in her thrilling veins;
> "Blossoms hang round the brows of morning, and
> "Flourish down...   (*To Autumn*)

As these interruptions impose a breathless pause on the verbal stream, reading suddenly becomes a sensuous, self-conscious event. In the same year Blake printed his *Sketches* (1783), Dr. Johnson published his complaint about Milton's blank verse being "verse only to the eye." Blake's blank verse reverses Johnson's valuation, as if exploiting Milton's own description of *Paradise Lost* as "sense variously drawn out from one Verse into another" through the visual potential of "sense" and "drawn out."[10]

At the opening of *To Spring* (E 408), the first poem of *Sketches*, Blake works this dynamic reflexively into the design of the poetic line, itself about drawing the motion of the eye:

> O thou, with dewy locks, who lookest down
> Thro' the clear windows of the morning; turn
> Thine angel eyes upon our western isle,
> Which in full choir hails thy approach, O Spring!
>
> (1–4)

"The Style that Strikes the Eye is the True Style," Blake refutes painter Joshua Reynolds's dictum (anno. Reynolds, E 638), and he elaborates philosopher Bishop Berkeley's remark "By the form everything is what it is," to insist that "Forms must be apprehended by the Sense or the Eye of Imagination" (anno. Berkeley, E 664). What is eye-striking in the poetic form of the invocation to Spring? The first enjambment – "lookest down / Thro' " – makes the reader's eye perform the action described: at *down*, we look down to the next line, then at the next enjambment – "turn / Thine angel eyes" – we turn our eyes, in advance of Spring's "angel eyes," from one line to the next. We ("all our longing eyes," the poet will describe us in his next stanza) effectively answer his invocation, his call "To Spring," with the way he gets us to read the verse of *To Spring*. The pivotal word, *turn*, tropes the visual form that defines poetry – the turn of words across a verse line – with a crosslingual punning on the Latin *versus: turning*.[11] So while the "thou" addressed is personified Spring, in the forming of the poetic line, "thou" is the reader hailed into action. If, as Geoffrey Hartman argues, the "energy of anticipation" in Blake's poetry is its ability to "envision what it calls for,"[12] an important factor is the way the poetic form calls forth what Wordsworth termed "the exertion of a co-operating *power* in the mind of the Reader."[13]

As the poet expands his call to Spring, he further draws the reader into imaging its arrival. The next stanza proceeds from the close of the first on the assurance that a

> . . . full choir hails thy approach, O Spring!
>
> The hills tell each other, and the list'ning
> Vallies hear; all our longing eyes are turned
> Up to thy bright pavillions: issue forth,
> And let thy holy feet visit our clime. (4–8)

The call "O Spring!" completes the first breath of syntax and the first stanza; but as we keep reading, we realize that the "!" is only a pause. The call spills into the next stanza, and as it does so, it forms the poem's sole end-rhyme – *Spring / list'ning* – a faint pair-*ing* across interstanzaic space that couples (and couplets) the sensuous harmony of the awaited spring and the awaiting world (and even chimes with the poem's title). The harmony gains a fleeting echo (if we're list'ning) in the next line's *longing*. The payoff is cued by the syntactic suspense (one of those unorthodox cuts) at "list'ning" itself: "list'ning" / blank page-space / "Vallies" (the listeners). The blank page-space is a visual punctuation, a pause of expectant, longing suspense. "The eye puts a cheat upon the ear, by making us imagine a pause to exist where there is only vacancy to the eye," complained John Walker in 1781, about Milton's enjambed syntaxes.[14] Blake would (perhaps did) agree, but with no grievance about the effect in making us imagine.

Such linear events occur with advertised eye-work in the quasi-sonnet *To the Evening Star* (PS, E 410). In *To Spring*, the "angel eyes" of the season are hailed to meet the "longing eyes" of its petitioners. Blake's "Evening" is a world of eyes: sweet eyes, glimmering eyes, glaring eyes, and across all of these, reading eyes.

> Thou fair-hair'd angel of the evening,
> Now, while the sun rests on the mountains, light
> Thy bright torch of love; thy radiant crown
> Put on, and smile upon our evening bed!
> Smile on our loves; and, while thou drawest the
> Blue curtains of the sky, scatter thy silver dew
> On every flower that shuts its sweet eyes

In timely sleep. Let thy west wind sleep on
The lake; speak si[l]ence with thy glimmering eyes,
And wash the dust with silver. Soon, full soon,
Dost thou withdraw; then the wolf rages wide,
And the lion glares thro' the dun forest:
The fleeces of our flocks are cover'd with
Thy sacred dew: protect them with thine influence.

The first enjambment – "while the sun rests on the mountains, light / Thy bright torch" – creates a field of sight: as the line-end meets the page-space, it not only conscripts this space as "light" but also suspends grammar, to make *light* seem adjectival to *mountains* (as if these looked light rather than heavy and dark). The clarification that *light* is a verbal imperative with a predicate is an emergence in syntax that corresponds to the transfer of light for which the poet calls, and himself sparks with a metrically stressed rhyming, across the line's turn, of *"light / Thy bright."* The syntactic shift enacts the subtle visual shifts and transitions of twilight, wherein forms shimmer in different aspects of perception.

One of the most remarkable events in this "verse to the eye" is the forming of "eyes" into the poem's only end-rhyme (by a re-sounding): as the flowers' "sweet eyes" shut, the evening's "glimmering eyes" shine forth. Between these metaphoric "eyes" Blake plays to the reader's eye with a dramatic enjambment, "sleep on / The lake" (8–9). Part of the drama is his ending the poem's second sentence half a line short, with a point about the timing, at "timely sleep," then running his new sentence on at exactly the point where sonnet tradition prescribes the close of an octave (8/6) or a second quatrain (4/4/4/2). "Let thy west wind sleep on" is more dramatic yet for the way its suspense (again) draws on page-space, as if to image the fields of sleep. When at the line's turn, the syntax gives "sleep on" a local habitation ("The lake"), this resolution does not so much revoke the open-endedness of "on" as leave a "phantom image," a "blurred superposition of the two syntactic alternatives."[15] Not just the evening star's but the reader's eyes are asked to "speak si[l]ence" in the glimmers of imagination. To Hartman this call is the poem's "strongest, most startling" figure: a silence that has to be sounded out "intimates presence, not absence" (p. 227).

Yet the presence is evanescent, and is so through the flux of sound. The poem's nonce first rhyme is not produced by any scheme of end-rhymes, but is a chime of the first two line-leading words, "Thou.../ Now." The vowel sounds ripple through *mountains, crown, our, our, thou, flower, thou,* alternating with another current of *while, smile, Smile, while, silence, sky, thy, eyes, timely, silence, eyes, widely, thine.* "Now" concedes impermanence, and the sonnet closes with the moment past, of silver "dust" lost to star-dost:

"Soon, full soon, / Dost thou withdraw." Without a beat, at the drop of a line, "soon" shifts from imminence to immanence, a present-tense vision of a dark world where "the wolf rages wide, / And the lion glares," and the flocks have only a poet's prayer for safety. With the poet's eye, the reader sees threats that sweetly shut eyes cannot.

The designs of rhyme

To the Evening Star invites a reader's eye, guided by the poem's speaker, to witness a chiaroscuro of enchanting protractions and sinister forebodings. The formal manipulation of doubleness can work otherwise – as in the severe night-world of *The Tyger* (*SE*, E 24–25). Here, Blake turns his reader's eye against his speaker's, by means of poetic patterns that induce a peripheral vision beyond what the speaker recognizes. The chief site is the framing question about eye-wrought art: "What immortal hand or eye, / Could frame thy fearful symmetry?" (its re-sounding at the close only shifting "Could" to "Dare"). Here, the key (and to Dr. Johnson, the necessary) signifier of poetry, rhyme, is not an aural but an eye-rhyme with "eye" itself. The signifier of poetic measure, "symmetry," plays no "same measure" but imposes metrical disproportion. The first line (following the stanza pattern) scans, almost mechanically

What im*mor*tal *hand* or *eye*

But (if we take the beat) the second stumbles

Could frame thy *fear*ful *sym*metry?

Eight syllables, not the pattern seven; three beats, not the percussive four. And in the midst lurks *thy*, to claim a sound-rhyme with *eye* in advance of and preempting the weak, unstressed *try* of "symmetry." The disorienting, ruptured verse-forms load the speaker's loaded questions with effects that make us wonder what this increasingly fraught song is really framing: is fearful symmetry the design of a malevolent Maker, or the perverse making of an overwrought questioner? The questioner envisions a fearful Framer; the reader's eye focuses on what the poetry is framing. Fearful symmetry may inhere in the fabulous tyger, or it may be imagination. Blake's pictorial image is no help: a side view (no symmetrical front view) of a not exactly frightening tiger, either mocking the questioner's anxiety with contradiction, or mocking us, with false safety.[16]

The Tyger reminds us that end-rhyme is a form for the eye as well as for the ear, sometimes in line with the eye, sometimes not, but always thickening the semantic work of words. Language in rhyme may be a sensuous enhancement of social harmony (love, dance, song), or it may figure law and order, even bondage – of prosody, and more. The only poem in *Poetical Sketches* that Blake sets in rhyming couplets, *Blind-Man's Buff* (E 421–23), teases at these possible allegories. Reversing Johnson's complaint about blank verse (it's only to the eye, with nothing for the ear to distinguish from unordered prose), Blake's tidy couplets report a game of all sound and no eye, where tyranny and wanton cruelty ensue, provoking a summary call for law and order and fair play:

> Such are the fortunes of the game,
> And those who play should stop the same
> By wholesome laws; such as all those
> Who on the blinded man impose,
> Stand in his stead; as long a-gone
> When men were first a nation grown;
> Lawless they liv'd – till wantonness
> And liberty began t' increase;
> And one man lay in another's way,
> Then laws were made to keep fair play.
>
> (61–70)

To Dryden's conservative, post-Miltonic argument that rhyme "Bounds and Circumscribes" an "Imagination" prone to run "Wild and Lawless,"[17] Blake's reply is that rhyme may pattern a cruel game as well as the homilies of fair play. Miming the forms of children's rhymes, he even implies the genesis of man's designs ("blind *man*" is a child's role) in childish games, whose local mischief, tricks, and blood-letting confusions rehearse worldly power-plays.

No wonder that in other *Sketches* rhyme patterns stories of capture by delusive art, showing how (as Hollander paraphrases the Miltonic case) "the sort of linkage it enforces" may become "allegorized as bondage":[18]

> With sweet May dews my wings were wet,
>   And Phoebus fir'd my vocal rage;
> He caught me in his silken net,
>   And shut me in his golden cage.

This is stanza 3 of *Song* ("How sweet I roam'd from field to field"), about a seduction by "the prince of love" (E 413). Love's trap is disclosed when the unsensed fetters, "net" and "cage," catch the verse in rhyme, turning the pattern into "the icon in which the idea is caught."[19] The subtler rhyme in this network is *He / me*, a succinct monosyllabic report of the insidious bondage. The singer's freedom is past tense, before love ("How sweet I roam'd..."); by stanza two "I" is the object *me*, bound in rule and rhyme by *He*: "He

shew'd me lilies...He led me through his gardens" (5, 7); "He caught me
.../ And shut me" (11–12). The loss named by *liberty* (its rhyme syllable
unstressed) is no challenge to the rule of *me* by *He*:

> He loves to sit and hear me sing,
>   Then, laughing, sports and plays with me;
> Then stretches out my golden wing,
>   And mocks my loss of liberty.   (13–16)

The weakness of the rhyme is no Miltonic portent of liberty but a cruel
mockery of his trope.

The force of form over lost self-possession inspires another lover's *Song*:

> My silks and fine array,
>   My smiles and languish'd air,
> By love are driv'n away;
>   And mournful lean Despair
> Brings me yew to deck my grave:
>   Such end true lovers have.   (1–6)

There are two forms of the self, a past one of "fine array" and "languish'd
air" and the present one of stylized "Despair." Cleanth Brooks sees the
evenly measured song as a "discipline of form," a "ritual performance"
of anguish, rendering it "precise and deft, graceful and yet resonant."[20] Yet
the disciplinary array may also spell only an illusion of control. If regular
trimeters rule the rhymes, their letters tell other stories. "Despair," making a
rhyme by imprisoning "air," rules with a vengeance over former insouciance.
The lady's ruefully punning "brings me yew" (evoking the lost "you") names
the new array, in this fatally wrought formalism:

> When I my grave have made,
>   Let winds and tempests beat:
> Then down I'll lie, as cold as clay.
>   True love doth pass away!
>   (15–18)

In this final stanza, rhyme pattern interacts with treacherous repetitions:
"I my grave have made" answers the poem's first (almost muted) couplet,
grave / have (5–6), tightening its fatalistic link into impending fate, while the
singer's self-regard in a tale of "true lovers" (6) ends and echoes in, and as,
the final alien abstraction of a fugitive "True love."

A sense of fatal repetition infuses poetic form in the historical pieces of
Poetical Sketches that follow the *Song* group: *Gwin, King of Norway; King
Edward the Third; Prologue, Intended for a Dramatic Piece of King Edward
the Fourth*. Not just about these war-making kings, these sketches also map

England in the 1780s, when the empire was suffering erosions of prestige at home, being weakened abroad by rebellions and then by full-scale war with America, as well as by new conflicts with long-standing enemies, Spain, and especially France.[21] *Gwin* (E 417–20) addresses this double reference with a modernized ballad, evoking the tradition of balladry as cultural history and using the recent emergence of the "literary ballad" to stage a critical reading of its poetic forms. It opens in a language of fable, implying a repeatability, not only through culture but also across history. A caution to tyrannical "Kings" is prelude to the ancient days of Gwin, oppressor of the "nations of the North" who provokes "Gordred the giant" to lead a rebellion, in which he slays Gwin. The revenge-tale enacted by two symbolic figures is less the ballad's point than the universal carnage that displaces all hope of political reform.

Blake's poetics of repetition and links of rhyme convey the warning. The systematic tyranny of the "Nobles" who "feed upon the hungry poor" (5–6) courts a vengeful return: the starving poor roar like "lions' whelps . . . / Seeking their nightly food" (19–20). Noble arrogance earns its violence and blackness back in kind: the poor roll "like tempests black" (17–18) to meet the oppressor's "host as black as night" (55); the rebel army advances "Like clouds, come rolling o'er" (36) while Gwin's troops "Like clouds around him roll'd" (60). The same simile serves both forces, a provocation and reaction Blake stresses by putting both in the same stanzaic position, the last line. The inevitability of such returns abides in the punning phonemes in *Gordred*. The cry of Gwin's watchmen, that the army of Gordred is "rolling o'er!" (36) almost says (and has the letters of) *rolling gore*. The gory latency soon erupts in "fields of gore" (46) and echoes in the report that "Earth smokes with blood, and groans, and shakes, / To drink her childrens' gore" (73–74). Allied with blood, *Gordred* releases not only *gore* but also *Gore-dread* and its nearly redundant cause, *gored red* – the second word distilled in the image of the battle's "red fev'rous night" (84).

In the field of this meaning-making sound lurks the *gore*-rhyme *war*, as word and event. Once it sounds (62), the reproduction of violence appears as a first cause, a "god of war . . . drunk with blood" (93), but no more theological than indifferent natural violence:

> And now the raging armies rush'd,
>   Like warring mighty seas;
> The Heav'ns are shook with roaring war,
>   The dust ascends the skies! (69–72)

As sounds and actions, "warring" and "roaring war" blur, and they blend visually into "gore / A sea of blood; nor can the eye / See to the trembling shore!" (74–76). What the eye can see is limited, in a grim pun, to this "sea":

> Steed rolls on steed, and shield on shield,
> Sunk in this sea of strife!　(91–92)

"Human forces actually become what they formerly were merely like"; "they are enveloped in the element and annihilated by it."[22] Tenors and vehicles merge: the armies are seas; the sea is a "wild sea" (p. 77), a sea of strife. "By the time Gordred cleaves Gwin's skull," suggests Robert Gleckner, "the social and political 'meaning' of that victory has paled to insignificance – even irrelevance"; "Visionary history inheres in the 'vale of death' and in the 'river Dorman' as the loco-descriptive symbols of the universal battle's 'sea of blood.' "[23] This bloodbath may not so much pale politics into visionary history as evoke an appalling visionary politics, a transhistorical anxiety about the human cost of historical conflict.[24]

> The river Dorman roll'd their blood
> Into the northern sea;
> Who mourn'd his sons, and overwhelm'd
> The pleasant south country.　(113–16)

The fable's persons (already iconic or undifferentiated) are replaced by one personified blood-inheriting sea, a mourner whose only work is to "over-whelm" – emotionally and literally – the rest of the world with its sur-plus. The weak closing rhyme ("country") allows another chord to prevail: *Dorman, northern, mourn'd*, all elegiac echoes of the sounds of *war, gore, Nore*, and *Gordred*. Without morally equating cruel tyrants and desperate subjects, Blake's rhymes and repetitions nonetheless spell the repayment of tyranny in kind.

Forms of repetition; repetition of forms

Repetition is the chief form in the political text of *King Edward the Third* (E 423–38). Its setting, Crécy before the battle of 1346, not only recalls the Shakespearean stage of England's wars with France but also hints at a scarcely altered contemporary situation. This historical trajectory, extend-ing from Edward's to Blake's day, at once defines the sketch's political per-spective and implies a logic for its macroform: its open-endedness. The six scenes occupy the hours before the battle, with this climax unsketched. This truncation is a formal determination, not a sketch left a "fragment."[25] Although England did prevail at Crécy, as it would in another cycle of his-tory at Harfleur and Agincourt under Edward the Third's descendant, Henry the Fifth, Blake's refusal to report these outcomes functions semantically as a refusal of triumphalism, the mode of nationalistic self-satisfaction. His sketch draws us, instead, into various critical perspectives on the interests that impel England's history of military adventurism.

The poetic form of the sketch, blank verse, is set with similar critical effect against its Miltonic tradition of prosody as politics. Blake's counter-perspective is not the conservative lens of eighteenth-century formalism that would expose liberty as lawlessness, but a modern lens of suspicion about the motivated rhetoric, craft, and intentional designs in the cant of "Liberty."

> Let Liberty, the charter'd right of Englishmen,
> Won by our fathers in many a glorious field,
> Enerve my soldiers; let Liberty
> Blaze in each countenance, and fire the battle.
> The enemy fight in chains, invisible chains, but heavy;
> Their minds are fetter'd; then how can they be free,
> While, like the mounting flame,
> We spring to battle o'er the floods of death?
> And these fair youths, the flow'r of England,
> Vent'ring their lives in my most righteous cause,
> O sheathe their hearts with triple steel, that they
> May emulate their fathers' virtues,
> And thou, my son, be strong; thou fightest for a crown
> That death can never ravish from thy brow,
> A crown of glory: (1: 9–23)

So King Edward exhorts his nobles and army, massed on the French coast. Readers have been troubled by the oration, its rhetoric striking S. Foster Damon as a reflection of Blake's "uncritical patriotism" in the years leading up to England's war with France in 1788, Mark Schorer as "an extended defense of war and national interests," and Northrop Frye, as "simply 'Rule Britannia' in blank verse."[26] Yet as a *poetic* rhetoric, Blake's form is not simple and not uncritical. It is subtly subversive. The visible forming of the line sets the cant of "Liberty" at odds with a not-quite-invisible chain of special interests (recall Blake's insistence that blank verse is still "Poetry Fetter'd"). Edward's manipulative eloquence and pulse-quickening rhythms are sketched as a political rhetoric, one Blake exposes with a semantics of rhyme in the midst of the blank verse: the chime of *Liberty / enemy / heavy / free* (11–14). Edward's cant links *enemy* and *heavy* to the "fetter'd" minds of France and *Liberty* and *free* to England; but in Blake's verse, one chord joins all. These phonics signify what the sketch stages at large: British minds, fettered by political and moral self-justification, are chained to a war machine that serves special interests while pretending universal libertarian value.[27]

The chain includes even Edward's blithe description of "Liberty" as "the charter'd right of Englishmen" (9) – a claim that would resonate for readers in the 1780s with emerging critiques of the tyranny veiled in ideologies of "charter'd" rights, including Blake's bitter song, a decade later, about London's "charter'd" streets and "charter'd Thames" (London; SE).[28] Blake's ironic view of chartered rights forecasts the patent economic self-interest staged in scene 2. As Edward exhorts his army in France, another son, the Duke of Clarence, celebrates chartered English business, imagining that from abroad his father looks homeward to see

> commerce fly round
> With his white wings, and sees his golden London,
> And her silver Thames, throng'd with shining spires
> And corded ships; her merchants buzzing round
> Like summer bees, and all the golden cities
> In his land, overflowing with honey ...   (2: 9–14)

This language of shining romance, enhanced by the flow of enjambment "round" the boundaries of the lines, is inseparable from terms of expanding economic power. In such a world, poetic language flows in justification of commercial self-interest, so much so that the Prince can crow, in a poetry of sensuous immediacy:

> my blood, like a springtide,
> Does rise so high, to overflow all bounds
> Of moderation; while Reason, in his
> Frail bark, can see no shore or bound for vast
> Ambition   (3: 234–38)

Here a Miltonic enjambment is not a form that tropes liberty of spirit. Blake is staging Dryden's complaint of immoderation: even as the suspension of "vast" at the end of the line romantically conscripts blank space into the unbounded field the Prince imagines for his enterprises of ambition, the figuring of enjambment in "overflow all bounds" (in syntax and sensibility) makes an opposite point about costly intemperance. "In a Commercial Nation Impostors are abroad in all Professions," Blake ranted some years later (PA, E 582). The Prince is an impostor poet of specious romance, joined by a Bishop unembarrassed to declare "England is the land favour'd by Commerce" (2: 30) and to invoke Heavenly sanction: we are "sovereigns / Of the sea" as

> our right, that Heaven gave
> To England, when at the birth of nature
> She was seated in the deep, the Ocean ceas'd
> His might roar; and, fawning, play'd around
> Her snowy feet, and own'd his awful Queen.
> (2: 79–83)

With such crass public poetry, no art is safe from contamination by commerce. No wonder Blake was provoked to a sneering rhyme (c. 1808–10) of "Brittannias Isle" with "Fiends of Commerce smile," or, in a variant, "... Brittannias Shore / ... Commerce roar" ("Now Art has lost its mental Charms"; E 479, 858).

King Edward presents a world of such impostor poets, most caustically in scene 4. The King's minstrel has composed a war-song that has so pleased the Prince (who has an affection for the genre) that he has "made [him] a 'squire" – a reward that inspires another song "about all us that are to die, that we may be remembered in Old England" (4: 44–50). "Where any view of Money exists Art cannot be carried on, but War only" (*PA*, E 275). Scene 6, the play's last, gives the proof of this credo in the war-song itself. It's in sextains of blank verse, the line of liberty now fashioned to song-fuel for a war machine. The word *war* is, significantly, the inaugurator of the only strong nonce rhyme chain: "cloath'd in war" (1); "covered with gore" (11); "strewn upon the shore" (31). The chain extends back across *Sketches* as a repetition: *war/gore* is one of the key rhymes of *Gwin*. Indeed, a host of verbal and imagistic repetitions draw Edward's army, those modern "sons of Trojan Brutus," back to Gwin's brutality. Again we hear of "thunder," of "Rolling dark clouds," of a "sickly darkness," of the "wrath and fury" of "wild men, / Naked and roaring like lions," of "savage monsters rush[ing] like roaring fire," of "red lightning, borne by furious storms," and a "molten raging sea" (2–31). Even as the war-song envisions a coming prosperity, its language is caught in records of violence past: the promise of "plenty" in "vales in rich array" (46–7) refigures the "firm array" of the massed Trojan invaders of Albion (13, 25). The final stanza's icon of Liberty, imagined in the song of Trojan Brutus himself, bears the legacy of violence recorded in the minstrel's opening stanzas:

> "Liberty shall stand upon the cliffs of Albion,
> "Casting her blue eyes over the green ocean;
> "Or, tow'ring, stand upon the roaring waves,
> "Stretching her mighty spear o'er distant lands;
> "While, with her eagle wings, she covereth
> "Fair Albion's shore, and all her families."
> (55–60)

Everything is repetition: the roaring waves Liberty eyes as her domain evoke the "roaring" armies that resisted the invading Trojans (22, 26, 27); and the iconography of the mighty spear, its imperial(ist) thrust, and the eagle, recalls the "spears" of the fathers and their spoil of "mighty dead" (34–35), as well as the aggressive "empire"-building that has them roaming "Like eagles for the prey" (42–45). And most of all, there is is the repetition of the cant of "Liberty," the King's mantra now contextualized in the history of violence it sustains and perpetuates.

Another war-song of sorts follows *King Edward the Third* in *Poetical Sketches*: the sixteen-line *Prologue, Intended for a Dramatic Piece of King Edward the Fourth* (E 439). Blake's dark joke is that "the Fourth" is not Edward the Third's son (who predeceased his father by a year), but a king born almost a century after Crécy. The thwarted succession is scarcely felt, however, for the link between the two sketches is a raging thirst for war, reaching across generations, across centuries. *Prologue* gives this language a succinct, ritualistic form, in which repetitions are not only of previous sketches and war-chants but also of history itself:

> O For a voice like thunder, and a tongue
> To drown the throat of war! – When the senses
> Are shaken, and the soul is driven to madness,
> Who can stand? When the souls of the oppressed
> Fight in the troubled air that rages, who can stand?
> When the whirlwind of fury comes from the
> Throne of God, when the frowns of his countenance
> Drive the nations together, who can stand?
> When Sin claps his broad wings over the battle,
> And sails rejoicing in the flood of Death;
> When souls are torn to everlasting fire,
> And fiends of Hell rejoice upon the slain,
> O who can stand? O who hath caused this?
> O who can answer at the throne of God?
> The Kings and Nobles of the Land have done it!
> Hear it not, Heaven, thy Ministers have done it!

The echo of the famous opening of *Henry V* ("O for a Muse of fire, that would ascend / The brightest heaven of invention...") amplifies the indict-ment: the allusion to Shakespeare's subject (its era located between Blake's two Edwards, again with France as enemy) makes war the inevitable stage of power. Blake's reiterated syntactic form "When...who can stand?" reaches a stunning modulation in line 13, where interrogation shifts to agency – "O who hath caused this?" The answer indicts "Kings and Nobles" and Heaven's Ministers together. The syntactic repetition, forged in the shadow of the couplet-summation of a Shakespearean sonnet, calls on the reader (if no other) to "hear."

A verse to the eye in the heart of hearing shapes a succinct song that calls the war home, to London and to the reader: *London* (*SE*, E 26–27). At its very heart, Blake shakes our senses with dark poetic invention. Here is its third stanza, framed by the last line of 2 and the first line of 4:

> The mind-forg'd manacles I hear
>
> How the Chimney-sweepers cry
> Every black'ning Church appalls.
> And the hapless Soldiers sigh
> Runs in blood down Palace walls
>
> But most thro' midnight streets I hear

How does one "hear" a mind-forg'd manacle? Manacle (in an age of legal slave-trade) is a strongly visual image of a constraining form, even with the psychological tenor of "mind-forg'd." The extravagant metaphor is precisely Blake's point: the manacles are invisible in the social and institutional forces of their forging; it is their consequences, a city where "every Man" (the syllable caught in "manacles") cries in pain before sighing into death, that is the devastating recognition. We have to see into what we hear and hear an indictment in the symbolic translation of what we see: the last sigh of a living body becomes blood on the walls of a death-demanding institution. The "Chimney-sweepers cry / Every blackning Church appalls" is a headline that superimposes visual on aural crimes. The sweepers' fatal lot is to remove black soot, from Church chimneys, among others. As a visual project, the effort to appall ("make pale" or lighten) the Church's blackness is rendered futile and poignant by its ever(y)-blackening coal-fires; as an ethical problem, the death of boys in this service should appall a Church that seems immune to indictment. The institution, Blake's syntax insists, is the agent of contamination: it blackens.

These intercalations of seeing and hearing are literally spelled out. The word that leads into stanza 3, *hear*, framed on the other side at the end of 4's first line, *hear*, is a visible "extra" rhyme (actually a repetition). "I hear" becomes a strangely compelling "eye-hear" in the frame Blake makes of the letters on the left vertical side of the stanza, the acrostic HEAR.[29] This brilliant forging of poetic form arrests attention, forging what we hear and see into a haunting "marriage *hearse*" (*London*'s last word) of information. Language in poetic form is no static product for Blake; it is an action that compels awareness of the form of our readings – not only of a poet's book but also of the world that such books penetrate and engage.

Notes

1. Morris Eaves, *William Blake's Theory of Art* (Princeton: Princeton University Press, 1982), p. 159.
2. David Erdman, *A Concordance to the Writings of William Blake*, 2 vols. (Ithaca: Cornell University Press, 1967), vol. I, pp. 739–46; vol. II, p. 2,181.
3. John Hollander, *Vision and Resonance: Two Senses of Poetic Form* (New York: Oxford University Press, 1975).
4. For "the nature and value of form" in the visual art, see Anne Mellor, *Blake's Human Form Divine* (Berkeley: University of California Press, 1974). Even as Blake was "rejecting as a Urizenic tyranny the outline or 'bound or outward circumference,'" Mellor argues, his visual mode was "above all a matter of outline, of an image realized almost entirely through a strong, clear, bounding line" (pp. xv–xvi).
5. W. J. T. Mitchell, "Visible Language: Blake's Wond'rous Art of Writing," *Romanticism and Contemporary Criticism*, ed. Morris Eaves and Michael Fischer (Ithaca: Cornell University Press, 1986), pp. 83–84.
6. Vincent De Luca, *Words of Eternity: Blake and the Poetics of the Sublime* (Princeton: Princeton University Press, 1991), pp. 89–90.
7. Santa Cruz Blake Study Group, "What Type of Blake?" *Essential Articles for the Study of William Blake, 1970–1984*, ed. Nelson Hilton (Hamden, CT: Archon, 1986), pp. 306–7. A notable exception is the decision of Susan Wolfson and Peter Manning (inspired by Santa Cruz) to follow the plate arrangements in the *Longman Anthology of British Literature*, vol. II (2nd edn. New York: Addison, Wesley, Longman, 2002), pp. 135–48.
8. De Luca, *Words of Eternity*, p. 70.
9. Robert Essick, "How Blake's Body Means," in *Unnam'd Forms: Blake and Textuality*, eds. Nelson Hilton and Thomas A. Vogler (Berkeley: University of California Press, 1986), pp. 215–16. This text is also noted by Santa Cruz (pp. 308, 323) and Nelson Hilton, "Becoming Prolific Being Devoured," *Studies in Romanticism* 21 (1982), pp. 417–24.
10. Johnson, "Milton," *Lives of the English Poets* (1783); ed. George Birkbeck Hill, vol. I (Oxford: Clarendon Press, 1905), p. 193. For a good discussion of these poetics, see Hollander, "'Sense variously drawn out': On English Enjambment," *Vision*, pp. 91–116.
11. With like punning, Wordsworth meditates on how "forms . . . circumfus'd" with "Visionary Power" are mysteriously conveyed "through the turnings intricate of Verse" (1805 *Prelude* 5.625–27).
12. Geoffrey Hartman, *Beyond Formalism* (New Haven: Yale University Press, 1970), pp. 193–204.
13. Wordsworth, "Essay, Supplementary to the Preface" [of 1815], *The Prose Works of William Wordsworth*, ed. W. J. B. Owen and Jane Worthington Smyser, vol. III (Oxford: Clarendon Press, 1974), p. 81. Wordsworth's argument for this agency is more Blakean than Blake recognized when he disparaged this Preface and Wordsworthian theorizing in general for giving in to Nature over Imagination (anno. Wordsworth, E 665).
14. Walker, *Elements of Elocution, Being the Substance of a Course of Lectures on the Art of Reading*, vol. II (London: Walker, 1781), p. 212.

15. Hollander, *Vision*, p. 115.
16. See Hollander's discussion of these effects, *Melodious Guile: Fictive Pattern in Poetic Language* (New Haven: Yale University Press 1988), pp. 32–34.
17. Dedicatory epistle to *The Rival Ladies* (1664), *The Works of John Dryden*, ed. H. T. Swedenberg, Jr., 19 vols. (Berkeley: University of California Press, 1961–79), vol. VIII, ed. John Harrington Smith and Dougald MacMillan (1967), pp. 100–101.
18. *Melodious Guile*, p. 184.
19. See William K. Wimsatt, "One Relation of Rhyme to Reason" (1944); *The Verbal Icon: Studies in the Meaning of Poetry* (Lexington: University of Kentucky Press, 1954), p. 165.
20. Cleanth Brooks, "Current Critical Theory and the Period Course," *CEA Critic* 7/7 (Oct. 1950), pp. 5–6.
21. David Erdman notes the contemporary relevance in *Blake: Prophet Against Empire* (Princeton: Princeton University Press, 1954), p. 18. That "nations black" (p. 35) are Gwin's oppressed subjects, moreover, shows Blake's anti-slavery politics taking shape some years in advance of the formation of the Society for the Abolition of the Slave Trade (1787).
22. De Luca, *Words of Eternity*, p. 77.
23. Robert Gleckner, *Blake's Prelude:* Poetical Sketches (Baltimore: Johns Hopkins University Press, 1982), p. 119.
24. See William Keach, "Blake, Violence, and Visionary Politics," *Representing the French Revolution: Literature, Historiography, and Art*, ed. James A. W. Heffernan (Hanover: University Press of New England, 1992), pp. 24–40.
25. The play is usually regarded as "unfinished" or a "fragment": see H. C. Robinson's initial remark of this kind (1811; *William Blake: The Critical Heritage*, ed. G. E. Bentley, Jr. [London and Boston: Routledge and Kegan Paul, 1975], p. 163), followed by (among others) Erdman (*Prophet*, pp. 18, 56, 63–64), Harold Bloom (E 969), and Gleckner (*Blake's Prelude*, p. 96). Yet nowhere does Blake himself term *King Edward* a fragment; nor does he apply a typographical sign to denote an unfinished text.
26. Damon, *A Blake Dictionary: The Ideas and Symbols of William Blake* (1965; New York: E. P. Dutton, 1971), pp. 228–29; Schorer, *William Blake: The Politics of Vision* (1946; New York: Random House, 1959), p. 165; Frye, *Fearful Symmetry: A Study of William Blake* (1947; Princeton: Princeton University Press, 1969), p. 180.
27. Erdman notes a similar Ode of the Bard of Albion, published 4 June 1778, "urging British troops to fight in France to 'guard their sacred homes' " (*Prophet*, p. 70).
28. During the 1780s the language of "chartering" was focusing ever sharper critical discussion. By 1792, Tom Paine was insisting in *The Rights of Man* that "it is a perversion of terms to say that a charter gives rights. It operates by a contrary effect, that of taking rights away," leaving them "by exclusion, in the hands of a few" (*Two Classics of the French Revolution* [New York: Anchor/Doubleday, 1973], p. 458).
29. See Nelson Hilton, *Literal Imagination: Blake's Vision of Words* (Berkeley: University of California Press, 1982), p. 64.

Further reading

Brooks, Cleanth. "Current Critical Theory and the Period Course." *CEA Critic* 7/7 (Oct. 1950): 1, 5, 6.

De Luca, Vincent Arthur. *Words of Eternity: Blake and the Poetics of the Sublime.* Princeton: Princeton University Press, 1991.

Eaves, Morris. *William Blake's Theory of Art.* Princeton: Princeton University Press, 1982.

Essick, Robert. "How Blake's Body Means." In Hilton and Vogler eds., *Unnam'd Forms: Blake and Textuality.* Berkeley: University of California Press, 1986. 197–217.

Fogle, Aaron. "Pictures of Speech: On Blake's Poetic." *Studies in Romanticism* 21 (1982): 217–42.

Hartman, Geoffrey. "Blake and the Progress of Poesy." 1969. *Beyond Formalism.* New Haven: Yale University Press, 1970. 193–204.

"The Discourse of a Figure: Blake's 'Speak Silence' in Literary History." *Languages of the Unsayable: The Play of Negativity in Literature and Literary Theory.* Ed. Sanford Budick and Wolfgang Iser. New York: Columbia University Press, 1989. 225–40.

Hilton, Nelson. "Becoming Prolific Being Devoured." *Studies in Romanticism* 21 (1982): 417–24.

Hilton, Nelson and Thomas A. Vogler, eds. *Unnam'd Forms: Blake and Textuality.* Berkeley: University of California Press, 1986.

Hollander, John. *Melodious Guile: Fictive Pattern in Poetic Language.* New Haven: Yale University Press, 1988.

Vision and Resonance: Two Senses of Poetic Form. New York: Oxford University Press, 1975.

Mitchell, W. J. T. *Blake's Composite Art: A Study of the Illuminated Poetry.* Princeton: Princeton University Press, 1978.

"Visible Language: Blake's Wond'rous Art of Writing." *Romanticism and Contemporary Criticism.* Ed. Morris Eaves and Michael Fischer. Ithaca: Cornell University Press, 1986. 46–86.

Ostriker, Alicia. *Vision and Verse in William Blake.* Madison: University of Wisconsin Press, 1965.

Santa Cruz Blake Study Group. "What Type of Blake?" *Essential Articles for the Study of William Blake, 1970–1984.* Ed. Nelson Hilton. Hamden, CT: Archon, 1986. 301–33.

Wolfson, Susan J. *Formal Charges: The Shaping of Poetry in British Romanticism.* Stanford: Stanford University Press, 1997.

5

DAVID BINDMAN

Blake as a painter

Blake and history painting

Recent commentary on Blake has tended to find the core of his achievement in the prophetic books of the 1790s and in the later prophecies, *Milton* and *Jerusalem*. These books speak now to a world that relishes their complexity, unresolved nature, and play between image and text. Yet they represent only a part of his achievement, and were the focus of his attention, as far as we know, only between 1788 and 1796, and again between 1804 and c. 1820. He was more continuously preoccupied with his work as a painter in tempera and watercolor of biblical and literary subjects, usually in series. Blake's "illustrations" are not a secondary activity but are quite as personal and imaginative as his prophetic work. It is true that there were artists like Blake's friend Thomas Stothard who made a living from designing illustrations to novels and other works, and Blake often engraved from the drawings. But such illustrations were clearly subordinate to the text. Blake's designs, on the other hand, constitute an active engagement with each text by an artist who never doubted that he was the peer of any author. Furthermore, his designs are informed by assumptions and traditions that belong to discourses of art rather than literature. They look back to the Italian Renaissance and to ancient Greece, and in later years to Gothic and even Hindu traditions. The fact that the starting point for almost all of Blake's temperas, watercolors, and some separate prints was a text written by another author no more diminishes them than Michelangelo's use of the Bible diminishes the Sistine Chapel. Blake argued that each of his tempera or watercolor designs had the potential to be hugely enlarged, and that his method of "portable Fresco" (E 527) would enable him to produce public paintings on a monumental scale.

If Blake's prophetic works might suggest that he was an alienated outsider, his tempera and watercolor designs to the Bible and other literature reveal an artist making his way with some success in the competitive London art world. He exhibited watercolors and temperas at the Royal Academy on six occasions in 1780, 1784, 1785, 1790, 1800, and 1808, and at most periods in his career he had loyal patrons who provided commissions, though never as many as he felt he deserved or needed to make a comfortable living. The prophecies reveal a fervently radical and apocalyptic figure, anxiously searching in the events of his time for signs that the biblical prophecy of Revelation was about to be fulfilled. The watercolors and temperas, on the other hand, do not, on the surface at least, suggest a revolutionary spirit, though as we shall see they do express the same underlying convictions.

Blake in later life vigorously denounced Sir Joshua Reynolds, who had been President of the Royal Academy during the whole of Blake's early career, in the privacy of his notebook and in the margins of books (E 635–62), but this did not mean that he was hostile towards the principles upon which the Royal Academy stood. Blake had been briefly a student at the Royal Academy in 1779–80 – probably for less than a year – after he had completed his apprenticeship as an engraver. Reynolds had been President from 1768 until his death in 1792, giving the *Discourses on Art* as a means of promoting the Elevated Style, the style of Raphael, Michelangelo, and the canonical sculptures of antiquity. Reynolds's aim, shared by many others at the time, was to make Britain the home of high art, as Italy had been in the Renaissance. "History" painting was to raise the morality and taste of the public through their exposure to paintings of virtuous and heroic conduct from the great ages of mankind. Blake often talked of the need for art to inspire youth to emulation of great deeds, and his work to the end of his career displays the influence of precisely the same models advocated by Reynolds, namely Raphael, Michelangelo, and antiquity.

Blake's anger at Reynolds was not so much directed at the principles or models he advocated as against his hypocrisy in not putting his ideals into practice. Reynolds painted relatively few history paintings, preferring instead making acclaimed portraits of the wealthy and powerful. He allowed the walls of the Royal Academy exhibitions to be covered, though never exclusively, by landscape, portraits, and sentimental scenes, all of which Blake despised as mere imitations of nature. In fairness to Reynolds, it is not clear what else he could have done in the absence of more than a few patrons with an informed taste for history painting. Blake and the painters he admired, like the Irishman James Barry, the Swiss Henry Fuseli, and the American Benjamin West, all of whom held high office in the Academy, are best understood as true loyalists to the ideals that Reynolds was unable or unwilling to fulfill himself.

Blake, however, set himself apart from the painters of the Academy in one important – perhaps fatal – respect. He refused from early in his career to paint in oils. He later rationalized this extraordinary decision as a moral preference for a clarity that could be achieved in line engraving and water-color, but was impossible in the "blotting and blurring" medium of oil (e.g., DC, E 546). Blake's watercolor technique until late in life involved making what are in reality tinted drawings, in which the color is contained within a pen outline. Without oils he was cut off from the lucrative business of por-traiture and from the prestigious practice of large-scale history painting. He was thrown back for his daily living on reproductive engraving, for which he had served a seven-year apprenticeship, but engraving was a "mechanical" art, regarded as a subordinate craft rather than an independent profession.

Financial dependence on engraving had one enormous advantage: it saved Blake from the hazard of confusing routine paid work with that which ex-pressed his deeper ambitions. He was able to maintain a clear division be-tween the "potboiling" labor of reproductive engraving and his imaginative and visionary work. Oil painters with ambitions to paint history were forced into the position of either producing decorative pictures or portraits, or be-coming socially adept at persuading rich patrons to buy history paintings, like Fuseli, who cultivated a sophisticated circle of wealthy admirers.[1] Those who tried to ignore the imperatives of the marketplace, like James Barry, or later Benjamin Robert Haydon, died in poverty. Reproductive engraving gave Blake a kind of independence, but at a heavy price. He had the drudgery of engraving other artists' designs day after day, a low level of income and low social status (he was known condescendingly as "Mr Blake the Engraver"). In recompense he could follow his imagination where it led, to experiment with new printing and painting techniques, or produce books in illuminated printing. He could persuade himself that he was immune to the taste of the town, and there was always the hope that unusual patrons might respond to his imagination, as a few were to do. The problem was, as we shall see, that the engraving work began to diminish in his middle years.

The young history painter, 1779–88

Blake's surviving early drawings reveal enormous ambition but no natural ease with the medium. They are mainly in a pen and grey wash technique, closely resembling drawings by his close friend the sculptor John Flaxman, later Professor of Painting at the Royal Academy. The two young artists shared a romantic taste for medieval art, English history, and unorthodox Christianity, and they both distanced themselves as far as they could from the prevailing materialism, though Flaxman was obliged to work for the pioneering capitalist and potter Josiah Wedgwood.[2] The friendship came to a temporary halt with Flaxman's extended period in Rome, 1787–94, where he was able to study the original works of the Renaissance and antiquity that Blake could only experience through engravings.

Most of Blake's early drawings appear to come from incomplete or abortive projects, but one can observe the emergence of some of his mature themes. His series of watercolors of *The History of England* (Butlin 51–69) was begun at least as early as 1780, for in that year he exhibited *The Death of Earl Goodwin* (Butlin 60) at the Royal Academy. Though the series was never finished – he was evidently still thinking of engraving some of the designs as late as 1793 – some themes can be discerned. Just as the pamphlets of c. 1788, *There is No Natural Religion* and *All Religions are One*, challenged the rationalist theology of the Church of England, so the *History of England* series' emphasis on myth and divine intervention challenged the new miracle-free British history of David Hume and others.

The early drawings for the Bible, the history of England, and Milton's *Paradise Lost* anticipate Blake's lifelong concern with the apocalyptic history of modern times as the fulfillment of biblical prophecy. Early watercolor drawings such as two versions of *Pestilence* (Butlin 184–85), which probably begin as part of the *History of England* series, anticipate several versions of the same theme in his mature years. It is, like the subjects *Plague*, *Famine*, and *War*, to which he returns often in his later career, a theme that can be found in the prophecies of the Old Testament, the Book of Revelation, and the recent history of England.

The most important and revealing of Blake's early works is the series of three watercolors of *The Story of Joseph* (Butlin 155–57), exhibited at the Royal Academy in 1785. They are unusually large watercolors, 15 × 22 inches, and they fit well into the elevated mode practiced in oils by Barry and West, whose art had been formed in the international atmosphere of 1760s Rome. The subjects are biblical, itself not unusual at the time, though the ones chosen are virtually unique. The sculptural forms of the figures, often referencing classical sculptures, reveal Blake's learned, even scholarly approach to his art. In the first watercolor (Fig. 10) Joseph's gesture in raising his cloak to hide his emotions echoes a familiar veiling motif in Roman sculpture. The female figure carrying a large basin on her head is an unmistakable reference to a Raphael wall painting in the Vatican, and so on. The firm outline that bounds the figures, and the measured if histrionic gestures, are especially close to the work of Barry at this time. Barry's passion for public art had led him only a few years before to volunteer to paint free of charge the monumental series of wall paintings entitled *The Progress*

Figure 10 *Joseph's Brethren Bowing before Him.* Pen and watercolor over pencil, exhibited 1785.

of Human Culture, for the Society for the Encouragement of the Arts, Manufactures and Commerce in London,[3] and for Blake he was an exemplary victim of Reynolds's tyranny.

Blake was in a sense, then, a conservative artist, looking back to the artistic past, even prepared to quote from it as a writer might from Horace. But a taste for classical, especially Roman, art was in the late eighteenth century often associated with radical and even apocalyptic politics. The obvious example is the great French painter Jacques-Louis David, a revolutionary leader and regicide who, in painting and in life, invoked the ideals of Republican Rome as a model for the France that would emerge from the Revolution. The respectable appearance of Blake's story of Joseph might also conceal if not a subversive subtext, then at least personal anxiety. The story is of the biblical Joseph, a man of prophetic powers, whose success achieved in exile obliged him to disguise his real self from his family, unaware that the "Egyptian" official is their own long-lost brother. In the final scene Joseph reveals himself, but only the brother closest to him embraces him; the others remain uncomprehending. Blake's choice of this subject may be connected with his own Joseph-like career to date. By 1785 he had achieved public success in exhibiting at the Royal Academy and was admired by some of his own contemporaries, but we can conjecture that the "disguise" of a respectable Royal Academy exhibitor threatened to alienate him from his "true" prophetic self. Only a few of Blake's biblical and literary designs appear to have an autobiographical subtext, but his designs often provoke an interpretation against the grain of their ostensible meaning.

The series of twelve wash drawings in illustration of *Tiriel* (Butlin 198) of c. 1788, are unique in Blake's work in illustrating a grim Lear-like tale of his own invention, for which a manuscript text survives. The *Tiriel* project, with its clear separation of text and design, is transitional in being an example of the conventional method of combining text with design implicitly rejected by Blake in developing the method of illuminated printing. He probably abandoned the series because his new technique took him beyond what had now become for him an obsolete method.

From the great color prints to the Butts Bible, 1795–c. 1810

Blake's invention and development of illuminated printing in 1788–94 meant that he made very few separate drawings or watercolors in this period. But there are signs, particularly in 1794–95, of an assertion of the independent power of images in works of illuminated printing. The prophetic books that deal with the early history of the world, *The First Book of Urizen, The Song of Los, The Book of Los*, and *The Book of Ahania*, are notable for containing a number of eloquent and densely printed plates completely without text. Pride in his new color-printing technique also led him to issue sample plates without text from a range of illuminated books and a few other designs. These were issued in two copies of the Small and Large Books of Designs (Butlin 260–67), though he does claim it was "to the Loss of some of the best things. For they when Printed perfect accompany Poetical Personifications & Acts, without which Poems they never could have been Executed" (E 771).

Notable among these designs, and *not* connected with a prophetic book, is the famous design often called *Glad Day* but known more correctly as *Albion Rose*. It exists in two color-printed impressions, c. 1794–96 (Butlin 262 1, 284; Fig. 11), and as an unusually free etching, probably c. 1804, though bearing the date 1780, inscribed "Albion rose from where he labourd at the Mill with slaves / Giving himself for the Nations he danc'd the dance of Eternal Death" (Essick, *Separate Plates*, VII; Fig. 12). It is an affirmative image of liberation – in 1780, in the lost original version, perhaps as the hopeful outcome for the American Revolution, in c. 1795 for the French Revolution, and in c. 1804–5, if that is the right date, for his own proclamation of personal regeneration.[4] Affirmation is rare in Blake's art of this time, particularly as his hopes for world revolution were being blighted, but it is a reminder that the prophecy of Revelation looks forward not only to the destruction of the earth, but beyond to the building of the New Jerusalem.

In 1795 he began work on the Large Color Prints (Butlin 289–329), a series of twelve magnificent monotypes using his color printing to dramatic effect, the method allowing him up to three impressions of each design. They are unusually large, about 17 × 21 inches, and they are of biblical and literary scenes, with a few taken from his own myth. Their overall theme and order are uncertain, but they appear to represent the spiritual history of man, from the *Elohim Creating Adam* to the baleful domination of *Newton*, the presiding genius of the materialism of Blake's era, crouching in his cave measuring, and thereby reducing, the world with a pair of compasses (Fig. 13).

The dominant artistic presence for Blake in the 1790s was Henry Fuseli. A snatch of conversation recorded by Joseph Farington on 12 January 1797 gives a sense of Fuseli's reputation in the Royal Academy and Blake's relationship with him: "We supped together and had laughable conversation. Blakes eccentric designs were mentioned. [Thomas] Stothard [painter and early friend of Blake] supported his claims to Genius, but allowed He had been misled to extravagance in his art, & he knew by whom."[5] Fuseli is clearly meant here. His art is characterized by emotional extremism derived from his origins in the *Sturm und Drang* (Storm and Stress) movement in

Figure 11 *Albion Rose*. Color-printed etching, c. 1794–96.

Switzerland and Germany, which advocated the direct expression of emotion, venerating Shakespeare as a genius who had defied the rules of classical composition.[6] Fuseli treated subjects from Milton and Shakespeare as worthy of history painting, and his mark on Blake can be seen most clearly in the latter's adoption in the 1790s of a body-type that can contort itself to express violent emotion. Fuseli taught Blake to think of the body as like a

Figure 12 *Albion Rose*. Etching, c. 1804 or later.

coiled spring that can retreat into itself, like *Newton,* or can extend itself
fully in exultation as in *Albion Rose.*

Blake attracted two important commissions in the later 1790s for watercolor illustrations, one possibly through Royal Academy contacts, the other
commissioned by Flaxman. The first, from the publisher Richard Edwards,

Figure 13 *Newton.* Color-printed drawing, 1795.

was for a series of illustrations to Edward Young's *Night Thoughts*, poetic reflections on life, death, and immortality, published in the 1740s. The idea was to produce an impressive illustrated book in the manner of John Boydell's *Shakspeare* [sic] *Gallery*. Blake after about two years' work produced an astonishing 537 watercolors (Butlin 330–34), almost all of which were drawn on enlarged pages of a text of the poem. Despite the potential monotony of the task, and signs of distaste for the clergyman–poet's conventionality, Blake responded with sustained invention both to the seriousness and to the wit of the text. The designs for Young are important as Blake's first attempt to make illustrations act as a commentary that "corrects" the text. This is, of course, often hard to discern, and has led some scholars into grotesque over-interpretation, finding Blakean meanings in virtually every mark. Blake's views are nonetheless evident in the caricatural rendering of the "author," and in occasional references to apocalypse, studiously omitted by Young. In the spectacular title page to Night VIII (Butlin 330 345), "the Man of the World [is] Answer'd" by Blake with a powerful and politically challenging image of the Whore of Babylon riding the Beast of Revelation, whose heads are of the ecclesiastical and political powers of the world, the company, Blake suggests, kept by Young himself.

The publication of the *Night Thoughts* was not a success. A volume containing forty-three engravings by Blake, selected from the first four of the nine Nights did appear in 1797, but nothing further, a victim to changed economic circumstances caused by the French War. Blake's illustrations to Thomas Gray's poems (Butlin 335), containing 116 watercolors surrounding the page as in *Night Thoughts*, are very different in spirit, and reveal an unexpected flair for comic horror, especially in the illustrations to the "Gothick" tale, *A Long Story*. They were commissioned by John Flaxman as a birthday present for his wife Nancy in 1797–98, and may have been a welcome diversion from Blake's fears of arrest in the government campaign against radicalism.

Blake's economic position seems to have declined sharply in the mid-1790s. Engraving work was hard to find, and was to remain so for most of the rest of his life. He was fortunate to find a savior of sorts in Thomas Butts, chief clerk in the office of the Muster-Master General, who in 1799 commissioned from Blake a series probably of fifty tempera paintings in illustration of the Bible (Butlin 379–432), but then went on to buy more than 100 biblical and Miltonic watercolors from Blake over the next nearly twenty years. The tempera technique, called by Blake quite incorrectly "fresco," had virtually nothing in common with Italian fresco, but it was the third of Blake's great technical innovations after relief etching and color printing. The medium was unstable, and the carpenter's glue he used as a medium caused the paint

Figure 14 Butts tempera series: *The Nativity*. Tempera on copper, c. 1799–1800.

to darken and lift. As a result most of the tempera paintings are in poor condition and several are lost altogether. In the better preserved ones the clear outline and beautifully luminous effects reveal what Blake hoped to achieve. His experiments with tempera followed from his desire to combine outline with the density of surface that he may have observed in fifteenth- and early sixteenth-century Italian paintings on exhibition in London from the great Orléans collection.[7] The Butts tempera series is clearly typological in paralleling Old and New Testament scenes in the medieval manner, but its surviving glory is in a number of memorable images. Among the most extraordinary are the motif in *The Nativity* (Butlin 401; Fig. 14) of the Christ child apparently springing from the Virgin's womb in a radiance of light, to be caught by Anne's outstretched hands, and the astonishing Miltonic serpent who enfolds Eve in *Eve Tempted by the Serpent* (Butlin 379). It seems that after the completion of the tempera series in 1800 Butts was prepared to pay Blake a guinea for any biblical watercolors he delivered to him over a period of about ten years. As a result the Butts Bible watercolors do not make up a coherent series; there are clear sub-groups of different sizes within them, the largest being a group illustrating the Book of Job (Butlin 550). Some of the designs for the Book of Revelation, though now scattered, make up a stylistically coherent group (Butlin 519–22), as do episodes from the passion and resurrection of Christ.

Over the years, significant shifts in style and content reflect important changes in Blake's thought. In early 1803 he remarks to Butts that "I have recollectd all my scatterd thoughts on Art & resumed my primitive & original ways of Execution in both painting & engraving, which in the confusion of London I had very much lost & obliterated from my mind" (E 724). This sense of artistic regeneration is associated with a rediscovery of the person of Jesus. As he had written to Butts previously in late 1802, "Tho I have been very unhappy I am so no longer I am again Emerged into the light of Day I still & shall to Eternity Embrace Christianity and Adore him who is the Express image of God" (E 720). These remarks suggest a kind of "Gothic Revival" in Blake's art that parallels the interest at this time in the Gothic among German painters like the Nazarene group, Caspar David Friedrich, and especially Philipp Otto Runge,[8] though he had no direct contact with any of them. In a letter to William Hayley a year later, he specifically associates seeing a collection that contained a number of fifteenth-century or "Gothic" paintings with his sense of the spiritual renewal of his childhood: "Suddenly, on the day after visiting the Truchsessian Gallery of pictures, I was again enlightened with the light I enjoyed in my youth, and which has for exactly twenty years been closed from me as by a door and by window-shutters."[9]

This Gothic revival can be seen in Blake's use of a more hieratic compositional structure in which the left-hand side of the picture exactly mirrors the right. This heightens the almost medieval spirituality of such works as *The Magdalene at the Sepulchre* and *Christ in the Sepulchre, Guarded by Angels* (Butlin 504, 500), both c. 1805; symmetrically placed angels create an architectural effect both austere and ethereal.

The Butts watercolors also move towards a more emphatic use of pen outline. This is particularly evident in *The Repose of the Holy Family in Egypt*, 1806 (Butlin 472), where the vegetation and landscape are meticulously contained within a sharp, even, and rhythmical penwork. There is also in 1805 and after a shift towards a greater transparency and luminosity, exploiting the properties of watercolor itself against the whiteness of the paper. The full impact of many of the Butts watercolors has been diminished by fading, caused by careless exposure to light, but even so a startling range of expressive effects can be discovered among them. The possibilities of light enabled Blake to tackle subjects, like the visions described by the prophets themselves, that had since the middle ages been regarded as untranslatable into visual imagery. Blake was arguably the first major artist since Dürer to attempt a comprehensive picturing of the fantastic imagery of the Book of Revelation and the biblical books of prophecy, rather than representing them by figures of the prophets themselves *writing* the visions. Blake offers, for instance, a magnificent image of Ezekiel's actual vision in all its extraordinary complexity and richness in the watercolor *Ezekiel's Wheels*, c. 1803–5 (Butlin 468; Fig. 15). The Butts watercolors also show Jesus as an active redemptive presence in the world. In the 1790s prophetic books, Jesus makes only an indirect appearance subsumed within the revolutionary identity of Orc in *Europe a Prophecy*. In the Butts watercolors Jesus now represents, as Blake tells us elsewhere, forgiveness of sin. His force lies in his gentleness, and Blake reverts to a figural type familiar from the painting of Raphael (though not of Michelangelo) and his Italian forebears.

Butts also commissioned some series of illustrations to Milton, but he was anticipated in this by another more shadowy patron, the Rev. Joseph Thomas, who came to Blake through Flaxman. Thomas had commissioned from Blake a *Comus* series (Butlin 527) as early as 1801, and was to commission a series of twelve watercolors for *Paradise Lost* in 1807 (Butlin 529). The following year Butts then commissioned a larger *Paradise Lost* set (Butlin 536), and these, despite their faded condition, represent the high point of Blake's "outline" style. A firm pen outline is used to give the figures and natural details a determinate and rhythmical character that implicitly reproaches the current English school of watercolor landscape painting, with its atmospheric effects achieved by fluid application of color and imprecise

Figure 15 Butts watercolor series: *Ezekiel's Wheels*. Black chalk, pen, and watercolor over pencil, c. 1803–5.

forms. The linearity of the larger *Paradise Lost* series represents a partial return to the neoclassical manner of the Joseph watercolors, signaled by his claim in letters to Butts (above) to have regained the light of his youth. But line is now used with greater confidence and skill, creating such effects as the weaving of the forms of vegetation into a magical tapestry in *Raphael*

Warns Adam and Eve (Butlin 536 6), while reinforcing the monumentality of the human figures.

The Butts *Paradise Lost* series expresses the intensity of Blake's relationship with Milton, reinforced, so Blake tells us, by visits from the older poet in spirit at Felpham. To Blake his watercolor designs to Milton were a conversation of equals, a dialogue conducted on his part in images. All have been the subject of interpretation and over-interpretation, applying Blakean ideas gathered from the prophetic books to tease out a detailed commentary on Milton. But Blake's commentary is best understood by following *pictorial* suggestions. In the *Paradise Lost* designs for Butts, for example, Blake shifts Milton's emphasis on Satan to Christ, "correcting" the poem according to the long-held belief that Milton had made Satan the hero of the poem. Blake makes the central axis of the watercolors in which both Christ and Satan appear into a field of contestation. The latter occupies the field in the first two plates, but after Jesus' decision to relinquish his position in Heaven to return to earth (Butlin 536 3), Satan is revealed as a pathetic creature watching the endearments of Adam and Eve, while embracing onanistically the serpent, an emblem of his own true self (536 4; Fig. 16). Christ's superior power is asserted in his dramatic rout of the rebel angels (536 7), his clear identification as the God who creates Eve (536 8), his central position in the judgment of Adam and Eve (536 10), and in Michael's prophecy of the Crucifixion (536 11). In the early 1790s Blake had claimed that Milton "was a true Poet and of the Devil's Party without knowing it" (*MHH* 6, E 35), approving Milton's rejection of conventional Christianity. By 1808 he had clearly identified the merciful Christ as the all-encompassing God, and relegated Satan to his rightful place.

The evidence in Blake's letters and watercolors of a growing sense of spiritual renewal in the years 1802–8 contrasts with his irascibility in dealings with others, for he was unable to regain his previous practice as an engraver after his return from Felpham in 1803. His old friends at the Royal Academy were still prepared to support him and were behind a scheme to publish, as a showcase for him, a series of his designs for Robert Blair's *The Grave*,[10] like Young's *Night Thoughts*, a popular poem on death and mortality first published in the 1740s. Blake produced a series of watercolors for the book (Butlin 609–38), and the original idea was for him to engrave them himself as he had with the *Night Thoughts* volume. The publisher, Robert Cromek, however, was evidently shocked by a proof of *Death's Door* (Essick, *Separate Plates*, XIII) in a white-line etched technique close to that used in *Jerusalem*, and had Blake's designs engraved in a conventional manner by Luigi Schiavonetti. It is hard not to sympathize artistically with Blake, but he was

Figure 16 *Paradise Lost* series: *Satan Watching the Endearments of Adam and Eve.*
Pen and watercolor, 1808.

clearly becoming extremely touchy and filled with a sense that his friends
were betraying him.

Public failure and private success, c. 1809–c. 1820

Blake's exhibition of 1809 (Butlin 649–66) was a desperate attempt to regain
an artistic reputation that had been effectively lost since going to Felpham

in 1800. His *Descriptive Catalogue of Pictures, Poetical and Historical Inventions, Painted by William Blake* (E 529–52) made the sensational claim that he had rediscovered "the ancient method of Fresco Painting" (E 529). Of the sixteen paintings in the exhibition, nine were in "fresco," and the rest were watercolors borrowed back from Butts for the occasion. There was also a version of the early *Penance of Jane Shore* watercolor (probably Butlin 69) to demonstrate that "the productions of our youth and of our maturer age are equal in all essential points" (E 550). Some of the "fresco" paintings are lost, like *The Ancient Britons*, showing the three survivors of Arthur's last battle, "the Strongest Man, the Beautifullest Man, and the Ugliest Man," and so is the "drawing" *The Brahmins* ("Mr. Wilkin, translating the Geeta; an ideal design, suggested by the first publication of that part of the Hindoo Scriptures, translated by Mr. Wilkin" (E 542, 548)).

The fresco paintings that do survive have all darkened quite badly, but they remain legible and impressive. The paired paintings *The Spiritual Form of Nelson Guiding Leviathan* and *The Spiritual Form of Pitt Guiding Behemoth* were designed, Blake tells us, to demonstrate the possibilities of "portable Fresco" (E 527). They were intended as trial pieces for immense versions, also in fresco, to be commissioned for public places like the Houses of Parliament, "on a scale that is suitable to the grandeur of the nation, who is the parent of his heroes" (E 531). It is usually understood that the reference to "heroes" was meant ironically, but the real point is that Pitt is described by Blake as the Angel from the Book of Revelation, who "pleased to perform the Almighty's orders, rides on the whirlwind, directing the storms of war" (E 530). These paintings, in their proposed incarnation in a public place, would act as a reminder that a patriotic victory was not a matter of personal glory, but a step on the way to the final apocalypse and redemption.

The *Descriptive Catalogue*, which was on sale at the exhibition, is the nearest thing we have to Blake's artistic credo, and it gives important insights into Blake's ideas about art. Outline has an absolute moral force; it is "the hard and wiry line of rectitude" (E 550), for clarity is necessary for vision. This view clearly affected his art at this time, as we have seen, but he softened his insistence on it in his later practice. He also proposes the strange theory, not unique to Blake but known to James Barry, that art was invented by the Jews, whose possession of the Divine Vision was manifested in sculptures on the Temple as well as in the Old Testament. The lost Hebrew works were copied by the Greeks in the canonical sculptures, like the Vatican *Laocoön* (the subject of a late print by Blake; Essick, *Separate Plates*, XIX), which can, therefore, despite Greek paganism, be admired as reflections of great lost "Originals." The Greek canon thus provides reflected archetypes of humanity that recur in every generation: "Chaucer's characters live age after age" because "every one is an Antique Statue" (E 536). Apart from the Greeks, "Milton, Shakspeare, Michael Angelo, Rafael... Gothic, Grecian, Hindoo and Egyptian" (E 544) also had access through memory to the lost "Originals"; hence Greek art need not be privileged over, for example, the Gothic. On the other hand artists who Blake claimed did nothing more than imitate nature, like Rubens, Rembrandt, and the Venetians, had no access to vision at all: "As there is a class of men... so there is a class of artists [Venetian and Flemish], whose whole art and science is fabricated for the purpose of destroying art" (E 538).

The fresco painting of *The Canterbury Pilgrims* (Butlin 653) was the basis for the famous extended account in the *Descriptive Catalogue*. A pungent and rambling text on engraving, the *Public Address* (E 571–82), suggests that he was planning a parallel publication on engraving, with a similar aim of self-justification and rehabilitation. It is centered around the magnificent *Canterbury Pilgrims* engraving (Essick, *Separate Plates*, XVI), which he put forward as an example of old-fashioned line engraving of the kind he had learned in Basire's workshop. It is, as Blake claims it to be, a masterpiece in the most ancient manner of the craft, of "Marc Antonio & Albert Durer," and a rejoinder to the imitative style of engraving practiced by his more fashionable contemporaries, as he quaintly put it, "What is Calld the English Style of Engraving such as proceeded from the Toilettes of Woolett & Strange," those "heavy lumps of Cunning & Ignorance" (E 573).

The 1809 exhibition was a catastrophe, and the *Public Address* overflows with acrimony, yet Blake's artistic ambitions seemed to grow ever larger. The *Canterbury Pilgrims* painting and engraving can be compared in their synoptic ambitions with *Jerusalem*, and it appears that he was working at this time on a great fresco painting of *The Last Judgment*. It is now lost, but it survived for the biographer J. T. Smith to see it in the possession of Blake's widow in the late 1820s. It contained "upwards of one thousand figures, many of them wonderfully conceived and grandly drawn. The lights of this extraordinary performance have the appearance of silver and gold."[11] There are fortunately enough versions in drawing and watercolor, and written descriptions by Blake, to give a good idea of what it was like. If *Jerusalem* encompasses all myths of humanity, and *Canterbury Pilgrims* all human types, then *The Last Judgment*, particularly in its lost final form, provides a summation of all the moral episodes of the Bible, within the frame of a Last Judgment heavily weighted towards the Book of Revelation. The composition is Michelangelesque, but the flame-like movement, both up and down, make it more Gothic in feeling. All versions have Christ in the judgment seat, Adam and Eve beneath on either side of the central axis, with the Whore of Babylon seated (in the Petworth House and National Gallery of Art, Washington versions [Butlin 642, 645]) on a cave in which the Great Red Dragon or Satan is finally imprisoned. The Petworth version was commissioned from Blake, through the agency of the portrait painter Ozias Humphry, by the Countess of Egremont, to join the greatest collection of British contemporary art gathered in Blake's time.

Blake's numerous attempts around 1809–10 to reclaim his position in the London art world failed utterly. He progressively fell out with his artist friends, though Flaxman sent him the odd engraving job, and an old friend George Cumberland, an amateur author and printmaker who lived in Bristol, kept in touch. Butts's patronage seems to have fallen off a little, but he continued to commission biblical tempera paintings around 1810–11, the most notable of which is Blake's largest surviving tempera (about 5 × 4 feet), the impressive if battered *Allegory of the Spiritual Condition of Man* (Butlin 673). The text on which the picture is based has been lost, but it is evidently a meditation on the subject of Faith, Hope, and Charity.

Butts commissioned, probably in 1816, six watercolors illustrating Milton's *On the Morning of Christ's Nativity* (Butlin 542), a revised version of the 1809 series for the Rev. Joseph Thomas (Butlin 538). He also commissioned the set of twelve watercolors illustrating *L'Allegro* and *Il Penseroso*, c. 1816 (Butlin 543), of which there is no other version. These small watercolors are painted in a minute and exquisite technique, with a sense of atmosphere calibrated precisely to the poems' contrasting moods of lightness and melancholy. The watercolors are given wider meaning by Blake's decision to make the two poems into a spiritual biography of Milton, as Blake's written commentary accompanying the series makes clear (E 682–85). The six scenes of Mirth and Melancholy are numbered continuously, so that they read as the story of Milton's descent from the joyful youth of his pastoral poems through the disturbances of his adult life, to his final redemption as a prophetic poet, blind to this world but open to the world beyond. The series is full of imaginative effects: in *The Sun at His Eastern Gate* (543 3) an immense Apollonian sun god in his radiance sets his toe on a mountain top, illuminating a beautiful pastoral landscape; in the final scene of *L'Allegro*, *The Youthful Poet's Dream* (543 6) the youthful Milton writes in a book, seeing "in his Dream the more bright Sun of Imagination," contrasted in visual richness and scale with the merely physical sun. In the realm of Melancholy, in *The Spirit of Plato* (543 9), Milton's head is burdened by an extraordinary outpouring of figuration that is both true to Plato's text yet elucidates it in its complexity. Finally in *Milton in His Old Age* (543 12), the blind poet, seated "in his Mossy Cell Contemplating the Constellations. surrounded by the Spirits of the Herbs & Flowers. bursts forth into a rapturous Prophetic

Strain." It represents the final reconciliation between the troubled spirit of Milton and Blake's own artistic imagination.

The landscape painter John Linnell's rediscovery of Blake in 1818 eventually provided him with an enthusiastic promoter, ambitious for him to achieve public recognition by his imagination. The first project Linnell obtained for Blake was for the seventeen tiny wood engravings for Robert Thornton's *Pastorals of Virgil*, 1821 (Essick, *Commercial Illustrations*, LIII), a schoolbook. It was an extremely modest commission, but the luminous effects Blake achieved opened up possibilities for wood engraving even beyond Thomas Bewick. In 1821 Linnell also singled out the Job watercolors (probably c. 1805 from the Butts biblical series, Butlin 550), ordering watercolor copies (Butlin 551)). He then persuaded Blake to engrave twenty-one plates plus title page in the early Italian manner, without etched underdrawing, with the intention of making an edition for sale. Blake copied the watercolor designs on a smaller scale, and set each one within a border containing lightly and freely drawn figures, decoration, and quotations from the Book of Job and other parts of the Bible as a commentary on the main image.

The *Illustrations of the Book of Job*, which did not appear until 1826, provide a singularly rich interpretation of the biblical story, using a method similar to the *L'Allegro* and *Il Penseroso* series. The motivations in the biblical story are notoriously hard to fathom: why does God punish Job, why does Job endure it so patiently, and why is he redeemed? Blake offers an imaginative solution by interpreting the story in terms of the fall and redemption of humanity, paralleling the story of Albion in *Jerusalem*. Blake uses the remarkable device of giving Job, Jehovah, and the Redeemer identical physiognomies, stressing that the God Job worships is created and transformed by Job's perceptions of him. In plate 1, Job is a conventional churchgoer reading the Bible with his family, according to the inscription on the altar beneath, in the letter rather than the spirit. Job enters into a Fall, and is tormented by Satan acting for an apparently arbitrary God, corresponding to Job's belief in the vengeful God of the Old Testament. In the median plate 11, Job realizes at last the Satanic nature of the God who has tormented him, and in his epiphany, "his Soul [is brought back] from the pit to be enlightened with the light of the living." He now understands the true God to be Jesus Christ, and is able, through Christ's sacrifice, to throw off the tepid religiosity into which he had fallen. This involves entering into a higher and mixed form of communication; in plate 20 Job converses with his daughters not just in words but also in pictures, and in the final plate the restored family praises the Lord exultantly through instrumental music, song, and possibly dance. Art and prayer thus become one and the same.

Once Blake had finished work on the Job engravings Linnell gave him the ambitious task of making 100 watercolors for Dante's *Divine Comedy* (Butlin 812), with the aim of producing also a series of engravings. The work was not completed before his death in 1827. Only a small number of the Dante watercolors are finished; some are barely sketched in, and only seven engravings reached proof form. Even so the Dante watercolors are among Blake's richest achievements, engaging fully with the problem of illustrating a poem of such complexity. The mastery of watercolor has reached an even higher level than before, and is used to extraordinary effect in differentiating the atmosphere of the three states of being in the poem. In *The Vestibule of Hell and Souls Mustering to Cross the Acheron* (12) (Butlin 812 5), there are literally dozens of figures in discrete groups but showing individualized forms of distress. The setting suggests the infinite gloom of the infernal rivers and lakes, though as yet none of the full torments of Hell has been experienced. Even the sketchiest of the Hell scenes creates an atmosphere that not only distinguishes Hell from Purgatory and Heaven, but also precisely expresses the ghastly and ever-changing climatic conditions within the nine circles of Hell, in which the victims roast, bake, freeze, and flounder in their own excrement, within their own micro-climates. Nothing could convey more plainly a sense of the primeval dankness of the mire in which the gluttons swim than *The Circle of the Gluttons with Cerberus* (11) (Butlin 812 *11*); it is like a grim parody of one of J. M. W. Turner's Swiss views.

The disjunctions, fragmentations, and mutilations of Hell give way eventually to Purgatory and feelings of tenderness replace pain, anger, rage, and pity. In *The Angelic Boat Returning after Depositing the Souls* (75) (Butlin 812 72; Fig. 17), nothing could be more moving than the sketchily drawn sequence of events: the group of figures arrives from the angelic boat, Dante embraces his friend the musician Casella, who then sings a deeply affecting song of love, while the angelic boat moves away in radiance against a sky that is now blue and infinite.

In Purgatory Blake draws attention in every scene, as does Dante, to the time of night and day in which each event takes place. Paradise is, of course, beyond time; it is, as Dante tells us, light itself, an idea conveyed by Blake with precision in *Beatrice on the Car, Dante and Matilda* (90) (Butlin 812 87), from the gorgeously flowery carpet of the earthly Paradise seen from Purgatory, to the glimpse of Beatrice's train across the Lethe. Paradise is expressed most fully in the astonishing vision in *Dante Adoring Christ* (94) (Butlin 812 90), where Christ is both the source and meaning of light. The Paradise sequence comprises only ten watercolors to illustrate thirty-three cantos, and the final image, *The Queen of Heaven in Glory* (102) (Butlin 812 99) hardly provides a clear resolution to Dante's journey.

Figure 17 Dante, *Divine Comedy* series: *The Angelic Boat Returning after Depositing the Souls*. Pen and watercolor over pencil, 1824–27.

Such an inconclusive ending, as well as the remark penciled on *Homer Bearing the Sword, and His Companions* (7) (Butlin 812 7): "Every thing in Dantes Comedia shews That for Tyrannical Purposes he has made This World the Foundation of All & the Goddess Nature & not the Holy Ghost"

(E 689), mark Blake's dissent from Dante's admiration for the poets of pagan Greece, and from the vengefulness of Dante's Hell. Blake was fervently anti-Catholic, and it is clear that he sees Dante's quest for Beatrice and return to faith in the Catholic Church as a form of nature worship and submission to the tyrannical "God of this world." Yet there are also abundant signs of Blake's relish for Dante's imagery and creation of atmosphere, and also sympathy for Dante's hatred of the corruption of power and of materialism. An extraordinary sequence of seven watercolors is devoted to only two cantos on the subject of the punishment of thieves (Butlin 38–44). They reveal a vivid appreciation of the imaginative transformations of Dante's text and its grim humor, but also reinforce the poet's condemnation of the destructive moral effect of the pursuit of material gain.

The unfinished Dante watercolors bring out clearly the way that many of the great themes of Blake's art and myth are as much present in his designs for other authors as they are in works wholly of his own invention. Yet they are also in their visual language acutely sensitive to artistic as well as literary traditions. It is no longer a question of quotation from earlier masters as it was in the early work, nor identifiable stylistic borrowings; he has achieved a confident, well-absorbed, and developing visual method. The demands of illustrating Dante are enormous, given the intricacy and profusion of his imagery, and the importance of physical atmosphere, but Blake does more than fulfill those demands. For each completed image in the series, and this applies just as forcefully to the biblical watercolors and those to Milton, is itself a history painting that would be persuasive on any scale, despite the "low" medium of watercolor. Each image belongs both singly and as a group to the succession of Raphael and Michelangelo, just as *Milton* and *Jerusalem* are epic poems in succession to Milton and his classical forebears.

Notes

1. Gert Schiff, *Henry Fuseli*, exhibition catalogue (London: Tate Gallery, 1975).
2. David Bindman, ed., *John Flaxman* (London: Thames and Hudson, 1979).
3. W. L. Pressly, *The Life and Art of James Barry* (New Haven and London: Yale University Press, 1981), pp. 86–119.
4. He wrote of having been "a slave bound in a mill among beasts and devils," but is now "again enlightened with the light enjoyed in youth" (letter to Hayley 23 Oct. 1804, E 756).
5. K. Garlick and A. Macintyre, eds., *The Diary of Joseph Farington*, vol. III (New Haven and London: Yale University Press, 1978–96), p. 745.
6. Schiff, *Fuseli*, pp. 9–10.
7. David Bindman, *Blake as an Artist* (Oxford: Phaidon Press, 1977), pp. 127–30.
8. David Bindman, *William Blake: His Art and Times* (New Haven: Yale Center for British Art, 1982), pp. 28–31.

9. E 756; Bindman, *Blake as an Artist*, pp. 140–41.

10. Robert N. Essick and Morton D. Paley, eds., *Robert Blair's* The Grave *Illustrated by William Blake* (London: Scolar Press, 1982).

11. J. T. Smith, *Nollekens and his Times*, 2nd edn. (London, 1829), p. 480.

Further reading

Bindman, David. *Blake as an Artist*. Oxford: Phaidon; New York: Dutton, 1977.

William Blake: His Art and Times. Exhibition catalogue. New Haven: Yale Center for British Art; Toronto: Art Gallery of Ontario, 1982–83.

Blunt, Anthony F. *The Art of William Blake*. New York and London: Columbia University Press, 1959.

Butlin, Martin, ed. *The Paintings and Drawings of William Blake*. 2 vols. New Haven and London: Yale University Press, 1981.

Essick, Robert N. *William Blake, Printmaker*. Princeton: Princeton University Press, 1980.

William Blake: Chambers of the Imagination. London: Tate Britain, 2000.

6

SAREE MAKDISI

The political aesthetic of Blake's images

Reading William Blake's illuminated books is, to say the least, an uncanny experience. Some people find it unappealing. Not seeing any immediately obvious meaning, not even recognizing in Blake's text any of the conventions and cues which normally guide readings along, they find themselves repelled by the text's seemingly obscure words and bizarre images, and ultimately find reading Blake a tiring and unrewarding activity, involving a great deal of effort and very little definite accomplishment. Other readers admire Blake's work for the very same reason: confronting the seemingly impenetrable wall of words and images, they arm themselves with formidable scholarly guides, dictionaries and code books, writings of long-forgotten mystics and visionaries, and they seek out the text's buried treasures, relishing the extraction of what they take to be the mysterious knowledge contained within, access to which is seemingly barred to all but those who have passed certain (presumably secret) rituals of initiation.

However, neither of these approaches to the illuminated books is consistent with Blake's own assessment of his work and habits of reading. Blake had nothing but contempt for ritualistic mystery and hidden knowledge. Indeed, he recognized these as the essential features of priestcraft and the repressive power of what he called "State Religion," which he associated with such notorious "State Tricksters" as the conservative Bishop of Llandaff – best known for his attack on the radicalism of Tom Paine – and with that version of the Bible which had been repeatedly deployed as "a State Trick, thro which tho' the People at all times could see they never had the power to throw off" (anno. Watson, E 612–16). Against the closed texts and the careful regulation of knowledge and power which he took to be essential to state trickery, Blake offered a series of "open" texts, suggestive of a kind of reading that would open out from the text, rather than trying to seduce the reader into its hidden confines: a revolutionary model of reading better suited to the uninitiated and the uneducated, and hence to "the People," than to the servants of power. Jesus, Blake writes, "supposes every Thing to be Evident to the Child & to the Poor & Unlearned" (anno. Berkeley, E 664). But although Blake once pointed out to a dissatisfied customer complaining of his work's obscurity that "that which can be made Explicit to the Idiot is not worth my care," he explained that the best kind of writing and art is that which "rouzes the faculties to act." He also pointed out that his own work has been particularly well elucidated by children, who "have taken a greater delight in contemplating my Pictures than I even hoped" (letter of 23 August 1799, E 703).

This may be of little consolation to postmodern readers making their first approach to the illuminated books. It does suggest to us, however, the need to think through a new approach to Blake's work, one that would involve "unlearning" whatever it is that makes us "learned," or taking seriously Blake's implicit suggestion that our very "learning" is what stands in the way of our reading his work with all the freshness of a child, whose "rouzing" faculties are uninhibited by paradigms of reading and by literary and aesthetic conventions, and perhaps even by the regulations of "State Trickery" itself. It may be, in other words, that the very way we have learned to read is precisely what prevents us from reading Blake properly; in which case, perhaps embracing – rather than recoiling from, or vainly trying to normalize – those aspects of his work that make it special or unusual might enable not merely greater appreciation for it, but also actual pleasure in reading it.

Of all the special characteristics of Blake's illuminated books, surely the most unusual is the way in which they are constituted by the dynamic relation of words and images. Here again, however, Blake's work pushes us to question whatever conventions might govern the ways we associate words and images, and even what we think of the nature of words, images, and narrative itself. We are reminded by Robert Essick in chapter 13 of this volume that the linear and sequential sense of time essential to narrative, even on those occasions when it is present, is undermined and subverted in Blake's work. This – as Blake's detractors have often pointed out in frustration – is exactly what so often makes them "impossible to follow."[1] Moreover, the pictures in Blake's books rarely simply illustrate the words that they accompany, and even when they do, such "simplicity" is often confounded. Most often, especially in the prophetic books, the words and images seem to operate more or less autonomously from each other, more often than not pulling away from each other and tracing different trajectories.[2] It may be useful to think of the illuminated books not as finite texts, contained within a closed circuit of interpretation as defined by some cage of mutually illustrative (and hence reinforcing) words and images, but rather as *virtual* texts, constituted by, even suspended in, the indefinite and expansive gap between words and images – a gap kept resolutely alive by the open nature of Blake's work.

Thus, in reading the illuminated books, we necessarily find ourselves mediating between words and images, generating active and vital meanings from this very process of mediation. What I am proposing here is of course a very different mode of reading than that undertaken by those readers of Blake who, like archaeologists entering a tomb, try to recover what they take to be the text's inert and hidden meanings, which they presume to be buried and simply waiting to be discovered by someone sufficiently clever, educated, and erudite. In our mode of reading, on the contrary, the "meaning" of Blake's text emerges from the process of reading itself – the kind of reading towards which the illuminated books "rouze" our faculties. Rather than resisting the open logic of Blake's work, our mode of reading accepts this logic and takes it as far as possible, by locating much of the meaning of the work in the very logic animating it, the kinds of connections it allows us to make, the freedom of thought and of energy that it enables.

Indeed, if we follow the open logic of the illuminated books far enough, we will quickly discover that reading Blake involves not just mediating between the words and images on a particular plate of one of the books – a kind of openness already daunting enough to some readers – but rather taking the openness even further, mediating between words and images on different plates of the same book, and even between words and images in altogether different books. For, after all, if we are willing to follow the logic of Blake's work far enough to explore the possibility that our reading is located in the unmediated gaps between words and images, why should we foreclose interpretive possibilities by limiting our exploration of such gaps only to particular plates of a single book? Once we can accept that our reading of Blake's illuminated books necessarily takes place in the gaps between words and images, there is no particular reason to suppose that such gaps open and close only on a plate-by-plate basis. For if we can agree that the images on a particular plate often do not illustrate the words next to them, one possibility that we are left with is that they might actually relate more closely to words printed elsewhere. Thus, for example, the image accompanying plate 10 of *America* (a devilish youth rising in flames from the bottom of the page) seems to fit much more closely with the speech on plate 8 (E 54: "The terror answerd: I am Orc") than with the text that appears on plate 10 itself (E 55: "Thus wept the Angel voice") – which itself is better illustrated by the image on plate 8 (a mournful and godlike old man: Urizen, Orc's antagonist)!

Much of the experience of reading one of the illuminated books, then, involves alternating between reading words and reading images, and turning back and forth through the plates, tracing and retracing different interpretive paths through the gap between words and images. This is a kind of reading – really an ongoing re-reading – that is essentially incompatible with the straightforward linear sense of time, and indeed the very habits of reading, to which we have been generally conditioned. In fact, since another part of the experience of reading one of Blake's books is that we seem to keep stumbling across words, lines of text, characters, figures, images, or even poems that we have seen before in other works by Blake, this process of tracing and retracing interpretive paths – that is, the process of reading Blake – can hardly ever be confined to a single text or book. It is, for example, an altogether different experience to read *The Little Black Boy* of the *Songs of Innocence* alongside *The Chimney Sweeper* of *Innocence* than to read *Little Black Boy* on its own. Skin color and identity are treated similarly in both, though in the former as a question of race and in the latter as a question of class and occupation. If we take it into account, this relationship might lead us to question the conclusion drawn by certain critics that *Little Black Boy* is an inescapably "racist" text, since *The Chimney Sweeper* reminds us that becoming "white" is not simply a matter of "race" in the narrow sense, and, in any case, ought perhaps to be read with some measure of irony.[3]

Moreover, reading *The Chimney Sweeper* of the *Songs of Innocence* alongside *The Chimney Sweeper* of the *Songs of Experience* is a different experience, and generates different meanings, from reading either one on its own. This is by no means to suggest that one "version" alone is somehow less "complete" than the two together, but rather that to read both alters our reading of each. Similarly, what begins as a mediation between word and image in one plate can shift into a mediation between words and images in two different plates. This process is of course amplified by the way in which even reading different copies, of, say, *The Chimney Sweeper* of the *Songs of Experience* on their own also offers us a different experience of the "same" plate. But perhaps this particular point would be better illustrated if we consider, for example, what might happen to our reading of *The Little Black Boy* if we try to take account of the fact that in some versions of the plate the little black boy is indeed colored black or brown, and in others white or pink. Does that alteration in *image* – between different versions of the "same" plate – in turn alter the meaning of the *words* themselves, given the multiple overlapping racial and colonial contexts in which the plate was produced? Can we any longer think of the words (which initially seemed, unlike the image in this case, to be constant rather than variable) as stable holders of meaning, or has something happened in our experience of reading the *images* to alter the way in which we think of reading the *words*? Are the same words really the "same" in the sense that they convey the same meaning? Or must we acknowledge that a seemingly identical imprint – whether verbal or visual – can be seen to generate multiple meanings according to the context in which it is read, a context constituted not only by various important cultural, historical, and political factors, but also by the path of reading that the reader has developed in tracing and retracing various paths between words and images through the *Songs of Innocence?*

As a result of such re-readings, the "same" plate can become other to itself – that is, no longer identical to itself – in the sense that it gradually becomes much more difficult, even impossible, to think of it as a single, definite, stable entity. What we can think of as the gap between different plates (such as *Chimney Sweeper* in *Innocence*, *Chimney Sweeper* in *Experience*) can thus be compared to the gap within the same plate (such as two copies of *The Little Black Boy*), and, in turn, the gap within the same work (like the multiple non-identical copies of *Songs of Innocence and of Experience*). Thus the stable self-containment of a single illuminated book is superseded by the wide virtual network of traces among different plates, different copies, different illuminated books; *virtual* because it is not always necessarily activated, and, even when it is, not always activated in the same way. This is also the case with the many images, phrases, and lines of text that we see repeated and recycled in Blake's work. When we encounter apparently the same line of text, or the same image, in multiple contexts (whether multiple versions of the same plate, or altogether different plates), our reading can expand to draw together these multiple appearances. Determining the meaning of a particular text (whether verbal or visual) involves reading it in an ever-expanding – though not an unlimited – number of contexts.

In order to make our discussion a little less abstract, let us take some further examples from the illuminated books themselves. It has often been pointed out that the opening line of *America* ("The Guardian Prince of Albion burns in his nightly tent") reappears as the closing line of *Africa* in *The Song of Los* (pl. 3, E 52; pl. 4, E 68). Most critics assume that this signals the continuity of the same narrative of progress from the end of *Africa* to the beginning of *America*. But there is no need to impose progressive time – or cyclical time – on Blake's work just in order to make sense of such repetitions. For this appearance of an apparently identical line in *America* and *Africa* might suggest a very different relationship between the two works, an indication of their respective locations in a larger network of expansive relations. By undermining the autonomy of each work to tell its own story, such a connection does not merely occasion a one-time retroactive link to another work, but rather reminds us of the array of perpetually open channels, the network of continually firing synapses, linking Blake's works to each other. A similar movement occurs on plate 6 of *America*. The last line of the text ("For Empire is no more, and now the Lion & Wolf shall cease") also appears, slightly modified, in *A Song of Liberty* appended to

The Marriage of Heaven and Hell (E 53; pl. 27, E 45). In turn, the last line of *A Song of Liberty* ("For every thing that lives is Holy") reappears, once again slightly transformed, two plates later in *America* ("For every thing that lives is holy, life delights in life..."), and again on the last plate of *Visions of the Daughters of Albion* ("Arise and drink your bliss, for every thing that lives is holy...") (E 45; pl. 8, E 54; pl. 8, E 51).

Of course, any artist or writer can repeat and recycle images, characters, and concepts, and maybe even whole phrases and lines of text. But there is a consistency in the way Blake effects this kind of repetition which contributes to his work's characteristic flavor. And as someone who earned his living (such as it was) as a reproductive engraver – whose professional obligation was at least in principle to faithfully copy prior images into a new medium where they could be rapidly and accurately reproduced in print – Blake was used to thinking of repetition in a particular way. The logic of copying through repetition was essential to the reproductive engraving business.[4] However, it was essential not only to engraving, but also to the modern industrial form of production as a whole, to the logic animating each of those "dark Satanic Mills," which were already in Blake's lifetime dotting England's "green & pleasant Land" (*Milton* 1, E 95–96).

For when Charles Babbage, one of the great early theoreticians of the modern assembly line, was looking for the conceptual ancestor of the modern factory, he found it in the logic of engraving. "The impressions from the same block, or the same copper-plate, have a similarity which no labour could produce by hand," Babbage writes in his notes on reproductive engraving; "the minutest traces are transferred to all the impressions, and no omission can arise from the inattention or unskilfulness of the operator."[5] If "uniformity and steadiness in the rate at which machinery works, are essential both for its effect and its duration," Babbage adds, "nothing is more remarkable, and yet less unexpected, than the perfect identity of things manufactured by the same tool." Thus, he concludes from his appeal to the logic of reproductive engraving, the key principle "which pervades a very large portion of all manufactures, and...one upon which the cheapness of the articles produced seems greatly to depend," is "that of COPYING, taken in its most extensive sense."[6] According to Babbage, then, the efficient modern factory should ideally reiterate this very logic, producing a stream of identical copies based on the same original impression; or at least that is how the process is supposed to work in principle, even if, like reproductive engraving itself, it rarely attains such perfection in practice. The industrially produced commodity represents a kind of "image," a copy, of a prior prototype. Thus the image becomes for Babbage the central concept driving the production process in even the earliest proto-industrial factories. Here the commodity itself can be thought of as a kind of image; or, to put it the other way around, the mass-produced and circulated image may be recognized as the ultimate commodity.[7] We will shortly return to all this to see what significance it might have for our understanding of Blake.

In the meantime, however, we can probably see that these material considerations greatly increase the significance of the persistence of forms of repetition, including those of words and whole phrases, within Blake's own work. However, whereas the reproductive logic of copying essential to commercial engraving as celebrated by Babbage generates a series of more or less identical standardized replications faithful to a prior original, in the illuminated books the copying – the *reiteration* – of the "same" text or image between and among several different contexts changes the meaning not only of the reiterated text itself, but of the contexts in which it appears in each of its iterations. Such reiteration amplifies the meaning of the "same" text, and transforms it as it is channeled through a number of different circuits of signification. As a result, what we might cautiously refer to as the "usual" relationship of text and context, from which meanings are generated, is amplified by the process of reiteration – just as we have already seen with reference to some of the *Songs*.

Even as students and admirers of Blake, of course, we should in all honesty pause here and admit that in principle there is actually nothing unusual about Blake's work. Whenever a text of whatever kind is cycled through – read in – different contexts its meaning changes; that, after all, is what reading is all about.[8] In this sense, all texts are open rather than closed, all texts are virtual rather than definite, fixed, finite in meaning! What is unusual about Blake's work, however, is that it literalizes this principle of reading: by reiterating the same texts or images in a variety of contexts it presents the principle in actual form rather than solely as potential, though in so doing it always reminds us of this potential. On the one hand, this paradoxically ends up looking like an attempt to circumscribe and limit the principle of reading, by anticipating, containing and channeling the circuits of interpretation through a wide – but not unlimited – number of contexts. On the other hand, what is special about Blake's work is not just the text itself in a narrow sense, but rather the mode of reading, indeed the consciousness of reading, towards which the text "rouzes" us. Far more than most literary and artistic work, Blake's reminds us of the extent to which all texts are open and virtual; and hence, far more than most, it frees us from the determinism of those texts that pretend to be closed and definite – texts which are, for example, constitutive of "State Trickery."

Thus the kind of repetition we see in the illuminated books is quite distinct from repetition in any ordinary sense. It multiplies the text and amplifies its significance rather than merely replicating it. What might look like a process of reproductive copying or printing – which, through his rolling-press, is how all of Blake's illuminated books came into the world – turns into one of transformation. One result is that any possible distinction between "original" and "copy" (no matter how fraught with difficulties those terms are) breaks down. Those lines, images, and fragments of text are all simultaneously copies and originals, and hence neither quite copies nor quite originals. Indeed, by repeatedly differing a repeated, literally reprinted, text from whatever might have been considered its "original" or proper meaning, Blake's process of reiteration ends up subverting the fundamental basis of what Babbage and others identified as the industrial logic of reproduction. And indeed the products of his printshop emerged in anything but a stream of identical copies, since, after all, there is no real "original" or prototype of the *Songs of Innocence* to distinguish from the various "copies." For the etched copperplate was merely one element or tool – and the initial printing itself only one step – in Blake's production process.[9]

Perhaps we can find the closest aesthetic relative of Blake's work not in print or visual culture, but in music, and especially in jazz. The way different copies of Blake's books relate to each other, for example, is something like the way different versions of a late John Coltrane tune relate to each other. Coltrane's modal "sheets of sound," driven by harmony rather than melody, exist only as repeated and widely divergent improvisations unchained to a prior original, a text, or even a rehearsal. This is a good point to recall some questions that have come up repeatedly in Blake studies: what, or where, is, for example, Blake's *America*? Is it all of the copies that exist? Is it the lost copperplates? Is it the concept underlying the seventeen surviving copies? Is it the lowest common denominator unifying all the copies? Is there one particular copy that is more original or more definitive than the others? Does *America* exist as a kind of multiple of the many variants that Blake produced, some with different inks, some with different color washes, some with missing elements, others with added elements, some with missing plates, others with extra plates? Or is *America* at one and the same time all of the copies and each of the copies, both one and many, constant and changing? Indeed, can *America* even be distinguished as such from the vast interlocking network of synapses and relays, the visual and verbal reiterations that link *America* physically to *The Marriage of Heaven and Hell*, *Visions of the Daughters of Albion*, and other works, each of which in turn exists in multiple non-identical copies? Such questions become even more difficult when we consider Blake's color-printed pages (for example, the title page of *The Song of Los*), in which separate prints are barely based on a permanent plate image, and by the time of the large color prints first executed in 1795, are either based on a lightly scratched outline or printed from unetched copperplates or millboards.[10]

It turns out that our investigation of the "meaning" of Blake's work – the way in which we read it – must move between, on the one hand, an account of various textual contexts "within" the work, and, on the other hand, the patterns of reiteration, including the material patterns of reiteration, linking those contexts together. For, as Nelson Hilton puts it, "how his [Blake's] text works is what it means;" or, as Paul Mann has argued very suggestively, "The 'meaning' of any Blake book is thus, first and foremost, that Blake made it, and made it *this way*, not just textually, not even only as a composite art, but fully, materially, as 'Itself & Not Intermeasurable with or by any Thing Else.'"[11] But while Mann and to a certain extent Hilton seek to shift critical attention towards the materiality of the object, I want to shift our attention beyond the object and instead towards the materiality of Blake's textual practice, the process of both textual and material reiteration in Blake's work. For Blake's work may be seen as the ideal site for a reunification of aesthetic and political–economic analysis. This would ultimately allow us to discuss simultaneously the poetic or artistic "vision" proposed in Blake's work *and* the material processes that articulated that vision (and were articulated by it in turn).

With this in mind, let us take an example of the way in which reading the gap between image and words on a particular plate of one of the books ultimately refuses to be self-contained and instead pushes us towards an examination of the broader issues that have come up in our treatment of Blake's work. We will see how our reading of the relation between words and images on one plate pushes us beyond the edge of the plate, not only to other plates and books by Blake, but to the world beyond. For our example, let us turn again to plate 6 of *America* (Fig. 18).

Taking full advantage of the fluidity of his own technique – and demonstrating its profound differences from the conventional commercial combination of typographic print with separately engraved illustrations, whose political, economic and aesthetic parameters, and division of labor he contests in the prophetic books – Blake often unifies the plate's verbal text with its visual "background," especially where the ends of various letters adapt to and even merge with the roots or shooting vines that frame the text. Although the verbal text on plate 6 seems to be framed by the visual elements at the top and bottom of the plate – the grave-like mound on which the youth is resting and the undergrowth at the bottom of the plate – it can also be seen to open a new dimension in the space of the plate.

For it is not exactly the case that the verbal text here is depicted as lying "beneath" or "within" the space of the grave. Because of the flowers and

Figure 18 *America*, plate 6. Copy E.

animal life at the very bottom of the plate, which mark a location in the
open air rather than either an underground scene or a merely stylized frame,
the verbal text produces a distortion in the plate's visual field. Its effect is
to push down (in the two dimensions of the printed page) what ought by
rights to be extended toward the reader/viewer (in the multiple dimensions

of the outside world). In other words, the plant and animal life that occurs on the bottom of the page is suggestive of a kind of foreground for the scene of the youth resting on the small mound, but here they are pushed vertically downwards on the page by the presence of the verbal text. Just as the verbal text is contained by the preceding and successive plates (which frame and define the speech as Orc's), and is at the same time suggestive of an opening away from Orc and the narrative of the American War, the verbal text, though framed by the plate's visual elements, opens up a new moment by generating this distortion in the plate's visual field. In the fourth – temporal – dimension figured in this distortion of the visual field, the verbal text opens up into a moment that is out of synchrony with the visual elements surrounding and framing it. Much of the verbal text is taken up with action and movement (shaking, moving, awakening, springing, running, laughing, singing), but the visual image here is one of rest, more suggestive of a pause than of strident (revolutionary) action. In this respect, of course, the visual imagery seems once again to mesh with the verbal imagery of momentary and eternal pauses.

The plate's verbal and visual texts are simultaneously integrated and disjointed. On the one hand, the words are literally woven into the plate's visual fabric. Moreover, there are many ways in which the verbal and the visual seem to correspond to each other (the line "the grave is burst," for example, seems to be illustrated here, and just as the text reads "let him look up into the heavens," we see a young man looking upwards). On the other hand, the relationship between visual and verbal also suggests a certain kind of unevenness and lack of synchronization. Where is the mill that the text refers to? Are the mill and the grave the same? If so, why is the richness of the metaphor (if that is what it is) reduced to only one of its two terms? If this young man is the freed slave, he looks far too young to have been laboring for "thirty weary years." If he is supposed to be celebrating his freedom in the "bright air" and the "fresher morning" (all pl. 6, E 53), why is the sky here so cloudy, why is the dark gloominess so accentuated in those copies that Blake went on to hand color? Where are the wife and children? Where is the open field? Where are the sun and moon, which play such important roles in the iconography of the verbal text?

What turns out to be the verbal/visual disjuncture that we witness in plate 6 is enhanced by the fact that the relationship of design and text varies from copy to copy along with variations in inking and coloring. And the variation is vastly amplified by the fact that the image of the resting youth is by no means unique to this plate of *America*. On plate 21 of *The Marriage of Heaven and Hell*, which was composed and etched before *America*, we see the same figure, in a similar position, though again there are multiple copies of that plate as well, and hence extensive differences in inking, coloring, and background illustration (Figs. 19 and 20). The same figure will also appear later on plate 4 of *Jerusalem*, and finally, with some minor alterations in stance, as the top half of Blake's illustration for Blair's *The Grave* (1805) (Fig. 22), as well as an initial white-line etching produced by Blake (Fig. 21) – which was rejected by the commissioning editor Robert Cromek, and replaced by the more fashionable engraving (based on Blake's illustration) which Cromek subsequently commissioned from Louis Schiavonetti.

The *Grave* illustrations open another series of relays which we must pursue through Blake's work. The figure of the old man entering "death's door," which constitutes the bottom half of Blake's *Grave* illustration, appears in a separate illustration called "Death's Door" in Blake's own *For Children: The Gates of Paradise* (1793) (Fig. 23), as well as in a contemporaneous pencil drawing in his private notebook. This figure of the old man is also strikingly reminiscent of the figure similarly robed, bearded, and on one crutch, being helped through city streets by a small child in *London* (*SIE*) and *Jerusalem*. The rising youth and the old man entering death's door were apparently first joined together in one image, precisely as they would later appear in the *Grave* illustration, in a much earlier pencil sketch which must have dated from around the time of *America* (Fig. 24).[12] They would reappear in an undated pencil sketch later traced over in ink, with a pyramid background reminiscent of the pyramid in the background of plate 21 of copy D of the *Marriage*. Finally, of course, the old man appears on his own, still – as always – hovering at the entrance to death's door, on plate 12 of *America* itself (Fig. 25).

Thus the passage on plate 6 acquires a new, and yet equally provisional and contingent, frame. Here it is set within the moment defining the gap between the youth's apparent emergence from the grave and the old man's hesitant entrance into the embrace of death. However, the parameters open up beyond the young man and the old man in their specific iterations within the body of *America* to embrace the rest of Blake's work. It is therefore at this continually provisional moment, at this point of contact between entrance and exit, that the speech rests. It is a moment – no longer contained by or within even the multiple copies of *America* – that is always on the brink of happening: a specific and yet highly variable moment that Blake would return to repeatedly through the corpus of his work. In this eternal and infinitely extended moment, the young man will never actually emerge from his expectant crouch, and the old man will never actually find his way into the grave that awaits him, even though all the tempests of time are pushing him towards it.

Figure 19 *The Marriage of Heaven and Hell*, plate 21. Copy D.

The temporal displacement figured in the *Grave* illustration is amplified by the extent to which the images of the old man and the youth are dispersed in a wide network through so much of Blake's work. For just as Blake establishes the existence of this network by producing multiple iterations of

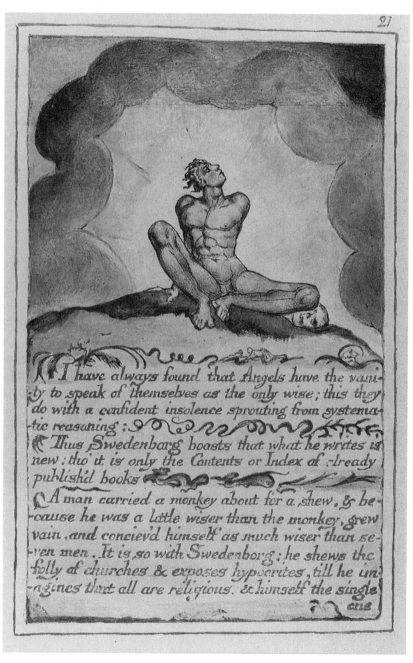

Figure 20 *The Marriage of Heaven and Hell*, plate 21. Copy E.

Figure 21 *Death's Door*. White-line etching, 1805.

Figure 22 *Death's Door*, engraved by Louis Schiavonetti after Blake for Robert Cromek's edition of Robert Blair, *The Grave* (1808).

Figure 23 *Death's Door* from *For Children: The Gates of Paradise*, c. 1793 (revised and reissued 1820 as *For the Sexes: The Gates of Paradise*), pl. 15. Copy D.

similar visual lines or verbal fragments in many different contexts (e.g., "every thing that lives is Holy," "One Law for the Lion & Ox," "the Guardian Prince of Albion burns in his nightly tent"), he gives the network greater reach and power by his repeated insertions of similar pictorial images in several different contexts. This is important because it affirms the extent to which Blake works with words and pictures in very much the same way, disrupting the commercial division of labor that separated typography (and hence words) from engraving (and hence pictures).[13]

We must now further specify some of the ways in which the verbal and visual networks of Blake's work coincide with and amplify each other. Through the complex series of relays linking Blake's different works, the verbal and pictorial elements of these works constitute what I have been calling a virtual text. While each textual fragment interacts with the particular context in which it happens to make an appearance, its meaning can be determined not only in terms of the immediate context of each such iteration, but also in terms of the context constituted through the broader network of verbal and visual reiterations running through the relays and synapses tying *America* to *Visions* to the *Marriage* to the *Grave* illustrations. The extent of this network of reiterations is amplified because of the ways in which most of these works exist in multiple discontinuous and non-identical copies, many with their own unique finish, look, color, sequence.

Figure 24 *Death's Door*. Drawing, c. mid-1790s.

Blake's similar treatment of the verbal and visual components of the illuminated works now takes on new significance. Not only have both word and picture been printed and painted together in his unique method, thereby uniting the separate realms of printing and illustration into what Mitchell

Figure 25 *America*, plate 12. Copy E.

identifies as a "composite art." Word and picture also take on a kind of crystalline hardness literally grounded in the materiality of the copperplate from whose acid-washed surface they emerged together in Blake's material practice as an engraver. However, not only do Blake's words strain to become graphic forms while his calligraphic letters take on a graphic significance. Blake's words also function both as syntactical devices (however problematic) and – in addition to being the graphic objects that Hilton and Mitchell describe – as full-fledged images, whose status we must now further specify. Just as the properly pictorial elements of the prophetic books demand reading in a textual sense, they also assume a non-pictorial function, as images whose significance, like that of their verbal counterparts, is derived from their iterability, whether actual or merely potential. In other words, the verbal phrases and components ("every thing that lives is Holy") that we often encounter in multiple iterations throughout Blake's work function much like the pictorial images that we see similarly reiterated, repeatedly broken up and reunited from work to work. What we encounter in Blake's prophetic books, then, is a number of actually or potentially reiterated images, both verbal and pictorial, and yet neither solely pictorial nor verbal: that is, similar but heterogeneous *graphemes* capable of – and subjected to – multiple iteration.

When we read the illuminated books (and associated prints), the principle of iterability and repetition must be considered as simultaneously material and philosophical: at once a technical concern and an interpretive one. The figural reiteration of images between works in Blake is inextricably related to the material reiteration of images among versions of the "same" work. Even my tentative distinction between figural and material reiteration is misleading because each act of reiteration is in fact both figural and material. For example, the line "every thing that lives is Holy" had to be not only etched separately on the plates of the *Marriage* and *America* (and elsewhere), but also printed separately in different copies of these books. Thus what I first called the figural reiteration of an image between the *Marriage* and *America* also became a matter of material reiteration as the different editions of the two works were printed – which in turn enables our figural comparisons between the two. Figural and material here slip into each other. This is why there is more than a merely intuitive relationship between, on the one hand, reading *America* alongside *Visions* or the *Marriage*, and, on the other hand, reading *America* copy G alongside copy D or copy A. The philosophical principle of iterability by which a text assumes different meanings in different contexts – which holds true not just for Blake's texts, of course – is here enacted as a material principle as well.

Perhaps inevitably, this discussion brings us to a consideration of Blake's unique mode of literary and artistic production, which of course both depended on and altered the existing technology of print reproduction. As Joseph Viscomi elaborates in chapter 3 of this volume, Blake's method of printing "in the infernal method" allowed him smoothly to integrate words and designs – which in conventional printing were divided into the separate realms and reproductive sequences of typography and engraving – in the same original composition. It is important to remember that both conventional typography and engraving were in Blake's time essentially reproductive activities, used, as Babbage saw, primarily for the dissemination of a series of more or less identical copies of original texts and images. Blake never used his special "infernal" method for commercial reproductive engraving.[14]

It would be a terrible mistake to isolate the process of copying within and among Blake's texts from the *material* process of copying – involving copper, acid, paper, and ink – by which Blake actually produced those texts in multiple iterations in his printshop. In other words, thinking about how Blake copied the "same" text from context to context, thereby repeatedly transforming that very "sameness," should help us to think about the materiality of his mode of production and his use and abuse of copying technology more generally, to which Robert Essick, Joseph Viscomi, Morris Eaves and others have drawn our critical attention.[15] Thus what is especially significant and distinctive about Blake's work is the way in which it takes advantage of the principle of iterability so central to his craft, and yet distorts it at the same time. The question of iterability here pushes us to the point at which aesthetic and material questions, matters of philosophy and of political economy, converge and must be considered together (for it would also be a mistake to discuss the question of repetition and reproduction in a strictly material sense without reference to broader conceptual and philosophical concerns).

How Blake's text works may be part of what it means – but what it means is certainly part of how it works and how it was made. For, as we have seen, if we try to read one of the illuminated books as a self-contained object, we will almost inevitably be frustrated. We will have greater success if we try to read it as a part of a virtual network of relations that opens away from itself and undermines its own autonomy. In reading Blake it is important to consider the concepts he was working with, and the degree to which the technical and material aspects of Blake's production practice are inseparable from the conceptual matrix associated with them. Thus Blake's critique of industrial production is to be found not only in his relatively late and resentful work (notably the *Public Address*), but also in the very method by which he distorted the relationship of copy and original which Babbage said was the conceptual heart of industrial production. In other words, Blake's critique of industrial production is simultaneously philosophical and materialist, aesthetic and political. That the variability of Blake's mode of production "rouzes" us to question and become more conscious of our very mode of reading is not a problem for the generation of meaning, but a meaning in itself. For Blake developed a mode of production that necessarily produced heterogeneous products at precisely the historical moment when manufacturers – not just those in the art world – were seizing on the potential offered by another mode of production that would ultimately reorient not only the ways in which people work but the entire cultural and political organization of societies all over the world in order to spew out a stream of identical "Good for Nothing Commodit[ies]" (*PA*, E 576–77).

Blake himself consistently refused to distinguish between artistic, political, and economic matters. Many students of Blake are familiar with his declaration in the last year of his life that "a Line is a Line in its Minutest Subdivision Strait or Crooked It is Itself & Not Intermeasurable with or by any Thing Else...," which is clearly an intervention in the realm of aesthetics. But it is worth remembering the continuation of the very same sentence: "... but since the French Revolution Englishmen are all Intermeasurable One by Another Certainly a happy state of Agreement to which I for One do not Agree. God keep me from the Divinity of Yes & No too The Yea Nay Creeping Jesus from supposing Up & Down to be the same Thing as all Experimentalists must suppose" (letter of 12 April 1827, E 783). For Blake, evidently, the question of intermeasurability, and the concepts of exchange, reproduction, and equality from which it cannot be meaningfully separated, are simultaneously matters of religion, politics, economics, philosophy, technology, and not just art. As Jon Mee reminds us in his contribution to this collection, this ultimately placed severe limits on Blake's relations with the London radicals of the 1790s, including Tom Paine, who were more willing to separate the realms of life and activity from one another.

Blake was, of course, an artisan whose livelihood as well as aesthetic values were being challenged in this period by the rise of a commodity-based consumer culture with whose economy his own bizarre works were ultimately incompatible. And he may have had some sense that a society increasingly oriented towards the production of intermeasurable things – a logic of production repudiated in his own highly differentiated artworks – would ultimately turn all of its members into equally homogeneous and intermeasurable units, and perhaps even into *things* themselves. It is against this industrial logic of commodification, the reification both of objects and of subjects, that I believe Blake based his own understanding of freedom. This remains, of course, an understanding of freedom that is incompatible with, and hence so often incomprehensible in, the social system that we presently inhabit, whose wealth takes the shape of an immense collection of commodities – and of images.

Notes

I would like to thank Robert Essick, W. J. T. Mitchell, Morris Eaves, and Richard Dienst for comments on earlier versions of this essay.

1. W. J. T. Mitchell, *Blake's Composite Art* (Princeton: Princeton University Press, 1978), p. 35.
2. Mitchell, *Composite Art*, pp. 3–39.
3. See Morris Eaves, "On Blakes We Want and Blakes We Don't," *Huntington Library Quarterly*, 58: 3 and 4 (1997), pp. 413–39, esp. pp. 428–39.
4. Robert Essick, *William Blake, Printmaker* (Princeton: Princeton University Press, 1980), p. 27. See also pp. 118–19, 136–64.
5. Charles Babbage, *On the Economy of Machinery and Manufacture* (London: 1832), p. 48.
6. Babbage, *Economy*, pp. 22, 48, 51.
7. See Richard Dienst, *Still Life in Real Time* (Durham, NC: Duke University Press, 1994).
8. See Jacques Derrida, *Limited Inc.* (Evanston, IL: Northwestern University Press, 1988).
9. Michael Phillips has recently presented evidence to suggest that two versions of *A Song of Liberty* appended to *The Marriage of Heaven and Hell* might have been prepared for large-scale cheap publication during the 1790s. See "Blake and the Terror, 1792–93," *The Library* 16, no. 4 (1994), pp. 290–95.
10. See Robert Essick, "William Blake, William Hamilton, and the Materials of Graphic Meaning," *ELH* 52 (1985), p. 852.
11. Nelson Hilton, *Literal Imagination: Blake's Vision of Words* (Berkeley: University of California Press, 1983), p. 11; Paul Mann, "Apocalypse and Recuperation: Blake and the Maw of Commerce," *ELH* 52 (1985), p. 2.
12. See Robert Essick and Morton Paley, eds., *Robert Blair's The Grave, Illustrated by William Blake: A Study with Facsimile* (London: Scolar Press, 1982), pp. 68–69; and Essick, *Separate Plates*, pp. 49–52.
13. Mitchell, *Composite Art*, pp. 14–39.
14. Essick, *Printmaker*, p. 118.
15. See the list of further reading below.

Further reading

Eaves, Morris. *The Counter-Arts Conspiracy: Art and Industry in the Age of Blake.* Ithaca: Cornell University Press, 1992.

Essick, Robert. *William Blake, Printmaker.* Princeton: Princeton University Press, 1980.

Hilton, Nelson. *Literal Imagination: Blake's Vision of Words.* Berkeley: University of California Press, 1983.

Mann, Paul. "Apocalypse and Recuperation: Blake and the Maw of Commerce." *ELH* 52 (1985):1–32.

Mitchell, W. J. T. *Blake's Composite Art.* Princeton: Princeton University Press, 1978.

Picture Theory. Chicago: University of Chicago Press, 1994.

Viscomi, Joseph. *Blake and the Idea of the Book.* Princeton: Princeton University Press, 1993.

7

JON MEE

Blake's politics in history

Blake has been called Britain's greatest revolutionary artist. He is also routinely described as a visionary or mystic, a man more concerned with spiritual than political matters. Many critics subscribe to the intermediate position that Blake's early enthusiasm for the French Revolution transformed itself into a Romantic concern with the creative power of the imagination or a version of John Milton's "paradise within thee, happier far."[1] This chapter suggests, on the contrary, that Blake was always a deeply political writer, even if he was one who viewed the distinction between spiritual and political matters as the product of a fallen human consciousness, but whether he is understood as a political radical, a mystical genius, or a disillusioned fellow traveler, the judgment is complicated by a paucity of biographical information. Unlike the annotations he made on various books he owned, which regularly refer to political matters, the few Blake letters that survive rarely mention politics. One which does, written in the final year of his life, suggests that Blake defined himself as a "Republican" artist:

> I know too well that a great majority of Englishmen are fond of The Indefinite which they Measure by Newtons Doctrine of the Fluxions of an Atom. A Thing that does not Exist. These are Politicians & think that Republican Art is Inimical to their Atom. For a Line or Lineament is not formed by Chance a Line is a Line in its Minutest Subdivision[s] Strait or Crooked It is Itself & Not Intermeasurable with or by any Thing Else . . . but since the French Revolution Englishmen are all Intermeasurable One by Another Certainly a happy state of Agreement to which I for One do not Agree.
>
> (letter of 12 April 1827, E 783)

Of course, the meaning of "Republican" is far from clear in this passage. It could refer to the French Republic, defunct when Blake was writing the letter, but a source of inspiration to him in the 1790s. It might equally represent a continuing allegiance to an older tradition of English republicanism, identified with Whig suspicions of the power of the Crown and proud of the traditional liberties of Parliament. Yet because they are predicated on the active role of the individual citizen, however defined, both of these traditions of republicanism have rather too much stress on the sovereign individual to fully encompass Blake's concern with what he called "universal brotherhood." Neither fits squarely with the practice of Blake's "Republican art."

Blake's lifetime saw both English and French republican traditions struggling to come to terms with the advent of a commercial society, welcomed, if not unequivocally, by Thomas Paine's *Rights of Man* (1791–92). Paine's book was in many ways the bible of the radical movement emerging in Britain in the 1790s, and Blake had many things in common with Paine, as we shall see, but the side which lent itself to the developing discipline of political economy was not one of them. Blake's attack on intermeasurability may well be a reference to the reduction of human beings to socioeconomic units by "the dismal science." Even so Blake's suspicion of the heartless calculations of "Politicians" cannot simply be read as the sign of a Romantic retreat from politics. His republicanism may have been opposed to the abstract individualism of emergent nineteenth-century liberalism, but it was no less political for that. What Blake definitely shared with Painite republicanism was a hatred of the institutions of arbitrary power. His sense that a culture of conformity had manifested itself in England after the French Revolution may have as much to do with his antipathy to "the English Crusade against France" (anno. Watson, E 613) as with any critique of political economy. From around 1792 William Pitt's government began to suppress political opposition of all kinds, fearing the spread of revolution from France. When the two countries went to war in 1793, the pressure to conform intensified and was to last more or less to the end of Blake's life. Above all else Blake's "Republican art" would seem to be pitted against this uniformity of "One King one God one Law" (*Urizen* 4:40, E 72). I have by no means exhausted the possible ways of understanding what Blake's letter means by Republican art, but in what follows I want to pursue some of the questions it raises in relation to Blake's writing and designs in the contexts in which they appeared. The meaning of "Republican" for Blake may be difficult to pin down, but his distinctiveness should not be taken as mere artistic eccentricity or even a sign of the individuality of genius. Too narrow a definition of what politics might have meant to Blake and his contemporaries ignores the fact that, for one thing, radical opposition during his lifetime was a heterogeneous matter. Not all republicans were in any simple way disciples of Paine. The individual freedoms of commercial society were far from being the sole or even major objectives of radicals in the first few decades of the nineteenth century. Blake's brand of prophetic politics has much in common with other ways of conceiving the New Jerusalem of liberty and, for all its concern with

"Eternity," never loses touch with political matters of concern to his time and ours.

Blake's background was in the socially mobile world of eighteenth-century London artisans and tradesmen, a world in which, as E. P. Thompson has put it, "the self-educated journeyman might rub shoulders with the printer, the shopkeeper, the engraver or the young attorney".[2] This urban culture prized independence above all else. Its artisans and tradesmen, including engravers such as Blake, prided themselves on the skills and secrets of their trades, and often had a strong sense of the moral rather than the market value of their products. The republicanism of this world often took less the form of a coherent ideology than a visceral suspicion of the encroachments of the Crown on the rights of the people. This spirit of independence moved Londoners to involvement in the popular resistance to the Crown's authority associated with John Wilkes in the 1760s, and more problematically in the bloody violence and destruction of the anti-Catholic Gordon Riots of 1780. Not least in relation to the idea of a just price for the "labours of the artist" (Prospectus, E 692), the same spirit of independence is to be found everywhere in Blake's work. Even his earliest poems, published in *Poetical Sketches* (1783), seem already deeply republican in the informal sense outlined above. The ballad *Gwin, King of Norway*, for instance, tells the story of a "num'rous" people rushing to "Pull down the tyrant" (E 418), while the unfinished dramatic fragment *King Edward the Third* represents the Hundred Years War against France as the disastrous result of royal ambition and pride. From a more strictly literary perspective, the poems in this early collection also participate in the tradition of English poetry that self-consciously espoused the idea of "the republic of letters." Although this phrase became a standard trope of eighteenth-century writing, it could also refer to a specifically republican ideal in which "the public" was defined in terms of the patriotic endeavors of private individuals rather than royal authority or patronage. Eighteenth-century poets who influenced Blake, such as James Thomson and Thomas Gray, wrote deliberately in this tradition, stressing the idea that the arts flourished only in a free society, and routinely presenting their poetry as part of a broader moral and political regeneration. Complaining at the loss of the power of "bards of old" (E 417), poems such as To the Muses from *Poetical Sketches* may represent juvenile imitations of these poets, but they also participate in this regenerative ideal. A key difference is that as an artisan engraver, rather than an independent gentleman, Blake was extending the boundaries of the republic of letters in a way that would have alarmed both Thomson and Gray. The tradition that associated poetry with liberty had its parallels in the idea of a "republic of the fine arts" promoted by artists such as Blake's hero the Irish history painter James Barry.[3] "England expects that every man should do his duty, in Arts, as well as in Arms, or in the Senate" (*DC*, E 549) is a statement derived from a republican perspective in which the nation is constituted not by the authority of the Crown but by the patriot population. Yet where those patriots are governed by the interests of "a Commercial Nation" (*PA*, E 582) or their membership is subject to a restrictive definition, the republican vision of the unity of the nation is an empty one for Blake.

In Blake's *Jerusalem* the voice of the Atlantic asks: "Are not Religion & Politics the Same Thing? Brotherhood is Religion" (*J* 57, E 207). "Religion & Politics" were certainly seen as intimately connected in Blake's time. Religious Dissent was typical of the social and geographical milieu into which he was born. Although he was baptized and married under the auspices of the Church of England, Blake was buried in the Dissenters' graveyard at Bunhill Fields and there is no record of his ever attending Anglican services. We can now discount claims that Blake's mother was one of England's small number of Muggletonians, a religious sect with its origins in the radical ideas of the Civil War, but it does seem that his family was associated in some way with Dissenters who worshipped outside of the framework of the national Church.[4] Throughout his life Blake seems to have been committed to the idea that "every man may converse with God & be a King & Priest in his own house" (anno. Watson, E 615), but as with many other Dissenters this sturdy independence was combined with a communitarian vision in which the people were gathered together in a struggle against the Beast of Revelation embodied in his concept of "State Religion" (anno. Watson, *passim*). Here are the origins of the emphasis on brotherhood that distinguishes his version of republicanism from more individualistic ones. Dissent was perhaps inevitably hostile to the political order that excluded it from full participation in public life on the basis of religion. Although prosperity encouraged quietism among many Dissenters in the eighteenth century, others played an important role in the revival of radical politics from the middle of the century and began to campaign actively for the repeal of the legislation that barred them from public life (without success until 1828).

Much of this political activity, as well as the important contributions made by Dissenters to scientific and educational change, were associated with the publisher Joseph Johnson, who operated in London as the center of a national web of mainly Dissenting intellectuals from the late 1760s. At different times this loose circle included the likes of Paine, Mary Wollstonecraft, and William Godwin. By 1790 Johnson had also become the Blake's most important employer of Blake as a copy engraver.[5] The publisher had a particularly close association with the Unitarian minister and polymath Joseph Priestley, a key figure in the scientific enlightenment in England and perhaps the most public face of radical Dissent in Britain from the 1770s. Priestley was a trenchant critic of the religious and political establishment. His *History of the Corruptions of Christianity* (1782), as its title suggests, was a hugely detailed and scholarly attack on the way that priests and politicians had combined through the ages to usurp what Priestley took to be the reasonableness of Christ's message. He was also a supporter of the American colonies in the War of Independence, an advocate of parliamentary reform, and sympathizer with the French Revolution who took the spread of political liberty from America to France as a sign of the fulfillment of biblical prophecy. These opinions brought him a great deal of hostility; his home and laboratory in Birmingham were burnt down by a hostile mob in 1791, and he was forced into exile in the United States in 1794. Many of Priestley's political and religious ideas find detailed echoes in Blake's poetry and art. For instance, Blake's attack on the dualism of body and soul on plate 4 of *The Marriage of Heaven and Hell* may owe something to Priestley's belief that the doctrine of a soul as a substance distinct from the body was a corruption adopted by Christianity from pagan religions. For both Priestley and Blake the radicalism of Christ had been obscured by the religious institutions set up in his name. Yet there were important differences in the way they conceived the truth of Christianity.[6]

Our only concrete evidence for Blake having direct contact with any dissenting religious group is his signature on a document circulated at a General Conference of Swedenborgians during Easter week 1789. The document comprised a series of resolutions among other things approving the writings of the Swedish prophet Emmanuel Swedenborg as "genuine Truths, revealed from Heaven" (*BR* 35). Blake had probably been interested in Swedenborg's writing from the early 1780s, most likely drawn by its millenarian proclamation of a New Age, its hostility to priestcraft, its positive view of human sexuality, and its visionary reading of the material world in terms of spiritual correspondences.[7] As *The Marriage of Heaven and Hell* and Blake's annotations to Swedenborg's own writings attest, however, he quickly became disillusioned with the institutionalization of the New Church. Believing that the "Whole of the New Church is in the Active Life & not in Ceremonies at all" (anno. Swedenborg, E 605), Blake is unlikely to have sympathized with the desire of Swedenborg's followers to constitute themselves into a new Church. The process would have seemed to him only the latest in a long history of the priest usurping the role of the poet–prophet (see plate 11 of *The Marriage of Heaven and Hell*). Soon after the 1789 conference, fissures appeared in the movement, the deepest of which were provoked by Swedenborg's controversial vision of an overtly sexual heaven and his tolerance of concubinage. At least two of those expelled from the movement,

Augustus Nordenskjöld and Carl Wadström, were ardent abolitionists and supporters of the French Revolution, a political development that the majority of the movement seem to have feared.[8] Both the political sympathies expressed in poems such as *The French Revolution* and his hostility to the idea that "Womans love is Sin" (*Europe* 5:5, E 62) suggest that Blake had much in common with the expelled members. His reservations about the development of Swedenborgianism almost certainly provided the impetus for *The Marriage of Heaven and Hell*, which may have originated as a separate pamphlet made up of what are now plates 21–23.[9] Blake had probably thought to find its initial audience with both the Swedenborgians themselves and their critics among the Dissenters associated with Johnson. From 1788 the *Analytical Review*, a journal published by Johnson, had been criticizing what it called Swedenborg's "ingenious reveries".[10] Joseph Priestley himself joined the fray in 1791 with his *Letters to the Members of the New Jerusalem Church*. These attacks shared *The Marriage of Heaven and Hell*'s satirical skepticism about the New Church's claim that it had been divinely ordained, but Blake more generally was open to the continuing possibility of prophetic illumination. "Divine Vision" was something Blake regarded as more than simply ingenious reverie. His lifelong enthusiasm for visionary experiences and a correlative skepticism about the power of Reason mark an important difference between Blake and many of those associated with the Johnson circle. This issue brings us to the question of Blake's response to the Revolution in France and his relationship to the politics of the Johnson circle more generally.

Although more work needs to be done on the specific extent to which a shared political language circulated in the writing published by Johnson, there is no doubt that Blake's books are part of a critical dialogue over the French Revolution. Blake's most direct contribution to the intellectual ferment responding to events in France takes the form of the first book of what seems to have been a projected seven-book epic called *The French Revolution* (1791). The poem now exists only in the form of page proofs, which bear Johnson's name as the publisher. We don't know why, but Johnson seems never to have published the poem, although we now know copies of Blake's illuminated books were on view in Johnson's shop in the early 1790s at least.[11] Blake's poem, like much else published by Johnson at the time, treats the French Revolution in millenarian terms. Throughout his life, Blake was given to treating contemporary politics in terms of biblical precedents. Liberty is always identified with the New Jerusalem in Blake's writing, and many others responded in the same way to events in France in the 1790s. Shortly before his emigration to the United States, Priestley published a sermon with Johnson under the title *The Present State of Europe Compared with the Ancient Prophecies* (1794), which interpreted the turmoil of contemporary Europe precisely in terms of the Second Coming. Yet for all their interest in prophecy, Dissenters such as Priestley sharply differentiated themselves from visionaries such as Swedenborg in so far as they represented their opinions as the products of rational enquiry in the guise of historical and philological researches. Blake seems to have been curiously uninterested in making his millenarianism safer in this way. When the illuminated books *America* and *Europe* declared themselves on their title pages to be prophecies, they were abrogating the conventions of enlightened public debate which many radicals and loyalists thought they shared. Priestley may have responded to the Revolution in France in explicitly millenarian terms, but he would never have claimed that his own writings were prophetic. Nor is this important distinction just a difference between poetry and scholarly prose. Samuel Taylor Coleridge, writing under the influence of rational Dissent in the 1790s, was as careful in poetry as was Priestley in prose to distinguish his millenarian politics from prophetic illumination. In his "Religious Musings," for instance, written in 1795–96, Coleridge interprets the French Revolution along with other advances in politics and science as signs of the coming fulfillment of biblical prophecy. The poem is full of evangelical fervor but in the end disclaims the power of prophecy itself, accepting that mere mortals do not enjoy divine inspiration:

> I haply journeying my immortal course
> Shall sometime join your mystic choir. Till then
> I discipline my young noviciate thought
> In ministries of heart-stirring song.[12]

This kind of "discipline" is far from being a feature of Blake's millenarian politics or of his poetry and art more generally. For all the imaginative intensity of his poem, Coleridge perpetuates an eighteenth-century fear of "enthusiasm." "Enthusiasm" was the favored term used to describe pejoratively latter-day claims to divine inspiration, especially when the claims came from popular religious movements such as Methodism. The word was also often used to describe what were taken to be the untethered and volatile passions of the mob more generally, but it could be applied to any "visionary" scheme – political, scientific, religious, or otherwise – which looked beyond the world as it was. The latter sort of enthusiasm was, it is true, not always regarded negatively – there was a saying that "nothing great was ever achieved without enthusiasm" – but the transport out of the familiar world that this aspiration entailed was always treated warily. Even in poetry, which many took to depend precisely on this kind of transcendence of the known world, the concern shown in Coleridge's poem to distinguish poetic aspiration from vulgar enthusiasm was common. If the sublimity of enthusiasm could provide a newly invigorated sense of self, there remained an anxiety that the continuities of identity should not be destroyed in the process. To put it simply, the idea of transport was always haunted by the fear it might not come with a return ticket. What was true for poets was perhaps even truer for political writers, especially if they were committed to radical visions of the world made anew. Politically speaking, Dissenters such as Priestley and Deists such as Thomas Paine were equally wedded to an idea of the autonomous individual. Blake in contrast seems to have been prepared to hazard the sense of a continuous and definitive subjectivity in the interests of political and other kinds of transformation. Indeed his later writing regards the casting-off of selfhood as essential to the experience of universal brotherhood: "Annihilate the Selfhood in me, be thou all my life!" (*J* 5:22, E 147). Such sentiments in Blake's later writing are sometimes regarded as a retreat into Christian orthodoxy, but from as early as *The Marriage of Heaven and Hell* (pl. 21, E 43), which celebrates a Jesus of "impulse" rather than the discipline of "rules," Blake was willing to put the self into hazard in the interests of his prophetic vision to an extent that would have alarmed both Coleridge and Priestley. The same holds true for Blake's treatment of sexuality, in both his ability to accept the unruliness of sexual desire in poems such as *Visions of the Daughters of Albion* and his readiness to depict sexual difference as an unstable rather than a fixed part of human identity. These are enduring features of his verbal and visual art which might be taken to measure Blake's distance from the enlightenment feminism of Mary Wollstonecraft in the same way as his enthusiasm measures his distance from the politics of Deism and Dissent.

Some critics see Blake as alienated from radical politics in the period precisely because his stress on the divine nature of his own inner light could find no echo in the broader radical movement. While it has proven impossible to find concrete connections between Blake and other radical groups beyond the Johnson circle, we should not be led into assuming that radicalism in the 1790s was a coherent movement, dominated by the rationalism of Priestley or even Thomas Paine's more populist and often knockabout version of enlightenment Reason. It is certainly the case that the irreverent Deism of Paine's *The Age of Reason* (1794–5) was very influential in the London Corresponding Society, the main popular radical organization in London from 1792 until it was outlawed by Parliament in 1799. Nevertheless, not everyone in the movement was keen to accept the enlightenment principles of the better-known leaders. The stress on sober respectability that characterizes, perhaps for tactical reasons, most of the official publications of the London Corresponding Society was by no means the hallmark of the entire radical movement. Thomas Spence, for instance, who for all his fierce hatred of the priestcraft of religious institutions often presented himself as a kind of prophet figure, was frequently dismissive of Paine's attachment to private property. His calls for land reform were usually couched in a manner that appealed to the exuberant spirit of popular millenarianism. The irreverent satire and righteous indignation of much of Spence's work calls to mind the heady cocktail of satire and prophecy in Blake's *The Marriage of Heaven and Hell*. Nor is it the case, as is often assumed, that those with strong religious feelings were necessarily the most politically moderate members of the movement. Take Richard "Citizen" Lee, for instance, one of the wilder spirits associated with Spence's periodical *Pig's Meat*, who was arrested in 1795 for publishing a handbill called *King Killing*. Lee saw in the French Revolution the triumph of "the Rights of God," and directly attacked those in the radical movement drawn to Paine's Deism, but his religious enthusiasm was expressed with an anti-clericalism extremely violent in its language, and as capable of irreverent satire as Paine. Its lack of regulation was far from what a Christian such as Priestley would have regarded as respectable. With Lee we are entering into the kind of world in which it is often difficult to make clear distinctions between anti-clerical skepticism and religious enthusiasm. Lee believed the Bible to be the essential foundation of any republican politics, but he also thought of his own visionary politics as the proper form of Reason. Call it prophetic inspiration or the light of Reason, what was often more important in the circles in which Lee and Spence moved was the idea that the poor and uneducated had as much right to express themselves as the elite. As one Spencean pamphlet put it: "Let us at last *think for ourselves – act for ourselves*; and then we shall cease to *drudge* and *sweat* for courtiers, and their cringing creatures."[13] For Blake likewise the beauty of the Bible was that "the most Ignorant & Simple Minds Understand it Best" (anno. Thornton, E 667). He was also quite capable of welcoming Paine's Deist attacks on "State Religion" for their own brand of enthusiasm or "Energetic Genius" (anno. Watson, E 613). Paine is no "modest enquirer," a phrase which suggests the sober deliberations of a Priestley, but "a worker of miracles" who defeated "all the armies of Europe with a small pamphlet" (E 617). This kind of positive appreciation of Paine as a latter-day prophet helps us to understand how the conservative critic of the French Revolution Edmund Burke could use the term "enthusiasm" to attack both the skeptical and religious wings of the radical movement. From a Burkean perspective, the likes of Spence, "Citizen" Lee, Paine, and their followers were all equally guilty of cutting themselves off from common sense, moving out of the safe houses of deference and tradition, and sacrificing a determinate social self to an illusory dream. No doubt, had he ever seen them, he would have regarded the enthusiasm of Blake's illuminated books as equally unregulated.

The comments above should have indicated that Blake's religious enthusiasm is a complex matter in itself. His stress on personal inspiration should not be mistaken for a straightforward Christian zeal. Blake could handle the Bible quite as roughly as Thomas Paine, who in *The Age of Reason* dismissed it as a priestly distortion of Hebrew folk tradition: "The Hebrew Nation did not write it," echoed Blake in his notebooks, "Avarice & Chastity did shite it" (Notebook, E 516). Paine was a hero to Blake for attacking the "Perversions of Christs words and acts" (anno. Watson, E 611). What seems to lie behind this opinion is the idea that liberation of the spirit of the Bible is of more importance than following the letter of the law. Also echoing Paine in *The Age of Reason*, Blake represented the powers of the prophecies more in terms of poetic than supernatural inspiration:

> Prophets in the modern sense of the word have never existed Jonah was no prophet in the modern sense for his prophecy of Nineveh failed Every honest man is a Prophet he utters his opinion both of private & public matters/Thus/If you go on So/the result is So/He never says such a thing shall happen let you do what you will. (anno. Watson, E 617)

Blake's application of biblical figures to contemporary politics seems to have been predicated upon the idea of the Bible as a kind of inspired political archive, that is, a collection of "sentiments and Examples which whether true or Parabolic are Equally useful as Examples" (E 618), rather than a prediction of specific events. Thus Blake believed "whenever any Individual Rejects Error & Embraces Truth a Last Judgment passes upon that Individual" (*VLJ*, E 562). The destinies both of individuals and nations could be illuminated by the prophecies of the Bible. They were not necessarily fulfillments of them. This attitude might seem to take Blake close to Joseph Priestley's view that the Second Coming need not refer to a literal intervention of Christ in human history.[14] Nevertheless Blake was no mere instrumentalist in his attitude to the Bible. It may have been no more holy than "the Edda of Iceland the Songs of Fingal the accounts of North American Savages (as they are calld)" (anno. Watson, E 615), but in so far as they are works of the human imagination, and so to be read as "poetic tales" rather than "forms of worship" (*MHH* 11, E 38), all of these bibles are the products of a divine inspiration. It is their reification into scripture, abstracted from a productive human context, a process that seems to be described in the "Africa" section of *The Song of Los*, which continues to appall Blake. Where Blake differs crucially from someone like Paine is that he sees the enlightenment cult of Reason as the latest manifestation of this dire process. Where Reason is reified into an abstract god, as Urizen seems to do in the mythology Blake develops from the mid-1790s, then it too is no more than another delusive object of worship. If radical politics abstracted the individual from the sum of human brotherhood in its stress on the autonomy of the reasoning power, then it perpetuated a "Mystery" as destructive of human potential as the "State Religion" it wished to displace.

These are real differences from the emergent forms of what we might call radical liberalism, ones which seem to have increasingly occupied Blake after the 1790s, but these differences should not blind us to his engagement with politics per se. Nor was Blake alone in his contempt for the cold individualism that he saw emerging out of the revolutionary decade. Paine himself is more complex than I may have been making him sound. In London's seething underground of enthusiasm, among those who welcomed *Rights of Man* so positively, various kinds of projectors and visionaries entertained ideas about the powers of the mind and the nature of society which were much more complex than a limited notion of Reason would allow. In these contexts, which have been opened to literary scholars by the work of historians such as Iain McCalman, Blake's combination of political, religious, and sexual revolution starts to look much less exceptional than it once did. Nevertheless there is no doubt that, in practical terms, Blake found himself increasingly isolated as the decade went on. The experience was not untypical for men and women committed to republican principles of whatever kind. By the end of the decade, like many others, he found himself in a kind of internal exile, fearing for his own safety: "To defend the Bible in this year 1798" he wrote in his annotations to Bishop Watson, "would cost a man his life" (E 611). This may seem the paranoid exaggeration of a timid literary man, but public opinion generally was deeply shocked when in the same year Joseph Johnson was sentenced to nine months' imprisonment for publishing an anti-war pamphlet. The prison sentence effectively marks the end of the publisher's circle of progressive intellectuals. Blake's main intellectual and political haven, however partial it may have been, was gone. In 1799 Blake wrote to George Cumberland that "I am laid by in a corner as if I did not Exist...Even Johnson & Fuseli have discarded my Graver" (E 704). The war with France was depressing the book market, especially the luxury illustrated editions on which Blake's livelihood depended, and the innovator of the late 1780s and 1790s who was confident that his new artistic techniques would find an echo in a reborn political world increasingly represented his surroundings in terms of darkness and imprisonment. After 1795 Blake engraved no new illuminated books for a decade, but his view of the world continued to be structured by his political affiliations. Even in the illustrations for Edward Young's pious *Night Thoughts*, commissioned by the publisher Richard Edwards in 1795, Blake chose to express his antipathy for kings. Edwards claimed to be bringing out his edition "to solicit the attention of the great for an enforcement of religious and moral truth" (*BR* 56). Blake, of course, always held to a view that the Bible was "filld with Imaginations & Visions from End to End & not with Moral Virtues" (anno. Berkeley, E 664), but his re-visioning of Young does not end there. Several of Blake's designs foreground "the death of tyrants," to use the title of one of "Citizen" Lee's poems. Indeed, where an illustrated version of Young's poem brought out in 1793 had presented Death as a King, Blake illustrates exactly the same lines from *Night Thoughts* with Death trampling on the bodies of Kings.[15] Any consideration of the politics of Blake's work has to take into consideration his position in a culture of surveillance where engravers, writers, and publishers faced imprisonment or harassment if they showed signs of political disaffection. The publisher of Blake's *Night Thoughts* engravings, Richard Edwards, seems to have been a committed loyalist who published Church-and-King pamphlets. His father signed a declaration against sedition in 1792 eagerly supported by other publishers. Given these political affiliations, a concern that his engraver was using his book to express radical sentiments may have played some part in the publisher's decision not to continue with any further volumes of his illustrated *Night Thoughts* after the first.[16]

If the *Night Thoughts* illustrations represent at least a partial attempt to communicate a republican warning to the wealthy purchasers of illustrated books, the privacy of the manuscript of *The Four Zoas*, which Blake began to work on at about the same time, offers an intensely apocalyptic view of contemporary society. From the perspective of Urizen, "the God of this World," the social order is the fulfillment of a providential plan, but Blake's poem invites its readers to recognize this point of view as false consciousness. Where Urizen sees only his "wondrous work flow forth like visible out of the invisible" (*FZ* 33:10, E 321), the figure of Enion offers a more radical vision that reveals Urizen's creation to be founded upon death and destruction:

It is an easy thing to laugh at wrathful elements
To hear the dog howl at the wintry door, the ox in the slaughter house moan
To see a god on every wind & a blessing on every blast
To hear sounds of love in the thunder storm that destroys our enemies house
To rejoice in the blight that covers his field, & the sickness that cuts off his
    children
While our olive & vine sing & laugh round our door & our children bring
    fruits & flowers
Then the groan & the dolor are quite forgotten & the slave grinding at the
    mill

And the captive in chains & the poor in the prison, & the soldier in the field
When the shatterd bone hath laid him groaning among the happier dead
It is an easy thing to rejoice in the tents of prosperity
Thus could I sing & thus rejoice, but it is not so with me!

(*FZ* 36:3–13, E 325)

Disillusionment with France after 1795 as a potential liberator for "the captive in chains & the poor in the prison" is a familiar part of the story of the
Romantic reaction to the Revolution, but there is evidence that Blake har-
bored hopes from that quarter as late as 1800. A recently discovered letter to
George Cumberland, written in September of that year, suggests that Blake
continued to conceive of France as more receptive to his visionary politics
than the prison-house of Britain:

> ... Rending the manacles of Londons Dungeon dark
> I have rent the black net & escap'd. See My Cottage at Felpham in joy
> Beams over the Sea, a bright light over France, but the Web & the Veil I have
>   left
> Behind me at London resists every beam of light; hanging from heaven to Earth
> Dropping with human gore. Lo! I have left it! I have torn it from my limbs
> I shake my wings ready to take my flight! Pale, Ghastly pale: stands the City
>   in fear[17]

This millenarian view of France may or may not have survived Napoleon's
crowning as Emperor four years later, but even so Blake found that the
consequences of his republican politics and sympathy for France were to
pursue him when he left the dungeon of London for Felpham and the
patronage of William Hayley in 1801. The details of his arrest and trial
for seditious libel in Sussex during 1803–4 are presented elsewhere in this
volume. Had material such as his letter to Cumberland from 1800 fallen
into the hands of the prosecution, his acquittal might have been much less
certain.

The events surrounding Blake's trial have often been seen as accelerating
a retreat away from the political into the private world of mythology that
dominates his great epics *Milton* and *Jerusalem*. Blake dated both books to
the traumatic year of 1804, although neither was first printed until several
years later. Yet David Erdman and other scholars have shown that whatever we make of his mythology, it continued to respond to the events of
his own time. That is not to say that the books are to be understood as
an extended commentary on contemporary history, but it does mean that
he continued to concern himself with questions of freedom and community
in relation to the world in which he lived. His politics, as we have seen,
were always of the kind that stressed the importance of the imagination in

human freedom, but he also remained wary of the dangers of reifying even the most liberating of energies. There is no simple privileging of the Romantic imagination over the material world of politics in these later books. The imagination itself can be imprisoning for Blake if it is abstracted from experience. "Eternity" in Blake's great epics, remains "in love with the productions of time" (*MHH* 7, E 36). Escape into the idylls of the imagination may have been a real temptation for Blake, but he was aware of this dangerous allure, and identified it with the dreamy state of "Beulah." "The moony habitations of Beulah" (*Milton* 30[33]:13, E 129) offer respite for the afflicted soul in the later prophecies, and can even preserve the ideal of liberty, but they also tempt the prophet away from "Mental Fight" (*Milton* 1, E 95).

Jerusalem is a book concerned above all with what the children of Albion called "Liberty." Indeed its vision of the awakening of Albion is one of national revival and the rekindling of the liberties of England. The poem's intense concern with the fate of Albion has been read as a conservative, even imperialist development by some critics, but they anachronistically assume that Blake's patriotism is a variant of modern nationalism. In fact, throughout the book, Blake offers an open and expansive notion of national identity. Rather than a narrow definition, predicated on "State Religion," the poem offers a vision of Britishness in more inclusive terms. A nation has been described as a group with many things in common but also with many things it has forgotten. *Jerusalem* aims to recall what has been forgotten, that is, the differences suppressed in the name of "One King, One God, One Law." At the center of this process of suppression, Blake places Stonehenge: "A building of eternal death: whose proportions are eternal despair" (*J* 66:9, E 218). Its eighteenth-century form is the gallows at "Tyburn," "Albions fatal Tree" (*J* 82:60, E 240) the place where the unity of the nation is built upon the judicial murder of some of its members. The gallows for Blake are a place where difference is suppressed so that the bogus integrity of the nation may be preserved. To return to the letter with which I began this essay, Blake seeks to unmask the terrible process by which that "happy state of Agreement" which has made Englishmen "Intermeasurable One by Another" has been maintained. *Jerusalem* recalls his readers to what has been lost or suppressed in this process, and also to the infinite possibilities that remain in the idea of the nation. Towards the end of the poem, when Los gives his vision of the "Briton Saxon Roman Norman amalgamating / In my Furnaces into One Nation the English: & taking refuge / In the Loins of Albion" (*J* 92:1–3, E 252), Blake gives us a quite different conception of the nation in which every individual finds space and identity. This inclusiveness extends not just to the dynamics of the British Isles, but also to Albion's place among the nations. For the poem represents London as a Babylonian center of Empire, literally a marketplace for human souls, which must be apocalyptically transformed in order that Jerusalem may awake and "overspread all Nations as in Ancient Time" (J 97:2, E 256).

There is no doubt, as I suggested earlier, that the republican tradition of identifying liberty with the flourishing of the arts informs most of Blake's statements on the subject. When he wrote to George Cumberland in 1795 that "Peace & Plenty & Domestic Happiness is the Source of Sublime Art" (E 700), he was making a direct criticism of the two-year-old English war against republican France. Blake takes a nation whose artistic life is in a healthy state to be one in which freedom is flourishing too. There remains the question of whether the arts were or became an end in themselves in Blake's mind. Perhaps there was a slippage, at least in emphasis, here for Blake, especially later in his life. One might parallel this slippage to the way that in some passages from the later prophecies the idea of the "Female Will" seems in danger of being abstracted out of the more complex thinking about sexuality and women's rights found elsewhere. Isolated and driven back onto his own resources as he was from the mid-1790s, it may be that his own right to practice as an engraver, painter, and poet came to be substituted in Blake's mind for freedoms more capaciously and democratically conceived. Yet Blake's poetry continues to insist that it is all too easy to forget the sufferings of others. Moreover his scattered comments on the writing and painting of others always took their politics into account. Bacon is condemned for forgetting "Every Body hates a King" (anno. Bacon, E 623). Reynolds is damned as the hireling of the "King & Nobility of England" (anno. Reynolds, E 636). Even Dante, whose genius Blake admires and whose poetry he would redeem, cannot entirely be forgiven the fact that he "gives too much Caesar he is not a Republican" (anno. Boyd, E 634). Insisting on the centrality of politics to his artistic achievement might seem like a philistine insistence on ideology, but Blake himself never forgot such matters when assessing the achievements of his great predecessors. Eternity may well have been the ultimate object of Blake's politics, but he was enough of a follower of Milton to believe that it was less likely to be gained in the cloistered virtue of Beulah than in the historical struggles of the "wars of truth".[18]

Notes

1. John Milton, *Paradise Lost*, XII: 587 in *John Milton*, ed. Stephen Orgel and Jonathan Goldberg (Oxford: Oxford University Press, 1990), p. 617.
2. *The Making of the English Working Class*, rev. edn. (Harmondsworth: Penguin, 1968), p. 23.

3. On the relationship between Barry and Blake, see John Barrell, *The Political Theory of Painting from Reynolds to Hazlitt: "The Body of the Public"* (New Haven: Yale University Press, 1986).

4. Keri Davies, "William Blake's Mother: A New Identification," *Blake/An Illustrated Quarterly* 33 (1999), p. 42.

5. Robert N. Essick, *William Blake's Commercial Book Illustrations: A Catalogue and Study of the Plates Engraved by Blake after Designs by Other Artists* (Oxford: Oxford University Press, 1991), p. 7. For fuller details of Johnson's career, see Gerald P. Tyson, *Joseph Johnson: A Liberal Publisher* (Iowa City: University of Iowa Press, 1979).

6. On Priestley and the body as distinct from the soul, see Jon Mee, *Dangerous Enthusiasm: William Blake and the Culture of Radicalism in the 1790s* (Oxford: Oxford University Press, 1992), p. 138 and *passim*.

7. For a summary of the possible reasons why Blake found Swedenborgianism attractive, see Viscomi, "The Lessons of Swedenborg; or, The Origin of William Blake's *The Marriage of Heaven and Hell*" in Thomas Pfau and Robert F. Gleckner, eds., *Lessons of Romanticism: A Critical Companion* (Durham: Duke University Press, 1998), p. 176.

8. For details, see Morton D. Paley, " 'A New Heaven is Begun': William Blake and Swedenborgianism," *Blake/An Illustrated Quarterly* 13 (1979), pp. 64–90.

9. See Viscomi, "The Evolution of *The Marriage of Heaven and Hell*," *Huntington Library Quarterly* 58 (1997), pp. 281–340.

10. Viscomi, "Lessons," p. 181.

11. See Keri Davies, "Mrs Bliss: a Blake Collector of 1794" in Steve Clark and David Worrall, eds., *Blake in the Nineties* (New York: St. Martin's Press, 1999), pp. 212–30.

12. Samuel Taylor Coleridge, "Religious Musings" in *Samuel Taylor Coleridge*, ed. H. J. Jackson (Oxford: Oxford University Press, 1985), p. 23.

13. Anon., *An Address to the English Nation* (London, 1796), p. 2. For further details of Lee, see my "The Strange Career of Richard 'Citizen' Lee" in T. Morton and N. Smith, eds., *Radicalism in British Literary Culture, 1650–1830: From Revolution to Revolution* (Cambridge, Cambridge University Press, 2002), pp. 151–66.

14. Mee, *Dangerous Enthusiasm*, p. 42.

15. See Edward Young, *Night Thoughts*, ed. Rev. Edward de Coetlogon (London: Chapman and Co., 1793), p. 8. De Coetlogon's edition is specifically oriented against what he calls "liberty perverted and abused," p. 363. Both Blake and the anonymous engraver of this design in de Coetlogon's edition illustrate Night I, l. 212 of Young's poem. De Coetlogon's engraving shows death as a crowned skeleton. Blake's (*Night Thoughts* 20) shows a robed figure standing on the bodies of two crowned figures.

16. For further details on Edwards, see G. E. Bentley, Jr., "Richard Edwards, Publisher of Church-and-King Pamphlets and of William Blake," *Studies in Bibliography* 41 (1988), pp. 283–315. Thomas Edwards signed a "determined Resolution utterly to DISCOUNTENANCE and DISCOURAGE all Seditious and Inflammatory Productions." See Michael Phillips, "Blake and the Terror 1792–93," *The Library* 16 (1994), p. 272.

17. Now in the possession of Robert N. Essick, the letter was reproduced in Essick and Morton D. Paley, " 'Dear Generous Cumberland': A Newly Discovered Letter and Poem by William Blake," *Blake/An Illustrated Quarterly* 32 (1998), pp. 4–13. Erdman, *Blake: Prophet Against Empire*, 3rd rev. edn. (Princeton: Princeton University Press, 1977), pp. 316–17, believes that the reptilization of Orc in *The Four Zoas* Night VIIb is a revision in the light of Napoleon's coup of 18th Brumaire (9 November) 1799. I think this letter suggests that as late as the autumn of 1800 Blake still had hopes of Napoleon.

18. *Milton*, ed. Orgel and Goldberg, p. 269.

Further reading

Bruder, Helen P. *William Blake and the Daughters of Albion*. Basingstoke: Macmillan, 1997.

Clark, Steve, and David Worrall, eds. *Historicizing Blake*. Basingstoke: Macmillan, 1994.

DiSalvo, Jackie, G. A. Rosso, and Christopher Z. Hobson, eds. *Blake, Politics, and History*. New York and London: Garland, 1998.

Erdman, David V. *Blake: Prophet against Empire*. 3rd rev. edn. Princeton: Princeton University Press, 1977.

Ferber, Michael. *The Social Vision of William Blake*. Princeton: Princeton University Press, 1985.

Harrison, J. F. C. *The Second Coming: Popular Millenarianism 1780–1850*. London: Routledge & Kegan Paul, 1979.

McCalman, Iain. *Radical Underworld: Prophets, Revolutionaries and Pornographers in London, 1795–1840*. Cambridge: Cambridge University Press, 1988.

Makdisi, Saree. *Romantic Imperialism: Universal Empire and the Culture of Modernity*. Cambridge: Cambridge University Press, 1998.

Matthews, Susan. *"Jerusalem and Nationalism." Beyond Romanticism: New Approaches to Texts and Context, 1780–1832*. Ed. Stephen Copley and John Whale. London: Routledge, 1992. 79–100.

Mee, Jon. *Dangerous Enthusiasm: William Blake and the Culture of Radicalism in the 1790s*. Oxford: Oxford University Press, 1992.

Thompson, E. P. *The Making of the English Working Class*. Rev. edn. Harmondsworth: Penguin, 1968.

Witness Against the Beast: William Blake and the Moral Law. Cambridge: Cambridge University Press, 1993.

8

ROBERT RYAN

Blake and religion

In the originality, comprehensiveness, and sheer energy of his analysis of the religious dimension of human experience, William Blake's artistic achievement is matched in Western literature only by that of Dante and Milton. Religion was, arguably, the primary theme and motive of all his art, poetic and pictorial. But to compare Blake's art with the work of other poets and painters soon makes clear that his own artistic program and vision differed strikingly from what is commonly understood to be the purpose of religious art. His poetry, and the illuminations that enrich it, only rarely are expressions of devotion. Although one catches glimpses of personal piety in his letters, and senses it in his more conventional pictorial art, Blake's illuminated verse is primarily social in its concerns, focusing on the historic and psychic origins of religious faith and on religion's influence on human behavior. Blake was convinced that religion profoundly affects every aspect of human life – political, economic, psychological, and cultural – and that its influence has generally not been a positive one. He detected flawed religious thinking at the root of most of the social disorders afflicting England in his time, and found that even the highest virtues associated with religion – "Mercy Pity Peace and Love" (E 12) – were routinely misconceived or manipulated for destructive ends.

Blake's usual religious posture, then, is not submission but protest; his poetry is a sustained prophetic denunciation of the cruelties, mental and corporeal, everywhere perpetrated in the name of God by those who claim to be doing his will. It is a detailed indictment of the collaboration of all the churches in the exploitation of the poor, the degradation of labor, the subordination of women, the abridgment of political liberty, the repression of sexual energy, and the discouragement of originality in the fine arts. In a time of intense political agitation he came to believe that a radical transformation of the nation's religious consciousness was the first prerequisite to serious political or economic reform.

The atmosphere of religious crisis that pervades Blake's poetry is partly a reflection of the times in which he lived. It is not generally remembered that the passions driving the ideological conflicts of the 1790s were religious as well as political in character. The British Constitution in Church and State was in large part a product of chronic religious antagonisms that began with the Protestant Reformation and manifested themselves with increased violence in the revolutionary upheavals of the seventeenth century. At the heart of these quarrels was a dispute over the legitimacy of the State's effort to monitor and control public religious practice in its own interest. The specific occasion of conflict in the 1790s was the increasingly insistent demand by Protestant Dissenters for removal of the civil disabilities they incurred by their refusal to accept the doctrine and liturgy of the Established Church. The emotions raised in this dispute intensified the domestic debate over the French Revolution and broke out violently in the "Church and King" riots of 1791, which were fomented by Anglicans and directed primarily at Dissenters. It seemed to many that not since England's revolution of the 1640s had religious conflict posed such a threat to social stability.

At first, Dissenters were among the most vocal admirers of the Revolution in France because they saw in the disestablishment of the Catholic Church a pattern that might be followed in England. When Edmund Burke in his *Reflections on the Revolution in France* (1791) was defining the terms of the national debate on the Revolution, he made the Dissenters his primary domestic targets, reminding his readers of the danger religious separatism had posed to legitimate government in the past. Much of the passion (and the organizational infrastructure) of the radical opposition to government in the 1790s did in fact come from Dissenters, and from other more radical religious sectaries, antinomian fringe groups that could trace their origin to the days of the Puritan revolution and Cromwell's Protectorate. Spokesmen for this religious underworld preached a radical social egalitarianism that exempted Christians from all law, judicial and moral. Some denied fundamental Christian doctrines such as the Trinity and rejected the authority of the Bible itself. Many of Blake's most radical religious ideas were common enough in London when he lived there, and he seems to have been borrowing the rhetorical style of the antinomians when he wrote: "The Bible or Peculiar Word of God, Exclusive of Conscience or the Word of God Universal, is that Abomination which like the Jewish ceremonies is for ever removed & henceforth every man may converse with God & be a King & Priest in his own house" (anno. Watson, E 615).

The national mood of religious dissent was heightened by the evangelical revival, which had been fostered mainly by the preaching and organizational talents of John Wesley. By the 1790s the Methodists had constructed a nationwide network of independent chapels that acknowledged no allegiance to the Church of England and drew increasing numbers of adherents from among those who had been neglected by the regular clergy's ministry. Soon the older Dissenting churches, the Baptists, Independents, and Presbyterians, caught the new evangelical enthusiasm, and their numbers and activity visibly increased during the 1790s.

Religious fervor had always been a volatile element in British political life, and schismatic activity brought disturbing memories of old insurrections. Another destabilizing element was a renewal of the millenarian spirit that manifests itself in the final years of every century and often accompanies religious revivals, but which was driven to unusually high levels of intensity by the extraordinary events in France that were easily seen as fulfillment of the apocalyptic prophecies in the Bible. From the books of Daniel and Revelation as well as certain passages in the Gospels, millenarians learned to expect a series of cosmic catastrophes that would precede the second coming of Jesus Christ and the establishment of his kingdom on earth, which would last for a thousand years until the final judgment brought time to an end. Religious pessimists saw the world as so steeped in wickedness that its destruction by a wrathful God was unavoidable; optimists believed that the millennium might be inaugurated peacefully by steady progress in piety and virtue. But the idea of doomsday appealed to the imagination of most believers, and throughout Europe people on all levels of society were avidly searching the scriptures to find the specific prophecies that were being fulfilled in their troubled times. Many of them seemed genuinely to believe that they were living in the last days of the world.

The prospect of cataclysmic upheaval, to be followed by "a new heaven and a new earth" as promised in the Book of Revelation (21:1), gave comfort to those who were discontented with the current social, economic, and political order and encouraged radical visions of what the ideally constituted society of the future would look like. Millenarianism thus fostered increased impatience with imperfect systems of government (whose days were precisely numbered) and made the possibility of violent revolution seem less disturbing, since the impending calamities would accomplish the will of Providence. Recent historians have seen popular millenarianism as an expression of political discontent among the exploited classes, a demand for radical social change disguised in religious language, but it should be noted that during the 1790s millenarian thinking was as common among the wealthier, more educated classes as it was among the poor.

For example, Joseph Priestley, England's foremost exponent of "rational Christianity," delivered a sermon in 1794 entitled "The Present State of Europe Compared with Antient Prophecies," which insisted that the "great convulsions and sudden revolutions" taking place at the time were without doubt the upheavals predicted in the Bible as leading to the millennium. Priestley, an optimistic Dissenter, took evident satisfaction in the doom that was about to fall on Antichrist, which he had no trouble in identifying as the "idolatrous ecclesiastical establishments of Christianity" – the Church of Rome and the Church of England – "in which power is claimed to prescribe articles of faith [and] make laws to bind the consciences of Christians."[1] Clearly the apocalypse could be interpreted freely according to one's religious politics. It is worth noticing that this sermon was published by Joseph Johnson, who employed Blake regularly as an engraver.

Blake would have agreed with Priestley's criticism of the Church of England, but his own concept of reformation was not as simple or as optimistic as Priestley's. He saw religious error as so profoundly ingrained in the human psyche that disestablishment of one corrupt form of it would not begin to effect the radical change that was needed. True reformation would require a mental apocalypse more unsettling than any earthquake or revolution that had so far attracted the attention of millenarians. In most of Blake's early prophetic books there is a sense of impending crisis, an atmosphere of gathering evil and repressed passion waiting for release, and each of his three longer prophecies – *The Four Zoas, Milton,* and *Jerusalem* – climaxes in a cosmic and psychic convulsion that transforms the earth, puts an end to time, and brings humanity into the life of Eternity with Jesus, who has triumphed over the enemies of mankind.

What would precipitate an apocalyptic transformation, and what necessitated it, was the total corruption of Christianity by what Blake sometimes called state religion and sometimes natural religion or Deism. He referred to state religion as "The Abomination that maketh desolate" (anno. Watson, E 618), a phrase from the Book of Daniel (11:31) suggesting that to Blake's apocalyptic imagination the Established Church was a tool, if not an embodiment, of Antichrist. "Deist" was a name originally applied to a group of religious scholars of the late seventeenth century whose disgust with doctrinal conflicts inspired a search for more enlightened conceptions of the Supreme Being than the biblical ones that were being fought over by various Christian factions. Isaac Newton's revelation of a perfectly designed universe encouraged belief in a detached deity whose orderly cosmos provided the pattern for an earthly hierarchy of social classes, each assigned to its preordained economic orbit. Resignation to the inevitability of the existing social order was made easier (for those in control of it) by the prosperity generated by the new capitalist economy and easier still by a theological sophistication that ignored or derided the primitive religion of the Bible, with its strong prophetic injunctions against social injustice. In the new dispensation religion was entrusted to the guidance of reason and what Blake called "the Selfish Virtues of the Natural Heart" (*J* 52, E 201).

Over the years, an ideology that was initially developed as a critique of Christianity penetrated the Christian churches themselves. The clearest symptom of the Deistic infection, for Blake, was a surrender to economic injustice and military conflict as unavoidable, even necessary, aspects of the natural order of things. Efforts to ameliorate poverty were considered not only naive or counterproductive (as the Reverend Thomas Malthus demonstrated in 1798) but indicative of impious discontent with the dispensations of an all-wise Providence. The theological complacency that made social inequalities seem inevitable had no trouble in sanctifying a twenty-two-year war against France. "Natural virtue" manifested itself in a vindictive morality that inhibited sexual freedom and punished with increasing severity the crimes of the poor and the protests of religious and political dissidents – all in the name of preserving the blessings of a Christian society.

Against this "pretence of Religion to destroy Religion" (*J* 38[43], E 185) Blake proclaimed what he understood to be the true religion of Jesus, the distinguishing qualities of which were a radical demand for social justice, the cultivation of mutual love and forgiveness, and the fostering of creative freedom in religion, morality, and the arts. The difficult mission that Blake undertook was to combat the deformed Christianity that had become the national religion of Britain, to take religion back from the priests who had subordinated it to the political, economic, and cultural agenda of the ruling classes, and to make it a truly revolutionary force in society.

And he undertook to accomplish all this through the media of poetic and pictorial art. One might characterize this program as another Romantic retreat from political activism to the quiet detachment of an artist's life, but it was not disillusionment, timidity, or naïveté that made Blake believe in the capacity of art to affect the national character by altering its religious vision. He was convinced that Milton's *Paradise Lost* contributed substantially to the religious ideology that dominated life in Britain by its reinforcement of belief in a distant, judgmental God who took pleasure in crushing rebellion against authority and who required the future death of his only Son before he could bring himself to pardon the sin of Adam and Eve. In the poem Blake named for him, Milton realizes the extent of his baneful influence and returns from Eternity to undo the harm his errors have done on earth. If the art of poetry could thus influence the national religion in negative ways, Blake reasoned, it should have power to change it for the better. He had always understood religion and poetry to be intimately connected. *The Marriage of Heaven and Hell* argues that religion originated in poetry, that priests abstracted theological systems from poetic tales and "enslav'd the vulgar"

(*MHH* 11, E 38). *Milton* goes further to suggest that religion exists on earth as the fallen form of the eternal art of poetry. In a sense it works like poetry, "with bounds to the Infinite putting off the Indefinite / Into most holy forms of Thought" (pl. 28[30], E 125).

To repair the damage done by the fall of humanity, then, would entail transforming religion back into poetry. Blake's strategy resembled what twentieth-century theologians would call demythologization – the practice of detaching the Christian faith from the mythical world picture of the first century so that it could be reimagined in more modern terms. Blake's way of recovering the gospel message was to remythologize it in terms of his own tale of the Zoas. This had the effect of defamiliarizing the Christian revelation, freshening its impact, and detaching it from the religious practices of institutional churches.

In Blake's myth of the origin of the universe, the most radical theological premise is that religion ought not to exist at all, that its presence in the world is a disastrous consequence of humanity's fallen condition. This vision of religious history is developed in *The [First] Book of Urizen*, a sometimes sublime and sometimes comical retelling of the biblical creation story. It "reveals" that the human race as we know it and the cosmos we inhabit are the products of an outbreak of psychic warfare among a community of beings whom Blake called the Eternals, one of whom, Urizen, rebelled against the collaborative community of which he had been a part, inaugurated a new, separate, enclosed universe, and assumed control of it as sole presiding deity. It is at this point in cosmic history that the Genesis story begins, but we have learned from Blake that the God who presides over creation in the biblical account is actually only a fragment of a more complete eternal being, a damaged psyche that is unduly concerned with authority and obedience. As Urizen began to impose control over the cosmos that resulted from his conflict with the other Eternals, a new element appeared in the universe of things, extruding from him as from a spider's abdomen:

> None could break the Web, no wings of fire.
> So twisted the cords, & so knotted
> The meshes: twisted like to the human brain
> And all calld it, The Net of Religion.
> (pl. 25, E 82)

The net tightened and hardened until it resembled the impenetrable ceiling of a dome, and the human beings confined within this enclosed cosmos "bless'd the seventh day, in sick hope: / And forgot their eternal life" (pl. 25, E 83).

What the Christian world adored as God, then, is a defective, limited being whose worship requires denial of much of what is needed for psychic balance. Urizen's moral code rests on a dichotomy between holiness and sinfulness, both of which qualities he conceived before having any experience of humanity and was then disappointed to find that no human being "could keep / His iron laws one moment" (*Urizen* 23, E 81). Nevertheless, humanity has willingly embraced this religion of sin and reproach with its preference for the spiritual over the carnal, for repression over fulfillment, and for humility over intellectual curiosity. Long before Ludwig Feuerbach and Sigmund Freud, Blake was pondering the mind's tendency to project and submit to inhuman, oppressive divinities.

Urizen, the god of laws and penalties whose worship thrives on human fear and need, is one of the most recognizable images in Blake's pictorial art. He is usually depicted as an old man with a white beard, the isolated paternal deity of traditional Christian iconography. Blake sometimes gives him a measure of patriarchal dignity and occasionally an element of pathos, but most often he is presented as a menacing, punitive power, even when apparently blind and senile. One can see Blake meditating on this baleful divinity in a set of prints that were completed in 1794 and 1795, just around the time when Urizen was appearing in the Lambeth Books. In *God Judging Adam* (Butlin 294), the divine Judge and the mortal who bows in submission to him are identical in features, a simple illustration of the proposition that the gods to whom we surrender our freedom are created in our own negative self-image. In *Elohim Creating Adam* (Butlin 289), an apparently sightless creator hovers oppressively over a wretched Adam, who has been brought to life already in the coils of the serpent. His head is being forced down onto the earth by his heavy-handed creator, whose wings and superincumbent position suggest Blake's Covering Cherub, the guardian at the gate of Paradise who prevents exiled humanity from re-entering. Blake's print invites comparison with that other "Creation of Adam," Michelangelo's Sistine Chapel fresco, in which life is bestowed with the touch of a single finger by a God who does not intrude on the space that will be needed when his creature rises to his proper height. Blake gives us a more flattering portrait of the Creator in the well known *The Ancient of Days* (Butlin 271), but it too contains its quota of ironic commentary. The Divine Architect employs a compass to draw his lines and boundaries, perhaps unaware that he himself is confined within a circle and that his hair is being blown by a wind that suggests sources of power outside his control.

In Urizen, Blake embodied his objection to the entire theology of submission, self-denial, contrition, and expiation that institutional Christianity fostered. Humility and docility were to him suspect virtues, encouraged by those who would diminish the freedom of others, and he had as little use for the morality of prudence and asceticism that went with them. "Men are admitted into Heaven," he wrote, "not because they have curbed & governd their Passions or have No Passions but because they have Cultivated their Understandings" (*VLJ*, E 564). Blake's most persistent objection to Urizenic religion was the fear of sexual passion that became a defining element of Christianity as early as the time of Saint Paul (see 1 Cor. 7). The premium placed on virginity seemed to him particularly wrongheaded, and he showed his disdain for it on many occasions, whether in the Proverb of Hell that proclaimed "The nakedness of woman is the work of God" (*MHH* 8, E 36) or in his elaborate and moving repudiation in *Jerusalem* of the traditional teaching on Mary's virginity (pl. 61, E 212). *Songs of Experience* protested against the "Priests in black gowns...walking their rounds,/And binding with briars, my joys & desires" (E 26) and offered no consolation to the "Youth pined away with desire,/And the pale Virgin shrouded in snow" (E 25), who remain unfulfilled even after their repressed lives are over. The prohibition of extra-marital sex created a society where brothels were "built...with bricks of Religion" (*MHH* 8, E 36) and where married women too were "pining in bonds of religion" (*America* 15, E 57).

Blake's most sustained and withering attack on the Urizenic religion of chastity was *Visions of the Daughters of Albion*, in which Oothoon, the victim of a rape, having been scorned by the rapist and rejected by the man who once loved her, delivers a searing indictment of the entire moral system in which she has been trapped, concluding with a bold advocacy of free love. In lines that still have power to shock, she speaks of masturbatory acts and asks, "Are not these the places of religion? the rewards of continence?/ The self enjoyings of self denial?" (pl. 7, E 50). In another remarkable speech she traces the connection between Christian theology and clerical privilege and the social injustices they foster, moving in quick imaginative progression from tithes to marriage as related manifestations of the same oppressive system:

> With what sense does the parson claim the labour of the farmer?
> What are his nets & gins & traps. & how does he surround him
> With cold floods of abstraction, and with forests of solitude,
> To build him castles and high spires. where kings & priests may dwell.
> Till she who burns with youth. and knows no fixed lot; is bound
> In spells of law to one she loaths: (pl. 5, E 49)

The cause-and-effect connection suggested by the word "till" shows that all of these theological, political, economic, and sexual situations are re-lated products of an erroneous conception of God, and Oothoon intuitively follows the intricate web back to its source in "Urizen! Creator of men! mistaken Demon of heaven" (pl. 5, E 48).

Oothoon's strong protest does not free her from the various forms of bondage she endures. A more formidable and effectual challenge to Urizen's repressive regime comes from Orc, the revolutionary spirit who inspired rebellion in America and France and who, like Oothoon, sees clearly the link between religion and political repression. Orc proclaims in *America*:

> The fiery joy, that Urizen perverted to ten commands . . .
> That stony law I stamp to dust: and scatter religion abroad
> To the four winds as a torn book, & none shall gather the leaves;
>
> (pl. 8, E 54)

The rhetoric is impressive enough, but in Blake's illumination of the text Orc's manifesto appears beneath an image of Urizen that shows him still very much in control. A religion that is so intricately "twisted like to the human brain" is not easily disposed of, and Blake will observe in *Milton* how "those who contemn Religion & seek to annihilate it" can themselves become "causes & promoters" of religions that are as oppressive as the ones they have tried to eliminate (pl. 40[46], E 141). While he was composing *America*, Blake might have observed the dechristianization campaign in France sponsoring an alternative "religion of nature," a cult that would later be used by Robespierre to sanction and sanctify the Terror.

As the French political experiment continued to degenerate into partisan violence and militarism, and Blake grew more aware of the negative aspects of revolutionary and iconoclastic passion, he began to devote more attention to the cultural processes by which a better human society might be developed, processes that in his mythic system were associated with Los, the Zoa of prophecy and artistry. In *The [First] Book of Urizen*, Los is deputed by the Eternals to limit the damage caused by Urizen's defection, a work of salvage that was endlessly frustrating, since the fallen world provides only damaged and inadequate materials for the artist's use. Still he struggles to reshape what Urizen has marred, if only to give finite form to errors that may then be perceived clearly for what they are. This task of defining the errors of Urizen is, of course, the one Blake himself has undertaken, and from this point on he identifies himself ever more explicitly with Los's effort to redefine religion, transforming it into a more humane system than the one devised by Urizen. Los's response to Urizen is more constructive than Orc's and finally more productive. One can see the difference illustrated on plate 18 of *Milton*, a well-known image that at first glance might appear to represent Orc getting ready to stamp the stony law to dust and its author with it. But the following plates reveal that the nude figure confronting Urizen is actually the repentant poet Milton, who is "Creating new flesh on

the Demon cold, and building him, / As with new clay a Human form..."
(pl. 19[21], E 112):

> ...Silent Milton stood before
> The darkend Urizen; as the sculptor silent stands before
> His forming image; he walks round it patient labouring.
> Thus Milton stood forming bright Urizen...
>
> (pl. 20[22], E 114)

If religion cannot be eliminated from the fallen world, it must be altered for the better. Artists are thus encouraged to follow Milton's example and work to change Urizen's darkened image into something brighter.

Transferring the stewardship of religion from Urizen to Los suggests that it might become more than a psychic prison maintained by willing inmates. Seen as a defective product of creative energy, religion becomes a potentially more benign dimension of human experience. Each of mankind's many gods is said to be "a fallen Son of the Spirit of Prophecy" (pl. 24[26], E 121), an unsuccessful attempt at imagining what a god might be. Another of Los's sons, more surprisingly, is Satan, who in *Milton* replaces Urizen as the promoter of delusional, destructive religion. By acknowledging paternity of this large, heterogeneous family, Los accepts responsibility for the religious condition of the world, recognizing that the existence of baneful or foolish creeds is only a misdirection or a failure of imaginative energy. The task of the prophetic imagination is to call humanity from its inhuman beliefs toward more positive visions of its spiritual potential. In an early expression of this insight, *Songs of Experience* begins with an invitation from the Bard summoning Earth to embrace the freedom that is hers by right, an offer that Earth rejects, complaining that she is forever imprisoned by a jealous god who has complete control of her destiny (E 18–19).

In the address "To the Deists" that begins the third chapter of *Jerusalem*, Blake wrote, "Man must & will have Some Religion; if he has not the Religion of Jesus, he will have the Religion of Satan, & will erect the Synagogue of Satan. calling the Prince of this World, God; and destroying all who do not worship Satan under the Name of God" (J 52, E 201). Blake's Satan is not the malevolent supernatural power of Christian tradition who tempts human beings to sin. It is the name he gives to the self-destructive and anti-social instincts that exist within every individual and stand in the way of imaginative health and psychic integration. Satan is the will to power that encourages us to use others for our own advantage, that dissolves the bonds that should unite the human community, hindering love, compassion, and mercy. Ultimately, Satan exists in each of us as the barrier preventing access to the Paradise within (see *Paradise Lost* 12:585–87) where we would rediscover our full humanity and our freedom as eternal beings.

Blake sometimes calls Satan "the God of this world." He is the God most Christians actually worship and persecute others for not worshipping. The religion of Satan is the one that is practiced in most churches on most Sundays, an ideology that accepts the present defective order of the world as a manifestation of God's eternal will. It serves the State's need for security by assigning chaplains to its armies and prisons and by providing a religious rationale for any public policy that requires one, from genocide and slavery to subtler forms of racism and economic injustice. Usually defining morality in sexual rather than in ethical or economic terms, it encourages repression and submission rather than liberation. In short it discourages its adherents from imagining or even desiring a world order much different from the one at hand.

But who is the Jesus that Blake opposes to Satan and invokes as the exemplar of a more liberating religion? In *The Marriage of Heaven and Hell* the character and teaching of Jesus are matters of dispute between angels and devils, each party claiming him as an exponent of its own moral and theological position. His name is mentioned only once, briefly, in the other books that Blake produced during the 1790s. But in *The Four Zoas, Milton,* and *Jerusalem*, Jesus is given unparalleled eminence as the Eternal Divine Humanity who must intervene at a moment of apocalyptic crisis to save the human race from eternal death. He is called "the image of the Invisible God" and "God the dear Saviour who took on the likeness of men:/ Becoming obedient to death, even the death of the Cross" (*Milton* 2, 22[24], E 96, 118). Although Blake's poetry seems more interested in the Jesus of Eternity than in the man who walked the earth twenty centuries ago, the gospel stories are recalled frequently enough to suggest that he did not want the historical life of Jesus to be forgotten:

> The Divine Vision still was seen
> Still was the Human Form, Divine
> Weeping in weak & mortal clay
> O Jesus still the Form was thine.

> And thine the Human face & thine
> The Human Hands & Feet & Breath
> Entering thro' the Gates of Birth
> And passing thro' the Gates of Death
> (*J* 27, E 173)

Blake's pictorial representations of Jesus in the illuminated prophetic books and in scores of prints and paintings are generally quite traditional in conception, resembling most likenesses of Jesus produced in Western Europe since antiquity. Only occasionally is there a suggestion of Jesus' role in the Zoas myth, for example in *The Nativity* (Butlin 401), which depicts the holy infant as an Orc-like figure, radiating light as he stands poised in mid-air, his back turned toward his fainting mother and disapproving foster father. In the next, more typical painting of the series, *The Adoration of the Kings* (Butlin 402), he has settled back comfortably into his mother's arms like a conventional Bambino.

Blake's conception of a divine human being who intervenes to save humanity from its fallen condition and restore it to a prelapsarian state of spiritual life is close enough to orthodox doctrine to be called authentically Christian, at least by the loose theological standards that were applied in a time when the Established Church feared doctrinal disputation and the evangelicals tended to reduce the conversion experience to an emotional acceptance of Jesus Christ as Savior.[2] Even a scrupulous theologian like Samuel Taylor Coleridge found it possible to formulate a brief doctrinal description of Christians as those "who receive Christ as the Son of the Living God who submitted to become Man in the flesh in order to redeem mankind."[3]

The only qualification Blake might make in this formulation would be to insist, as Emmanuel Swedenborg did, that Jesus was himself the Living God, embodying in his Divine Humanity the fullness of the Godhead. The Swedenborgians adopted as a defining doctrine the belief "that there is only One God, One Person, in whom is the Divine Trinity, called Father, Son, and Holy Spirit, like the human trinity of soul, body, and proceeding operation, in every individual man; and that the Lord and Saviour Jesus Christ is that God."[4] This formulation approximates fairly closely Blake's way of speaking about Jesus. Part of the attraction of Swedenborg's emphasis on the Humanity of God was that it stood in radical opposition to the Deist notion that "God in the dreary Void / Dwells from Eternity, wide separated from the Human Soul" (*J* 23, E 168). A God who is truly human is less likely to turn into a monster of vindictive holiness, like the Power that presides over the religion of Satan.

Jesus appears in the later prophecies as an eternal being who contains within himself all who participate in the life of eternity. The concept of a Divine Man who contains multitudes could have had many sources, including Swedenborg, but the most obvious would be the epistles of Saint Paul (e.g., 1 Cor. 12:12–31; Eph. 1:20–23), which first introduced the notion that all believers are united in the body of Christ. It may be worth noting that

Blake does not adopt Paul's notion of Christ as head of this extended body. The poet's idea is less explicitly hierarchical: Jesus embodies all humanity; he does not govern it.

> Then those in Great Eternity met in the Council of God
> As one Man for contracting their Exalted Senses
> They behold Multitude or Expanding they behold as one
> As One Man all the Universal family & that one Man
> They call Jesus the Christ & they in him & he in them
> Live in Perfect harmony in Eden the land of life
> Consulting as One Man... (FZ 21, E 310–11)

The primary activity of the universal family is a strenuous engagement in the arts of imagination. Blake actually defines the true religion of Jesus as an unconstrained use of imagination. "I know of no other Christianity and of no other Gospel than the liberty both of body & mind to exercise the Divine Arts of Imagination" (J 77, E 231). And human existence in Eternity, likewise, is defined in terms of imagination. "I rest not from my great task!" Blake writes in Jerusalem, "To open the Eternal Worlds, to open the immortal Eyes/ Of Man inwards into the Worlds of Thought: into Eternity/ Ever expanding in the Bosom of God. the Human Imagination" (J 5, E 147).

That last apposition repeats an unconventional theological conception that persists in Blake's writing from first to last, the identification of God or Jesus with the human imagination, an equation that is interpreted by some readers as a denial of genuine transcendence to Jesus. The association of imagination with divinity appears very early; his first illuminated text (1788) declares: "The Religions of all Nations are derived from each Nations different reception of the Poetic Genius which is every where call'd the Spirit of Prophecy" (ARO, E 1). In his annotations to Swedenborg's Divine Love and Divine Wisdom, possibly dating from the same year, Blake twice substituted "the Poetic Genius" where Swedenborg used "the Lord" and "God" and then wrote: "He who Loves feels love descend into him & if he has wisdom may perceive it is from the Poetic Genius which is the Lord" (E 603). Later, in Milton, this "poetic genius" is described in more specifically Christian language:

> The Bard replied. I am Inspired! I know it is Truth! for I Sing
> According to the inspiration of the Poetic Genius
> Who is the eternal all-protecting Divine Humanity
> To whom be Glory & Power & Dominion Evermore Amen
> (pls. 13–14[14–15], E 107–8)

Elsewhere in *Milton* and *Jerusalem* Imagination is called "the Divine Body of the Lord Jesus. blessed for ever" (*Milton* 2, *J* 5, E 96, 148), and individual human imaginations are "those Worlds of Eternity in which we shall live for ever; in Jesus our Lord" (*Milton* 1, E 95). The identification of the Eternal Jesus with the human imagination is further developed in Blake's *Vision of the Last Judgment*:

> This World of Imagination is the World of Eternity it is the Divine bosom into which we shall all go after the death of the Vegetated body . . . All Things are comprehended in their Eternal Forms in the Divine body of the Saviour the True Vine of Eternity The Human Imagination who appeared to Me as Coming to Judgment. among his Saints & throwing off the Temporal that the Eternal might be Establishd. (E 555)

The narrative structure and conceptual argument of *Jerusalem* seem to posit an ontological gap between the best efforts of the human imagination, as represented in the creative and prophetic activity of Los, and the salvific power of Jesus who must intervene to save Los when he is in mortal peril. But Blake equates Jesus with the imagination so persistently that the reader is faced with an unusually taxing interpretative challenge. Even with a very large expense of mental energy, it seems impossible to stabilize that metaphor, the two terms of which may constitute the ultimate set of Blakean contraries, the final demonstration of his dialectical theology. The Eternal Living God, the Savior without whom humanity would remain forever in its fallen state, may be regarded as an act, a construction, of the human imagination. This assertion can be read in two ways. A theist might acknowledge that any religious conception is the product of the imagination in the sense that sacred scripture is the work of various imaginations acting under the inspiration of the Holy Spirit. Blake always saw the imagination as the conduit of religious truth, for it is imagination that puts us in touch with Eternity with its complete, fourfold vision of reality.

But Blake's equation may be read in a way that is not so amenable to a positive religious interpretation. He may be suggesting that the Divine Savior is simply a very noble figment of the human imagination. This is a possibility that occurs even to Jerusalem, the Bride of the Lamb, in the poem that Blake named for her. Imprisoned in the dungeons of Babylon, she cries out to her "Lord & Saviour,"

> Art thou alive! & livest thou for-evermore? or art thou
> Not: but a delusive shadow, a thought that liveth not.
> Babel mocks saying, there is no God nor Son of God

That thou O Human Imagination, O Divine Body art all
A delusion. but I know thee O Lord when thou arisest upon
My weary eyes even in this dungeon & this iron mill.

(*J* 60, E 211)

It seems that the experience of faith must be tested continually by the challenge of doubt. Blake said that Swedenborg repeated old religious errors
because "He conversed with Angels who are all religious, & conversed not
with Devils who all hate religion" (*MHH* 21, E 43). Radical skepticism may
be an essential intellectual shield when confronting "Urizens Dragon form"
(*FZ* 111, E 385), the entrenched power of organized religion. In order to
challenge the errors that dominate the religious world, we must be ready to
entertain the possibility that all religious belief is delusional.

Blake was aware that artists themselves must be on guard against their
own personal beliefs, those resting places of the mind that he called the
Spaces of Beulah. As Harold Bloom observed, "the health of the creative
life lies in the willingness of these forms and extra-artistic beliefs to sacrifice
themselves so as to revive the mind's power to visualize fresh appearances."5
While belief is essential for Blake, beliefs are suspect. A particular belief held
firmly in the mind can inhibit one's imaginative freedom and thus act as an
obstacle to discerning true Christianity.

When the focus of his sympathy shifted from Orc to Los, Blake came to
understand the history of religion as the story, not only of perpetual antagonism between authoritarian dogmatism and radical iconoclasm, but of a
more complex three-way interaction in which the imaginative, prophetic impulse in humanity arbitrates, even cultivates, a continuing conflict between
belief and skepticism. The creative, prophetic Los struggles to clarify the
religion of Jesus, freeing it from the dogmatic, repressive structures imposed
by Urizen and from the skeptical, materialist reductions of Orc/Luvah. Los
mediates between them, "Striving with Systems to deliver Individuals from
those Systems" (*J* 11, E 154). So Blake's religion of Jesus can never be a
collection of dogmas, rituals, and moral prescriptions. It is an endless imaginative negotiation between conflicting mental impulses, the goal of which
is a momentary clarity of vision. This is not a dialectic of the Hegelian kind
that anticipates a synthesis of opposing elements; it is a dialectic in which
both tendencies, belief and denial, remain in permanent antagonism and are
never reconciled, like those contraries in *The Marriage of Heaven and Hell*,
without which there is "no progression" (pl. 3, E 34). For Blake, discord was
the guarantor of religious truth and vitality. In a healthy dialectic, nothing is
protected from contradiction. No doctrine or pious belief is sacred enough
to be beyond criticism. Blake had no use for Deism, but he defended Thomas

Paine's Deistic critique of the Bible in the *Age of Reason* when it was attacked by a bishop of the Church. "Christ died as an Unbeliever. & if the Bishops had their will so would Paine... let the Bishop prove that he has not spoken against the Holy Ghost who in Paine strives with Christendom as in Christ he strove with the Jews" (anno. Watson, E 614).

Blake himself claimed a freedom in interpreting the Bible that no Church in his time would have tolerated. He admired the scriptures as a supreme example of imaginative art, an illustration of his conviction that the inspired artist communicates directly with Eternity. "The Hebrew Bible & the Gospel of Jesus are not Allegory but Eternal Vision or Imagination of All that Exists" (*VLJ*, E 554). He admired the courage of the prophets and their vision of Jehovah as champion of the poor and helpless, and he found in the apocalyptic literature a rich source of ideas and images. But he reserved the right to read the Bible critically and to condemn vigorously much of what he found there, particularly in the Old Testament. For example, commenting on Joshua's invasion of Canaan, he wrote: "To me who believe the Bible & profess myself a Christian a defence of the Wickedness of the Israelites in murdering so many thousands under pretence of a command from God is altogether Abominable & Blasphemous" (anno. Watson, E 614). He would allow no nation or religious community to claim the right to express definitively "the word of God universal." "That the Jews assumed a right Exclusively to the benefits of God. will be a lasting witness against them. & the same will it be against Christians" (E 615).

No one has a monopoly on religious truth, which emerges only in the conflict between opposing viewpoints. Belief walks a perilous path between credulity and skepticism, which are mutually corrective. Blake's commitment to this kind of dialectical theology where truth is looked for in the tension between opposing claims accounts for the striking disagreements among his critics as to the real character of his theological beliefs. Those who attempt to understand Blake's religious opinions must accustom themselves to the way different dramatic voices express conflicting theological views, so that his verses can be quoted convincingly on both sides of any important religious question. What seem to be earnestly pious or derisively skeptical pronouncements are usually discovered to be argumentative "contraries" that will be balanced by contradictory statements made elsewhere. When, for example, in *The Marriage of Heaven and Hell* we come upon the assertion that "All deities reside in the human breast" (pl. 11, E 38), it appears to be a denial of belief in any transcendent divine power. But the meaning of "reside" seems to shift when in *Jerusalem* the Saviour says to Albion: "I am not a God afar off, I am a brother and a friend; / Within your bosoms I reside, and you reside in me" (*J* 4, E 146). In short, the reader of Blake is forced into the same negotiation between faith and skepticism that Los adopts in his dealings with Urizen and Luvah. That the final determination of Blake's personal creed is left so much to the reader is a striking illustration of the poet's respect for the inviolable freedom of the individual religious imagination.

Discussing the religious dimension of William Blake's artistry, one continually confronts a series of ironies and paradoxes. He saw that all religion posed a formidable danger to human welfare, and yet believed that one must cultivate certain forms of it in order to keep others from triumphing. He thought skepticism an essential defense against the delusions of faith, and yet feared it as dangerously corrosive of humanity's best imaginative instincts. And although Blake was passionately dedicated to his religious (or anti-religious) mission, he does not appear to have derived much comfort from it in his life as an artist. Blake was not even given the satisfaction of knowing that his prophetic denunciation of the Christian churches was being heard. For this he had to blame his own choice of a hermetic style and a mode of book production that insured a limited audience. But even with wider circulation, he must have known that his critique of religion was too idiosyncratic and too radical to be effective in the public sphere where religious reformation happens. Blake had no noticeable influence on the religious consciousness of his society to compare with the impact of other poets like Wordsworth and Byron. His own fierce integrity provided the only consolation he knew. He might have said for himself the words he attributed to the prophet Isaiah: "As I was then perswaded. & remain confirm'd; that the voice of honest indignation is the voice of God, I cared not for consequences but wrote" (*MHH* 12, E 38).

Notes

1. *The Present State of Europe Compared with Antient Prophecies*, "A Sermon, preached at the Gravel Pit Meeting in Hackney, February 28, 1794, Being the Day Appointed for a General Fast" (London: J. Johnson, 1794), pp. 7, 13, 21–22.
2. I have argued the case for Blake's orthodoxy in some detail in *The Romantic Reformation: Religious Politics in English Literature 1789–1824* (Cambridge: Cambridge University Press, 1997).
3. *Collected Letters of Samuel Taylor Coleridge*, ed. E. L. Griggs, vol. VI (Oxford: Clarendon Press, 1956–1971), p. 622.
4. Robert Hindmarsh, *Rise and Progress of the New Jerusalem Church, in England, America, and Other Parts*, ed. E. Madeley (London, 1861), p. 24. That this emphasis on the Divine Humanity is not intrinsically heterodox is suggested by its reaffirmation in the twentieth century by the Christian theologian Karl Barth, who wrote: "The incarnation discloses in history what God is 'eternally and

antecedently in himself.' God is essentially what he shows himself to be in Jesus. There is no other God than this, nor is he God in any other way than he here makes known... The Word, and therefore God Himself, does not exist for us apart from the human being of Christ" (*Church Dogmatics*, trans. G. T. Thomson and Harold Knight, I, 2 (New York: Scribner, 1956), p. 166.

5. Harold Bloom, *Blake's Apocalypse: A Study in Poetic Argument* (Garden City, NY: Doubleday, 1963), pp. 214–15.

Further reading

Altizer, Thomas J. J. *The New Apocalypse: The Radical Christian Vision of William Blake*. East Lansing: Michigan State University Press, 1967.

Bottrall, Margaret. *The Divine Image: A Study of Blake's Interpretation of Christianity*. Rome: Edizioni di Storia e Letteratura, 1950.

Bradley, James E. *Religion, Revolution and English Radicalism: Non-conformity in Eighteenth-Century Politics and Society*. Cambridge: Cambridge University Press, 1990.

Clark, J. C. D. *English Society 1688–1832: Ideology, Social Structure and Political Practice during the Ancien Régime*. Cambridge: Cambridge University Press, 1985.

Damrosch, Leopold, Jr. *Symbol and Truth in Blake's Myth*. Princeton: Princeton University Press, 1980.

Davies, J. G. *The Theology of William Blake*. Oxford: Clarendon Press, 1948.

Garrett, Clarke. *Respectable Folly: Millenarians and the French Revolution in France and England*. Baltimore: Johns Hopkins University Press, 1975.

Gilbert, Alan D. *Religion and Society in Industrial England: Church, Chapel and Social Change, 1740–1914*. London: Longman, 1976.

Hole, Robert. *Pulpits, Politics, and Public Order in England 1760–1832*. Cambridge: Cambridge University Press, 1989.

Jacob, Margaret C. *The Newtonians and the English Revolution 1689–1720*. Ithaca: Cornell University Press, 1976.

John, Donald. "Blake and Forgiveness." *Wordsworth Circle* 17 (1986): 74–80.

Lincoln, Anthony. *Some Political and Social Ideas of English Dissent 1763–1800*. 1938; rpt. New York: Octagon, 1971.

Mee, Jon. *Dangerous Enthusiasm: William Blake and the Culture of Radicalism in the 1790s*. Oxford: Clarendon Press, 1992.

Paley, Morton D. *Apocalypse and Millennium in English Romantic Poetry*. Oxford: Clarendon Press, 1999.

" 'A New Heaven is Begun': William Blake and Swedenborgianism." *Blake/An Illustrated Quarterly* 13 (1979): 64–90.

Priestman, Martin. *Romantic Atheism: Poetry and Freethought, 1780–1830*. Cambridge: Cambridge University Press, 1999.

Riede, David G. *Oracles and Hierophants: Constructions of Romantic Authority*. Ithaca: Cornell University Press, 1991.

Ryan, Robert M. *The Romantic Reformation: Religious Politics in English Literature 1789–1824*. Cambridge: Cambridge University Press, 1997.

Soloway, R. A. *Prelates and People: Ecclesiastical Social Thought in England 1783–1852*. London: Routledge & Kegan Paul, 1969.

Thompson, Edward P. *Witness Against the Beast: William Blake and the Moral Law*. New York: New Press, 1993.

Wilkie, Brian, and Mary Lynn Johnson. *Blake's Four Zoas: The Design of a Dream*. Cambridge: Harvard University Press, 1978.

9

DAVID SIMPSON

Blake and Romanticism

For a number of years in the long middle of the twentieth century the term *Romanticism* conjured up for students of English literature two dates and half a dozen names. The dates became so self-evident that no one remarked on their oddness. Neither 1789 nor 1832, the standard limits of the period, were chosen for literary-historical reasons. The first commemorates the French Revolution, the second the Great Reform Bill that extended the vote to many affluent males who had not had it before. George Crabbe, Jeremy Bentham, and Sir Walter Scott all died in 1832, but their passing has not been used as the measure of the end of an era. 1789 happened to be the year of William Blake's *Songs of Innocence*, but its appearance has not usually been regarded as foundational for Romanticism: that honor has much more commonly been bestowed upon Wordsworth and Coleridge's jointly authored first edition of *Lyrical Ballads* (1798). This has had the effect of distancing the literary from the political revolution, leading to lively arguments about what the politics of *Lyrical Ballads* (and Romanticism generally) might be given its appearance during the British counter-revolution, after the widespread loss of faith in French republicanism and following the government's repressive measures against British radicals. Blake has nonetheless mostly counted as one of the names that the mention of Romanticism has been supposed to invoke, along with Wordsworth, Coleridge, Keats, Shelley, and Byron. All poets, all men. Jane Austen was usually left out of any efforts at categorizing Romanticism, along with all the other novelists of the period: she has tended to appear in literary history as an isolated genius in the story of the nineteenth-century novel. The drama was even further distanced: the common consensus was that there was not much of it and that what was there was not very interesting.

There have been some visible consequences to the periodization of Romanticism just described. By 1832 such figures as Tennyson, Carlyle, Macaulay, Darwin, and Disraeli were already in print. But these writers have traditionally been part of Victorianism, and are discussed as such when they are discussed at all. Wordsworth's *The Prelude* was not published until 1850, though it is seldom studied as anything other than a central document of Romanticism. Wordsworth's other long poem, *The Excursion*, appeared in 1814 but has not usually figured in popular literary histories or the college courses running alongside them. The 1820s have been something of a missing decade – after the "great" Romantics but before Dickens – as have the 1780s at the other end of the common chronology. Thus Robert Burns and William Cowper have not been crowned as exemplary, foundational Romantics, even though one distinguished literary historian, Hippolyte Taine, thought they were. The limitations of periodization are evident with this body of literature as with all others: writers tend not to live, publish, and die at times that fit neatly into latterday critical schemata (though Dryden obligingly passed away in 1700 and thus allowed us to make the "age of Dryden" coincide with the end of the seventeenth century). But these are not the only limitations that have accompanied the invocation of something called *Romanticism*, which has always been described not simply as a period but as the essence of that period, that whereby it is most true to itself. To call a writer a *Romantic* has thus traditionally been to signal an interest in such categories as genius, nature, childhood, and imagination, perhaps along with some assumed response to the French Revolution. Those who wrote in the Romantic period but wrote about other things or demonstrated other priorities have then come to be, oddly, not Romantic in this particular sense. At best they achieve the specific dignity of being anti-Romantic, as Byron visibly was in his attacks on the Lake Poets and in his deliberate celebration of the rhyming couplets and satirical style associated with Pope and the Augustans (though Byron has also been seen as the arch-Romantic in his dramatic presentation of the figure of the solitary, tortured genius). Otherwise the un-Romantics just fall between the cracks, as did George Crabbe, who shared Byron's formal preferences for rhyme but made no polemical issue of it and led a relatively ordinary personal life.

The six major Romantics according to the long-standing assumptions were, as I have said, all male poets. But not all of their poetry has counted as essentially Romantic. The definitional preference has been for lyric poetry, a fashion cultivated by Matthew Arnold in his editing of Wordsworth and by the popularity of Palgrave's *Golden Treasury of Songs and Lyrics*, the standard nineteenth-century anthology, and sustained of course by the attention span (actual or imagined) of countless common readers and students. There are some fairly profound reasons for this. The lyric mode is the one in which the predicament of self-consciousness can most dramatically and economically be explored, and this is one of the characteristic priorities of what we have come to call Romanticism. Schiller, for example, in his important critical essay *On Naive and Sentimental Poetry* (1796), proposed that all essentially modern poetry must be self-conscious, aware of itself as lacking the integrity and oneness with nature that was available to the ancients, for whom the social division of labor and the general disenchantment of the world had not yet set in. The modern poet, that is to say the Romantic poet, must confess the ultimate inaccessibility of what he most wants, and either make a virtue of this necessity or subside into a terminal melancholia. (I say *he*, since this was an aggressively male-gendered syndrome). The incremental sense of isolation that the canonically Romantic poet demonstrates was further theorized by Hegel in his posthumously published lectures on aesthetics and fine art as the outcome of a long process commencing in the Christian middle ages, whereby the emphatic attention to the spiritual world and to the afterlife worked against any sense of proper satisfaction with ordinary experience. So literature, as the least materialized of the media of art (music did not count as this for Hegel), came to the fore as world-historical expression, and lyric poetry came fully into its own as the least materialized kind of literature. Add to this critical argument the felt pressures of a mass market in which the writer or artist, increasingly unconnected to personal patrons, had to make a reputation or at least a living, and one can see the appeal of the Protestant-related paradigm of anxious self-inspection offered by Schiller and Hegel as the essence of the Romantic and the modern self.

Hegel's schema for the history of art is also, then, a model of the history of the world, and his argument for the emergence of what he called Romanticism (along the lines set out by the Schlegels and by Madame de Staël) makes it the central motif in the development of modernity itself. With this application of the term, the referent has become much larger and grander than a mere period of literary culture exemplified by a few English poets. It has become the guiding energy of several hundred years of European history, a history that has itself come to be significantly exemplified in literature. Hegel did not formulate these ideas by sheer coincidence, of course, for he thought and wrote for and within a generation that was obsessively preoccupied with historicism, with tracing patterns in the past and projecting them into the future, and with explaining why the world had turned out one way and not another. Our continued contemporary preoccupation with such terms and concepts as *culture, ideology, nation,* and *society* is very much the result of the critical articulation of post-enlightenment historicism. Writers and critics then became newly invested in ideas about what the Germans called the *Zeitgeist* and what Shelley and Hazlitt liked to call "the spirit of the age." To live, to think, and to create is to do so in time and place, but mostly not in ways that can provide the writer with an existentially supportive sense of sure foundation, for what is in time and place cannot be assumed to be for other times and places or for others within the same time but occupying different places.

This equation of Romanticism and modernity is, however, not yet the grandest narrative to make use of the term, which has entered the common language to denote an enduring state of mind and being – "ah, he is a romantic" – assumed to be forever available and thus beyond history itself. The same fate has befallen (and had already befallen) some of the critical terms – *imagination, the sublime,* and *genius* for example – which the critics and theorists of the late eighteenth century sought to pin down and distinguish from their more threatening near-cognates or close relatives (like *fancy, beauty,* and *common sense*). So that when we turn, as I now do, to the question of William Blake and "Romanticism," what is meant? For readers inside the schools and universities it is unlikely to be the common language associations, to which I have just alluded, that come to mind, although they do create a definite pressure to imagine Romanticism in ways that fit with these ordinary usages. But something of each of at least three other representative possibilities is at stake: Blake as (Hegelian) Romantic, the poet of modernity itself; Blake as an affirmative and exemplary figure (the arch-Romantic) in a narrower period (most commonly 1789–1832, but one could argue for other dates); and Blake as a more complex or conflicted spirit working within a historical formation, perhaps as both a Romantic and an anti-Romantic, perhaps in ways that entirely refuse this sort of categorization. There is at least a fourth, one I have not yet mentioned. For Blake figures not only in literary history but in art history, which is a history with its own specific periodizations and content categories. (Blake can be counted as participating in at least three of them: painting, engraving, and book illustration.) In each of these four constructions of Romanticism Blake can be (and has been) made to figure, and in ways that range from representative genius to marginal eccentric. It is hard to keep these categories completely separate, but I shall try for the purposes of clear exposition to do just this.

Blake's continued presence in both the common and academic imagination owes much to a number of devoted artists, writers, editors, and scholars: the Rossettis, Alexander Gilchrist, Swinburne, Yeats, Arthur Symons, and Sir Geoffrey Keynes are certainly among them. Few of his early commentators had, however, any extended interest in his relation to something called Romanticism. The need to specify what that is or was or should be has been the preoccupation principally of professional literary critics and scholars in the universities. Because Blake's creative circle – the persons with whom he kept company and shared ideas – was made up of artists and engravers, the literary Blake has often looked like a loner, a mystic, a visionary, and it was the image of Blake as this sort of Romantic (the sort to which the

Modernists would find themselves so antagonistic) that first appealed to those who kept alive his reputation. Thus Henry Crabb Robinson wrote of him in 1811 as the latest in the line of "ecstatics, mystics, seers of visions, and dreamers of dreams" whose principal task was to give "bodily forms to spiritual beings".[1] The image of the mystic is of a figure outside history, even if it is also associated with one version of a specifically Romantic imagination. S. Foster Damon, one of the founding fathers of academic Blake criticism, brought him into literary history as precisely such a "mystic," one of the "eternal Types of Humanity" and one that shows a "surprising sameness, no matter from what culture or creed they may have sprung."[2] From this perspective questions about periodization are unimportant. Blake's exceptionalism, and his apparent commitment to a language and style beyond or above the merely historical, came fully into contact with literary-historical conventions for the first time in Northrop Frye's monumental study of 1947, *Fearful Symmetry*.

Frye sought to account for Blake as something more than "an interruption in cultural history, a separable phenomenon," and a "literary freak."[3] In pursuing this goal he felt the need to establish some kind of periodization for Blake's poetry. He found it neither in Augustanism nor in Romanticism, but in something chronologically between the two whose guiding spirits were Berkeley, Sterne, Percy, Gray, Collins, Ossian, and others; something that could for want of a previously accepted term be called "the age of Blake" (pp. 167–68). The literary conventions that must be understood for us to read and appreciate him are allegory and satire; neither of them favored Romantic (or modern) resources. Allegory has (and had already in the later eighteenth century) become anachronistic: had Blake been born "between, say, 1530 and 1630, he would have found a large public able to speak his language." But since he was not, he could only be accused of developing a "private symbolism".[4] His other preference, for satire, put him in the company of "Rabelais and Apuleius" and in what for Frye could well have been "his real medium" (p. 193), one that informs the epics, the *Songs of Experience*, and *The Marriage of Heaven and Hell*, this last standing as "perhaps the epilogue to the golden age of English satire" (p. 201).[5] But it does not put him in the company of Wordsworth, Coleridge, Shelley, and Keats: it could be said to afford him an odd comradeship with Byron, but with Byron he shares almost nothing else. In this way, Frye put Blake into literary history but took him out of one of its major subdivisions, the one called Romanticism. The idea of a period called "the age of Blake" has never quite taken off, partly because it does not contain a literature that has seemed to many to require designation, and partly because such terms as Preromanticism and early Romanticism have competed for the same space.[6] And indeed, looking back at his book, Frye himself played up Blake's connections not so much to history but to literary theory and to his "understanding of literature as a whole".[7] In this way any negative consequences of Blake's exclusion from a favored period called Romanticism could be overcome by making him the prototype of literature in general, and a testing ground for the kinds of theories we need to devise to make sense of it.

This capacity of Blake's work to stand for the whole of literature and as a sort of encyclopedia of its various techniques implicitly affiliates Frye's Blake with Hegel's Romanticism, given that what Frye (and the rest of us) assume by the term *literature* has been the ongoing product of the same long cycle of history that Hegel called modern-Romantic. The evolution of the discipline of psychoanalysis in the last 100 years or so has further emphasized the potential in Blake's books to expound something that is transhistorically human (as it had been for Damon), rather than critically specific to time and place. Blake's epics have often been read as myths or protomythologies, as guidebooks to the eternal struggles within the human psyche. The sheer difficulty of reading them at all has contributed to the desire for this sort of coherence, and it is a desire apparent in Frye's book, over half of which is devoted to the longer poems, and above all in its concluding reflections on the usefulness of Blake for a modern life that can be seen as once again a "great mythopoeic age" (p. 423) whose analysis is going on in psychology and anthropology as well as in literature and criticism. Blake's work could, it is proposed, provide the key to uniting the "whole pattern" of contemporary thought (p. 425): its potential is "archetypal" (p. 427). These priorities are also apparent in Harold Bloom's *Blake's Apocalypse* (1963), fully a quarter of which is given over to an account of the "mythic structure" of *The Four Zoas*.[8] And in this same sense Bloom has written that "modern poetry, in English, is the invention of Blake and Wordsworth."[9] Of course, the same general identification of Romanticism with modern life could involve the more or less complete exclusion of Blake, as it did (for example) for Morse Peckham, whose preference for a governing paradigm of "dynamic organicism" had no place for Blake's eclectic and bewilderingly allusive satirical–allegorical range of styles.[10] Peckham's Blake was but a "failed Romantic . . . the Enlightenment dissolved around him, but he retreated in fear to an early sixteenth-century position" and to a "closed system" made up of "neo-Platonic and Hermetic" doctrines of redemption.[11]

We move, then, from the long Romanticism that is identified with modern life to the shorter Romanticism whose limits are only some thirty or forty years apart across the turn of the nineteenth century. Frye, as we have seen, thought that Blake did not fit in here, and Peckham expressed his irritation at the results of others' efforts to make him fit, while for Bloom he was a

major presence. One can find the same range of estimations in other constructions of a narrowly periodized Romanticism, the exposition of which
has principally been of interest to literary scholars based in North America
rather than in Britain. There are many reasons that could be suggested
for this. They would surely include the historical coincidence between the
Romantic period and the cultural and political establishment of an independent United States after 1776, and the relatively high level of interest in
European Romanticism among nineteenth-century American writers. There
is also the fact that the most forceful academic attempts at defining Romanticism came not from professors of English but from a historian of ideas and a
scholar of comparative literature, Arthur O. Lovejoy and René Wellek. Neither of these fields was established in British universities. It is also the case
that the evolution of British literary criticism has been marked by a strong
Modernist and anti-Romantic ethos for most of the twentieth century.

Lovejoy set out to try to tidy up a vocabulary wherein "Romanticism"
was everywhere and therefore nowhere. His trenchant recommendation was
that we should always speak of Romanticisms, in the plural, and never of
a single structure of ideas that can be found in all the national traditions.
Indeed, even within a single national culture no one definition fits all the
varieties of artistic expression, and certainly not one based in exclusively literary analysis: "The first great revolt against the neo-classical aesthetics was
not in literature at all, but in gardening; the second, I think, was in architectural taste".[12] Most of Lovejoy's examples come not from British literature
but from French and German, and a similar cosmopolitanism is apparent in
Wellek's response to his essay, which does try to make the case for a single
and coherent movement of mind that can be called Romanticism. Wellek's
1949 article "The Concept of Romanticism in Literary History" remains an
indispensable resource in its range of reference, summary, and argument. It
covers a variety of European national cultures, not just the obvious ones; it
offers a very useful history of the term *Romanticism*; and it puts the case for
a unified spirit of the age based in imagination, nature, and symbol/myth.[13]
Wellek prefers *Preromanticism* to Frye's "age of Blake" (pp. 159–60), but
he puts Blake as first in line for inclusion in Romanticism properly so called
(p. 178): notwithstanding Blake's objections to contemporary nature poetry
(p. 182), he comes out powerfully in favor of imagination and the
"mythopoeic" (p. 188), and thereby fully satisfies two of Wellek's three defining priorities.

By 1963, in his "Romanticism Re-examined," Wellek is singing a different song. He still holds to the idea of a unitary Romanticism, but now it
is one from which Blake is excluded: "we shall not, I think, make much
progress with the problem of romanticism if we seek its prototype in such

an exceptional and lonely figure as Blake, who seems to me rather a survival from another century, however much he may anticipate the issues of our own time".[14] Why the shift of opinion? New work in comparative criticism by E. D. Hirsch, Paul de Man, and Geoffrey Hartman seems now to have persuaded Wellek that the primary paradigm of Romanticism is philosophical and epistemological: "the great endeavor to overcome the split between subject and object, the self and the world, the conscious and the unconscious" (p. 220). This is not only a philosophical problematic of fitting and fitted that Blake happened to refuse in famously belligerent language; it is also one explicitly based in German sources and models, of which Blake knew next to nothing. And it is an alternative to the "prophetic" strain exemplified by Blake according to Bloom, whom Wellek refutes (p. 217). The match with "nature," we remember, did not work for Blake in Wellek's 1949 schema; now that nature has become the primary item for the definition of Romanticism (it is the sphere in which epistemological questions are rehearsed), Blake's place is obviously not tenable. Something else seems to be at stake, though. Bloom is faulted for minimizing "both the Christian and the Hellenic components of romanticism" (p. 218) in favor of the "visionary." Blake indeed made a big case for Gothic (faith, imagination) against Greek (pagan, rational) inspiration; and even within the sphere of the Gothic his prickly, idiosyncratic kind of Christianity was based in antinomian, dissenting subcultures rather than in broad Church principles, and could not be made the foundation for any general, consensual theology, either as literal doctrine or as metaphor. Blake's learning may well have been profound and cosmopolitan, but it was hardly systematic or obviously coherent, so that he can credibly be presented both as the heir of the densely Greek and Latin Milton and the Hebraic Old Testament and as the significantly anglophone genius that Bloom (among others) made him out to be (T. S. Eliot, as we shall see, had similar concerns). Blake for these reasons seems anti-cosmopolitan, even stridently nationalistic, and definitely at odds with the ethos of departments of Comparative Literature as international, multilingual, and committed to high culture and high philosophy and to a demanding and formal education. Wordsworth, who despite his university education might be thought to have known a lot less than Blake did, still demonstrates in his poems the problem of the mind's relation to nature that later critics have made constitutive of Romanticism, and he is in this way conformable with the post-Cartesian tradition's inquiry into the complexities of self–other relationships. Anxiety in Blake can often seem to take the less inviting form of bluster. We are back to Blake's predilection for satire, once again at odds with the preferred priorities of Romanticism.

By 1963 there was already another persuasive and influential model of Romanticism in circulation, expounded in M. H. Abrams's *The Mirror and the Lamp* (1953). Here it is the expressive imagination that is offered as the defining energy in Romanticism; and while Blake fits the model very comfortably, it is through Wordsworth and above all Coleridge that the case is made. Discussions of Blake in this densely documented and widely respected literary history would, if strung together, amount to only a couple of pages out of four hundred. Once again the emphasis is on a coherent history of ideas drawn out from eighteenth-century British aestheticians and German philosophers. Blake does not refer extensively to the first and refers not at all to the second. Abrams produced at least two other important interpretations of Romanticism. In 1963 there was an essay on "English Romanticism: The Spirit of the Age," in which Wordsworth's turn from youthful political radicalism to personal transformation through the imagination is offered as the typical Romantic reaction to the loss of faith in the French Revolution.[15] Blake is again peripheral; and indeed, the dating of Wordsworth's turn to around 1797 would not fit the arguable shift in Blake's views several years earlier. Then, in 1971, Abrams published another long book, *Natural Supernaturalism*, with only an eight-page discussion of Blake's myth of the universal man. Blake's myth, it is said, "has neither prototype nor parallel".[16] It thus offers no material for literary history.

Another philosophically derived or affiliated version of Romanticism made up the avant-garde alternative to Abrams's humanistic model in the 1960s and 1970s: the one that came to be described as "deconstruction." Its two major exponents, Geoffrey Hartman and Paul de Man, are very different, but they share a sense of Blake's marginality to their own interests and priorities. Again, they are both comparatists, both committed to a multilingual, European field of reference and application. De Man took much of his inspiration from French and German sources (Rousseau and Benjamin), and wrote attentively on Wordsworth and Shelley; Hartman, an extraordinarily learned literary historian, made Wordsworth, not Blake, the center of attention for a renewed theory of Romanticism.[17] These critics were major influences on the reception of Romanticism at the same time as Blake was being rediscovered as a 1960s-style radical whose "Proverbs of Hell" were appearing as highbrow graffiti on library walls in British and American colleges: it was to Blake that many student readers turned (however partially) for a literary legitimation of free love, anti-war sentiment, and radical action. And while it would be hugely reductive and insulting to suggest a simply reactive relation between these two kinds of attentiveness, it seems likely that the relative marginality of Blake to the "official" critical establishment was part of his

appeal to the counterculture, and that this appeal was reciprocally a contribution to the renewal of interest in a Wordsworth who was felt to have
turned away from politics, a language-based Shelley, and a philosophically
absorbed Coleridge.

If so, then this would simply be one more instance of criticism's demonstration of the prickly relationship between Blake and its constructions of
Romanticism. Bloom seems to stand alone among American critics in his
sense that Blake is a fundamental figure for its adequate periodization. Frye's
peculiar sense of Blake as central to literature, though not to Romanticism
itself, is an important though more complex recognition, and one that gestures toward removing him from any dominantly historical representative-
ness. Models of an occult or mystic Blake have had the same result. And
given that Bloom's Romanticism is one that includes and contains modern
poetry, it too is not much concerned with the elaborations of any precisely
substantial or limited use for the term. Blake is of course by no means the only
excluded figure in the reigning typologies of Romanticism: Clare, Crabbe,
Cowper, Burns, Scott, much of Byron, and a host of women writers come to
mind. But he is unusual for having been, for much of the twentieth century,
the outside insider, the writer who is mentioned, quoted, and taught (while
others have been ignored completely) but mostly not placed at the center of
the spirit of the age. It is as if he cannot be ignored but cannot be quite integrated: the traditions which we need to know to make some sense of him are
not the traditions that have gone into the favored models of Romanticism.

British literary critics have been much less interested in defining Romanticism than their American contemporaries, partly because of a prevalent anti-
systematizing ideology, and partly because the Modernist prejudice against
Romantic writers proved especially enduring in the British universities, so
that Romanticism has been most commonly invoked as something that might
better not have happened. Eliot's brief estimate of 1920, that Blake's isolation made him "eccentric" and "inclined to formlessness," so that he wrote
"great poetry" only by way of "unpleasantness," has remained implicitly
popular.[18] Eliot's essay is explicit in its contextualization of Blake within the
wider debate about English culture and its history. Blake exemplified the dis-
sociation of sensibility that set in at the time of the Puritan revolution, and
that produced the mythological "thinness" with which he was compelled
to work. He needed but lacked "a framework of accepted and traditional
ideas that would have prevented him from indulging in a philosophy of his
own," and that could have made up for what was otherwise "a certain mean-
ness of culture".[19] Poetry like Blake's, that is to say, is what is written when
natural genius is deprived of a sustaining intellectual and social environment. The Romantic individual is here interpreted as the sorry outcome of

a culture gone wrong. And the fault line is one established in political as much as literary history: the English Civil War (sometimes called a Revolution) of the 1640s, which divided king against parliament and commons, then commons against parliament, and destroyed any hope of reconciliation between state-sponsored and dissenting forms of Christian faith.

Eliot's own Anglo-Catholic sympathies are well known, but his analysis of a lapsed coherence in British culture was convincing to many who did not share his preferences. F. R. Leavis, probably the most influential figure in twentieth-century British literary criticism, also found that Blake suffered from not having access to "adequate social collaboration."[20] Leavis located the fault line in British culture in the eighteenth century, with the onset of Augustan notions of high culture and politeness, though he also had notorious problems with Milton's language. He approved of the bourgeois society and its dissenting imaginations, some aspects of which Blake's work exemplified, but he had little time for Romanticism. British criticism after Modernism mostly found in the Elizabethan and seventeenth-century metaphysical poets the high point of the national literary imagination, connecting a crucial moment in political history (the consolidation of the State and the beginnings of empire) with the figure of a unified consciousness, an undivided sensibility, and a classless personality. In the popular figment of the Shakespearean theater there was room for all regardless of class, wealth, or professional expertise, and the poetry of the time was taken to display a similar inclusiveness. It stood forth as the literature of undivided labor. But it was also (as in the work of John Donne) ferociously difficult, enough so to require the efforts of the professional literary critic.

Because Romanticism, whatever it was, came well after this great divide, it has not seemed widely important to British critics to establish its precise periodization. One major figure for whom it was, however, crucial was Raymond Williams, whose 1958 *Culture and Society* was a major contribution to the debate about English (and British) national history and identity. Williams found the "lifetime of Blake" to be the "decisive period" in the onset of the Industrial Revolution with all its consequences for culture and imagination.[21] Like Eliot, Williams related Romanticism to "problems in experience" (p. 54), but for him they were profoundly social–historical and embedded in the "wider social criticism" (p. 49) of commercial and industrial society. His five-point summary of the Romantic moment (pp. 49–50) is complex enough to take the question beyond the merely judgmental and certainly beyond the limits of a purely literary or philosophical history. But what matters here is not the conclusive definition of something called Romanticism but the insistence upon a besetting historical crisis that was simultaneously economic, cultural, artistic, and experiential. Literature here does not transcend the terms of ordinary experience but rather brings them to formal representation; and there cannot be a history of literature that is not also a history of everything else that was happening around it.

There have been other forms of attention on both sides of the Atlantic that are not premised on one or another version of a literary Romanticism. We may call them, for want of a simpler or familiar term, *empirical–historical*. Blake has, I think, fared better with this kind of scholarship, which is less preoccupied with periodizing literary history than with working out the most precise possible terms in which writers and texts are affiliated with specific events in place and time. Such efforts are of course not innocent of theoretical assumptions, nor is the "history" that they depend upon to be taken as providing simple and direct access to how things were, to what really happened. But in directing attention away from such questions as "how much of a Romantic was Blake?" they have kept alive an alternative tradition of commentary on his work, one that takes for granted its importance to a tradition of radical dissent and political reference. David Erdman's *Prophet Against Empire* (1954) is the founding text in a tradition that shows no sign of exhaustion; and E. P. Thompson's *The Making of the English Working Class*, a major study of the social and political history of the period, has had a significant influence on our understanding of Blake as not an alienated visionary (as he has seemed to those schooled only in high cultural references) but "the original yet authentic voice of a long popular tradition.²² The recovery of Blake's historical referentiality has been ongoing, and is arguably now more vigorous than ever in response to the historical turn taken by literary criticism and theory in recent years. Marilyn Butler's 1981 *Romantics, Rebels and Reactionaries* is symptomatic of much recent work in its willingness to give up on the search for a "closely coherent body of feeling" in favor of a more dispersed and various categorization of Romantic writing.²³ Blake appears in this account in a new format, sharing a chapter with Wordsworth and Gillray and compared with Boydell and others as a barometer of market forces (pp. 39–68). Blake's books now have a "corporate author... the urban sub-class which emerged through its opposition to Britain's national policy" (p. 43). Recent critical attention to issues of empire and slavery shows signs of reviving interest in the epic and thus in Blake's long poems, while the scrutiny of the sex–gender system in Romantic culture is also bound to account for Blake's complex and difficult writing on that topic. Among literary critics, then, Blake's work seems likely to flourish and remain unignorable in roughly inverse proportion to the compulsion toward defining a Romanticism.

There remains the matter of what Romanticism has meant to art historians, and what Blake has meant to them in the light of their opinions.

I am not an art historian, but I will offer some remarks that will I hope be helpful and suggestive. It is apparent in Butler's decision to discuss Blake in relation to Wordsworth *and* Gillray that those of us who are literary scholars should pay more attention to the other half (or more than half?) of Blake's career. And much of the most important recent work on Blake has been "art historical" in emphasis.[24] As such it has mostly eschewed the question of what Romanticism is and is not, for many of the same reasons that explain the recent priorities of the literary critics. It could be said, in fact, that the discussion of Romanticism has been even more unresolved and tentative for art historians than it has been for literary critics. It is of course much harder to write the history of art as an exclusively national tradition, given the nature of the artist's training and the art market itself. And as soon as one attends to different national traditions the problems of accurate periodization can seem insurmountable. What the French call Romanticism in literature began later (and had different emphases) than the movement called by the same name in Britain; add in the visual arts and the plot seems to thicken beyond the point where a narrative can be maintained. At the same time the international and canonical training of the painter might be thought to produce a more coherent range of styles that are not as subject to the pressures of national agendas as are works of literature. But the knowledge that everyone learned to draw by studying Michelangelo, for example, is not of itself of much use in trying to find the common ground between the likes of Turner, Friedrich, Delacroix, Goya, or Blake, any one of whom might be advanced as the exemplary Romantic. E. H. Gombrich argued some time ago that all the efforts at specifying periods in art history were simply "a series of masks for two categories, the classical and the non-classical."[25] This position does have the virtue of freeing us from overzealous efforts at narrow periodization. But there will always remain the question of art's relation to its place and time, and to other arts of the same place and time, even if we choose not to pursue a rigid definition of something called Romanticism.

Art historians have in fact often replicated literary history's paradigms in their efforts at such periodizations. Hugh Honour, for example, cites the French Revolution and Kant's philosophy as the critical influences on Romanticism, and notices a preference for expressive over mimetic conventions.[26] The first idea comes from Friedrich Schlegel, the second from M. H. Abrams. For Honour, Blake figures as a "visionary" and "arch nonconformist" (p. 286) whose closest artistic peer (besides his follower Samuel Palmer) is Philipp Otto Runge, whose work he almost certainly never saw (pp. 73–74). William Vaughan does not attempt to pin Blake down to a limiting series of quintessentially Romantic traits, offering instead a summary of the career and its various inspirations, though he does position Blake as the founder of a tradition of spiritual landscape art.[27] And John Barrell has argued for a Blake who is not to be understood (despite his notorious annotations to the *Discourses*) as antithetical to Reynolds in some sort of classic–Romantic face-off, and who does not fulfill the terms of Abrams's famous expressive individuality but adheres instead to a model of republican civic solidarity.[28] Peter Ackroyd, author of a recent biography, also claims that Blake "continued to think of himself as a public artist" throughout his career.[29]

The media in which Blake worked have further complicated the question of his relation to anything we might call Romanticism in the visual arts. Morris Eaves, in a fine essay on the relations between verbal and visual representations in the period (which he deliberately does not try to summarize as a thematized Romanticism) writes that "Blake lived and died in a socioeconomic network of painters and paintings, line engravers, stipple engravers, mezzotinters and printers."[30] No one has so far dreamed of founding something called Romanticism on any except the first two categories here listed: painters and painting. The others, the bread and butter of Blake's career (for his poems sold only in very small quantities), were directly responsive to the middle-class market and its appetite for affordable but acceptably genteel commodities for private display. These artifacts certainly embodied some of the "spirit of the age," but they are a far cry from the philosophically dense, elite identity of lyric poetry upon which most literary constructions of Romanticism have been fashioned. Their popularity indeed could well have contributed to the high-cultural credo of anti-visuality at a time when the visual was coming more and more to represent the mass market and the uneducated consumer. But even if one were to focus on painting and painters as the core of a Romanticism within which Blake might figure as exemplary, the effort would be equally unpromising. The most important genres in British painting at the end of the eighteenth century were portrait, landscape, and history painting. This last was felt to be a problem for British painters, faced with representing a highly contested religious and political tradition to a culture increasingly committed to commerce and the bourgeois private life rather than to the deeds of great men.[31] They did, however, excel at landscapes and portraits; but Blake did his principal work in none of these genres. He did no formal portraits and his views on Wordsworthian nature-worship were distinctly hostile. The aesthetics of the sublime, also very popular at the time, might be affirmatively related to Blake's visionary images, but the smallness of scale and intimacy of format in, for example, the prophetic books makes them rather remote from the manner typified conventionally by the paintings of Turner and Martin. It would seem, then, that despite the appeal of Blake's designs as cover art for all sorts of books about Romanticism, his place in a visually based periodization is likely to remain eccentric.

And what of the near future? The extraordinary actual and potential contribution of the electronic William Blake Archive based at the University of Virginia would seem to offer an unprecedented opportunity to close the gap between verbal and visual in the traditional academic appreciation of Blake's work. At the same time, the sheer density of (virtual) presence that each page of Blake's work can now assume for the viewer–reader, as one page is compared back and forth with other pages, line by line, image by image, seems likely to keep us very much at a distance from large and general claims about what about them is properly Romantic and what is not. There are, however, other and grander narratives that are keeping alive the debate about Romanticism, and Blake participates in at least two of them, those concerning empire and gender (and he has at least a tangential place in the debate about ecology). The recent interest in Romanticism as coincident with massive imperial and colonial expansion has revivified critical attention to the epic, the traditional genre of empire, and Blake wrote epics, idiosyncratic though they may be. Stuart Curran has argued for *Jerusalem* as "truly *the* British national epic – of this period, perhaps of all periods," but notes at the same time that it opposes the heroism of violence traditionally embodied in the epic form.[32] Blake's examinations of the sex–gender system of his age are arguably more complex and exigent than those of his contemporaries: the exposure of today's students to the *Visions of the Daughters of Albion* produces confusion and discomfort rather than the ideological self-imaging that figures so largely in the average classroom. Blake, it seems, will remain on the front line for critical-literary history only as long as the front line has room for the margin. There is no sign yet of any simple consensus about *how* Blake represents empire and gender, but there is every sign that his representations cannot be ignored. Given the now habitual awareness of the intricacies and varieties of history itself, best addressed by exhaustive local description rather than by confidently periodized and always somewhat metaphysical categories, it is probably going to seem less important than it once was to try to fix his or anyone else's place in a clear or exclusive entity called *Romanticism*. But the rhetorical and substantial legacies of our previous efforts to this end are unlikely to disappear.

Notes

1. G. E. Bentley, ed., *William Blake: The Critical Heritage* (London and Boston: Routledge and Kegan Paul, 1975), pp. 157, 160. An appreciative anonymous critic writing in 1830 coupled Blake with Coleridge and opined that he would

have been more at home in Germany, the best place for such spiritualized "works of the mind"; see pp. 201, 205.

2. S. Foster Damon, *William Blake: His Philosophy and Symbols* (Boston: Houghton Mifflin, 1924), p. 1.

3. Frye, *Fearful Symmetry: A Study of William Blake* (1947, rpt. Boston: Beacon Press, 1962), pp. 3, 147.

4. Frye, *Fearful Symmetry*, p. 161. The most powerful case for allegory's persistence into Romanticism has been made by Paul de Man (following Benjamin), but de Man had no interest in Blake. Frye himself, in an essay written in 1963, modified his case by explaining Blake's own negative estimate of at least one kind of allegory, wherein the ideas evoked are more important than the manner in which they are represented, potentially leading to a view of poetry as principally "didactic." Frye here finds that the poetry is best described as "mythopoeic" rather than "allegorical": see "The Road of Excess" in Harold Bloom, ed., *Romanticism and Consciousness* (New York: W. W. Norton, 1970), pp. 127, 130.

5. Cleanth Brooks, *Modern Poetry and the Tradition* (1939; rpt. New York: Oxford University Press, 1965), also defined Blake as a periodic anachronism, a writer with "the daring of Elizabethan metaphor" and "something very close to metaphysical wit" (p. 235).

6. The most vigorous recent case for the first is Marshall Brown, *Preromanticism* (Stanford: Stanford University Press, 1991), though Blake does not figure as part of it. Frye's own *Study of English Romanticism* (New York: Random House, 1968) more or less ignores Blake.

7. Frye, *Fearful Symmetry*, preface.

8. Bloom, *Blake's Apocalypse: A Study in Poetic Argument* (1963; rpt. Ithaca: Cornell University Press, 1970), p. 189.

9. Harold Bloom, *The Ringers in the Tower: Studies in the Romance Tradition* (1968; rpt. Chicago and London: University of Chicago Press, 1971), p. 17.

10. Morse Peckham, "Toward a Theory of Romanticism," *PMLA* 66 (1951), pp. 5–23. See also "Toward a Theory of Romanticism: II Reconsiderations," *Studies in Romanticism* 1 (1961), pp. 1–8, where the claim is made for the continued operation of Romanticism in/as modern culture.

11. Morse Peckham, *The Triumph of Romanticism: Collected Essays* (Columbia, SC: University of S. Carolina Press, 1970), p. 213; *Romanticism and Behavior: Collected Essays II* (Columbia, SC: University of S. Carolina Press, 1976), p. 28.

12. A. O. Lovejoy, "On the Discrimination of Romanticisms," *PMLA* 39 (1924), p. 241.

13. René Wellek, "The Concept of Romanticism in Literary History" (1949), *Concepts of Criticism*, ed. Stephen G. Nichols, pp. 128–98; see p. 161.

14. Wellek, "Romanticism Re-examined," *Concepts of Criticism*, ed. Stephen G. Nichols (New Haven and London: Yale University Press, 1963), p. 218.

15. M. H. Abrams, "English Romanticism: The Spirit of the Age," in Harold Bloom, ed., *Romanticism and Consciousness*, pp. 91–119.

16. M. H. Abrams, *Natural Supernaturalism: Tradition and Revolution in Romantic Literature* (New York: W. W. Norton, 1971), p. 257.

17. See Paul de Man, *Blindness and Insight: Essays in the Rhetoric of Contemporary Criticism* (New York: Oxford University Press, 1971), and Geoffrey H. Hartman, *Wordsworth's Poetry, 1787–1814* (New Haven and London: Yale University Press, 1964).

18. T. S. Eliot, *Selected Essays* (New York: Harcourt, Brace and World, 1960), pp. 278, 274.

19. Eliot, *Selected Essays*, p. 279.

20. F. R. Leavis, *The Common Pursuit* (New York: George W. Stewart, 1952), p. 188. The American scholar Hoxie Neale Fairchild, who is happy enough with the notion of "the Protestant origins of the romantic faith," nonetheless finds Blake incoherent in religious terms, and an example of "the decay of Nonconformity into a cult of human self-sufficiency": see *Religious Trends in English Poetry*, vol. III (New York: Columbia University Press, 1949), pp. 67, 135. Leavis's position had changed by 1971, when he decided that Blake – at least in his lyrics – had access to both high and popular culture, which he synthesized in a way that remains important. See "Justifying One's Valuation of Blake," *William Blake: Essays in Honour of Sir Geoffrey Keynes*, ed. Morton Paley and Michael Phillips (Oxford: Clarendon Press, 1973), pp. 66–85.

21. Raymond Williams, *Culture and Society, 1780–1950* (1958, rpt. Harmondsworth: Penguin, 1971), p. 49.

22. Thompson, *The Making of the English Working Class* (1963; rpt. Harmondsworth: Penguin, 1976), p. 56.

23. Marilyn Butler, *Romantics, Rebels and Reactionaries: English Literature and Its Background, 1760–1830* (Oxford and New York: Oxford University Press, 1981), p. 184. Similarly, the recent *Oxford Companion to the Romantic Age: British Culture, 1776–1832*, ed. Iain McCalman (Oxford: Oxford University Press, 1999), does not contain an essay on Romanticism. The editor's introduction discusses the term as too restrictive and circular, and useful principally for its "ambiguities and complexities" (p. 5).

24. I am thinking of such books as Robert Essick's *William Blake, Printmaker* (Princeton: Princeton University Press, 1980), Morris Eaves's *The Counter-Arts Conspiracy: Art and Industry in the Age of Blake* (Ithaca and London: Cornell University Press, 1992), and Joseph Viscomi's *Blake and the Idea of the Book* (Princeton: Princeton University Press, 1993). Efforts at "reading" word and image together were significantly refigured in W. J. T. Mitchell's *Blake's Composite Art* (Princeton: Princeton University Press, 1978).

25. E. H. Gombrich, *Norm and Form: Studies in the Art of the Renaissance* (London: Phaidon, 1966), p. 83.

26. Hugh Honour, *Romanticism* (New York: Harper and Row, 1979), pp. 11, 20.

27. William Vaughan, *Romantic Art* (New York and Toronto: Oxford University Press, 1978), pp. 72–82, 153–58.

28. John Barrell, *The Political Theory of Painting from Reynolds to Hazlitt: The Body of the Public* (London and New Haven: Yale University Press, 1986), pp. 222–57.

29. Peter Ackroyd, *Blake: A Biography* (1995; rpt. New York: Ballantine, 1997), p. 77.

30. Morris Eaves, "The Sister Arts in British Romanticism," in *The Cambridge Companion to British Romanticism*, ed. Stuart Curran (Cambridge: Cambridge University Press, 1993), pp. 236–69; p. 246.
31. See David Solkin, *Painting for Money: The Visual Arts and the Public Sphere in Eighteenth-Century England* (New Haven and London: Yale University Press, 1992), esp. pp. 190–214.
32. Stuart Curran, *Poetic Form and British Romanticism* (New York and Oxford: Oxford University Press, 1986), p. 178. Curran also comments astutely on Blake's pastoral, which takes the form of "a determined and intellectually rigorous antipastoral" (p. 111).

Further reading

Abrams, M. H. *The Mirror and the Lamp: Romantic Theory and the Critical Tradition*. Oxford: Oxford University Press, 1953.
Natural Supernaturalism: Tradition and Revolution in Romantic Literature. New York: W. W. Norton, 1971.
Barrell, John. *The Political Theory of Painting from Reynolds to Hazlitt: The Body of the Public*. London and New Haven: Yale University Press, 1986.
Bentley, G. E., Jr., ed. *William Blake: The Critical Heritage*. London and Boston: Routledge and Kegan Paul, 1975.
Bloom, Harold. *Blake's Apocalypse: A Study in Poetic Argument*. 1963, rpt. Ithaca: Cornell University Press, 1970.
Bloom, Harold, ed. *Romanticism and Consciousness: Essays in Criticism*. New York: W. W. Norton, 1970.
Butler, Marilyn. *Romantics, Rebels and Reactionaries: English Literature and Its Background, 1760–1830*. Oxford and New York: Oxford University Press, 1981.
Curran, Stuart. *Poetic Form and British Romanticism*. New York and Oxford: Oxford University Press, 1986.
Curran, Stuart, ed. *The Cambridge Companion to British Romanticism*. Cambridge: Cambridge University Press, 1993.
Eaves, Morris. *The Counter-Arts Conspiracy: Art and Industry in the Age of Blake*. Ithaca and London: Cornell University Press, 1992.
William Blake's Theory of Art. Princeton: Princeton University Press, 1982.
Eaves, Morris and Michael Fischer, eds. *Romanticism and Contemporary Criticism*. Ithaca and London: Cornell University Press, 1986.
Eliot, T. S. *Selected Essays*. New York: Harcourt, Brace and World, 1960.
Essick, Robert. *William Blake, Printmaker*. Princeton: Princeton University Press, 1980.
Frye, Northrop. *Fearful Symmetry: A Study of William Blake*. 1947, rpt. Boston: Beacon Press, 1962.
Hegel, G. W. F. *Hegel's Aesthetics: Lectures on Fine Art*. Trans. T. M. Knox. 2 vols. Oxford: Clarendon Press, 1975.
Lovejoy, A. O. "On the Discrimination of Romanticisms," *PMLA* 39 (1924): 229–53.
McGann, Jerome J. *The Romantic Ideology: A Critical Investigation*. Chicago and London: University of Chicago Press, 1983.

Mitchell, W. J. T. *Blake's Composite Art*. Princeton: Princeton University Press, 1978.

Solkin, David. *Painting for Money: The Visual Arts and the Public Sphere in Eighteenth-Century England*. New Haven and London: Yale University Press, 1992.

Thompson, E. P. *The Making of the English Working Class*. 1963, rpt. Harmondsworth: Penguin, 1976.

Viscomi, Joseph A. *Blake and the Idea of the Book*. Princeton: Princeton University Press, 1993.

Wellek, René. "Romanticism Re-examined." *Concepts of Criticism*. Ed. Stephen G. Nichols. New Haven and London: Yale University Press, 1963. 199–221.

Williams, Raymond. *Culture and Society, 1780–1950*. 1958, rpt. Harmondsworth: Penguin, 1971.

II
BLAKE'S WORKS

10

NELSON HILTON

Blake's early works

"If a method of Printing which combines the Painter and the Poet is a phenomenon worthy of public attention, provided that it exceeds in elegance all former methods, the Author is sure of his reward," especially when the resulting productions are "of equal magnitude and consequence" with those "of any age or country" (E 692). So maintained thirty-five-year-old William Blake in an etched prospectus addressed "To the Public" and dated 10 October 1793, two weeks before the execution of Marie Antoinette would dominate the London news. "Works now published and on Sale at Mr. Blake's, No. 13, Hercules Buildings, Lambeth" comprised two "Historical Engraving[s]" – *Job* and *Edward and Elinor* – two "small book[s] of engraving" – *The Gates of Paradise* and *The History of England* (now lost or never actually published) – and, extending this range of concern with matters national, spiritual, and educational in diverse media: *America, a Prophecy*; *Visions of the Daughters of Albion*; *The Book of Thel*; *The Marriage of Heaven and Hell*; *Songs of Innocence* and *Songs of Experience*. In his only recorded use of the phrase now synonymous with his greatest achievement, Blake described these latter six books as "in Illuminated Printing." The prices ranged from three to twelve shillings (almost a laborer's weekly wage). Not advertised were the author's two conventionally type-set volumes, *Poetical Sketches* of ten years before and *The French Revolution* of 1791; missing also from the prospectus were Blake's five-year-old first experiments in illuminated printing, *All Religions are One* and *There is No Natural Religion* and, understandably, two manuscripts: a burlesque set in an island in the moon and a verse narrative about a mythic patriarch, *Tiriel*. None of the works he then advertised, which include those best known today, were to find a large market, but Blake later commented that sales were "sufficient to have gained me great reputation as an Artist which was the chief thing Intended" (letter of 9 June 1818, E 771).

According to several accounts, Blake was already composing accomplished poetry in early adolescence, some of which appears in the volume *Poetical*

Sketches published by admiring friends when Blake was twenty-five. The *SONG* which begins "How sweet I roam'd from field to field" (E 412) is in particular dated to Blake's fourteenth year, an attribution perhaps over-determined by the poem's adolescent-worthy mix of incipient genital sexuality and culture seen as both agent of repression and means of expression. The amorous roamer tastes at will until he or she beholds the courtly romance icon "the prince of love" with "gardens fair" – but then, experiencing "blushing" and with "wings" whet for sweet doings of May, is shut in a "golden cage" by the still greater cultural cliché of "Phoebus," who *loves*, relates the speaker, "to hear me sing" while engaging in teasing sexual "sporting," "playing," and then "stretching out" of a now singular "golden wing" and, to conclude on the key-word, "mocks my loss of liberty." The poem thus signals Blake's lifelong preoccupation with the tension between the liberty of seemingly unlimited, unconscious potential – roaming, tasting "all" – and its loss in the very limitations of form and consciousness which occasion and enable through whole libraries the articulation of that loss (though "Los" the prophet is not named until 1794).

   This *SONG* opens a set of eight which seem to experiment with and finally reject lyric expression. The bravura metrics and sound-effects of *Mad Song* (E 415) offer a telling example of Blake's remarkable facility with the verbal materials of his art. Other "songs" toy with the sentimentalism and narcissistic melancholy of an "age of sensibility"; the concluding "Song," *To the Muses*, takes a dig at the chauvinist relocation of the Muses to England in *Rule Britannia* and turns "the conventional diction of much eighteenth-century poetry... on itself":[1] "The sound is forc'd, the notes are few!" The selection of songs makes but one part of a volume sub-titled "miscellaneous poems" whose overall effect conveys, as T. S. Eliot observes, "what the poems of a boy of genius ought to show, immense power of assimilation."[2] The opening suite of the four season poems has been seen to foreshadow Blake's later fascination with the "fourfold," as if each vividly sketched season prefigured one of the four zoic essences. That interpretation reflects at least the felt "visionary" intensity of the pieces; for despite the deliberately conventional subject matter and trope of personification, the poems "originate not so much in [Blake's] response to natural objects or events as in a conception that demands a heightened perception of reality"[3] – a profound difference in degree which becomes one of kind. The "heightening" is accomplished by a heady mixture of libidinal suggestiveness, vivid realization, and a language studded with allusions to and echoes of the King James Bible, Spenser, Milton, and others in a dense pattern of images and actions. By the end of *To Spring*, for instance, the "dewy locked" lover out of Song of Songs (5:2) longed for at the beginning has already arrived, dramatically outspeeding the invocation of a poet left to record that the land's "tresses *were* bound up for thee" (emphasis added) – with the deft implication that these now unbound "tresses" are trees' budding boughs (E 408). "To Winter" breaks with the conventional seasonal cycle in this sometimes despairing artist's vision that it has a distinct essence and no guarantee it will release its sway.

Other forms Blake sketches out are the Gothic and the historical ballad (*Fair Eleanor, Gwin*), the Spenserian stanza ("Imitation of Spen[s]er"), and, at greatest length, Shakespearean historical drama in a subject it left untreated – *King Edward the Third*. Here Blake seems to make an appearance in the guise of a serving man, William, notable for his "great ambition to know every thing" (E 434). The three concluding "sketches" present the experimenting artist's parting gage in the innovative form of prose poetry. The last, *Samson*, deliberately courts comparison with that most formally experimental of Milton's works, and by its narrative shifts of perspective and expectation serves notice of a talent able not only to imitate the old but to present new things in new ways – despite whatever reservations concerning the printed volume seem to have discouraged Blake's distribution of it.

Blake's evident ambition receives its most grandiose formulation in his manuscript known by its opening words as *An Island in the Moon*, where Quid, the character closest to the author, asserts that "Homer is bombast & Shakespeare is too wild & Milton has no feelings they might be easily out done" (E 455). Though definite identifications of actual figures behind the characters are few, the piece evidently satirizes the salon acquaintances who had taken up the inventive artist (and now co-proprietor of a printshop) and sponsored his *Poetical Sketches*. It repays attention on many levels, not least for the revelation that "of all the Romantic poets, Blake had the most fully developed sense of humor,"[4] one sometimes exercised at the reader's expense. After relating how "Mr Inflammable Gass . . . set his hair all in a flame & ran about the room," the author confides a lesson to be kept in mind even through *Jerusalem*, "No No he did not I was only making a fool of you" (E 453). Characters' play with language and especially names – "Hang names . . . whats Pharoh better than Phebus," "An Easy of Huming Understanding by John Lookye" – announces an inveterate tendency (E 452, 456).

Sometimes the humor comes at the expense of the contrived and empty productions of the contemporary culture, as in the parodic encomium on "matrimony's golden cage" or the deformation of a popular song's sappy refrain:

A bleating flock, an humble Cot.
Of simple food a Store,
These are a blest, unenvy'd Lot. –
We ask the Gods no more

into the self-mocking refrain:

Honour & Genius is all I ask
And I ask the Gods no more[5]

In jest or not, references to envy and ambition recur insistently. At times, however, the humor drops away to reveal more profound concerns – as when, in the midst of "another merry meeting," one character sings what will in four years appear in *Songs of Innocence* as *Holy Thursday*, after which (half-recalling Rev. 8:1) "all sat quiet for a quarter of an hour." Two more future songs follow, including the later song of innocence *Little Boy Lost*, attributed finally to Quid after three manuscript alterations, as if the death of the author's father some months before in July 1784 was still difficult to confront even through a fiction ("O speak father speak to your little boy / Or else I shall be lost" [E 463]).

In the final paragraph Quid speaks abruptly about "Illuminating the Manuscript," a process which he relates to a new publishing scheme that would have "all the writing Engraved instead of Printing & at every other leaf a high finished print" (E 465). While this hardly fits the relief-etched method which mixes writing with design that Blake was soon to initiate, it may suggest what he intended for *Tiriel*. Together with its satiric and verbally exuberant predecessor, this manuscript is the early work most neglected but most revealing of Blake's overarching ambition to assert his "original & primitive" ways (letter of 10 January 1803, E 724). Once "King of the West," Tiriel has been deposed by his sons, and the piece opens with his having returned before the palace to make them witness the death of his wife and their mother, Myratana, and to curse them. He then sets off on a journey which takes him to the vales of his parents Har and Heva and their guardian Mnetha. Wandering on, Tiriel encounters in the wilderness his brother Ijim, and is borne before his sons whom he curses again, now with real effect, then forces his surviving daughter Hela to lead him again through the wilderness of another brother, Zazel, back to Har and Heva whom he curses and also himself and then dies. The poetic narrative in old-fashioned fourteen beat lines is only half of *Tiriel*, for Blake also finished twelve accompanying drawings, more than enough to have one "at every other leaf." These illustrations make plain the syncretic nature of the work: in the first, Tiriel supports the dying Myratana while the sons look on in a portico framed by Greek columns but with prominent Egyptian pyramids in the distance, while in another, depicting the aged "Har and Heva Bathing," Blake's design "quotes" a recent composition depicting "Zeus and Hera" by the painter James Barry whom he much admired. As one looks and listens more closely, the story turns into a prototypical Blakean "myth-mash" composite of classic narratives and more. A revealing moment occurs early on as Heva tells Tiriel that "we have many sports to shew thee & many songs to sing / And after dinner we will walk into the cage of Har" (E 279). Hearing "Har sing in the great cage" (recalling the speaker of "How sweet...") is reiterated as an attraction. Such imagery has long led some readers to feel that *Tiriel* suggests in part a commentary on the state of the arts in an age which could conceive of poetry as a golden structure built with "harmony of words, harmony of numbers" (John Dryden) and which viewed the annual art exhibition of the Royal Academy – including submissions by Blake in 1784 and 1785 – in the "Great Room." Tiriel's final speech seems to stress the point when, after describing the "weak infant...compelld to number footsteps" the meter shrinks for one line into monotonous but fashionable blank verse to crawl through the feet of "the drone" it condemns: "And *when* | the *drone* | has *reachd* | his *crawl* | ing *length*" (E 285). Exchanging the present for the past, *Tiriel* views late eighteenth-century English artistic material and practice as an impotent enterprise with nothing left but to curse its stultifying ethos of decorum and "improvement." Five years later Blake still wonders "what is the material world, and is it dead?" (*Europe* iii, E 60), but *Tiriel* shows already the dead-end of art compelled "to humble the immortal spirit" (E 285).

Around the same time Blake extensively annotated Johann Caspar Lavater's *Aphorisms on Man*, a work translated by an acquaintance who was to become increasingly close to Blake, the polymath artist Henry Fuseli, who also designed the frontispiece Blake engraved. The book recommended such annotating to create a kind of personality summary to be shared with friends and results in a unique opportunity to overhear Blake opining, "I hate scarce smiles I love laughing" (E 585) or, more profoundly, "our Lord is the word of God & every thing on earth is the word of God & in its essence is God" (E 599). In the final annotation Blake joins himself with those "who are philosophers" and thus aware that "what the laws of Kings & Priests have calld Vice" is not to be confused with "the vicious propensity" of "omissions of intellect springing from poverty" (E 601). His own philosophical inclinations also appear about this time in two aphoristic tractates which represent Blake's first, halting, postage-stamp-size experiments with relief-etched "illuminated printing." Both concern religion, one to declare that *ALL RELIGIONS are ONE*, the other that *THERE is NO*

NATURAL RELIGION. Summarized, both assume "all knowledge must derive from some source" but "certain kinds of knowledge are not attributable
either to experience or to reason," consequently there must be some other
source of knowledge;[6] this Blake identifies as "the Poetic or Prophetic
Character" of "an universal Poetic Genius" (E 3, 1).

Though it may not have preceded *Songs of Innocence* in the watershed
year of 1789, *The Book of Thel* has an economy which has led editors to
give it precedence despite the larger size of its plates. As with *Tiriel*, the action is quickly summarized: the virgin heroine laments her transience and is
answered in turn by a lily, a cloud, and a clod of clay who, in the final plate,
enables Thel to enter "the land unknown" from which, at the conclusion,
she flees back to *Tiriel*'s "vales of Har." However, many allusive suggestions
give *Thel* a surfeit of allegorical possibilities, as if Blake intended to create
a formula whose product varies according to the assumptions brought to
it. The title-page design illustrates this possibility with a "bi-stable" design
which – depending on the scale assumed by the viewer – offers either a scene
with an over-arching willow and life-sized pastoral heroine or, switching
the frame, a small tombstone graven with the work's title and an accompanying fairy-sized shepherdess (Fig. 26). The flowers and accompanying
figures constitute the visual conundrum as the viewer's attempt to make
sense of them leads instead to the discovery of two quite distinct and incompatible perspectives, neither of which resolves the graphic anomaly. So too
the first line describes Thel as one of "[t]he daughters of Mne Seraphim," a
name "myth-mashing" the Greek *Mnemosyne*, mother of the muses, and the
Hebrew angelic order of *Seraphim*. Thel confirms the problematic nature of
reference as her first speech unfolds nine successive similes in an attempt to
define herself:

> Thel is *like a* watry bow. and *like a* parting cloud.
> *Like a* reflection in a glass...
> ... *like a* smile upon an infants face
> (pl. 1, E 3 [emphasis added])

A related allegory of allegories dated the same year foregrounds a like concern with figuration by naming its heroine "Lyca" ("The Little Girl Lost"
and "The Little Girl Found" in *Songs of Innocence*).

Blake's interest in such free-floating allegory may in part reflect his acquaintance with Thomas Taylor, known as "the Platonist" for his fascination with Platonic and neo-Platonic philosophy. In 1789 Taylor published his
translation and commentary on Porphyry's elaborate allegorical exegesis of
a passage in Homer, "Concerning the Cave of the Nymphs," which describes
a "northern gate" for souls descending to earth similar to that which Thel
crosses for the altered-scale climax of her journey. Becoming a type of the

Figure 26 *The Book of Thel*, title page. Copy O.

"mole" recommended in the epigraph for its knowledge of "the pit," Thel encounters a kind of collective unconscious reality "where the fibrous roots / Of every heart on earth infixes deep its restless twists." She waits "oft beside a dewy grave" and, true to her title-page tombstone, listens "to the voices of the ground, / Till to her own grave plot she came, & there she sat down" to hear a "voice of sorrow breathed from the hollow pit" (pl. 6, E 6). Amid various possibilities, perhaps not least is that of Thel come to visit the virgin plots or plates of her book, calligraphed with the author–artist's etching "ground" in an early step toward revealing her (textual) body. At any event, the "voice of sorrow" utters a host of pseudo-courtly questions concerning the treachery of the senses which culminate in one English translation of Thel's Greek-rooted name: "Why a little curtain of flesh on the bed of our *desire?*" (pl. 6, E 6, emphasis added). The given name stressed on the title page ("The Author & Printer Willm Blake"), which encompasses another English translation of her name, "will," opens Thel's book as a meditation on the unending question as to the will and desire of the artist. Thel remarks to the cloud how in one hour it shall fade away and

> Then we shall seek thee but not find; ah Thel is like to thee.
> I pass away. yet I complain, and no one hears my voice.
>
> (pl. 3, E 4)

Carrying a latent self-comparison to Jesus, who says that "Ye shall seek me, and shall not find me" (John 7:34), Thel's lament resonates with Blake's self-description as "The voice of one crying in the wilderness" in the first plate of *ALL RELIGIONS are ONE* (an invocation of Isaiah 40:3 and its repetition in all the Gospels).

Songs of Innocence, also dated 1789, needs first to be approached as its own integral work, evidently created and for a few years published without thought of the later *Songs of Experience.* A collection of great metrical sophistication, it seems intended not so much for children as for those interested in that most influential of cultural practices much debated by the eighteenth century, the education of children. John Locke's arguments for the rational education of children and Jean-Jacques Rousseau's belief in the child's original goodness represent the century's two new alternatives to the pervasive Calvinist legacy of original sin in a contest whose high social stakes occasioned a proliferating variety of literature for children and for their teachers. The title-page image of a nurse or mother instructing a young boy and girl from a book epitomizes a concern throughout the collection with various such overt or implicit "scenes of instruction." Indeed, the conclusion of the work's *Introduction* highlights the fact that a child can only access or hear the "happy songs" through the uncertain medium of particular readers' voices and understandings, uncertainties of which the child is in no sense aware.

The collection may be imagined as a series of vignettes concerning the psyche's birth into language and protracted journey toward fuller awareness of the world of signs and sense exemplified and conveyed primarily by language. So the underlying narrative of the *Introduction* tells of individual and cultural progression from song as pure sound to a song of words, posing the question along the way of how this transformed object is "the same" as the other. Vocalization then gives way to written words, with the accompanying vanishing of whatever inspired the initial sound and the foregrounding of the "I" who pens it. This "I" – itself, like all deictics (for example, pronouns, demonstratives) a particularly curious effect of language whose reference depends upon its user – becomes literally the pipe or conduit by which the written words of the song reach the reader who, *playing* the "I," "reinspires" them so that "[e]very child may joy to hear." While readers today may think of the song's "glee" as invoking an aspect of childlike, joyful abandon, "glee" was more familiar to Blake as a genre of multi-part song so popular that it prompted the formation of numerous "Glee Clubs" in his lifetime. The intimation that "songs of pleasant glee" stipulates several different voices singing jointly from different degrees of literacy makes a useful *caveat* for all who would seek a single interpretation.

Printed editions of Blake make it easy to overlook the many different sequences in which *Songs* are presented – if the poems offer a "series of vignettes," Blake has the unsettling habit of re-shuffling them into quite different arrangements. By way of a modern analogy, however, one may note the object-relations psychoanalytic model for early development as the passage through a series of psychological states or "positions," none of which are left behind but rather accrete as a set of unconscious memories any one of which may at any time be affecting mood and consciousness in accordance with the frequently fluctuating age of one's childish "inner sense." Such an analogy may help explain why *Infant Joy*, very often found as the "vignette" argument would suppose early in the collection, may also be found toward the end (as in most printed versions) and sometimes middle. The song begins, most improbably, with a speaker who claims to have no name and to be but two days old. The reader may come subsequently to feel that these must be the projected thoughts of an infant's mother who assumes, as it were, both sides of a dialogue in the necessary first move initiating the *in-fans* or "unspeaking" (Latin) to "naming" and "calling." By custom, infants were baptized – with the accompanying legal recording of a name – on the third day after birth, so the poem's subject still exists in that exceptional and difficult-to-articulate space outside of official language. Perhaps, the poem may suggest, such is the unspeaking and unspeakable source of joy. While as an artist Blake deals continually with the creation of form, there is always the sense – as in *Thel*'s "voices of the ground" – that form or materialization carries a sorrowful burden of being never adequate to the whole.

The Lamb advances us to a position on the gradient of language acquisition from which the innocent can make simple inferences but cannot grasp figurative language. The overt scene of instruction presents the child's catechizing a lamb, but that action together with some evident allusions indicates another, antecedent scene where the young child – also a "lamb" in colloquial contemporary endearment – was somewhat similarly instructed concerning the *Agnus Dei* or Lamb of God. Singers of this particular glee can thus see parts for "the lamb" as young sheep, young child, Son of God and a text itself "called by his name." At the poem's end, in a move Blake sets up repeatedly, the bottom drops away, here via the uncanny exact repetition of a blessing which, coming directly after the culminating first-person plural ("We are called"), has the effect of drawing the focus back from that scene to an observer – or "maker," "poet" – potentially powerful enough to call into being and bless the "Little Lamb God" just seen:

> Little Lamb God bless you.
> Little Lamb God bless you.

With *The Little Black Boy* and *The Chimney Sweeper* the ubiquitous ideological use of language to rationalize instruction particularly oppressive for children moves to the fore. Another incarnation of the "lamb," "little Tom Dacre" treasures up the slightly older sweep's solicitous nonsense that soot cannot now spoil his white hair and cherishes it into a wish-fulfilling dream of angelic assurance that "if he'd be a good boy, / He'd have God for his father & never want joy." And, the poem insists, such an imaginary non-sequitur has the authentically real effect of making Tom "happy & warm" despite the cold morning. Again the conclusion opens out rather than ties up as the frame narrator – old enough to care for Tom as an other but still so young as to narrate largely by simple conjunctions – voices a conclusion which may be heard as at once innocent (literally, "free from harm"); ignorant, given the debilitated end which awaited sweepers like Tom and himself; and apocalyptically threatening the poem's art-purchasing, house-possessing ("your chimneys") readers with the mob vengeance of "thousands of sweepers Dick, Joe, Ned & Jack." "So if all do their duty, they need not fear harm" thus invokes multiple contexts, one of which would require nothing less than a complete change of the reader's perspective.

Influenced perhaps by pronunciation of his name, Blake seems to identify particularly with "black." The little black boy receives one of the collection's most intimate "scenes of instruction" from an actual mother whose kisses mingle emphatically with what she said ("kis*sed* me"). The mother's lesson turns on the idea that "we are put on earth a little space" in order to learn – in a remarkable formulation – "to bear the beams of love" and, with that, the ultimate inconsequence of racial coloring. "Beams of love" seems conventional enough (God shines with them in Isaac Watts's immensely popular

Hymns for Children), but that one must "learn to bear" them hints at their implication in a heavy ideological double-cross. Parting shots here are the omitted apostrophe which makes the black boy echo conventional malediction in imagining "Ill shade him," even as he fantasizes unreal "silver hair" for the white boy and, pathetically, the concluding wan hope that he will finally "be like him and he will then love me."

A number of songs are situated further along the language-awareness gradient and perilously close to experience of the self's linguistic constitution. These include *On Another's Sorrow*, which can be seen as enacting the ultimate stage of denial ("No no never... / Never never...") to defend against its real occasion, (not "Another's sorrow," but) "our grief.../...our grief," and several poems which a few years later were relocated away from *Innocence*: the two poems about "Lyca," already mentioned, which, like a pure allegory, resist translation to other words though touching pretty clearly on love, sex, adolescence, parenting, loss, prophecy, Demeter, Persephone, Jesus, and the poet's self-reference; *The School Boy*, whose sincerity evaporates in the elaborate artificiality of his plea to be released from "learnings bower"; and *The Voice of the Ancient Bard*, whose scene of instruction rends innocent faith in unmediated signification with its self-interested attack on other instructors.

More than perhaps any other of his works, *The Marriage of Heaven and Hell* played a central role in the mid-Victorian re-invention of Blake and has benefitted ever since from that positioning. The poet Algernon Swinburne's 1868 critical study found it "the greatest of all [Blake's] books...about the greatest produced by the eighteenth century in the line of high poetry and spiritual speculation,"[7] and today's reader can still relish the energy and verve of a text which sets out to raise a docile and gullible world "into a perception of the infinite." The evident case and point for Blake was his own recent infatuation with the work of Emanuel Swedenborg, ended through first-hand observation of the same dull institutional round at the new Swedenborgian Church and a more extended reading of the teacher's quickly predictable "correspondences" and tiresome "memorable relations." With the fervor of the recently undeceived, Blake ties together titles of two Swedenborgian works to derive one certain to offend the latest "true" religion – indeed, the final swash after *Marriage* which serves to center it on the page can be seen as marking a still more scandalous plural "*S*."[8]

The term "satire" is often used to describe *The Marriage*[*S*], whose potpourri of "Argument," prose, "Memorable Fancies," Proverbs, "Notes," and "A Song" recalls that term's derivation from Latin *satura*, a "medley" or "mixed dish": one genre for the imaginative artist is oppression. The satire focuses on the limitations of intellect and perception occasioned by our forgetting the nature of language and accepting the imposition of supposed teachers. An "Argument," for instance, should make things more evident (according to its etymology) and was thus the term adopted by Milton for the innovative short prose summary he prefixed to each book of *Paradise Lost*. In a gesture worthy of his earlier satire ("I was only making a fool of you"), Blake's free-verse before prose "Argument" clarifies little – unless the curious but thrice-emphasized "perilous path" invokes those "perilous paths the race of poets rove" that Blake would have encountered in a translation of Theocritus. "The just man" of the Argument who now "rages in the wilds" might thus reincarnate "the true Man" or "Poetic Genius" as yet another avatar of "one crying in the Wilderness."

The narrator begins by declaring that "Without Contraries is no progression" and offering examples from the physical world ("Attraction" and "Repulsion" figure in Newtonian dynamics) and individual psychology. These elemental forces have been recategorized into "what the religious call Good & Evil." Furthermore, according to "The voice of the Devil," the varying history of such reification can be read in *Paradise Lost* where "Reason is call'd Messiah," though "in the Book of Job Milton's Messiah is call'd Satan." The narrator later reminds us that the text we read does not escape the imposition it points to by reporting Ezekiel's comment that "we of Israel taught that the Poetic Genius (as you now call it) was the first principle." So *The Marriage* strives to take us past "apparent surfaces" of what something "is called" to an awareness of an "infernal" or contrary wisdom, method, and sense which undermine Swedenborg's pedestrian concern for the "internal" or "corresponding" sense of scripture. Varying the "what is called" motif, the narrator relates how he gathered some Proverbs while "walking among the fires of hell, delighted with the enjoyments of Genius; which to Angels look like torment and insanity" (*MHH* 5, E 35). Returning home "on the abyss of the five senses," his imagery opens another recurrent strand of Blake's discourse with reference to the practice of etching. On the shiny, angled metal plate or "flat sided steep" he sees reflected "a mighty Devil folded in black clouds" who "with corroding fires" writes a "sentence now percieved by the minds of men, & read by them on earth":

> How do you know but ev'ry Bird that cuts the airy way,
> Is an immense world of delight, clos'd by your senses five?
>
> (pl. 5, E 35)

Such knowledge comes, *Marriage* suggests, with recognition of the ultimate contrary to the errors of "All Bibles or sacred codes": "Energy is Eternal Delight."

As one might expect, the "Proverbs of Hell" run contrary to the generic notion of pithy, folk-authored formations of conventional prudence and morality. Blake's aphoristic genius creates what might be thought of as an inter-related collection of "koans" – those zen word-viruses or instructional devices designed to cut through muddied perceptions of everyday language. They attempt to exemplify, as the concluding proverb proposes, how "Truth can never be told so as to be understood, and not be believ'd." This formulation unpacks the connection of "belief" with "truth" (as in its cognates "troth" and "trust"), to circle around the point that "understanding" is already a matter of belief (since "Every thing possible to be believ'd is an image of truth."). The proverb is still more arresting in Blake's calligraphy where (printed transcriptions notwithstanding) commas and periods are sometimes with apparent deliberation indistinguishable, so that the proverb begins by informing us that "Truth can never be told so as to be understood." – as if truth, like joy, exists beyond the reach of words – before, reading on, we "understand" that this full stop "." may be a pausing "," and so believe we grasp the truth proposed. Blake plays constantly on such minute particulars of syntax and perception ("What is now proved was once. only imagin'd." confirms existence imagined or proved as identical except in time). "Sooner murder an infant in its cradle than nurse unacted desires," still shocks though it does little more than rephrase the early proverb that "He who desires but acts not, breeds pestilence" (with a legible comma). To "nurse" (the crucial word) unacted desires entails already the suicidal termination of possible "infant joys"; what disturbs most here, perhaps, is the proverb-maker's emphatic rhetoric to insist on individual response-ability to and for desire. The "desire of raising other men into a perception of the infinite," for instance, can carry its own unique and formidable responsibilities, as the narrator learns from Ezekiel (pl. 12, E 39).

Alternating "Memorable Fancies" and prose, the narrator, usually emphasizing a first-person involvement, relates various accounts and instances of the struggle between the institutionalized, "angelic" perspective of the media-controlling status-quo and the contesting, energetic, visionary perception of those artists outcast as "devils." While the yin-yang nature of the overall economy is clear, the narrator's sympathies show themselves through a discussion with the prophets, a justification for relief-etching or "printing in the infernal method, by corrosives, which in Hell are salutary and medicinal," the ability to counter an angelic "phantasy" of abjection with one of energetic co-existence, an exposition of unoriginal Swedenborg's "conceited notions," and, finally, the actual "conversion" of an angelic reader-surrogate. In one striking scene the narrator visits "a Printing house in Hell" and reports on the activities in a series of chambers which represent "the method in which Knowledge is transmitted from generation to generation." The first – literalizing famous statements by Locke and Dr. Johnson – shows the "clearing away the rubbish" of old conceptions. After a chamber of adornment comes another with "an Eagle with wings and feathers of air, he caused the inside of the cave to be infinite," an epitome of Blake's attempt by "image" to jump-start the reader's imagination. Subsequent chambers show metals taken from the infinite cave melted like lead for type into "living fluid" and, impossibly, "cast" by "Unnam'd forms" reminiscent of the printer's type-holding "formes" "into the expanse" where they "took the forms of books." The name or form of any great book, *The Marriage* knows as well as Milton's print-celebrating *Areopagitica*, embodies the metamorphosed "pretious life-blood of a master spirit, imbalm'd and treasur'd up on purpose to a life beyond life."[9]

The narrator concludes his participation in the book with the bold declaration that "I have also: The Bible of Hell: which the world shall have whether they will or no" and an assertion of necessary difference, "One Law for the Lion & Ox is Oppression." Sometime in 1790, the evident date for most if not all of *The Marriage*, Blake moved across the Thames to the suburb of Lambeth where he would live until 1800, and for this reason his early illuminated work is sometimes referred to collectively as "the Lambeth books." But the narrator's assertion has also given rise to an alternative title, "The Bible of Hell," the truest name for Blake's ambitious project. Itself a quasi-biblical variety in miniature, *The Marriage* ends with *A Song of Liberty*, whose lines seem to caption an invisible emblem book that outlines a Blakean myth of revolution in which "the new born wonder" or fiery force later named "Orc" suffers temporary defeat by a jealous "starry king" before a final triumph where "Empire is no more." The Song's "Chorus" reasserts the over-riding interpretative principle of questioning what we are taught to call things: those whom the Priest "calls free" should not set our boundaries nor "pale religious letchery call that virginity, that wishes but acts not!" (pl. 25, E 44–45).

For Blake, even more than for his contemporaries, the French Revolution seems to have been a personal event. In one "Memorable Fancy" the narrator, surrounded by insistent references to "black," sees "Leviathan" advancing "with all the fury of a spiritual existence" from "the east, distant about three degrees" – degrees which here refer not so much to Swedenborg's three as to the units of longitude which separated London from the ferment of revolutionary Paris. In 1791 Blake turned more directly to that recent history with *The French Revolution. A Poem, In Seven Books*. Only one copy of the first book survives, however, which suggests it was type-set by the publisher, Blake's sometime employer Joseph Johnson, for proof purposes rather than for publication. In over 300 lines of striking and novel anapestic septenary meter Blake turns the weeks leading up to the day after the fall of the Bastille into a visionary drama of monarchical "angels" and republican "devils" playing for real stakes in an updated Book of Revelation. With the exception of an allegorically described Bastille given towers and dens bearing names like "Religion," "Order," and "Darkness," the focus shifts between the King and his reactionary council (reminiscent of Milton's Satanic politicians) "each conversing with woes" and the people's assembly (E 286), meeting "like spirits of fire in the beautiful / Porches of the Sun" (E 288). Blake limits his personae to a few familiar names save for an allusive one he invents, "the ancientest Peer, Duke of Burgundy" (E 289), to satirize the celebrated Edmund Burke's recent conservative manifesto, *Reflections on the Revolution in France* (November 1790), and its lament that "the age of chivalry is gone." Another image intimates Blake's awareness of Adam Smith's fateful metaphor of "the invisible hand" for the emerging market economy as the King's scepter becomes "too heavy for mortal grasp. No more / To be swayed by visible hand" (E 286). Despite the haunting and emphatic presence of the "spirits of the dead," "The enormous dead," no one dies to achieve the happy prospect at the poem's conclusion. Such wishful thinking may have argued against publication as much as the unheard-of meter.

For Children: The Gates of Paradise, the small book of seventeen engraved designs published by Blake "and J. Johnson" in 1793, reminds us how profoundly images and words relate for Blake. Beginning with a frontispiece exclaiming "What is Man!" for the design of a figure with Blake-like features asleep in a cocoon, the sequence moves through sixteen representative states or stages of the human life-journey, including at the outset the four elements and ending past "Death's Door." Only at plate 13 does the cycle seem to break with the image of a family confronting the spirit of their recently deceased patriarch over the heading "Fear & Hope are – Vision."

Such a twofold ground ramifies through *VISIONS of the Daughters of Albion*, also dated 1793. It seems to concern, on the one hand, the pressing issues of slavery and the contemporary condition of women and, on the other, the uncertain personal perspective intimated in the epigraph of an eye seeing more than the heart knows, perhaps with special regard to Mary Wollstonecraft as both daring author of *Vindication of the Rights of Woman*, just published by Johnson, and victim of a neurotic infatuation with Blake's friend Fuseli. A number of Fuseli's designs and his impressive classical learning seem to be invoked by *Visions*, which can be seen as a kind of Greek tragedy whose three characters deliver set speeches more or less unheard and at cross-purposes with each other. The heroine Oothoon, whose name derives from Blake's reading of Ossian, dominates the poem's second half, and while her memorable lines about sexual freedom have impressed generations of a largely male audience ("Take thy bliss O Man!/And sweet shall be thy taste & sweet thy infant joys renew!" [pl. 6, E 49]), one can hardly fail to observe that in a no-win situation the achievement of vision tragically destroys her. That "[t]he Daughters of Albion hear her woes, & eccho back her sighs" serves choral notice of the unresolved, ongoing social dimension of the tragedy (pl. 8, E 51).

At some point after *The Marriage* Blake's thinking about "contraries" led him to create a series of poems which might respond to "innocence" as "Songs of Experience" and with it make a collection "Shewing the Two Contrary States of the Human Soul." The subtitle emphasizes "two" states, but these necessarily triangulate a third, unnamed perspective or state – the author's, at a minimum – which permits them to be described. Blake confirms as much in a later note which reads:

> Unorganizd Innocence, An Impossibility
> Innocence dwells with Wisdom but never with Ignorance
> (textual notes, E 838)

One ready device was to create some poems for "experience" which share the same titles as ones in innocence – or even, as in the case of *Nurse's Song* and *NURSES Song*, the same opening line. Such identical titles highlight what *Innocence* and *The Marriage* make plain, the relativity of perception to a potentially infinite context or frame of reference ("A fool sees not the same tree that a wise man sees"). The themes of desire and language discovery take a depressing swerve into finitude with *Experience*'s presentation of numerous speakers who, content with their acquisition of basic communication skills, "[i]n ignorance...view a small portion & think that All" (*J* 65, E 216). This lack of awareness applies especially to those supposed to know all, like "the Bard" who introduces *Experience* (pl. 30, E 18). Authoritative tones command, "Hear the voice of the Bard!", and most readers are so acquiescing that when "That might controll" arrives in the eighth line with three possible referents ("the lapsed Soul," "The Holy Word," the bard's voice) to solicit the reader's syntax-controlling power, "that might" goes unexercised. Other confusions multiply, and looking at the design, one finds that the "starry floor," far from "giv'n...till the break of day," is "barred" by the portentous injunctions and allusions written on a cloud. To attend truly to prophetic utterance may involve freeing the reader to hear instead the voice of "the barred" – the oppressed, the outcast, the thousands of sweepers crying "'weep 'weep" – and to see through the endless "errors of acquired folly" (anno. Lavater, E 600). *EARTH'S Answer*, which follows the *Introduction*, makes it clear that the Bard's is only one point of view.

The songs are dramatic and stage as much the consciousness of the speaker as the object spoken to or about. One should use the script to ponder what context could generate its speaker. What sort of mind would invoke "The invisible worm, / That flies through the night" (*The SICK ROSE*); include self-reference in six out of eight lines (*My Pretty Rose Tree*); or refer to a chimney sweeper as a "black thing" (*The Chimney Sweeper*)? *London* and *The Tyger* call for special attention – if the *Songs* are about learning language, these constitute the diploma-pieces. Each has occasioned voluminous commentary which cannot begin to be summarized here. *London*'s astonishing wager bets all on a scene of instruction where either the speaker is crazy (hearing so many voices) or the reader must acknowledge blindness and deafness before some heretofore unperceived pervasive ordering of social existence. Consequently the poem hinges on its ability to get us to hear and see or, minimally, admit as possible new marks and signs of a synaesthetic reality – how cries make white black churches, how sighs run down as blood on palace walls – and neatly enacts its parable via initial letters of the third stanza, where we see the verb insisted on elsewhere: "How . . . / Every . . . / And . . . / Runs . . .". The poem's termination with the sight *and* sound rhyme "hearse" (*hear-see*) asserts again the need to cleanse the doors of perception to grasp "the marriage[s]" of meaning and words, heaven and hell. As for *The Tyger*, it could have been spelled, as Blake does elsewhere, with an "i" except that it is not about a "tiger" any more than *The Lamb*, on whose reverse it is etched, concerns a young sheep. The famous first line insists immediately on a confrontation with metaphor. Or is it rather a metaphor of metaphors – involving neither what you call a "tiger" nor what you call "burning" nor the "roaring" energy of a stellar body (cf. *BL* 5:27 ff., E 94) but the very power of language to call into being and frame alternative worlds? The power of questions to reveal assumptions of a questioner appears unquestioned – unless, jumping frames of reference, one seeks an answer from the illustration, where a nonplussed tiger appears more than a little anxious under such demanding language and the responding desires to answer which have helped make *The Tyger* the most anthologized poem in English. If we imagine it as wondering who, really, is "only making a fool of you," the caricatured outline of the artist's face incorporated into the tree (copy U, Fig. 27 [parallel to the first stanza]) suggests one who might smile at the possibility.

If our folly is to study and return to Blake's early works, which include many pictures and notebook lyrics not mentioned here, we should, according to one Proverb, by persisting soon become wise – or convinced at least that while their ways defy straightforward explication, such "crooked roads without Improvement, are roads of Genius" (*MHH* 10, E 38).

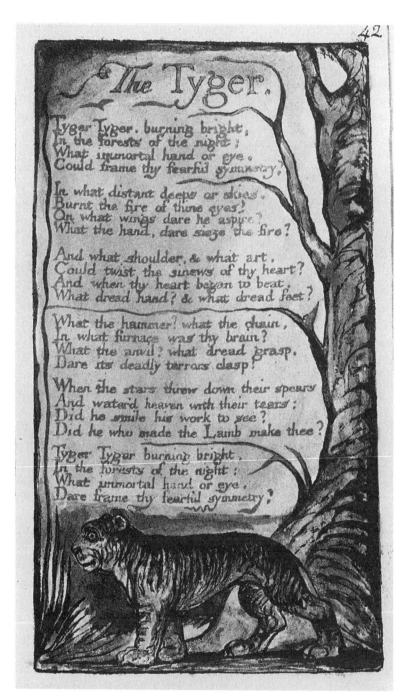

Figure 27 *The Tyger* (*SIE*). Copy U.

Notes

1. Harold Bloom, *Blake's Apocalypse: A Study in Poetic Argument* (1963; Ithaca: Cornell University Press, 1970), p. 21.
2. T. S. Eliot, "William Blake" (1920), *Selected Essays*, 3rd edn. (London: Faber and Faber, 1951), p. 318.
3. Robert Gleckner, *Blake's Prelude*: Poetical Sketches (Baltimore: Johns Hopkins University Press, 1982), p. 68.
4. E. D. Hirsch Jr., *Innocence and Experience: An Introduction to Blake* (New Haven: Yale University Press, 1964), p. 75.
5. E 452; cf. Blake's *An Island in the Moon*, ed. Michael Phillips (Cambridge: Cambridge University Press with the Institute of Traditional Science, 1987), p. 74.
6. Sheila A. Spector, *"Glorious Incomprehensible": The Development of Blake's Kabbalistic Language* (Lewisburg, PA: Bucknell University Press, 2001), p. 58.
7. Algernon Charles Swinburne, *William Blake: A Critical Essay* (1868; New York: Dutton, 1906), pp. 226–27.
8. Michael J. Tolley, "Marriages in Heaven and Hell: Blake's Enigmatic Title-Page," *Symposium on Romanticism*, ed. Deirdre Coleman and Peter Otto (Adelaide: Centre for British Studies, 1990), p. 12.
9. John Milton, *Areopagitica, The Prose of John Milton*, ed. J. Max Patrick (Garden City, NY: Anchor Books, 1967), p. 272.

Further reading

Blake, William. *The Early Illuminated Books*. Ed. Morris Eaves, Robert N. Essick, and Joseph Viscomi. Princeton: William Blake Trust/Princeton University Press, 1993.
An Island in the Moon. Ed. Michael Phillips. Cambridge: Cambridge University Press with the Institute of Traditional Science, 1987.
Songs of Innocence and of Experience. Ed. Andrew Lincoln. Princeton: William Blake Trust/Princeton University Press, 1991.
Tiriel. Ed. G. E. Bentley, Jr. Oxford: Clarendon Press, 1967.
Crisman, William. "Songs Named 'Song' and the Bind of Self-Conscious Lyricism in Blake." *ELH* 61 (1994): 619–33.
Ferber, Michael. *The Poetry of William Blake*. Penguin Critical Studies. London: Penguin Books, 1991.
Gillham, D. G. *Blake's Contrary States: The* Songs of Innocence and of Experience *as Dramatic Poems*. Cambridge: Cambridge University Press, 1966.
Gleckner, Robert. *Blake's Prelude: Poetical Sketches*. Baltimore: Johns Hopkins University Press, 1982.
Glen, Heather. *Vision and Disillusionment: Blake's* Songs *and Wordsworth's* Lyrical Ballads. Cambridge: Cambridge University Press, 1983.
Hilton, Nelson, et al. *Blake's* Songs of Innocence and of Experience: *Graphical Hypertext*. http://www.english.uga.edu/wblake (includes additional bibliography and further readings).
Leader, Zachary. *Reading Blake's* Songs. Boston: Routledge & Kegan Paul, 1982.
Paley, Morton. " 'A New Heaven is Begun': William Blake and Swedenborgianism." *Blake/An Illustrated Quarterly* 13 (1979): 64–90.

I I

ANDREW LINCOLN

From *America* to *The Four Zoas*

Like some other radicals in the 1790s, Blake saw the American revolution as igniting a process of liberation that would sweep around the globe, exploding repressive superstitions and causing despotic governments to crumble. Some envisaged this process as a fulfillment of the enlightenment that would establish universally acceptable principles of justice based on reason rather than on corrupt tradition. But Blake's antinomianism led him to see the enlightenment as an extension of the errors it aimed to dispel. He imagined global revolution not as universalizing the rule of reason, but as liberating desire and spreading "thought-creating fires" (*SL* 6:6, E 68).

The vision was certainly rebellious, but Blake himself cut an odd figure as a revolutionary. The links between his prophetic art and contemporary radicalism have been widely explored, but identifying a contemporary fit audience has proved difficult. When he composed *America* (1793), the first of his "continental prophecies," he may have thought of it as an intervention in the political debate stimulated by the French revolution. But the advertised price of 10s. 6d. (E 693) put it well out of reach of a popular audience. It was his most ambitious illuminated book to date, with plates more than four times bigger than the *Innocence* plates. His desire to develop his own vision seems to override the possibility of reaching a wide readership. The obscurity of his prophecies might be seen as a strategic protection against prosecution in increasingly dangerous times. But we are usually in little doubt when he is attacking kings and priests. Much of the difficulty lies elsewhere, in the handling of time and space, the use of mythical figures whose significance is never clearly explained, the unresolvable syntax, the multiple allusions, the uncertain relation between the figurative and the literal, or between text and design. As a prophet he seems to presuppose a reader equipped like himself. It seems unlikely that any such reader has yet appeared.

Global revolution

The *America* "Preludium" plunges us into a world that seems at once very strange and eerily familiar. The unusual metrical form (a seven-stress line used with considerable freedom), the cloudy atmosphere, the abrupt and violent action are typical of Blake's attempts to recreate an ancient bardic voice – one which speaks as if from beyond the limits that govern the vision of the present age. The identity and motives of Urthona are not explained: instead we are shown the consequences of his tyranny, and invited to speculate on its significance. The female that Orc embraces evokes an iron age, representations of America as an Amerindian female, as well as the forbidding, virginal, and pestilential nature of the newly discovered continent as described by European observers. Much contemporary writing on the American rebellion placed it in a broad historical perspective that looked back to the European "discovery" of the New World and to the early settlements, associating these with a decisive break from oppressive conditions in Europe. Orc's escape from his chains, then, might be related to the energetic awakening of that earlier period. To name Mexico and Peru in the context of Orc's rape of the female could evoke the history of conquest by which these American civilizations succumbed to European power. Before Orc breaks his chains he cries: "On the Canadian wilds I fold, feeble my spirit folds" (pl. 1:17, E 51). The enfeebled spirit of natural life in the New World was regarded by some Europeans as a scientific fact, while European conquest was assumed to have an invigorating effect on its wilderness. The female's ready response to Orc's fierce embrace can be related to the Amerindian women's supposed sexual complicity with their conquerors. Her response to Orc as a fallen image of God recalls reports of the Indians' response to Columbus.[1] If this Preludium can also be read as a representation of the American rebellion, that is because the rebellion promised to unleash a new era of colonization in the New World. In this context, then, Orc's fire can be seen as the natural energy that fuels discovery, imperial conquest, the rape of undeveloped nations, their development and spiritual conversion, as well as libertarian revolt. It is precisely because these things are related in the history of America that Blake needs a myth that will suggest their relationship. The work challenges discursive categories that would separate the positive from the negative aspects of this history. As we shall see, Blake often shows "both/and" relationships where we might expect "either/or" distinctions.

The Preludium, then, may suggest an alternative to the more hopeful Prophecy that follows, where Orc emerges from the Atlantic like the beast rising from the sea in Revelation 13. The fear-driven tyrant, Albion's Angel, identifies him as Antichrist, but Orc presents himself as a resurrected Christ, come to obliterate the stony moral law and offer an erotic liberty. We seem distanced from the political issues historically at stake. Contemporary observers emphasized the politicization of the Americans through public meetings, debates, publications. But in Blake's prophecy, most of the American leaders say nothing, while Washington has only seven lines in which to voice his fears of American degeneration under British domination (pl. 3:6–12, E 52). This revolution does not lead to independent legislation, but to the burning of the law-built heaven of Urizen (Blake's Jehovah-like sky-god) and the recovery of the lustful body. There are rage and burning on both sides of the conflict, but those who resist Orc's fires degenerate into reptile form, while the sign of liberation is nakedness. This conclusion is reinforced in the visual designs to the work, which has the highest proportion of naked bodies of any of Blake's illuminated works.

Blake's early experience of Swedenborgianism may have encouraged him to associate liberty with increased "sensual enjoyment" (*MHH* 14, E 39).[2] The emphasis on lustful fires allows him to imagine a universal revolution that begins in one country, without suggesting uniformity of vision. Orc spreads "heat but not light" (*America* 4:11, E 53); liberated desire must generate thought in each individual. Conversely, Blake sees the binding of desire as the means by which individuals are subjected to a uniform vision. We can see this in *Europe* (1794), which was planned as a sequel to *America* (its plates appear to have been prepared on the backs of the *America* plates). *Europe* approaches the French Revolution through an imaginative history of Christianity, and associates the birth of Christ with the harnessing and sublimation of desire into a transcendent, "feminine" world-view. Christianity is here a civilized religion, promoted by a refined angelic bard, Los, who represses by appealing to the appetites and affections rather than by harsh legislation and threats of force. Under the influence of Los, Orc's messianic energy is simultaneously elevated and bound. We might take as an example of such bardic activity Milton's ode "On the Morning of Christ's Nativity," which has often been cited as a model for Blake's poem. The captivating music and enchanting aerial atmosphere of Milton's ode seem to dematerialize the incarnation it celebrates; in Blake's terms, it represses as it idealizes.

Los's partner, the goddess Enitharmon, figures the ascendancy of "feminine" values in Christian ideology – maternal love, domesticity, chastity – values which privatize identity and desire. The vision of motherhood promoted by Christianity (gently coercive, seductively powerful, controlling through nourishment and joy) is first glimpsed in the Preludium, where it displaces the nameless shadowy female's horrifying vision of motherhood. This nameless female – turbaned, victimized, abandoned by her violent, enslaved progeny – might be the racial other of a dominant European civilization (Blake had worked on illustrations showing the horrors endured by black slaves in South America).[3] The cryptic sequence might suggest a conquest through conversion, the feminine counterpart of the masculine conquest in the *America* Preludium. In the Prophecy, Enitharmon's coercive power is expressed musically. Her rhapsodic song alludes to, among other things, eighteenth-century English hymns (some by women), which station the worshipper in nocturnal isolation, longing for a blissful dawn in an eroticized heaven. Her children are usually seen as the counterparts of the pagan gods in Milton's ode, banished by the birth of Christ. Here the evocation of their fantastic, exotic attributes enacts the celebration and binding of Orc, as intimations of (masculine) sublimity modulate into the (feminine) attributes of beauty and pathos.

The song encloses a compressed, enigmatic sequence (*Europe* 9:6–13:8, E 63–65) that can be read as a sequel to the historical allegory in *America*, where in resisting the American revolution, the forces of Albion's Angel were smitten with their own plagues (*America* 15:1–20, E 56–57). But it also offers a history of the harsh masculine tradition that institutional Christianity, for all its gentle feminine values, actually embraces. Here the ultimate cause of repression is a primeval retreat from desire, which leads to regulative social order. Blake suggests a continuity between Druid groves of consecrated mistletoe, the Romans who displaced them, and the scientific age ushered in by Bacon and Newton. The myth characteristically looks beyond the apparent opposition between barbarous superstition and enlightenment reason, to assert a fundamental kinship between them. The alliance between the masculine Urizenic tradition and the feminine tradition epitomized by Enitharmon is suggested in the remarkable illuminations that accompany the text. We begin with images of masculine power: the frontispiece with its patriarchal creator and compasses; a phallic serpent on the title page; two plates with sinister images of masculine aggression (pls. i–ii, 1–2). These are followed by figures of feminine pity and desire (pls. 3–4). Female angels attend a dark knight in scaly armor; others serve a monstrous enthroned Pope (pls. 5 [Fig. 28], 7). Dramatic images of famine, plague, and imprisonment expose the gap between the ideology of Christian love and the grim reality it governs (pls. 6, 7, 13). A comparable gap is exposed in *Songs of Experience*, first advertised as a single work in Blake's prospectus of 1793 (E 692), and incorporated into *Songs of Innocence and of Experience* by 1794. The *Experience* poems dramatize a world bound by "God & his Priest & King" (pl. 37, E 23), in which the divine virtues of *Innocence* are realized only as symptoms of dire repression: hypocritical mercy, "usurous" pity (pl. 33, E 19), fearful peace, selfish love.

Figure 28 *Europe a Prophecy*, plate 5. Copy E.

The Song of Los (1795) completes Blake's initial exploration of revolution by offering visions of "Africa" and "Asia" that may frame *America* and *Europe* to form a global sequence. "Africa" reduces the history of civilization to a concise bardic genealogy (the metrical irregularity perhaps suggesting bardic spontaneity). It relativizes different cultural traditions – Brama, Trismegistus, Chaldea, Greek philosophy, the Christian gospel, Islam – as so many stages in the completion of a minimal philosophy of human life. But still this vision of global history begins with Africa, the starting point of Mosaic tradition, and identifies Adam and Noah as the original patriarchs. It also ends with this tradition in "Asia," where the reaction of Asiatic despots to the spread of "thought-creating fires" (pl. 6:6, E 68) ushers in a universal resurrection, and Urizen finds Adam and Noah reduced to skeletal form – exploded myths. Blake seems to have assumed that, perhaps by derivation, "all nations believe the jews code and worship the jews god" (*MHH* 12, E 39). It is not surprising, then, that biblical tradition should have a central place in his longer explorations of the origin of error.

Origins

The authority of the biblical account of origins had already been challenged by developments in the natural sciences, by the speculations of Deists and *philosophes*, and by an emergent tradition of textual criticism. By 1794 such speculations were being condemned as seditious. But by imitating the appearance of the King James Bible's two-column chapter-and-verse format in his illuminated myths of origin, Blake made clear his own direct challenge to the "Authorized Version" of human history.

The *[First] Book of Urizen* is, among other things, a satirical version of Genesis, "The First Book of Moses." It retells the Mosaic history from creation to the entry into Egypt as a parable of progress. It has affinities with Rousseau's famous account of the rise of civilization as a disastrous fall into bondage.[5] Blake's Urizen is the archetypal patriarchal God. He resembles Jehovah, Zeus, Thor, and other supreme beings, as well as Milton's Satan and the fallen creator or "demiurge" represented in gnosticism (an influence on and rival to, early Christianity).

Creation begins with his retreat from the communal life of a fiery eternity in which the senses can expand and contract at will. As a "self-contemplating" shadow, he begins to think of the infinite self as finite, vulnerable, and bounded by death; self-preservation drives his search for a stable order. In three copies (A, B, C) he is expelled by eternals after attempting to impose "Laws of peace, of love, of unity" (pl. 4:34, E 72). The urge to unify the human community through law is therefore seen as an archetypal error, based on a limited understanding of identity.

After Urizen's fall the narrative moves into a more naturalistic mode of vision, in which human development is a matter of responding to and organizing an external world. The first power to preside over this realm is Los, the "Eternal Prophet," whose creativity is initially simply a capacity to adapt to and stabilize a mysterious, alien world. Blake seems fascinated by the problem of how order could evolve from such a limited being. The problem is explored more fully in a complementary myth, *The Book of Los* (1795), where Los is a helpless victim enclosed in a hellish vision of existence. This vision has its counterparts in the Epicurean theory of Lucretius, which derives human order fortuitously from a downward-moving universe of matter and vacuity, a world that presupposes no creator and no purposeful generative power (the "oblique" change in Los's "downward-borne fall" is like the swerve of the falling atoms in Lucretius which allows productive change to occur [pl. 4:42, E 92]).[6] As the science of Blake's own age demonstrated, a mechanistic vision of the world could also support the idea of a designing creator. Indeed, Moses had been identified as the "first author of the atomical philosophy."[7] We might read *The Book of Los* as an imaginative solution to the problem of how a mechanistic view of being could give rise to a view of the physical world as consciously created. It shows how Los moves from being a mere casualty of his world to become a conscious shaper of it, and how he learns to direct his energies until for the first time intimations of "joy" appear in the fallen world. The vast orb he makes, which apparently becomes the "self balanced" sun, represents nature as a stable mechanism. This conclusion echoes radical speculations that the earliest institutional religions were sun-religions.[8]

Urizen suggests that in a naturalistic vision, the imaginative powers awakened in Los must provide the basis for the world-view that Urizen will inherit, rationalize, and regard as its own creation. There, since Los reacts to his world without foresight, time does not express the will of a divine creator but becomes simply a measurable continuum, while the body is seen as the unforeseen product of time – emerging through a blind evolutionary process that binds and stifles human energies (pls. 10–13). As the body becomes a finite object separate from all others, feeling becomes attached to other finite objects which must be possessed and protected. This is the basis of the family. Love takes the form of an inherently possessive "Pity," which is seen as the origin of sexual difference: the female Enitharmon emerges as a secondary being and as a source of torment for Los (pls. 18:1–19:13, E 78–9). In this condition desire is alienated because its arousal is always potentially in conflict with the urge to maintain order. It erupts as an independent power, Orc, who is simultaneously nurtured and suppressed (pls. 19:14–20:25, E 79–80). The triangular relationship between Los, Enitharmon, and Orc is a remarkable anticipation of Freud's account of the Oedipal conflict, but while Freud developed a "scientific myth" to ground his theory, Blake shows that the tent of "Science" simply confirms a limited vision of nature (pl. 19:2–9, E 78).[9] The binding of Orc with the chain of jealousy enacts the commitment to deferred fulfillment, which provides the dynamic for material progress and confirms fallen humanity's separation from eternal desire.

The division of emotional life between a feminine "Pity" and a fiery masculine desire has important implications for Blake's developing mythology, as it defines the emotional ambivalence that pervades his view of fallen civilization. Orc's desire awakens the dormant Urizen, inspiring not only his search for mastery of an external world through the sciences, but also his urge to regulate desire through a religion founded on "Pity." Humanity is therefore trapped in a circle of repression: pity fosters the desire it must repress, just as desire stimulates repressive pity. This vision of the emotional dynamic of the social order is a grotesque counterpart of the benignly balanced opposition of selfish and sympathetic passions in enlightenment social theory.

In *Urizen*, then, civilization is founded on the brutal suppression of desire. Few works in English can express a more powerful sense of the body's capacity for pain. The book is filled with visual images of torment, of bodies cramped, buried alive, flayed, threatened with drowning, fire, or horrific metamorphosis (Fig. 29). The stylistic push towards extremity of posture and movement is rendered more striking by color printing. The direct visceral appeal of such images seeks to make readers conscious of their own bodies while provoking speculation about meanings. But *Urizen* not only depicts grotesque transformations in the human body: the narrative itself undergoes a continuous metamorphosis. At the beginning readers are denied intelligible spatial and temporal referents, or a clear sense of cause and effect – we are exposed to a linguistic chaos which may induce an anxious search for stable order. By the end of the narrative we have moved from the present tense, through unspecific "times" and "ages" into the calendar of "days" and "years," while the narrative eye has gradually zoomed out, bringing into focus the dark globe of Urizen, a body, a family, a mountain, a variegated landscape, cities, thirty cities, a continent (Africa), and the earth as a globe. As we move towards an increasingly naturalistic and "historical" perspective, so the expansion of the narrative horizon simultaneously represents the contraction of the human condition. We, that is, are being located in fallen time and space as diminished observers, our urge for order answered diagnostically.

Urizen concludes with the Moses-like Fuzon leading the "remaining children of Urizen" out of a condition of bondage they call Egypt. *The Book of Ahania* (1795) is a sequel in which Fuzon's fiery rebellion against Urizen recalls not only Moses's attempt to deliver his people from Egypt but also the revolt of Milton's Satan and of Absalom (2 Samuel 15–19). It can also be related to the progress of Robespierre in revolutionary France (the foot

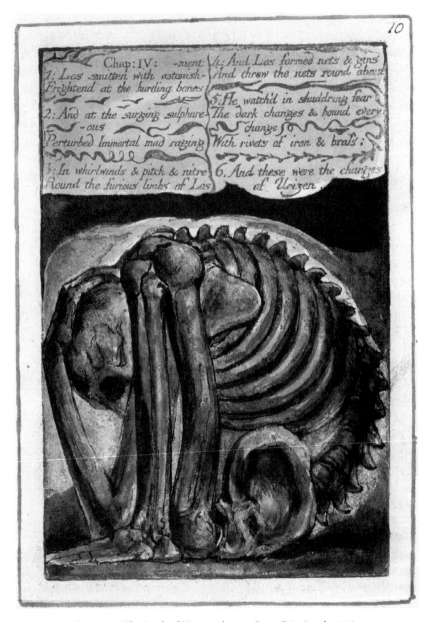

Figure 29 *The Book of Urizen*, plate 8. Copy G (printed 1818).

of plate 6 depicts a severed head and piled bodies). The political relevance of its account of the rebel's rapid transformation into the tyranny he opposes is perhaps the easiest part to grasp. More surprising is the direct connection between armed rebellion and the consciousness of sexual sin. For the work explores sexual repression as it afflicts the reasoning mind, and the language is laden with the fear and fascination of sexuality.

We can approach this issue by considering *Paradise Lost*. Milton shows that divine creativity is expressed partly through feminine beauty, which also takes on the appearance of seductive temptation. Milton's God is personally removed from such temptation: he has a son but no female companion. It seems that divine creativity both expresses and suppresses the sexuality associated with the female. But in expelling Satan, God is also repressing and expressing that will-to-power on which his own order depends. Both the aggressive male and softer female aspects of passion, it seems, are simultaneously embraced and condemned. At the beginning of *Ahania*, Urizen has not yet experienced the separation of the female that Los suffered in *Urizen*: he is, therefore, androgynous. But for the reasoning mind, the aggressive masculine aspects of experience assume a threatening separate form before the feminine aspects do. Like the Son in *Paradise Lost*, Fuzon is not born to a female. He is the "Son of Urizens silent burnings," a manifestation of Urizen's own unacknowledged desires and self-hatred (pl. 2:9, E 84). In relation to Fuzon's wrath and desire, then, Urizen is at once a rival masculine authority and in the position of a female whose virginity is no protection against rape (the "Lengthning" beam "tore through" Urizen's protective shield, his cold loins are divided, pl. 2:19–29, E 84). To maintain order Urizen quells his own orgasmic response by rejecting the female side of his own nature, Ahania, as sin. (She is between his knees in the frontispiece design – the child of his repression.) One consequence of this rebellion, then, is a myth of origins that associates sexuality – and especially female sexuality – with evil: Urizen's weapons are ribs and a serpent (which recall the patriarchal myth of Eden), and a rock that becomes Sinai, the origin of the Mosaic law.

But there is another side to Urizen's reaction. While rebellious desire must be seen as evil, the will that triumphs over it must be formally distanced from desire. Urizen's suppression of Fuzon cannot spring from lust for revenge. It must be reconciled with a supposedly compassionate justice (the Father who sacrifices his own Son in *Paradise Lost* speaks of mercy; Urizen acts in "bitter Contrition," pl. 3:3–4, E 85). Blake's narrative suggests that the doctrine of atonement springs from this necessity. The sacrificial victim becomes an object of a pity that, typically, seeks at once to foster and to repress its object: Fuzon is sanctified and condemned, "Lifted on high" and "nail'd" down (pls. 3:52, 4:8; E 86, 87). The elevation of Fuzon on the Tree of Mystery emphasizes the typological relationship between Adam, Moses, and Christ (Moses raising the brazen serpent in the wilderness is seen by John as foreshadowing the crucifixion [Numbers 21:6–9, John 3:14–15]). The myth of the fall, the

Mosaic doctrine of atonement and the crucifixion are seen as instruments of state power, aspects of a confused ideology in which love and mercy are both celebrated and ruthlessly suppressed. Once again the Eternal Prophet is seen in the service of priestly repression: Los enables Urizen's wet dream to bear fruit in the absence of a female (pl. 4:13–14, E 87), by putting flesh on the bare bones of Urizen's noxious vision of humanity, giving a semblance of life to abstract conceptions.

Ahania and The Book of Los were produced economically by Blake's standards. They are the shortest of these illuminated books, with only six and five plates respectively, and their texts are etched in intaglio (the standard technique, rather than relief etched, the unconventional technique used for all the other illuminated books), with many lines per plate. Perhaps Blake had begun to feel that his developing vision needed a much more extensive canvas than his own printing process would currently allow. Besides, his visual designs seem to have been more saleable than the poems. Around 1794–96 he reproduced designs without text in the color-printed Small Book of Designs (taken mostly from Urizen, Marriage, Thel), and the Large Book of Designs (which features designs from illuminated books, along with single prints such as Albion Rose and The Accusers [Butlin 262]). In 1795 he may have begun work on his magnificent series of large color-printed designs (although some were apparently produced around 1804–5) (Butlin 289–329).[10] The designs address some of the issues explored in the prophetic books. Humanity's subjection to patriarchal divinity, for example, is seen in Elohim Creating Adam, God Judging Adam, and even in Christ Appearing to the Apostles; Newton reveals the repressive aspect of science; Nebuchadnezzar and Good and Evil Angels develop designs from Marriage plates 4 and 24.

Over the next eight years Blake's professional fortunes varied considerably. In 1795–97 he was working on one of the biggest commissions he ever received, to design and engrave illustrations for Edward Young's popular reflective poem Night Thoughts (Butlin 330). The project was abortive, but probably led to an order from Blake's friend Flaxman for a set of 116 watercolor illustrations for Thomas Gray's Poems in the Night Thoughts format (each illustration surrounding a central text-panel) (Butlin 335–36). In both projects Blake took every opportunity to emphasize the spiritual and sublime potential of the poems, as in his treatment of Gray's Hyperion (in The Progress of Poesy) as a fiery sun god triumphing over darkness (Butlin 335 46). Blake's idea of sublimity did not suit all tastes: in 1799 the Rev. Dr. Trusler's unappreciative criticisms of his paintings of Malevolence and Benevolence provoked Blake's famous letter in defense of Imagination (letter of 23 August 1799, E 702–3). In the same year Blake was at work on a series of fifty tempera paintings on biblical subjects for Thomas Butts, two of which were exhibited at the Royal Academy exhibition (*The Last Supper*, May 1799; *The Miracle of the Loaves and Fishes*, May 1800, Butlin 424, 416). These were followed by another series of biblical illustrations for Butts, this time in watercolor, and, around 1801 a series of eight illustrations to Milton's *Comus* for the Rev. Joseph Thomas (Butlin 527). Such commissions gave scope for Blake's creativity, but in September 1800 he moved from Lambeth to Felpham, under the patronage of the poet William Hayley, who set tasks not commensurate with Blake's ambitions. They included illustrations for Hayley's *Life of Cowper*, designs for Hayley's own *Ballads* (Essick, *Commercial Illustrations*, XLIV, XLI), and a series of paintings of poets' heads for Hayley's library (Butlin 343). Convinced that Hayley intended to turn him into a "Portrait Painter" (E 725), Blake returned to London late in 1803.

Vala, or The Four Zoas

The major prophetic work of these years combined an exploration of origins with an account of universal revolution in an epic vision of universal history. Blake began to transcribe this poem in a manuscript illustrated with drawings in 1797, and he continued to work on it during his years at Felpham and perhaps later. The manuscript survives in a heavily revised condition, with much of the text written on proof sheets of Blake's engravings for Young's *Night Thoughts*. Blake's concern with the psychological effects of repression is amplified in an extraordinary way through some of the drawings. A nightmarish series of sketches on page 26, for example, which illuminates the relationship between patriarchal repression and the fetishizing of sexuality explored in the text, shows a human butterfly with breasts and vulva; a batwinged figure riding a huge erect penis; a winged monster with a mermaid tail, female genitals and curved neck and beak; a winged dragon with a woman's face and breasts (Fig. 30). Such images dramatize the fear of female sexuality that Blake sees at the heart of patriarchy. Other drawings seem less obviously related to the text, and some may predate it, perhaps originating as preliminary sketches for the *Night Thoughts* series. There is evidence that Blake tried to find appropriate matches between his text and the *Night Thoughts* designs, but the view of some critics, that this attempt produced cunningly detailed allegories, seems optimistic.

Like Young's poem, Blake's was to have nine "Nights," the last of which would be a vision of the Last Judgment. Originally conceived as *Vala*, the work eventually became *The Four Zoas*, a title referring to the four masculine powers that dominate its view of history. These powers, each with a female counterpart or emanation, are Urizen and Ahania; Los (here identified as a

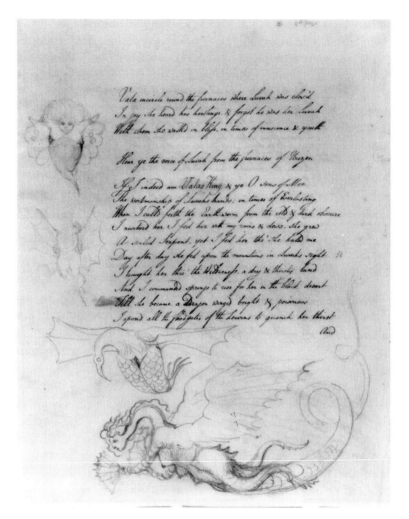

Figure 30 *The Four Zoas*, page 26.

form of Urthona) and Enitharmon; Luvah (the eternal form of Orc) and Vala, both associated with the passions; Tharmas and Enion, who are associated with the body, the senses, the realm of matter. Readers soon discover that no simple definition of these powers is adequate: they are what they do, and their roles vary according to context.

From the outset the poem appears to base its claim to universality on its eclectic synthesis of different traditions. An epigraph from the Greek Testament is soon followed by a reference to "heroic Verse"; the tone and settings of the poem often recall the murky, turbulent world of the Icelandic

Eddas and Ossian; other traditions – Neoplatonic, Gnostic, Hindu – are evoked in passing. The essential unity of humanity is suggested in the figure of the Universal or Eternal Man, whose sick body is the realm of fallen history and the grounds of identity underlying cultural differences. The figure implicitly confirms the secondary status of the female in Blake's vision.

As a universal history the poem explores a favorite subject of enlightenment historians – the rise and fall of civilization – and is shaped by the contemporary awareness that social development may be undermined by the same forces that promote it. The poem's history of fallen civilization can be divided into two major phases, which parallel each other. In the first (Nights I–III), the powers that shape human life are seen as divine, while the natural world comes to be organized as the living embodiment of divine order. This "Golden World" is designed to satisfy not only the spiritual need for beauty, harmony, and spiritual purpose, but also the intellectual need for an explanation of natural phenomena – especially astronomical phenomena. It collapses as a result of the inherent tensions between these purposes: the explanatory astronomical activities become increasingly specialized and impersonal, while the spiritual needs, including the need for a personalized providence, are met by religious institutions which promote fear and an appetite for mystery. Urizen's rejection of Ahania in Night III enacts the scientific rejection of teleological explanations and of religious authority, which leads to the collapse of the entire world view. In the second phase of fallen history (Nights III–VIII), the shaping powers are initially seen as merely natural, since the collapse of the Golden World plunges Man into the boundless and centerless world of pure materialism, where life and consciousness are seen to have evolved from the ceaseless flux of matter. From this starting point in "The Caverns of the Grave," the natural world eventually comes to be organized in empirical or scientific terms – a Universal Empire ordered by impersonal laws and forces rather than sustained by spiritual presences. But this can only come about by the reconstitution of reason as a power at once subject to the limitations of the body and established as the sole judge of experience in all things. The story of Urizen's restoration in *The Four Zoas* recasts and elaborates the central sections of *Urizen*. Whereas Urizen's Golden World collapses when its order and clarity have been clouded by a religious mystery that he rejects, at the heart of the second system he encounters a new and more powerful manifestation of mystery, Vala, whom he will eventually embrace. Whether the powers that govern human life are divine or natural, the major phases of civilization are based in part on creative and repressive labor. Unlike *Paradise Lost*, which minimizes the labor involved in the production of heavenly artifacts, and passes lightly over the incessant toil in hell, *The Four Zoas* places labor – with tools, chains, furnaces, looms, mills – at the center of human experience.

While this universal history may strive towards an eclectic synthesis of traditions, it is shaped most obviously by the Bible and *Paradise Lost*. In 1798 Blake annotated the Bishop of Llandaff's *Apology for the Bible*, a response to Tom Paine's assault on the authority of scripture. Although Blake did not share Paine's Deism, he was prepared to defend Paine's vigorous attack on a text that he himself described as "a Poem of probable impossibilities" (E 616). But still the Bible remained for Blake the most important guide to human destiny. His poem's vision of universal history is complemented and disrupted by an account of a providential intervention intended to redeem humanity from error, an account based explicitly on Christian tradition, whose universal significance is simply assumed. It describes the descent, crucifixion, resurrection, and second coming of Jesus, a story which represents not only the history of Jesus but also the larger history of Christianity itself. It constitutes a Blakean theodicy, in which the history of Christianity is itself a history of error. The "Council of God" (p. 21:1–7, E 310–11) is a republican alternative to the monarchial hierarchy of Milton's heaven in *Paradise Lost*. But when the horrified eternals react to the errors of fallen humanity by instigating a scheme of redemption, they are seen to learn from their own errors. Their appointment of Jesus as fallen Man's guardian, the last of seven such "Eyes of God," is an act of mercy, but also a consequence of their limited vision (p. 21:6–11, E 312). They themselves must descend before fallen humanity can rise (p. 118:40, E 388). The Daughters of Beulah, who provide "a mild & pleasant rest" from Eternity (p. 5:29, E 303), represent both the faith and patience that sustain the desire for redemptive action and the condition in which inspiration begins. If this elaborate reinterpretation of divine providence explicitly privileges the Christian tradition, an incomplete revision (involving the title page, a few local changes in Nights I–IV, and the addition of p. 25:6–33, E 314–17) represents a further shift away from eclectic synthesis: it identifies the Man as Albion, subsuming world history into a British perspective in a way that disconcertingly shadows contemporary attempts to widen British global influence.

The mythical narrative of *The Four Zoas* is, among other things, a satirical exploration of the power of mythical narratives to assume cultural authority, to predetermine thought and action, and to justify repression. The main narrative dramatizes the production and influence of dominant myths, while its own account is repeatedly interrupted or challenged by competing voices – from below (the Demons of the Deep, e.g. pp. 14:7–16:12, E 308–9), from above (Eternity, Beulah), and from within (in the conflicting reports, memories, and assertions of the main characters). Remarkably, the myths that dominate fallen history are also produced by conflicting voices, and reveal the opposed impulses and ideological contradictions that pervade systems of order in the fallen world.

The mythmaking in this poem arises from the need to come to terms with desire: much of it centers on Luvah and Vala, the god and goddess of love. In Enitharmon's "Song of Death," which provides the ethical basis for an emerging ideology, Vala is a seductive power who inspires possessive passion, jealousy, guilt and fear, while Luvah is an aggressive power who usurps the role of reason (p. 10:11–14, E 305). In Los's response, which provides the spiritual basis of the new world order, Vala is a pitiful, dependent figure who inspires sympathy as she weeps for "Luvah Lost," while Luvah is a deity who descends to her garden – like Milton's Son of God who descends to Eden as both redeemer and punisher (p. 11:5–14, E 306). Taken together these accounts reveal the emotional ambivalence that underlies social order in the fallen world: love is both a usurping and a redemptive power; it is both dangerously seductive and associated with the urge to give and receive comfort. The poem gives no indication of the veracity of such myths, but shows instead their function in fallen history. They provide a justification for the regulation of passion by reason and define a sense of dependence upon a transcendent god. The Golden World that Urizen constructs – which embodies divine purpose in a unified hierarchy – systematizes the vision of transcendence and dependence that Los has provided and the suppression of the passions that Enitharmon's song promotes. Luvah appears here as a transcendent power whose divine energy must be reconciled (by violence) with the fixed appearance of the natural world (pp. 25:40–30:7, E 317–19), while Vala appears as a figure of sorrowing dependence, whose protests and demand for comfort in the face of "incessant labouring" are actually a form of resignation which helps to consolidate the downtrodden members of Urizen's world into a submissive community (p. 31:6–16, E 320–21).

Urizen's second world order requires a more elaborate myth of the human condition, one more congruent with its empirical basis – reflecting a more historical consciousness, and a new awareness of the need to assert its universal relevance (pp. 83:4–84:42, E 358–60). Here Vala is once again seen first of all as the seductive power who drew Man out of paradise; she is apparently the tempting emotional indulgence that releases disruptive desire (Luvah) and must be rigorously suppressed. As such she provides a justification for the punitive violence that underpins law and for the military aggression that must shape and defend civilization. Such aggression is itself an expression of a fierce repressed passion: Vala must be subject to the rage of Orc. But in the Spectre of Urthona's complementary vision, "soft Vala" has become an ideal that can assuage the terrors of desire and so release humanity from the imperious appetites of the body, allowing a blissful reunion (p. 84:33–35, E 359). We see here, apparently, an emergent vision of a "Universal Manhood" that can be realized through self-denial (p. 84:11, E 359). The gentle passions (pity, mercy, peace, and love) become instruments of control by which natural passion can be restrained: Vala must be given to Orc so that he might lose his rage.

These contradictory myths of Vala, as sinful indulgence and as spiritual ideal, find expression in a new form of Vala, the Shadowy Female, a manifestation of the emotional ambivalence Blake sees at the heart of his own civilization. The most complex and most heavily revised part of the poem shows how, through the Shadowy Female, these myths exert their influence on all aspects of life in Urizen's world. For the visions of Universal Manhood associated with her appear in unexpected and conflicting forms – in the dream of Universal Empire (p. 95:15–30, E 360), in radical reactions to oppressive state power (pp. 88:19–89:17, E 361–62), and in the Christian vision of a Universal Family (p. 103:32–39, E 376).

In exploring the power of the Shadowy Female, the narrative presents a visionary counterpart to enlightenment analyses of the often paradoxical relationships between the material factors that promote social development and those that threaten to undermine it. In some contemporary social theory, war was seen as a positive shaper of social order as well as a threat to it. The rise of the arts and science could lead to internal conflict between authority and the urge for liberty, or between superstition and enthusiasm, a conflict that could liberalize the state but might also undermine it. The division of labor which spurred the economy could result in mental mutilation for the laboring majority. In Gibbon's account of Rome, pagan religions contributed to the social cohesion of the state, but Christianity emerged as a disruptive force which, with its otherworldly vision of destiny and its preoccupation with sinfulness, helped to weaken the empire.[11] In Blake's alternative analysis, the Shadowy Female is the spiritual power that governs such developments. She is the vision of love that allows fallen reason to control religion, to divert energy and skills into the arts of war, and into the physical drudgery that sustains commerce and industry. And she is the power that eventually undermines these activities.

Blake presents the historical revelation of Christianity as a reaction to this development, in a transformation of the prophet's role from restraining the passions to transforming them through works of art (p. 98:2–67, E 370–71). As a prophet of Christianity, that is, Los becomes an artist whose inspirational work is seen to liberate fallen individuals from their sleep of death and offer them reassurance through its "permanent" forms. Los presides over this spiritual rebirth in Golgonooza, a new Golgotha. The transformation allows a new delight in the body and a new sense of kinship with others to emerge, a new social fabric (woven by Enitharmon in Cathedron [p. 100:2–25, E 372–73]). Gibbon described the development of the early Church as an evolutionary process in which its original character was progressively and inevitably modified by material interests. Blake shows a comparable development, explaining the limitations of the Church in terms of its provenance. Since Los remains in his Spectre's power and clings to the vision of a finite world, his creativity eventually declines from vision to memory, while Christianity evolves into state religion (pp. 104:31–115:24, E 378–86). Once the Christian vision's transforming power has been absorbed in this way there is no escape from error except through the Last Judgment.

Readers who can sympathize with Blake's radical critique of civilization may become uneasy about the extraordinary vision of resurrection presented in Night IX. For this narrative begins with a letting go which releases Orc from all constraints, and one consequence of this release is chaotic violence. This vengeful fury, a reflection of the mob violence of Blake's own age, is ironically counterpointed with visions of redemption from above, the last remnants of a supervising providence (pp. 122:1–20–123:27–39, E 391–93). Beyond these, the myth works towards a condition in which each (masculine) individual will be able to see God in his brother's face. In the process the violence is offset by other consequences of the liberation of Orc – the renewal of sensual enjoyment and of labor.

In the Last Judgment agriculture is given precedence over the "Trades and Commerce" prioritized in Urizen's empire (a priority Blake shares with the agrarian capitalism of Adam Smith and the radical agrarianism of Godwin, Coleridge, Spence, and others). The zestful communal labor of the harvest and the vintage becomes the means by which humanity is to be resurrected, as pleasure in the body is recovered through work. But the underside of this invigorating activity is usually "rout & desolation" (p. 137:16, E 405). Labor never quite loses its oppressive aspect: its instrumentality, its inherent division between active agent and passive material to be processed, remains troublesome.

And sexuality, that activity that gives rise to some of the fascinating, hilarious, or nightmarish illustrations in the manuscript, also remains a problem that must somehow be passed through. In the progress towards brotherhood, the family and sexual relations have to be recreated only to be outgrown. The germination of the soul in a pastoral underworld is narrated as a myth of female development towards motherhood (pp. 126:18–131:19, E 395–400). This enclosed version of motherhood, the seedbed from which adult identity emerges, must be superseded by the less exclusive vision of motherhood represented by Enion (as earth mother, p. 132:24–35, E 401), and then by the brotherhood of the Eternal Men who shudder at the separate female form (p. 133:5–9, E 401). Luvah, having presided over the renewal of the family, now presides over its destruction in his winepresses – a horrifying vision of purgation through atrocity (pp. 136:5–137:4, E 404–5). What we see here, apparently, is not only the destruction of the limited self through the overwhelming power of love, but the satiation of sexual desire, including all its sadistic fury, in order that the narrative may leave sexuality behind. After the winepress orgy, females unite in the labor of weaving and spinning and in the praise of industry (p. 137:11–14, E 405). This is as close as the narrative gets to accommodating the female in its economy of regeneration. In brotherhood, apparently, desire transcends sexual expression. Blake might want us to see this as a progression from a less social to a more social expression of love. But the devil's account is that sexuality is sublimated in Blake's resurrected Man, subject to a new kind of repression, and that this is always implicit in Blake's relegation of the female to secondary status. At the end of the poem Men turn in thought on beds of sorrow from which women have apparently been eliminated, and Man rises, an Adam without an Eve, to converse with "Animal forms" (p. 138:12–19, p. 138:30–31; E 406). Visionary conversation and intellectual war become the models of eternal mutuality and community – gentlemanly models which depend on but displace both the sexual desires and the labor of the risen body.

Los's most liberating act in this poem is not the production of art but the destruction of the heavens, a gesture of blind despair rather than a work of vision (p. 117:5–9, E 386). Where, one might ask, does this conclusion leave Blake himself, as prophetic artist? In his later works, *Milton* and *Jerusalem*, Blake will return to the figure of Los in order to examine his own relation to the prophetic tradition – a tradition that has been responsible for so much that he condemns in his own civilization.

Notes

1. Abbé Raynal describes the sexual complicity of native American women in *A Philosophical and Political History of the Settlements and Trade of the Europeans in the East and West Indies*, vol. II (Dublin, 1784), p. 433. William Robertson discusses contemporary theories of American feebleness in *The History of America*, vol. I (London, 1777), p. 287. He notes that the Indians regarded Columbus and his men as "children of the Sun, who had descended to visit the earth" (vol. I, p. 92).
2. See Marsha Keith Schuchard, "The Secret Masonic History of Blake's Swedenborg Society," *Blake/An Illustrated Quarterly* 26 (1992), pp. 40–51.

3. The illustrations appeared in John Gabriel Stedman's *Narrative of a Five Years' Expedition against the Revolted Negroes of Surinam from the year 1772 to 1777*, 2 vols. (London, 1796).
4. "First" was deleted from the title page of copy G, and from the title page and Preludium title in copies A and G.
5. *A Discourse Upon the Origin and Foundation of the Inequality among Mankind* (London, 1761).
6. See Northrop Frye, *Fearful Symmetry* (Princeton: Princeton University Press, 1947), p. 257.
7. Ralph Cudworth, *A Treatise Concerning the Eternal and Immutable Morality* (London, 1731), p. 57.
8. The speculation appears in Constantin Volney's *The Ruins: or, A Survey of the Revolutions of Empire* (London, 1792). See Jon Mee, *Dangerous Enthusiasm: William Blake and the Culture of Radicalism in the 1790s* (Oxford: Oxford University Press, 1992), p. 139.
9. Freud developed his "scientific myth" to explain the origin of Oedipal conflict in *Totem and Taboo* (1912–13).
10. See Martin Butlin in "The Physicality of William Blake: The Large Colour Prints of '1795,'" *Huntington Library Quarterly* 52 (1989), pp. 1–17.
11. See David Hume, "On Superstition and Enthusiasm" (1741–42); Adam Smith, *The Wealth of Nations* (1776); Edward Gibbon, *Decline and Fall of the Roman Empire* (1776–88).

Further reading

Aers, David. "Representations of Revolution: From *The French Revolution* to *The Four Zoas*." *Critical Paths: Blake and the Argument of Method*. Ed. Dan Miller, Mark Bracher, and Donald Ault. Durham and London: Duke University Press, 1987. 244–70.

Ault, Donald. *Narrative Unbound: Revisioning William Blake's* The Four Zoas. New York: Station Hill Press, 1987.

Blake, William. *The Continental Prophecies*. Ed. D. W. Dörrbecker. London: William Blake Trust/Tate Gallery, 1995.

The Four Zoas: A Photographic Facsimile of the Manuscript with Commentary and Illustrations. Ed. Cettina Tramontano Magno and David V. Erdman. Lewisburgh, London, and Toronto: Bucknell University Press/ Associated University Press, 1987.

The Urizen Books. Ed. David Worrall. London: William Blake Trust/Tate Gallery, 1995.

Ferber, Michael. "Blake's *America* and the Birth of Revolution." *History and Myth: Essays in English Romantic Literature*. Ed. Stephen C. Behrendt. Detroit: Wayne State University Press, 1990. 73–99.

Lincoln, Andrew. *Spiritual History: A Reading of William Blake's* Vala *or* The Four Zoas. Oxford and New York: Oxford University Press, 1995.

Mann, Paul. "*The Book of Urizen* and the Horizon of the Book." *Unnam'd Forms: Blake and Textuality*. Ed. Nelson Hilton and Thomas A. Vogler. Berkeley: University of California Press, 1986. 49–68.

Mee, Jon. *Dangerous Enthusiasm: William Blake and the Culture of Radicalism in the 1790s*. Oxford: Oxford University Press, 1992.

Tolley, Michael. "Europe: 'to those ychain'd in sleep.' " *Blake's Visionary Forms Dramatic*. Ed. David V. Erdman and John E. Grant. Princeton: Princeton University Press, 1970. 115–45.

Wilkie, Brian and Mary Lynn Johnson. *Blake's Four Zoas: The Design of a Dream*. Cambridge and London: Harvard University Press, 1978.

12

MARY LYNN JOHNSON

Milton and its contexts

The best way into the time-twisting, identity-scrambling otherworld of Blake's *Milton: A Poem* (c. 1804–18) is to set aside guidebooks, including this one, take a deep breath, and follow the hero as he breaks through the surface of the title page – alone, without a "companion" – parting the syllables of his own name (and the poem's title) with one hand, sweeping back publishing details with the other, to brave the swirling abyss of the unknown (Fig. 31). The reader-resistant text billowing around Milton's nude figure scans vertically, bottom to top on the left, top to bottom on the right – a hint of the head-spinning reorientations to come. At the foot of the page, in much smaller lettering, a single upright line appears reassuringly straightforward: "To Justify the Ways of God to Men" (*Paradise Lost* 1:26).[1] But is Blake reaffirming – or co-opting – Milton's magisterial summation of epic purpose? Or is Milton, in flexing his left foot to take a second step into Blake's poem, leaving the secure foundation of his theodicy behind him? Should both poets – and their audiences – be interrogating, not justifying, God's ways? As the poem proceeds, readers find themselves clueless *in medias res*, thrown back on their own resources, as if subjected to a wilderness-survival test. But the neural overload helps cleanse the doors of perception, and the solo ordeal can be character-building. This chapter is meant to be put aside now and taken up again on the far side of "Finis" (*Milton* 43 [50]:2, E 144), after pulse and respiration have returned to normal.

Blake's *Milton* is the only extended literary work in English, or perhaps in any language, that features a poet as protagonist and title character. In European literature there are parallels of sorts, but no precedents: Moschus laments the death of Bion; Dante makes Virgil his spiritual guide; Jonson pays tribute to Shakespeare's memory; and many poets, including Milton, have been subjects of sonnets or other short works. In the visual arts too it is not uncommon for one artist to incorporate another, as model, into a new work of art. But Blake alone transforms a revered poet of an earlier

Figure 31 *Milton*, title page. Copy C.

time into a new kind of epic hero who embarks upon an inward-questing adventure, the outcome of which depends in part on the author's composition of this very poem. *Milton*, the only illuminated book Blake named after a publicly recognizable human being, has the further distinction of being his only overtly autobiographical work: not only does he interrupt the narrative to make first-person observations as scribe and witness (as in *Jerusalem* and elsewhere) but he depicts himself as "WILLIAM" (pl. [32]) and as "Blake" (pl. 36 [40]) and becomes fully engaged in the plot. Among Blake's works, the poem is also unique in that its denouement turns upon the courageous actions of a female character on a mission complementary to the hero's. Finally, *Milton* is Blake's most detailed and sustained consideration, in theological terms, of the remedy for humankind's separation from the "Eternal Great Humanity Divine" (pl. 2:8, E 96): in *Milton*, atonement occurs through Christlike self-giving to others, not through what Blake viewed as the Druidical blood-sacrifice of a surrogate.[2]

As the poem opens, the long-dead Milton (1608–74), obedient and uncomplaining, has been "unhappy tho in heav'n" for "a hundred years" while "pondring the intricate mazes of Providence" (pl. 2:17–18, E 96) – stuck forever, it seems, in the convoluted moral score-keeping system of the heaven he had imagined in Book III of *Paradise Lost*, and mired in his fallen angels' muddles on "Providence, Foreknowledge, Fate, and Will, / Fixt Fate, Free will, Foreknowledge absolute,...in wand'ring mazes lost" (*PL* 2:559–61). All this time he has been impassively viewing his estranged Emanation, Ololon (a composite of his poems, his loving impulses, and his all-female family) "scatter'd thro' the deep / In torment!"(pl. 2:19–20, E 96). It takes "a Bards prophetic Song!" (pl. 2:22, E 96) to move him to stake his soul on rejoining his Emanation, reversing the narrow path to immortality he had taken in his lifetime. This is possible only if he breaks through warps in time, space, and consciousness to correct his personal and doctrinal errors and rekindles, through Blake, the spirit of prophecy in Britain. In cinema-style jump-cuts, flashbacks, flash-forwards, and speeded-up and stop-motion replays, each poet participates in the self-transformation of the other, and both gain insight into unresolved contradictions in the historical Milton's life, work, and critical reputation that have impeded the transmission of his prophetic legacy to Blake's generation. These poet–poet interactions, complemented by poet–emanation encounters in the parallel plot, consolidate the creative powers of Milton, the Bard, Blake, and Blake's archetypal "Shadowy Prophet" Los, who seeks to return to "the Eternal bosom" (pl. 22 [24]:15–16, E 117). As the poem ends, the resurrected Milton, through Ololon, unites with "Jesus the Saviour," who – on another plane of reality – enters "Albions Bosom" (pl. 42 [49]:11, 21; E 143), the heart of England, to awaken Albion from the deathly sleep of human history, while Blake's soul returns "into its mortal state / To Resurrection & Judgment in the Vegetable Body" (pl. 42 [49]:26–27) in a world brought by these exploits to the verge of the biblical end-times, "the Great Harvest & Vintage of the Nations" (pl. 43 [50]:1, E 144).

Why Milton, rather than Chaucer, Spenser, or Shakespeare? Mainly, it's because Milton was the only one of Blake's great predecessors to align himself with those "more ancient & consciously & professedly Inspired Men" of the Bible (pl. 1 [i], E 95) whose influence on the arts, usurped in the neoclassical period by Greek and Latin models, is to be restored in the "New Age." As Elisha took up the prophetic mantle of his spiritual forebear Elijah, as Spenser drew from Chaucer's "well of English undefiled," Blake looks to the leading Protestant poet–prophet–patriot of the previous age for visionary empowerment. Blake's era is roughly analogous to the interval between the departure of a Tibetan lama's soul and its rediscovery, sometimes years later, in a new incarnation: the "line of vision"[3] has been blocked by what might be called the "line of memory," the dominant tradition of imitation-based art that has partially compromised even Milton's formidable creative powers. England's literary, religious, and political iconoclast has himself become an icon; the champion of liberty has become, through his critical legacy, an instrument of oppression; the theorist of sensory and spiritual fulfillment in marriage has become, in practice, an agent of misogyny; the purifier of corrupt state religion has become contaminated with his own puritanism. Only by rejecting this false identity can Milton the poet – rewritten in (and as) *Milton* the poem – reclaim the energy, including sexual energy, of Blake's Orc (the flawed but vital faculty that Milton misidentified as Satan in *Paradise Lost*), shake off the restraints of Urizen (misidentified as God), become whole with Ololon, and release the imaginative powers urgently needed by Blake.

As emphasized in *The Marriage of Heaven and Hell* – an excellent introduction to *Milton* – Milton's root error in *Paradise Lost*, as a "true Poet and of the Devils party without knowing it" (*MHH* 5, E 35), was to relegate revolutionary energy to the realm of the diabolic. Milton's Christ is not the dynamic, authority-challenging force for good who leaps from the pages of Blake's Bible but a coolly rational "Governor" who puts down Satan's rebellion and, on humanity's behalf, negotiates his own death to satisfy divine justice. Unlike the "Prophets Isaiah and Ezekiel," who dared "roundly to assert" that "God spake to them," the classics-saturated author of *Paradise Lost* invokes the Holy Spirit (Blake's "Poetic Genius") through the filter of the unnamed "Heav'nly Muse" who inspired Moses "on the secret top" of Sinai (*PL* 1:6–8) – the spirit of law, not prophecy.

England's great epic, then, is not a prophecy of liberation but a "history" of the restraint of desire (*MHH* 5, E 34): "in Milton; the Father is Destiny, the Son, a Ratio of the five senses. & the Holy-ghost, Vacuum!" (*MHH* 5, E 35). Yet this same Milton, in the works of his "left hand," blistered his opponents with anti-monarchical, anti-episcopal, and pro-divorce pamphlets and fearlessly attacked evils that Blake attributes to "God & his Priest & King" (*Songs* 37:11, E 23). It is this uncompromising "voice of honest indignation," strangely silent in Milton's poetry, that England needs to hear at the dawn of a new century, when the government is obsessed by Napoleon, the established Church is in the hands of crypto-Deists like William Paley, author of *Natural Theology* (1802), and liberty-loving Britons have nowhere to turn for patriotic and spiritual leadership. In *London, 1802* (published 1807), Wordsworth makes essentially the same point, in strikingly similar terms: "Milton! thou shouldst be living at this hour / England hath need of thee . . . / Thy soul was like a star, and dwelt apart."

In Blake's *Milton*, miraculously, this starlike soul crashes back to earth as a sign that history is coming to a close and "Eternity" is at hand. For Blake as character, most of the action takes place near "Blake's cottage at Felpham" (pl. 36 [40]), a real structure still standing in the Sussex coastal village where the historical William and Catherine Blake lived from September 1800 to September 1803, and where Blake's forcible removal of a drunken soldier from his garden led to his terrifying trial, and acquittal, in January 1804 on the serious charge of sedition. The Blakes had moved to Felpham to be near the versifier and biographer William Hayley, who had a history of befriending troubled artists, notably the painter George Romney (1734–1802) and the poet William Cowper (1731–1800). Hayley's commissions offered what seemed a heaven-sent opportunity for Blake to obtain both financial security and artistic autonomy: "I call myself now Independent. I can be Poet Painter & Musician as the Inspiration comes."[4] One of Hayley's first assignments for Blake, a particularly congenial one, was a portrait of Milton (among others) for his new library, in preparation for which Blake probably read Hayley's adulatory *Life of Milton* (1796) in tandem with Samuel Johnson's unflattering 1778 portrayal of a "surly and acrimonious republican" so "severe and arbitrary" in his domestic relations as to express in his poetry "something like a Turkish contempt for females."[5] By late 1802, however, Blake realized that in submitting to Hayley's patronizing micromanagement he had compromised his artistic integrity and imperilled his very soul. To "See Visions, Dream Dreams, & prophe[s]y & speak Parables . . . at liberty from the Doubts of other Mortals" (E 728), he would have to go back to scrounging for odd engraving jobs in London, even at the risk of doing without "Natural Bread" (E 724).

Blake's all-out commitment to artistic independence upon returning to London in 1803 – leading to a precipitous drop, after 1806, in commercial employment and an astonishing upsurge in creative productivity – is the defining event of what became his Decade of Milton, 1800–1810. This period encompasses, in addition to his portrait of Milton and *Milton: A Poem*, his study of Cowper's notes for an aborted edition of *Paradise Lost* ("the same that Fuselis Milton Gallery was painted for," E 727) and the launching of a significant body of visual commentary on Milton's major work (1801–16). Even Blake's 1803 biblical tempera "Riposo,"[6] "tho' not directly taken from a Poem of Miltons (for till I had designd it Miltons Poem did not come into my Thoughts)" reflects Milton's aura (E 729). In this Milton-inspired decade Blake produced well over 100 temperas and watercolors on biblical subjects for Thomas Butts (c. 1799–1809); illustrations of the Book of Job (1805–6); *The Mental Traveller* and other ballads of the Pickering Manuscript (1803–7); most of *Jerusalem* (1804–21); "apotheoses" of Nelson guiding Leviathan and Pitt leading Behemoth (c. 1805); at least five pictorial renditions of the Last Judgment (1806–9) and one of the Fall of Man (1807); designs for Robert Blair's *The Grave* (1805–7); illustrations of Shakespeare (1806–9); a panoramic tempera and engraving of Chaucer's Canterbury Pilgrims (1808–10); and a ten-by-fourteen-foot painting, now lost, of the three surviving Ancient Britons (c. 1808–11). Selections from this huge output formed the core of Blake's first and only one-artist exhibition, sixteen "Poetical and Historical Inventions" accompanied by a *Descriptive Catalogue* (1809) of "Opinions and Determinations" on themes also addressed in the Preface to *Milton*: the artist's responsibility to society, and society's to the artist, in a commercial–political–religious environment that devalues visionary art. These same concerns spill over into his annotations to Reynolds's *Discourses on Art* (c. 1798–1809), *Public Address*, *A Vision of the Last Judgment*, and *Blake's Chaucer* (1809–10).

Is biography, then, the key to *Milton*? Only a handful of family and friends could have guessed what Felpham meant to Blake, or spotted "Lambeth" (pls. 22[24]:11, 36[40]:22; E 117, 137) and "South Molton Street" (pl. 4:21, E 98) as his addresses before and after the Felpham experience, or detected Hayley's "Genteel Ignorance & Polite Disapprobation" (letter of 6 July 1803, E 730) behind the solicitous mask of the Bard's Satan. Still more deeply personal is Blake's full-page portrayal of his deceased younger brother and fellow artist "ROBERT" (pl. [37]) – not a character in the poem – as his spiritual double sharing his experience in the afterlife. But suppose these facts had never come to light. Blake, like artists in many fields, then and now, wove private allusions into his work that he probably never expected readers to recognize. And for the most important symbols, he includes interpretive contexts within the work itself. Blake's Felpham garden, for example – scene of his conversations with Milton and Ololon and the birds' and flowers' "lamentation of Beulah over Ololon" (pl. 31[34]:1–63, E 131) – is clearly a space charged with numinous intensity, a point of convergence between time and eternity, everyday appearances and ultimate reality, natural effects and spiritual causes.

Other apparent obscurities are intricate variations on Miltonic and biblical patterns that were, in Blake's time, entirely within the public domain. For example, the prose half of the Preface harks back to Milton's polemical pamphlets, with Blake's anticipated transformation of the "Daughters of Memory" into "Daughters of Inspiration" evoking the promise of Milton's masterwork "not to be obtained by the invocation of Dame Memory and her siren daughters" (Hughes 611) and his condemnation of "Hirelings in the Camp, the Court, & the University" echoing Milton's attack on "Hirelings" in the established Church (Hughes 856–79). In response, a new generation of free artists ("Painters! . . . Sculptors! Architects") is to "Rouze up," reject the values of the marketplace, abandon classics promoting "Corporeal War," and emulate Bible-inspired works encouraging "Mental" or spiritual combat in accordance with standards set by their "own Imaginations, those Worlds of Eternity in which we shall live for ever; in Jesus our Lord." This reference to "Jesus" provides a context for "those feet" in the famous opening line of the "Jerusalem" hymn, which constitutes the lyric half of the Preface. In this alternative national anthem for England as a spiritual and eternal state,[7] the soldier–builder–artist's vow to wield his spiritual weapons in "Mental Fight" blends the sword-carrying rebuilders of Jerusalem (Nehemiah 4:17–18) into Paul's metaphor of the "good fight" in a "war that is not carnal" (2 Corinthians 10:4, cf. Timothy 6:12). The concluding motto, also paraphrased by Milton in *Areopagitica* (Hughes 743–44), reaffirms Moses' rebuke of Joshua's complaint about upstart prophets, "Would to God that all the Lords people were Prophets" (Numbers 11:29).

To open the poem proper, Blake pointedly eschews Milton's graceful and ingenious Christianized adaptations of epic formulas: instead of visiting from Parnassus, or from the heavenly sphere of Milton's Urania, Blake's "Daughters of Beulah" descend into his pen- and burin-holding hand "down the Nerves of my right arm / From out the Portals of my Brain" (pl. 2:6–7, E 96). The artist's brain, as the physical seat of the imagination or "Eternal Great Humanity Divine," harbors a "Paradise" of shadowy poetic images – a variation on the "paradise within" that comforts Milton's fallen Adam and Eve (*PL* 12:587). Not only do the Daughters of Beulah offer a perfect vantage point for recording Milton's Emanation-seeking journey through their realm "in soft sexual delusions / Of varied beauty" (pl. 2:3–4) but their purview, bordering eternity, also encompasses the lower "vegetated" world of the "False Tongue" (derived from Psalms 120:3 and James 3:5), the domain of liars, defamers, and false prophets who made "Jesus, the image of the Invisible God" (pl. 2:12; cf. Colossians 1:14) "a curse, an offering, and an atonement" (pl. 2:13; cf. 2 Galatians 2:13).

Milton belongs to the same genre as *Paradise Regained*, the "brief" epic that Milton associated with the Book of Job (*Reason of Church Government*, Hughes 668); both Milton's Christ and Blake's Milton confront Satan at ever deeper levels and emerge purified and strengthened by their trials. But the orderly four-book structure of *Paradise Regained* presents Christ's three temptations in order of ascending difficulty and suspense, while the oddly asymmetrical two-book structure of *Milton* distributes Milton's and Ololon's complementary adventures unevenly, with many (but not all) of Milton's actions taking place in Book I, Ololon's in Book II. The most egregious symmetry-breaker is the "Bard's prophetic Song" (pls. 2:24–12:44), by far the hardest-to-understand section, which in its longest version occupies roughly half of Book I and almost a third of the whole poem. This outsized Song, repeatedly stretched to include parts of *The Four Zoas* creation story, may be the residue of Blake's earlier plan for a *Milton* "in 12 Books" (title page) that would have incorporated the whole of the *Zoas* myth into the framework of Milton's journey.[8]

The Bard's Song revolves around a dispute that ultimately challenges one of the foundational doctrines of *Paradise Lost*, and of most Christian denominations: Christ's vicarious atonement for the sins of fallen humanity through the substitute debt-payment of his innocent blood. Although we now know from *De Doctrina Christina* (first published in 1823, well after Blake's last revisions of *Milton*) that the historical Milton rejected the Calvinist predestination of Elect (saved) and Reprobate (damned), what is "decreed" by Milton's God suggests otherwise: "Some I have chosen of peculiar grace / Elect of all the rest" (*PL* 3:172, 183–84), while others who "neglect and scorn" the promptings of conscience will "hard be hard'n'd, blind be blinded more, / That they may stumble on, and deeper fall" (*PL* 3:199–201). Even if souls enter these states of their free will, the predestined overkill of the sinners' additional hardening and blinding (by God?) is patently abhorrent to Blake – and to like-minded Bible readers. In 1740, more than sixty years before *Milton*, the Methodist leaders John Wesley and George Whitefield had publicly split on this very issue, with the fiery Whitefield taking the Calvinist position and the temperate Wesley insisting, in his epoch-making sermon "Free Grace," that the predestination of elect and reprobate is such a "horrible Decree" that it could be issued only by a God "worse than the devil; more false, more cruel, more unjust." If Blake knew of the Wesley–Whitefield dispute, though, he ignores it in his depiction of the evangelists as the "two Witnesses" lying dead "in the Street of the Great City" (*Milton* [24]:56–59, E 118; Revelation 11:3). The titanic family brawl recounted in the Bard's Song concerns the responsibilities of three of Los's sons in the 6,000-year cycle of planting and harvesting human souls in the Vegetable World. As Los has set things up, Rintrah the "Reprobate" son, whose dominant passion is Wrath, opens the soil with his Plow; the "Redeemed" son Palamabron, whose passion is Pity, cultivates it with his Harrow; and – contrary to normal agricultural practice – both implements are also used in the harvest (pl. 6:13, E 99). The envious and hypocritically mild-mannered "Elect" son Satan, who has no part in growing anything, is supposed to run the Mill that grinds down the harvested grain, those "dark Satanic Mills" (pl. [i]:8, E 95) amalgamating the reductive mechanisms of British industry, Lockean philosophy, and Newtonian physics. But Satan wheedles his way into Palamabron's position, upsetting the cosmic order and bringing all productive work to a halt, then blames the upheaval on his brother. When Palamabron convenes a "Great Solemn Assembly" (pl. 8:46–48, E 102; cf. Joel 2:15, 2 Kings 10:20) to ensnare Satan in his lying accusations (Proverbs 6:2, Isaiah 28:13), the judgment of "all Eden" unexpectedly falls on "Rintrah and his rage: / Which now flam'd high & furious in Satan" (pl. 9:10–11, E 103) – the subject of a full-page design (pl. [10]). The surprise verdict, as at the climax of a courtroom drama, exposes the true villain.

Satan, now revealed as Urizen's alter ego, "rends off" his family affiliations and creates "Seven deadly Sins" or "principles of moral individuality" from the "uppermost innermost recesses" of his mind, accuses everyone else of violating them, and isolates himself in "a vast unfathomable Abyss" that opens within his bosom, which has grown "Opake against the Divine Vision" (pl. 9:19–35, E 103). In spectral form he sinks into a "Female Space" especially created by his mother to contain and protect him (pl. 10 [11]:1–11, E 104), and he sets "himself above all that is called God" (pl. 11 [12]:12, E 104; 2 Thessalonians 2:3–4). For intensive Bible-readers, this proclamation is a portent of the Second Coming: Satan/Urizen is the "son of perdition" unmasked as the hidden deity worshipped under the "Unutterable Name" (pl. 11 [12]:14, E 104). The Assembly mercifully sets limits of contraction (Adam's finite body and lifespan) and opacity (Satan's blocking of vision) and grants a finite time to Satan's finite space, the traditional 6,000-year span of human time that culminates in the seventh millennium of Christ's reign. These seven eras are presided over by a succession of "eyes of God," the first six being erroneous or incomplete realizations of the divine nature, the seventh the Eternal Great Humanity Divine at last made manifest in the person of Jesus as "Reprobate" and "Transgressor" (pl. 13 [14]:27, E 107).

Here the Bard digresses – and so shall I – to note that the Eternals' verdict raises the crucial question of why "The Innocent should be condemn'd for the Guilty" (pl. 11 [12]:16, E 105; cf. Proverbs 21:18). The answer is that "If the Guilty should be condemn'd, he must be an Eternal Death / And one must die for another throughout all Eternity" (pl. 11 [12]:17–18). As Milton later learns from the Seven Eyes of God – whose collective point of view is generally reliable in this epic of distorted, incomplete, and shifting perspectives – "States Change: but Individual Identities never change nor cease" (pl. 32 [35]:22, E 132). It will be Milton's task, in the main body of the poem, to end the cycle of guilt and condemnation by voluntarily submitting to "Eternal Death" as the first member of a newly created "State" of "Eternal Annihilation" (pl. 32 [35]:22–29). "States" are similar to "Classes" (such as Elect, Redeemed, and Reprobate) in that they exist only insofar as they are populated by "Individual Identities." In accordance with the Eternals' distinction between Negations and Contraries – expressed in the reverse (spirit-writing?) of Book II's half-title inscription: "A Negation is not a Contrary / Contraries are Positives" (pl. 30 [33], E 129) – the states of Redeemed (expressing pity) and Reprobate (expressing wrath) are "Contraries," or vital forces in fruitful opposition, while the Elect state (prideful envy masquerading as pity to conceal suppressed wrath) is only a "Negation" sucking up the Contraries' positive energy. The Elect class and the state Satan, Negations lacking innate existence, cannot be redeemed but must be "continually created" (by recruiting new members, as it were). When no more individuals are in the condition of negating self-righteousness, the Elect will become what a computer programmer might call a null class, a category void of content. Once it is no longer needed, the class itself, as Milton will learn, should be purged from the system: "The Negation must be destroyd to redeem the Contraries" (pl. 40 [46]:33, E 142).

In the second half of the Song, in what might be thought of as a negative "pre-capitulation" of the alternating male-female perspectives in the poem as a whole, the brothers' feminine counterparts take over. Satan's Leutha, modeled on Sin, Satan's daughter and incestuous mate in *Paradise Lost*, "Offering herself a Ransom" (pl. 11 [12]:30, E 105) for her condemned spouse/father, claims to be "Author" of his sin – as Palamabron's Gnomes had recognized (pl. 12 [13]:39, E 106; *PL* 2:760). In her version of events, the trouble started with her attempted seduction of Palamabron. To evade the "artillery" of Palamabron's jealous consort Elynittria, Leutha hid in Satan's brain, she says, and "stupefied the masculine perceptions," keeping "only the feminine awake" (pl. 12 [13]:5–6, E 105). In this effeminized condition

Satan developed the "soft / Delusory love to Palamabron" (pl. 12 [13]:6–7) that led to his downfall. Leutha's surprising confession prompts Elynittria to put down her weapons and bring her rival to Palamabron's bed, where in dreams Leutha bears evil offspring who later become characters in the poem proper. As Leutha is the guilty personification of Satan's "feminine delusion of false pride self-deciev'd" (pl. 11 [12]:26, E 105), however, her taking on his punishment is merely a parody of atonement; it is neither the vicarious sacrifice of an innocent lamb (the doctrine Blake is questioning) nor the self-sacrifice of one who loves another more than life (for Blake, the true meaning of Christ's death, now being rediscovered by Milton).

In response to this "Terrible Song" of charges and countercharges, the convivial heavenly gathering breaks up into theological debates and challenges to poetic authority that drive the Bard to take refuge in Milton's bosom. Whatever else this Song means, it means that art matters; poems have consequences. The nameless Bard, a Romantic extremist of the Shelleyan type, is purely a function: he exists to sing his song and thereby refute W. H. Auden's dictum that poetry makes nothing happen. His refrain, "Mark well my words! they are of your eternal salvation" (pls. 2:25; 3:5, 20; 7:16, 48; 9:7; 11 [12]:31), has put his listeners on notice that what they hear "sitting at eternal tables" is not to be judged by its entertainment value. The Bard, by following his Song into the heart of his fit audience of one, is nudging the hero and the world toward apocalypse – that instantaneous revelation of "Truth or Eternity" that, for Blake, may occur at any time, with the burning-up of error "the Moment Men cease to behold it" (*VLJ*, E 565). And indeed this poem-within-a-poem proves more effective as a conscience-catching device than Hamlet's play-within-a-play: with shock and revulsion, Milton recognizes the worst aspects of his own personality in the self-deceived, self-justifying villain of the piece: "I in my Selfhood am that Satan: I am that Evil One!" (pl. 14[15]:30, E 108); he has identified his whole being with his core ego (not to be confused with Blake's creatively subversive Devil in *The Marriage of Heaven and Hell*).

Having absorbed the Bard into his bosom, Milton understands that "without my Emanation" (pl. 14 [15]:28, E 108) only his Pharisaically self-righteous nuclear Selfhood had been ensconced in heaven. By reducing himself to this closed-in, self-defensive, self-preserving, emptied-out center, Milton had maintained a lifelong self-image of moral and artistic superiority – in morals, an abstemious "niceness of nature, an honest haughtiness and self-esteem" (*Apology for Smectymnuus*, Hughes 694); in art, a "lofty and steady confidence in himself, perhaps not without some contempt of others."[9] Belatedly, Milton grasps the Gospel truth that he who loves his life shall lose it, and in the first of a series of magnificent speeches expressing successively deeper levels of self-understanding, he twice announces, "I go to Eternal Death!" (pl. 14 [15]:14, 32; E 108). As he speaks, Milton "took off the robe of the promise, & ungirded himself from the oath of God" (pl. 14 [15]:13; cf. Isaiah 61:10, 1 John 2:25, Revelation 7:9, 14), a more radical action than his having been "Church-outed" for refusing to "subscribe slave and take an oath withal" to enter the Anglican priesthood (*Reason of Church Government*, Hughes 671). Milton's self-divestment from his Elect status, depicted in a full-page illustration (pl. [16]), begins a purgatorial process (defying Protestant doctrine) that will lead to a true state of blessedness, as suggested by the halo radiating from his head as he turns his back on the setting sun of a false heaven and takes the first step toward his lost emanation.

From this point on, the levels of action splinter into parallel universes as the fragmented and shape-shifting Milton, on multiple planes of reality, sloughs off his false nature, annihilates his hypermasculine ego, regains his personal and artistic integrity, and recovers his full humanity. To work out his sexual and gender confusions in Beulah, the realm of sexual fulfillment surrounding Eternity, he enters with "direful pain" into "his own Shadow; / A mournful form double; hermaphroditic: male & female / In one wonderful body" (pl. 14 [15]:36–38, E 108). As his Shadow falls into the "Sea of Time & Space" to enter Blake, "that portion named the Elect: the Spectrous Body" splits off into "Los's Mundane space" (pl. 20 [22]:21, E 114) and redounds as a "black cloud over Europe" (pl. 15 [17]:50, E 110), whereupon Milton realizes that he had already unknowingly seen Beulah on earth "In those three females whom his Wives, & those three whom his Daughters / Had represented and contained" (pl. 17 [19]:1–2, E 110), and (most important!) "they and / Himself was Human" (pl. 17 [19]:6). But at the level of Milton's "Mortal part" (pl. 20 [22]:10, E 114), his material body or fossilized corpse, the patriarch appears as Moses' "Rock Sinai," surrounded by his women-folk in the form of Canaanite "rocks of Horeb" writing his dictates (pl. 17 [19]:9–17, E 110). Here Blake alludes to Milton's enlisting one daughter as his night-time amanuensis and having two daughters read aloud to him in languages they did not understand – a "scene of misery," in Johnson's words, that Blake also knew from its recent entrance into the visual arts.[10]

Meanwhile, Milton's "Redeemed portion" (pl. 20 [22]:11, E 114), as depicted in a full-page wrestling/icon-toppling scene (pl. [18]) in which Milton splits the word "Self-/hood" with his right foot, struggles with Urizen on the banks of the Arnon, the river between Canaan and the Promised Land. Milton sculpts new flesh on his enemy with the "red clay of Succoth" (root meaning of "Adam" plus casting ground for Solomon's temple vessels, 1 Kings 7:46) while, breaking Urizen's hold on the Ten Commandments, he wards off a deathly brain-chilling baptism in the "icy fluid" of the Jordan (pl. 19 [21]:6–14, E 112). As if all this weren't enough, on still another level Milton's "Sleeping Body," assisted by "Spirits of the Seven Angels of the Presence" (pl. 15 [17]:3, E 109; Revelation 8:2) "now arose and walk'd with them in Eden, as an Eighth / Image Divine tho' darken'd" (pl. 15 [17]:4–6). From the perspective of Eternity, Milton's Shadow self, beneath the "couch of Death," resembles a "Polypus that vegetates beneath the deep" (pl. 15 [17]:8) and his "real and immortal Self" appears "as One sleeping on a couch / Of gold" (pl. 15 [17]:12–13), while from the perspective of the "shades of hell," the Shadow appears "a trail of light as of a comet" (pl. 15 [17]:19). But within Milton's own primary consciousness, "to himself he seemd a wanderer lost in dreary night" (pl. 15 [17]:16).

Instead of wandering, though, Milton is making a "track" (diagrammed on plate [36], E 133) through the "Mundane Egg" (pl. 19 [21]:15, E 112) or "Mundane Shell," the illusion of our confinement in space and time, a "vast Concave Earth: an immense / Hardend shadow" (pl. 17 [19]:21–22, E 110) defined by the two "limits" of Satan and Adam, opacity and contraction. In Milton's movement toward the mundane, which crisscrosses Blake's movement toward vision, space-time is accelerated, warped, and whizzed into multiple dimensions. Scattered visionary insights are gathered into a single moment, as when Los steps out of the sun in Lambeth (pl. 22 [24]:11, E 117) and whirls Blake to Felpham (pl. 36 [40]:22–24, E 127), while instantaneous glimpses of spiritual reality are anatomized, to be explored nanosecond by nanosecond by different participants, and by the same participant from different points of view. The focal point is the visionary "Moment in each Day that Satan cannot find / Nor can his Watch Fiends find it" (pl. 35 [39]:42–43, E 136), the here-and-now measured between human heartbeats. To Los, who can "walk up and down" throughout history, "Every Time less than a pulsation of the artery / Is equal in its Period & value to Six Thousand Years / For in this Period the Poets Work is Done" (pls. 28 [30]:62–29 [31]:1, E 127); similarly, "every Space larger than a red Globule of Man's blood / Is visionary," and "every Space smaller than a Globule of Man's blood opens / Into Eternity" (pl. 29 [31]:19–22). From the perspective of Eternity, the perception of the "reasoner" that Earth is "a Globe rolling thro Voidness" is a "delusion" (pl. 29 [31]:15–16). For Milton, as a "traveller thro' Eternity," heaven is "a vortex passd already, and the earth a vortex not yet pass'd" (pl. 15 [17]:35, E 109); "travellers from Eternity. Pass outward to Satans seat," where Milton is headed, "But travellers to Eternity. Pass inward to Golgonooza," where Blake is going. Because Blake's journey is the same as Milton's, his arrival at the city's Gate promises – if he acts upon his new insights after the poem's open-ended conclusion – to fulfill "an old Prophecy in Eden" that Milton "Should up ascend forward from Felphams Vale & break the Chain / Of Jealousy from all its roots" (pl. 23 [25]:37–38, E 119; cf.20 [22]:57–62, E 115).

Consideration of the bizarre image of Milton's meteoric entry into Blake's "left foot" at the "tarsus" (pl. 15 [17]:49, E 110) cannot be deferred indefinitely. Generally considered an allusion to the Damascus Road conversion of Paul (formerly the Pharisee Saul of Tarsus, Acts 9), it is depicted in a full-plate design (pl. [32]; Fig. 32) of the instant before impact: Blake's head and upper body are thrown back almost horizontally, his bent right leg buckling under the strain, his arms wide apart, as in paintings of saints receiving the marks of Christ's wounds in their palms and ankles. Although Blake reports first seeing Milton "in the Zenith as a falling star" (pl. 15 [17]:47; *PL* 1:745), his retrospective gaze suggests the broad trajectory of Milton's supposedly "perpendicular" (pl. 15 [17]:48) descent. Only later does he recognize its "vast breach," for "man cannot know / What passes in his members till periods of Space & Time / Reveal the secrets of Eternity" (pl. 21 [23]:7–10, E 115). On his smitten foot he sees the Vegetable World as "a bright sandal," which he binds on "to walk forward thro' Eternity" (pls. 21 [23]:12–14, 22 [24]:5; E 116); at this point, he is joined by Los, who steps out of the sun (pl. [47]) and infuses Blake's soul with "fury and strength" (pl. 22 [24]:6–14).

Meanwhile, in Milton's world, the hero's renewed concern for his emanation is bringing him closer to the moral level of his own Adam, who at the cost of his own salvation had willingly chosen Eve over Paradise (*PL* 9:958–59). Although Milton's vow to "redeem" Ololon still smacks of debt-payment, his self-giving expectation that he will "himself perish" is an "unexampled" form of self-sacrifice (pls. 2:21, E 96; 23 [25]:56–58, E 119) because he believes he will suffer the irretrievable loss of his immortal soul. What Milton does not yet know is that Ololon – who epitomizes the misunderstood and mistreated women in his life, the female figures of his poems (mainly Eve from *Paradise Lost*, Dalila from *Samson Agonistes*, and the chaste Lady from *Comus*), and the alienated and unfulfilled feminine and creative aspects of his still-unrealized full humanity – is simultaneously undertaking her own quest to rescue him. Milton's journey, patterned after Satan's journey from Hell through Chaos to Earth in *Paradise Lost*, recalls the Greek myth of the poet Orpheus's descent into Hades to save his dead wife Eurydice, while Ololon's reverse action – opening a "wide road...to Eternity" (pl. 35 [39]:35, E 135; cf. *PL* 2: 1025–26) – is like that of Alcestis, who gave up her life as a surrogate for her husband Admetus. Ololon's story is also, in effect, a rewriting of Milton's only real love poem, *Methought I Saw My Late Espoused Saint*, his sonnet about a dream of his veiled spouse (generally understood to be Katherine Woodcock, his second wife) "Brought to me like *Alcestis* from the

Figure 32 *Milton*, plate 31 (E [32]). Copy C.

grave." But instead of vanishing just as she is about to embrace Milton, as in the sonnet, Blake's Ololon-Alcestis engages him in an honest face-to-face discussion which ends with their mutually casting off impediments to their reunion. This is the "Mutual Forgiveness" that re-opens Paradise (*For the Sexes: The Gates of Paradise*, lines 1–2, E 259).

Operating like Milton on multiple planes of reality, Ololon (whose name probably derives from the same root as "ululation") is at once a mild and pearly river in Eden (pl. 21 [23]:15, E 115); the multitudinous inhabitants of a community along its banks (pl. 21 [23]:16) who, drunk with the spirit at the feast in heaven, miss hearing the Bard's Song and wrathfully drive Milton out of heaven (pls. 20 [22]:43–46, E 114; 21 [23]:31–34, E 116; 34 [38]:3–5, E 133); a sixfold composite of Milton's three wives and three daughters in the "deep" (pl. 17 [19]:1–2, E 100); a cluster of rocky Canaanite hills surrounding Milton/Mount Sinai in the "Desarts of Midian" (pl. 17 [19]:16); and a twelve-year-old virgin in conversation with Blake on earth in human time (pl. 36 [40]:16–20, E 137). The emphasis on Ololon's youthful virginity is probably a critique of Milton's exaggerated regard for chastity: he even insisted, as a widower, that his second and third wives be virgins to spare him from the "gross and indelicate" predicament of being a "second husband".[11] Some aspects of Milton's and Ololon's reunion remain private ("wondrous were their acts by me unknown / Except remotely," pl. 40 [46]:2–3, E 141), but their final climactic confrontation, witnessed by Blake, results in the simultaneous dissolution of her virginity and his puritanical "Selfhood."

Feminist critics have rightly concerned themselves with Ololon's submissive and contingent status in the dramatic concluding scene. But Ololon has already made independent contact with "the Family Divine as One Man even Jesus / Uniting in One with Ololon" (pl. 21 [23]:58–60, E 116), and she has been ordained, in the unmistakable voice of Jesus at the ascension ("Lo! I am with you alway," pl. 21 [23]:56; Matthew 28:20), to the ministry of the Holy Spirit: "Watch over this world, and with your brooding wings, / Renew it to Eternal Life" (pl. 21 [23]:55–56). It is her arrival in Blake's garden that precipitates Milton's final self-recognition and self-annihilation of Milton-as-Satan (imitating the Eternal Great Humanity Divine on a "Paved-work / of precious stones" (pl. 39 [44]:24–25, E 140; Exodus 24:10, Ezekiel 28:2–16). Only after resisting the temptation to destroy this ultimate Satan as something external to himself is Milton ready, in the "grandeur of Inspiration," to "wash off the Not Human," "cast off the rotten rags of Memory" and take off Albion's "filthy garments" of Bacon, Locke & Newton" (pl. 41 [48]:1–6, E 142) – an echo of "all our righteousnesses are as filthy rags" (Isaiah 64:6). Here Ololon, having been converted from wrath to pity in Book I, and now self-liberated from her virginity, takes the form of apocalyptic clouds that signal the Second Coming (pl. 41 [48]:7–15; Daniel 7:13, Matthew 24:30, 26:64, 1 Thessalonians 4:17, Revelation 1:7). Surrounding Milton, now one of the "Starry Eight" who "with one accord" merge into "One Man Jesus the Saviour," Ololon's clouds are "folded as a Garment dipped in blood / Written within & without in woven letters" (pl. 42 [49]:12–13, E 143) – another apocalyptic image, this time blending the Word of God's "vesture dipped in blood" (Revelation 19:13) with the book "written within & without" (Ezekiel 2:10, Revelation 5:1) – the Book of Revelation itself. And on the very last page (pl. 43 [50]) a female figure, probably Ololon, divests herself of her grain-covering to reveal her human form.

In an age culturally inured to the tone and conventions of biblical prophecy, we resist poetry that, in Keats's words, "has a palpable design on us," especially – in an academic setting – words of "eternal salvation" from a self-proclaimed "Inspired Man." The more Blake and his characters speak in this vein, the more analytical filters and buffers we are likely to employ in critically "processing" *Milton*: we hear not prophetic authority but authoritarianism, not exhortation but fanaticism, not a voice crying in the wilderness but the ravings of someone who has gone off his medication. But if we grant other poets their gods and heroes, fairies and dragons, vampires and werewolves, or Wordsworthian "Huge and mighty forms," perhaps we owe it to Blake, on the same basis, to suspend disbelief in the soul-saving rhetoric of lower-class evangelistic Protestantism.

But be warned: suspended disbelief can be risky. For Blake's self-representation as a prophetic visionary is more than a rhetorical device eliciting ordinary literary-critical responses. His purpose is to change lives, so that through those changed lives a nation and a world may be redeemed. It is easy, with twenty-first-century hindsight, to pounce upon Blake's failings and blind spots – but this eventuality, too, Blake has anticipated. As the Preface indicates, the New Age demands from its youth new works of imagination – possibly in the form of literary, graphic, or musical creations that would do for Blake what Blake did for Milton: correct his errors and free up his misdirected creative energies to regenerate contemporary society. If we are to achieve a more imaginative, humane, and forward-looking vision of gender equity and reconciliation, we must look to a new prophet – not an Ezekiel this time, but a new Deborah, perhaps, or a voice-hearing activist like Joan of Arc, someone with the strength to re-envision all that is liberating in Blake's work, release his energies, and seek correction, in her turn, by a still more far-sighted artist–prophet, male or female, of the yet more distant future. Meanwhile *Milton: A Poem* urges each reader, here and now, to make a start.

Blake paid a high personal price for his Decade-of-Milton achievements. Yet in choosing Art over Mammon, he made an excellent bargain. To the adoring young artists who brightened his impoverished later years, he was a model of cheerful industry; and he died in ecstasy, singing songs of his own composition, with the light of vision burning in his eyes. To seek that inspiration, even today, is the best reason for reading Blake at all.

Notes

1. Quotations of Milton are from *John Milton: Complete Poems and Major Prose*, ed. Merritt Y. Hughes (New York: Odyssey Press, 1957); poetry is identified by book and line numbers (e.g., *Paradise Lost: PL* 2:1025), prose by page numbers in Hughes (e.g., Hughes 611).
2. Concerning "the Atonement in the ordinary Calvinistic Sense," Blake remarked: "It is a horrible doctrine; If another pay your debt, I do not forgive it" (*BR* 548).
3. A coinage by Joseph Anthony Wittreich, Jr., ed., *Milton and the Line of Vision* (Madison: University of Wisconsin Press, 1975), to distinguish the "visionary tradition" from the "line of wit" that descends through Donne, Dryden, and Pope (pp. xiv, 98).
4. Robert N. Essick and Morton D. Paley, " 'Dear Generous Cumberland': A Newly Discovered Letter and Poem by William Blake," *Blake/An Illustrated Quarterly* 32:1 (summer 1998), pp. 4–13; for a roadside photograph of the partially obscured cottage (privately owned), see *BR* pl. LVII, opp. p. 561.
5. William Hayley, *The Life of Milton* (London: T. Cadell and W. Davies, 1796), "second edition, considerably enlarged," facs., intro. Joseph Anthony Wittreich, Jr. (Gainesville, FL: Scholars' Facsimiles & Reprints, 1970); Samuel Johnson, "Milton" (1778) in *Lives of the English Poets*, ed. Ernest Rhys, intro. L. Archer Hind, 2 vols. (London: Dent; New York: Dutton, 1925), pp. 55–114, esp. pp. 58, 65, 93.
6. *The Repose in Egypt* (now lost), Butlin 405.
7. See Nancy Goslee, " 'In Englands green & pleasant Land': The Building of Vision in Blake's Stanzas from *Milton*," *Studies in Romanticism* 13 (1974), pp. 105–25.
8. This scenario supports Blake's 1803 claims of having produced "an immense number of verses on One Grand Theme Similar to Homers Iliad or Miltons Paradise Lost" on his "Spiritual Acts" in Felpham and having "perfectly completed" a "Sublime Allegory" about his "trouble," "the Grandest Poem that This World Contains" (letters of 25 April and 6 July 1803, E 728, 730).
9. Johnson, *Lives*, p. 60.
10. Romney's idealized treatment of the scene, designed for Hayley's 1793 edition of Milton, and Fuseli's chilling work of the same year are reproduced in Gert Schiff, *Johann Heinrich Füsslis Milton-Galerie* (Stuttgart: Fretz & Wasmuth, 1963), pls. 63 and 62.
11. Johnson, *Lives*, p. 79.

Further reading

Milton: A Poem

Bracher, Mark. *Being Form'd: Thinking Through Blake's* Milton. Barrytown, NY: Clinamen Studies, Station Hill Press, 1985.
Cooper, Andrew M. "Blake's Escape from Mythology: Self-Mastery in *Milton*."

Doubt and Identity in Romantic Poetry. New Haven: Yale University Press, 1988. 54–76.

DiSalvo, Jackie. *War of Titans: Blake's Critique of Milton and the Politics of Religion.* Pittsburgh: University of Pittsburgh Press, 1983.

Erdman, David V. "The Steps (of Dance and Stone) that Order Blake's *Milton.*" *Blake Studies* 6 (1973): 73–87.

Essick, Robert N. and Joseph Viscomi, eds. *William Blake*: Milton a Poem *and the Final Illuminated Works*: The Ghost of Abel[,] On Homers Poetry [*and*] On Virgil[,] Laocoön. Blake's Illuminated Books. Vol. V. Princeton: The William Blake Trust / Princeton University Press, 1993.

Fox, Susan. *Poetic Form in Blake's* Milton. Princeton: Princeton University Press, 1976.

Grant, John E. "The Female Awakening at the End of Blake's *Milton*: A Picture Story, with Questions." *Milton Reconsidered: Essays in Honor of Arthur E. Barker.* Ed. John Karl Franson. Salzburg: Universität Salzburg, 1976. 78–102.

Howard, John. *Blake's* Milton: *A Study in the Selfhood.* Rutherford, NJ: Farleigh Dickinson University Press; London: Associated University Presses, 1976.

James, David E. *Written Within and Without: A Study of Blake's* Milton. Frankfurt: Peter Lang, 1977.

Mitchell, W. J. T. "Style and Iconography in the Illustrations of Blake's *Milton.*" *Blake Studies* 6:1 (1973): 47–71.

Newlyn, Lucy. "Milton." Paradise Lost *and the Romantic Reader.* Oxford: Clarendon Press, 1993. 257–78.

Riede, David. "Blake's *Milton*: On Membership in the Church Paul." *Re-Membering Blake.* Ed. Mary Nyquist and Margaret Ferguson. New York: Methuen, 1987, 257–74.

Rivero, Albert J. "Typology, History, and Blake's *Milton.*" *Journal of English and German Philology* 81 (1982): 30–36.

Rose, Edward J. "Blake's *Milton*: The Poet as Poem." *Blake Studies* 1 (1968): 16–18.

Sandler, Florence. "The Iconoclastic Enterprise: Blake's Critique of 'Milton's Religion.'" 1972. Rev. edn. *Essential Articles for the Study of William Blake, 1970–1984.* Ed. Nelson Hilton. Hamden, CT: Archon Books, 1986. 33–55.

Vogler, Thomas A. "Re: Naming MIL/TON." *Unnam'd Forms: Blake and Textuality.* Ed. Nelson Hilton and Thomas A. Vogler. Berkeley: University of California Press, 1986. 141–76.

Welch, Dennis M. " 'Cloth'd with Human Beauty': *Milton* and Blake's Incarnational Aesthetic." *Religion & Literature* 18:2 (1986): 1–15.

Wittreich, Joseph Anthony, Jr. *Angel of Apocalypse: Blake's Idea of Milton.* Madison, WI: University of Wisconsin Press, 1975.

Youngquist, Paul. "Criticism and the Experience of Blake's *Milton.*" *Studies in English Literature* 30:4 (1990): 555–71.

Illustrations of Milton's works

Behrendt, Stephen C. *The Moment of Explosion: Blake and the Illustration of Milton.* Lincoln: University of Nebraska Press, 1983.

Davies, J. M. Q. *Blake's Milton Designs: The Dynamics of Meaning*. West Cornwall, CT: Locust Hill Press, 1993.

Dunbar, Pamela. *William Blake's Illustrations to the Poetry of Milton*. Oxford: Clarendon Press, 1980.

Franson, John Karl. "Christ on the Pinnacle: Interpretive Illustrations of the Crisis in *Paradise Regained*." *Milton Quarterly* 10 (1976): 48–53.

Johnson, Mary Lynn. "'Separating What Has Been Mixed': A Suggestion for a Perspective on *Milton*." *Blake Studies* 6:1 (1973): 11–17.

Mulhallen, Karen. "William Blake's Milton Portraiture and Eighteenth Century Milton Iconography." *Colby Library Quarterly* 14:1 (March 1978): 6–21.

Pointon, Marcia R. *Milton and English Art*. Toronto: University of Toronto Press, 1970.

Tayler, Irene. "Say First! What Mov'd Blake? Blake's *Comus* Designs and *Milton*." *Blake's Sublime Allegory*. Ed. Stuart Curran and Joseph Anthony Wittreich, Jr. Madison: University of Wisconsin Press, 1973. 233–58.

Werner, Bette Charlene. *Blake's Vision of the Poetry of Milton: Illustrations to Six Poems*. Lewisburg: Bucknell University Press, 1986.

13

ROBERT N. ESSICK

Jerusalem and Blake's final works

Is *Jerusalem* unreadable? Several of its ringing declarations – "I must Create a System, or be enslav'd by another Mans / I will not Reason & Compare: my business is to Create" (pl. 10:20, E 153) – have become cultural mottoes in our time. But is *Jerusalem* more than a curiosity shop with some treasures amidst the clutter? Viewing the work from afar permits orderly schemes of supposed comprehension; but the closer we come to the poem's walls of words, the less clear our vision, the less certain our resolve to persevere through all 100 plates. To plunge into *Jerusalem* is to confront a profoundly unsettling experience.

The text of *Jerusalem* appears to be a narrative, replete with reasonably standard English syntax, a third-person narrative voice, named characters, and events. Yet these ingredients resist linkage into a chronology of represented actions constituting a story, much less a sequence of causes and consequences forming a plot. The characters seem like human personalities for brief passages, but they expand or contract into polymorphous personifications of psychic or cosmic categories resisting both stability and definition. These entities give speeches, but they constitute a series of monologues rather than conversations. Space is granted more than three dimensions, with Britain, Palestine, and fictive places mixed and matched like skewed map overlays. Time is also multiple, with moments and eternities each containing the other. The poem immediately assumes a command of Blake's private mythology, as though he had carried the epic tradition of beginning *in medias res* to a bizarre conclusion: not the middle of a famous action, but the middle (muddle?) of Blake's mind. Yet, for all its freedom from the consensus realities that make texts readable, *Jerusalem* is highly repetitious in its imagery and actions. We are tossed about with maximum sound and fury but appear to get nowhere until suddenly, on the last few plates, the poem ends with an apocalyptic big-bang. Perhaps we should decide that *Jerusalem* is a poem to be experienced, not understood, and allow Blake's long, irregular seven-stress lines to wash over us, their cadences both lulling and harsh detached from sense.

Did Blake himself presume to understand his creation? He claims on the third plate that the poem was "dictated" to him (E 145); amanuenses need not comprehend what they write. Was Blake writing for an audience, the "Public" he addresses at the start, or is his work an act of personal therapy? Such questions prompt us to put interpretation aside for the moment and consider the material base, the production history of the work, the biographical context of its composition, and the traditional paradigms and genres it tempts us to deploy as navigational aides. We can then move on to consider image patterns, characters, and themes. But let us not lose sight of our initial experience of the poem's verbal texture and of its whirlwind of pictorial images. And let us not even try to grasp *Jerusalem* the way we can at least pretend to understand Wordsworth or Dickens, but assume instead that Blake questions the very grounds of understanding – not just of his work, but of the world.

Even before leaving his cottage in Felpham and returning to London in the fall of 1803, Blake was working on a "long Poem descriptive" of the "Spiritual Acts of [his] three years Slumber on the banks of the Ocean" (letter of 25 April 1803, E 728). A few months later he commented on "a Sublime Allegory which is now perfectly completed into a Grand Poem" (letter of 6 July 1803, E 730). These references are probably to *The Four Zoas* manuscript rather than *Milton* or *Jerusalem*,[1] but these texts share many styles, themes, and passages. All three were shaped by Blake's difficult relationship with his patron in Felpham, William Hayley; the encounter with the soldier John Scolfield in August 1803 and subsequent trial for sedition; and Blake's later struggles, personal and professional. Seven of the twelve sons of Albion named in *Jerusalem* are in part veiled references to persons involved in Blake's trial; the name of another son, Hyle, is shorthand for Hayley, while Hand alludes to Robert Hunt, who wrote a damning review of Blake's 1809 exhibition of paintings. Several passages describing "Half Friendship" as "the bitterest Enmity," "deep dissimulation" as "the only defence an honest man has," and "General Good" as "the plea of the scoundrel hypocrite & flatterer" (pls. 1:8, 49:3, 55:61; E 144, 198, 205) are responses to Blake's own experiences with friendship, hostility, and the confusing presence of both in the same people.

The 1804 date on the title page of *Jerusalem*, like the same date on the *Milton* title page, marks Blake's first full year back in the maddening yet energizing hurly-burly of London. Blake was in the habit of dating his works according to their conception, or initial and partial composition, rather than the date of completion or publication. This certainly holds true for *Jerusalem*.

Progress was rapid at least until the summer of 1807 when George Cumberland noted that sixty plates had been finished (*BR* 187). Work then slowed considerably as Blake's days were dedicated to several commissioned series of watercolors illustrating John Milton's poems, preparations for his 1809 exhibition, and perhaps finishing *Milton*. Less productive events may have turned Blake away from *Jerusalem* and even led to its temporary abandonment. Dissension with Robert Cromek over the illustrations to Robert Blair's *The Grave* and over the *Canterbury Pilgrims* design, alienation from old friends such as Thomas Stothard and John Flaxman, the failure of the 1809 exhibition (no sales, and only Hunt's review), the sale of at most one copy of *Milton* shortly after its first printing in 1811, the probable failure of his 1812 exhibition of prints from *Jerusalem* to stimulate any interest in the work, and diminishing commercial engraving projects may have been enough to convince Blake, for all his dedication to his art in the face of public indifference, that there would be little purpose in completing *Jerusalem*. It was probably during these dark years that he gouged several lines from plate 3, including references to the blessings of "love" and "friendship." Blake left these wounds undisguised in copies of the book as silent witnesses to the doubts, even despair, against which he struggled.

The opening text plates of *Jerusalem* offer several comments on its composition, structure, and theme. The last is explicitly stated, in accord with epic conventions, at the poem's beginning: "Of the Sleep of Ulro! and of the passage through / Eternal Death! and of the awaking to Eternal Life" (pl. 4:1–2, E 146). Yet the implication that this will be a spiritual journey or quest-romance in three stages is not borne out by the poem's non-sequential narrative. Blake also describes the "Measure" of his poem, one that avoids "a Monotonous Cadence" and stresses "variety in every line" (pl. 3, E 145–46). These "numbers" will conform with three specified emotional and aesthetic modes: "terrific," "mild & gentle," and "prosaic" (pl. 3, E 146). The prefaces that begin each of the four chapters are indeed written in prose, but the few examples of the "mild & gentle" are overwhelmed by the "terrific" (sublimity, guilt, despair, lamentation) dominating the language of *Jerusalem*. The prosody, and presumably a good deal besides, are based not on strictly poetic requirements but on "the mouth of a true Orator" (pl. 3, E 146), a comment which emphasizes the oral dimension and rhetorical intentions of Blake's composition.

The most intriguing prefatory reflection also appears on plate 3: "Every word and every letter is studied and put into its fit place" (E 146). But how can we reconcile such a claim with the fact that Blake rearranged the sequence of plates of chapter 2 in the final two copies of *Jerusalem* he collated? It would seem that *Jerusalem* is responding to one of its own preliminary self-representations much as its author responded to Wordsworth's *The Excursion*: "You shall not bring me down to believe such fitting & fitted" (E 667). Blake's variant plate arrangements and their failure to produce any significant differences in meaning prompt us to hazard our own rearrangements. We could, for example, reconstruct chapter 3 as follows: plates 52–53 (which must come at the start), 69, 63, 73, 64, and then Blake's sequence minus the reordered four plates. Like many other almost-arbitrary collations one can invent, this does not transgress any principles of syntax or continuity, or any unities of voice and action, not already disrupted by the authorial arrangement. A poem so amenable to reconfiguration would appear to violate one of Blake's most direct statements about it, perhaps as part of a more general dynamic that undermines all principles of authority or even the author's intentions one usually assumes are directing literary production.

Like Blake's prelusive comments in and on *Jerusalem*, the basic format of the work offers a tempting display of orderliness. We begin with a frontispiece and title page. Next, four chapters, the first with twenty-three plates (but twenty-five if we include the two prefatory plates), the others with twenty-five plates each. Each chapter begins with a full-page design (the frontispiece filling this role for chapter 1) followed by a prose preface "To the Public [Jews, Deists, Christians]" on a single plate. All but the first preface includes a lyric poem. The work concludes, as it opened, with a full-page design. This comforting stability seduced many twentieth-century Blake scholars into believing that this four-part structure held the key to differences in audience or theme among the chapters and, at least by implication, to the poem's meaning. Several hypotheses were advanced: each chapter is appropriate to the audience addressed in its preface, each is modeled on one of the four Gospels, each is dominated by one of Blake's four Zoas, each deals with one of four stages of the fall or of an individual's life, or the whole poem constitutes "a drama in four acts: a fall, the struggle of men in a fallen world...the world's redemption by a divine man...and an apocalypse."[2] Unfortunately, none of these quaternaries bears close scrutiny. *Jerusalem* certainly includes the grand motifs just quoted, but these are not parceled out according to the chapters. A universal fall occurred before the poem began – although it is equally true to say that we witness repeated falls throughout *Jerusalem*. Chapter 4 indeed concludes with apocalypse; yet, like its companions, it is dominated by the horrors of fallen time and space. Each chapter includes visions of redemption and of prelapsarian and/or postapocalyptic eternities. The poem's conventional, well-ordered macrostructure becomes a bibliographic metaphor for the rationalist and quantitative ways of reading the world subverted by the text's microstructure and explicit declarations against the "excrementitious / Husk & Covering" (pl. 98:18–19, E 257) of enslaving systems.

A movement from structuralist to, broadly speaking, phenomenological approaches to *Jerusalem* was heralded by Curran's 1973 essay, "The Structures of *Jerusalem*" (see note 2). The same volume contains Roger Easson's "Blake and his Reader in *Jerusalem*," which considers the liberating effects the poem's anti-systematic rhetoric has on its readers. Fred Dortort's *The Dialectic of Vision: A Contrary Reading of William Blake's* Jerusalem perceives the poem's repetitions as multiple perspectives, each incomplete and subject to ironic readings, on the same archetypal events. Although differing in many ways, these approaches to *Jerusalem* all search for formulae that generated the poem's peculiar features or our responses to them. We can begin to uncover some of these underlying algorithms, capable of producing complex, repetitious, yet ever-various patterns, by tracing a single image cluster – threads/cloth/weaving/clothes – through the poem.

I will begin with the smallest unit: fibers and threads. *Jerusalem* offers many examples: "fibres" (many times), "iron threads" (which links this image cluster to another – metal-working), "chain" and "chord," "flax," "fibrous veins" (which intersects with another important image field – the human body), "muscular fibres" and even "fibres of thine eyes," "fibres" that take "root" (a link to agricultural imagery), and both "Fibres of dominion" and "Fibres of Brotherhood" (pl. 88:13–14, E 246). Blake weaves these threads into many objects made of cloth: "curtain," "linen," "woofs," "veil" ("vale" and the character Vala by punning extension), "garments of needle work," "net," "mantle," "vesture," "robes," "cushion," "pillow," "A sheet & veil & curtain of blood" (another intersection with the body). The list goes on and on, and can be extended into woven forms such as "wicker," "network," and other coverings, including "self*hood*." The final sub-category of the field is the manufacture of threads and cloth: "loom," "weaving," "mills" (another interface with metal-working), "shuttles," "needle," inter-, over-, and en- "woven," "spinning wheel," "reel," "spindles," "distaff," "treddles," and those animal weavers, the "Silk-worm" and "winding Worm."

This catalogue, only a selection from the entire cluster, is sufficient to indicate several important verbal phenomena. The associations that create the image field are metonymic. Metonymy – the linking of words through shared lexical categories – appears to be fundamental to Blake's "Divine Analogy" (*J* 49:58, E 199), if we can take that term as descriptive of his own methods. As I've noted parenthetically for a few examples above, some of the images in one cluster connect with others. These synapses can also form relationships among characters (e.g., Los, associated with forging metals, and Enitharmon, associated with weaving), and extend to the designs (e.g., nets on plates 4 and 45, women working threads on plates 59 and 100). *Jerusalem* becomes not a seamless but a multi-seamed fabric of interwoven metonymies. This textile extends beyond *Jerusalem* to become allusions to other texts: "Josephs Coat" (pl. 67:23, E 220) to Genesis 37, "an Ark & Curtains" to Exodus 26, and, by implication, all the weaving women to the classical Fates and all the veils to those Milton associates with Eve (e.g., *Paradise Lost* 4:304, 5:383, 9:425). The many references to the Bible, direct and veiled, become a form of extended typology linking the Old Testament, the New Testament, and Blake's own mythologies.

Metonymy has an inherent tendency to convert its terms into the vehicles of metaphors. A few are specified by *Jerusalem* – "Fibres of love" and "shuttle of war" (pls. 4:8, 66:62; E 146, 219) – but most arise through subtle networks of allusion and suggestion that become explicit only within interpretive acts by readers.[3] The image field I have been mapping serves as a metaphor for the texture of the text (from *textere*, to weave) and its apocalyptic impulses (from *apokalyptein*, to unveil), as the rhetorical excesses of this and the previous paragraph are meant to demonstrate. From that self-reflexivity we can move outward to Blake's life, including his profession as a commercial engraver, with its investment in woven patterns of hatching and crosshatching displayed as a white-line background veil on the title page of *Jerusalem*; his family connections (his father and eldest brother were hosiers); and the fact that plates 64 and 96 of *Jerusalem* were cut from a copperplate on which Blake had engraved an advertisement for a carpeting and hosiery firm. From the circumference of these metaphoric possibilities we can move both outward and inward to Blake's concepts: flesh as covering and outline of inner spaces, nature as obfuscating veil, and thought itself as a woven fabric of associations that finds expression through what P. B. Shelley called a "vitally metaphorical" language which "marks the before unapprehended relations of things."[4] Reading *Jerusalem* requires a journey through many such image fields, for all are strands of the "golden string" that will "lead you in" to the "gate, / Built in Jerusalems wall" (pl. 77, E 231). What we find there is closer to the linguistic functions of the brain, at the level of cells and synapses, than to the world of linear time and three-dimensional space we use our brains to construct.

Some further characteristics of *Jerusalem's* verbal dynamics and their thematic implications deserve recognition. The interconnected metonymies tend to collapse the binarisms (metonymy/metaphor, signifier/signified, vehicle/tenor) I have been using. The figural becomes literalized both in the specifics of Blake's language – a female cannot be "like" a loom when "every Female *is* a Golden Loom" (pl. 67:4, E 220) – and in the poem's larger conceptual orientation. The fundamental distinctions between the real and the imaginary, between objective reality and its verbal or pictorial representations, and between being and thinking also become fluid. Indeed, Blake privileges "Mental Things," which "are alone Real" (*VLJ*, E 565), over what we generally consider the realities of time and space, which Blake characterizes as allegorical projections of a fallen state of consciousness. Perceiving the physical universe as an ideological conspiracy authorizes the production of alternative ways of projecting mind into a world. *Jerusalem's* grammar of metonymies finally emerges into both a historical method, a way of investigating parallels among cultures to uncover their common origin, and a multi-dimensional cosmology imaginable through language unchecked by Newtonian physics. The result can be characterized as a psychodrama of being in which the principal forces take the form of prolific fragmentation countered by an anxious desire for everything to come to a grand unity.

My characterizations of the dynamics of *Jerusalem* have discomfiting similarities to attributes which, in the twentieth century, were seen as symptomatic of schizophrenia. Particularly telling in this regard is confusing patterns of thought with objective structures and believing that similarities indicate causation or conspiracy. Blake may have suffered from a mild form of schizophrenia which he could control on a daily basis by channeling its special energies and insights into poems like *Jerusalem*. He claimed that he heard voices and saw visions; both are indicators of unusual brain chemistry. We all hear a voice in our heads. Most of us believe this to be the stream of our own thoughts; the schizophrenic grants the voice independent identity. Blake told Thomas Butts that he had "written" his long "Poem from immediate Dictation twelve or sometimes twenty or thirty lines at a time without Premeditation & even against my Will" (letter of 25 April 1803, E 729) – a comment that should dissuade us from normalizing the reference to dictation in *Jerusalem* as only a traditional bow to the muse. Blake's belief, from about 1802 to 1810, that his friends were conspiring against him suggests the paranoia that frequently accompanies schizophrenia. His unwillingness to abandon his "visionary" poetry, in spite of much advice to do so, is typical of the schizophrenic's unwillingness to seek a cure and thereby suffer the loss of the extra-sensory powers the disease bestows. These personal proclivities find expression in *Jerusalem*: like Blake, Los "percieved that corporeal friends are spiritual enemies" and, with great effort, "kept the Divine Vision in time of trouble" (pl. 44:10, 15; E 193).

A symptomatic explanation for the origin of the poem's oddities does not constitute a devaluation of *Jerusalem*; there can be power, value, and method even in (especially in?) madness. The poem's tendency to merge thinking and being is an exaggerated version of one of the characteristics used to characterize Romanticism, from Immanuel Kant's definition of space and time as categories of consciousness to William Wordsworth's landscapes of the mind. Several texts have been suggested as precedents, even models, for *Jerusalem*. The Bible is of course the most important, especially Revelation, with Ezekiel's warnings about the fallen Jerusalem and his plans for the new (ch. 40–47) a close second. Morton D. Paley has convincingly demonstrated how the poem continues a tradition in the interpretation of Revelation that began with St. Augustine's statement that it contains "many obscure passages to exercise the reader's mind, but few clear enough to illuminate the meaning of others, mostly because the author appears to be saying different things when he is only saying the same thing in different ways."[5] Several seventeenth-century British scholars extended this view into analyses of Revelation as "visionary theatre" comprised of "Parallel-Acts" arranged into a non-chronological "Synchronism" – observations that ring true for *Jerusalem*.

A broad perspective on Blake's participation in religious utterance, both oral and written, can be helpful in contextualizing *Jerusalem*. In many passages, we hear the voice of the preacher, a voice mixing lamentation and rapture that began with the Old Testament prophets, found its most influential period as an expression of Protestant dissent in seventeenth-century England, and continued, in spite of increasing secular dominance of public discourse, into Blake's time and beyond. The Jewish tradition of midrash – the imaginative exegesis of sacred texts – also offers significant parallels. Like *Jerusalem*, the midrashic interpretation of sacred texts is founded on metonymy, for "the correspondences are not between things seen and their hidden or inner meanings, but between texts and the historical contexts in which they were produced or to which they apply, or texts and other texts; between signifiers and signifiers, not between signifiers and signified."[6] Much of *Jerusalem* can be viewed as an expansive commentary on intertextual relations, principally among the Bible, the legendary history of early Britain, and Blake's own mythology.

A third tradition, one specifically poetic, deserves consideration. The metonymic image fields in *Jerusalem* function much like the sound patterns shaping oral-formulaic poems like *The Iliad* and *Beowulf*.[7] Oral composition and its attendant formulae may also lie behind the repetitions in syntax and diction constituting biblical parallelism, first explored in Robert Lowth's *On the Sacred Poetry of the Hebrews* (1753). The images defining any one field in *Jerusalem* tend to cluster in passages of 10–30 lines rather than being randomly distributed throughout the text. This pattern suggests that one image served, like oral formulae, as a mnemonic cue for its associates: "thread" (or "gate" in the architectural image field, or "plow" in the agricultural) would call to Blake's mind other images in the same field. A number of phrases in *Jerusalem* appear to function in a similarly generative manner. "They became what they beheld" appears six times within three plates and becomes almost a refrain; a variant, "they became what they behold," is repeated three times. "Moral" is followed by "virtue" nine times; in the eight passages in which "moral" is without its companion, the word still conjures up formulaic variants (e.g., "morality and virtue," "natural virtue"). "Power" follows "reasoning" six times, twice on each of two plates. "The Starry Heavens are fled [or "were fled"] from the mighty limbs [or "awful Members"] of Albion" four times, and four times he "turns [or is "turning" or "had turn'd" or "should turn"] his back against [or "to"] the Divine Vision." These metonymic patterns and formulaic phrases contribute to the repetitiousness of *Jerusalem*, but they also help establish the myriad interconnections constituting the poem's complex of meanings.

My reference to Albion raises the specter of Blake's mythic characters, their speeches (often anguished) and acts (often futile). The cast is legion, but a simple list of the main characters – four males followed by three females, with thumbnail sketches of their allegorical roles – can provide a useful starting point.[8]

Albion. Humanity, fallen into error (often imaged as sleep), fragmented, resistant to salvation. Guilty about his own desires, he is tormented by "Shame & Jealousy" (pl. 28:27, E 174).

The Saviour/Jesus/Luvah. The emotions and acts necessary for salvation: love, forgiveness, self-sacrifice. Luvah can also represent their opposite: Albion's sons "assimilate with Luvah" and become "bound in the bonds / Of spiritual Hate" (pl. 54:11–12, E 203).

Los. The human imagination working, against great impediments, in the world of time and space. "Los is at the same time Old Testament Prophet, New Testament Evangelist, Miltonic Seraph, ancient British Bard, the classical Hephaistos/Vulcan, alchemist, blacksmith, and watchman."[9] To this list we can add Blake himself as he struggled to create *Jerusalem*.

The Spectre. That portion of each male character necessary to the accomplishment of his task in the material world and yet resisting that goal. From a psychological perspective, these are the powers of execution (e.g., etching skills) – but also "Pride & Self-righteousness" (pl. 8:30, E 151) – and their linked opposites, self-doubt and anxiety – that thwart creative acts. From an objectivist perspective, these are the materials (e.g., copperplates) and social relations (e.g., patronage) necessary for the embodiment of the imagination – but also the resistance of matter to mind and personal entanglements that thwart creative acts. The "othering" or reification of the Spectre and his assumption of an independent will shifts him from the productive to the destructive ends of these spectra.

Jerusalem. Woman, city, poem. Albion's "emanation" – the projected, alienated female portion of his identity. In her ideal form, "Liberty" (pl. 26:3, E 171) – the freedom of the imagination to fulfill itself within and without. The reunion of Jerusalem with Albion, one of the goals of the poem as quest-romance, will return Britain to its prelapsarian condition as one with biblical Palestine.

Vala. The female as absolute other, chief embodiment of the independent "Female Will" (pl. 30:31, E 176), Luvah's emanation (i.e., emotion objectified), and a compound of all the nature goddesses ever invented. Like the beauties of the physical world, her seductive desirability is a trap for the masculine imagination.

Enitharmon. Los's emanation, variously helpmate and hindrance, inspiration for and threat to his artistic/salvific labors.

Following Blake's lead, we must immediately complicate this list, one that already hints at overlapping among the players. The absence of a represented linear temporality in *Jerusalem* hinders the development of characters whose identities reside in consistency or self-sameness over time. The defining distinctions among the characters and their many dependants (e.g., Albion's countless sons and daughters) are at best semi-permeable; they tend to individuate and coalesce in disturbing ways. Jerusalem and Vala are antithetical representations of the female other, yet they are closely related: "...England who is Brittannia divided into Jerusalem & Vala" (pl. 32:28, E 178). Los's "Spectre is named Urthona" (pl. 44:4, E193), but ten lines later Los is "Urthonas Spectre." The differences among these spectres, "Albions Spectre" (pl. 8:34, E 151), and "the Spectre of Man" (pl. 10:15, E 153) are uncertain. Even "Sexual Organization" (pl. 30:58, E 177), a structure underlying many of the poem's conflicts, is transgressed by "Hermaphroditic Condensations" (pl. 58:11, E 207) and the "Male Females" (pl. 75:17, E 231). These disruptions of definitional boundaries find visual parallels in designs showing combinations of species, such as the lepidopterous women of the title page and the bird-headed man on plate 78.

Blake's mythic history of human consciousness offers one explanation for weak character differentiation. All of humanity was once part of a single, universal man: Albion in his prelapsarian condition; divided and contentious humans are his fragments. The generation of differences, memories of a lost unity, and the desire for its restoration mingle throughout *Jerusalem*. Such a narrative, like all chronologies, is at best half-hidden in the poem. Its more dominant synchronic structure suggests that these characters are parts of a single mind struggling to overcome the bipolar conflicts. Yet these unstable personalities also indicate a positive reconfiguration of identity. *Jerusalem* is misogynistic in its representations of female sexuality and agency, but also harbors a critique of the self-sustained, domineering masculine ego – what Blake calls the "Selfhood" and frequently identifies with the Spectre (e.g., pl. 58:48, E 208). The network of shifting characters suggests a radically anti-essentialist concept of the self as a distributed and interactive cognitive phenomenon rather than an individual ego. *Jerusalem* offers a model for what Blake, speaking *in propria persona*, asks from the Saviour: "Annihilate the Selfhood in me" (pl. 5:22, E 147).

From conflicts among the characters, and particularly among the perspectival orientations of their speeches, emerge some of *Jerusalem's* central themes. The range is vast, but many of the poem's core issues can be grouped under four broad topics: violence, sex, religion, and work. Entanglements among the first three underlie the tragedies of fallen time and space that Los, the Saviour, and Blake labor to resolve.

Much of *Jerusalem* is an excursion into the horrific sublime; it may be the most violent, blood- and entrails-splattered poem in English. Dismemberment is particularly important, for it bodies forth the psychic and cosmic fragmentation defining Blake's sense of the fall. The disemboweling of the male at the hands of females, pictured on plate 25, dramatizes the forced alienation of inner spirit into external nature. But violence extends beyond such obvious examples to include a proto-Freudian sense of repression as the wellspring of strife. For Blake, this process began with male/female division and continued into the delimitation of sexuality to "finite inflexible organs" (*BL* 4:45, E 92). As a result, "Sexual Generation swallow[ed] up Regeneration" (*J* 90:37, E 250) and the war between the sexes began. Sexual strife extends into gendered conflicts between mind and nature, inside and outside, most clearly dramatized through the speeches and actions of Vala, but implicit in all the poem's male/female interactions prior to a millennium when all "Embraces are Cominglings: from the Head even to the Feet" (pl. 69:43, E 223).

Blake's description of phallic/vaginal sexuality as "a pompous High Priest entering by a Secret Place" (*J* 69:44, E 223) signals its relationship to religions based on hierarchy and mystery. Violence as the basis of false religions assumes a more pervasive presence in *Jerusalem*. Blake makes only passing reference (pl. 63:30–31, E 214) to the symbolic substitution of animal for human sacrifice and instead introduces the supposed fall of the original patriarchal (and Christian) religion of Britain into Druidism, its dark forests and darker human sacrifices. His investigation of the disturbing nexuses between violence and the sacred extends to Christ's crucifixion and the doctrine of atonement. Self-sacrifice, as the annihilation of selfhood, and forgiveness are routes to salvation; others cannot die for one's own sins. Deism or natural religion is for Blake the contemporary form of Druidism: both sacrifice inner spirit to the worship of outer nature and create theologies of good and evil. The prefatory lyric in chapter 3 epitomizes, through the sufferings of a Christ-like monk, the violence of "Moral Law" when "from the Gospel rent" (pl. 52:18, E 202) and used by tyrants ancient and imperial (Titus, Constantine) or modern and rationalist (Gibbon, Voltaire) against revealed religion.

The labor in and of *Jerusalem* is directed toward overcoming the oppositions and "unnatural consanguinities" (pl. 28:7, E 174) just summarized. Revolutionary and restorative work is inherently mental but also intensely physical – an integration of inside and outside that in itself provides a model for artistic creation and a more fully human universe. Los is the major workman, enlisting the aid of his sons and his Spectre at key junctures, much as Blake turned to his etching skills to build *Jerusalem*. Some of Los's greatest endeavors are represented through images of cities and their buildings. In chapter 1 (pls. 12:45–13:29, E 156–57), he constructs Golgonooza – Blake's London transformed into the city of art – modeled on the New Jerusalem and its temple described in Ezekiel 40:7. It is possible to diagram some features of Blake's Golgonooza,[10] but its gates expand well beyond three-dimensional space to become a metaphor for the expanded senses and the multi-dimensional universe they perceive and in that perceiving create. The city is a quadrangle, but each side is "fourfold" because each side faces (and thus represents) one item from each of four categories: the "World[s]" in Blake's mythic geography of mental states (Ulro, Generation, Beulah, Eden), the four cardinal directions, the four senses, and four substances (gold, silver, brass, iron). Multiples of four (and more) expand until the city becomes less an architectural than a semiotic construct, as though space could be reinvented in accord with the metaphoric multiplicities of poetic language. This wildly dynamic city- and mind-scape epitomizes the tensions in *Jerusalem* between restrictive and magical numbers, between Los's (and Blake's) contrary desires to "deliver Individuals from...Systems" (pl. 11:5, E 154) and yet "Create" their own "System" (pl. 10:20, E 153), and between apocalyptic destruction and millennial reconstruction.

The tendency of fixed structures in *Jerusalem* to become mobile evolves into a visionary physics based on space-bending, dimension-multiplying processes. Expansions are inward as well as outward: "The Vegetative Universe, opens like a flower from the Earths center: / In which is Eternity. It expands in Stars to the Mundane Shell / And there it meets Eternity again, both within and without" (pl. 13:34–36, E 157). Human identity and its relationship to objectivity follow similar trajectories of simultaneous infolding and outfolding: "And Los beheld his Sons, and he beheld his Daughters: / Every one a translucent Wonder: a Universe within, / Increasing inwards, into length and breadth, and heighth" (pl. 14:16–18, E 158). To counter the "wheel without wheel" characterizing Newtonian physics, Blake proposes "Wheel within Wheel [which] in freedom revolve in harmony & peace" (pl. 15:18–20, E 159). *Jerusalem* reconstitutes the physical universe by balancing its outward and alienating expansion with an inward dynamic, one that does not leave a finite human mind stranded in an infinity of space, but rather quests for an interior realm united with that outer infinitude.

I have continued the main interpretive tradition by emphasizing the words and neglecting the pictures in *Jerusalem*. A full study of the work would give equal attention to designs which are as epic as the text in their range of graphic styles, iconographies, and cultural allusions. By considering just one design, I hope to indicate some of the basic issues that arise when we turn to the visual dimension of *Jerusalem*, particularly in regard to text/design relationships and the ways different contexts and the perspectives they generate lead to different interpretations.

Plate 76 is the full-page, white-line design that introduces the final chapter (Fig. 33). The inscription etched in the lower center, "Jesus," confirms the identity of the figure crucified on a fruit-bearing tree. Before him stands "Albion," also inscribed in the plate just below the figure, whose cruciform gesture suggests a traditional *imitatio Christi*, an act of reverence leading to salvation. The position of Albion's arms and legs also imitates his posture in *Albion Rose*, a separate plate designed in 1780 but not given its title inscription – one indicating that the figure represents heroic self-sacrifice – until late in Blake's career. The light emanating from Jesus' head and the similar but weaker rays on the left horizon suggest that the material sun is being replaced by the spiritual Son. A few white lines (like the fruit, difficult to see in most impressions) indicate the tree's roots; some jagged lines form triangles (trees? mountains?) center right. When we consider the figures, their gestures and emotional expression, from a perspective provided by the long tradition of crucifixion scenes in European art, we are led to a positive interpretation of plate 76.

One motif complicates the picture. Which of several trees named in *Jerusalem* are we to associate with the one pictured? It may be the "Tree of Life" (pl. 41:9, E 188) from Genesis 2:9 and Revelation 22:2. Popular religious prints of Blake's time show Jesus crucified on this tree as a double emblem of spiritual life.[11] But could it be the "Tree of Good & Evil," the "deadly Tree" of "Moral Virtue" and "the Law / Of God who dwells in Chaos hidden from the human sight" (pls. 28:15–16, 92:25; E 174, 253)? This tree merges in *Jerusalem* with the oaks, their "dark roots" and "stems of Mystery" (pls. 14: 8, 83:13; E 158, 241), on which the Druids sacrificed their victims; and with "Albions Tree" of "Atheistical Epicurean Philosophy" to

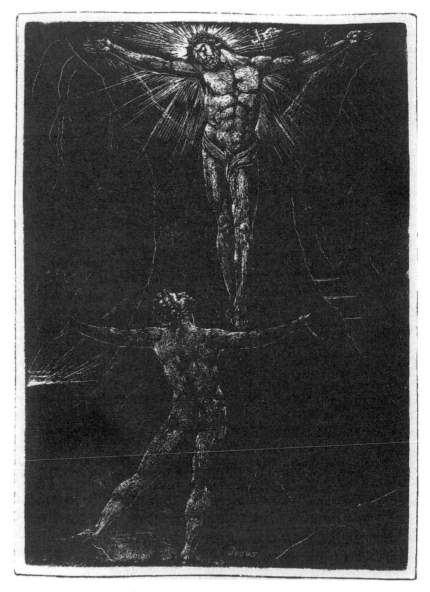

Figure 33 *Jerusalem* 76. Copy A. White-line etching, 22.4 × 16.3 cm.

which Luvah is "naild" (pls. 65:8, 67:13; E 216, 220). The crepuscular light of plate 76 and the dense inking of uncolored impressions find a textual nexus with a world where "the Sun is shrunk" and "the Trees & Mountains [are] witherd / Into indefinite cloudy shadows in darkness & separation" (pl. 66:50–52, E 219). Albion becomes what he beholds – a process associated with the fall in all nine of its appearances in the text. Do these negative associations convert the crucified Jesus into "A Vegetated Christ," an "Evil-One" who has become "the Satanic Body of Holiness" (pl. 90:34–38, E 250)? Or does his radiant self-sacrifice rise above the background of fallen nature?

A consideration of contexts offered by the poem leads us away from an initial response based on a general cultural perspective and into Blake's ambivalent attitudes toward the crucifixion, atonement, and imitation. More generally, the design becomes entangled in the same issues of interpretation haunting a text in which identities are fluid and perspectival differences resist dialectical synthesis. Yet, these characteristics, ones that make *Jerusalem* unreadable by conventional means and make how we understand what we perceive to be a major theme, anticipate the post-apocalyptic world envisioned at the end of the poem. There "All Human Forms [are] identified even Tree Metal Earth & Stone" (pl. 99:1, E 258). All forms are identified *as* human and thus subject to human will – a condition foreshadowed by the liberty the work grants its reader to "Create a System" of meanings out of the *materia prima* of *Jerusalem*. All humans, incorporated into the body of Albion, are perpetually "going forth & returning" as we cross definitional boundaries between "Years Months Days" and "Immortality" (pl. 99:2–4, E 258). The problems encountered by readers of *Jerusalem* become imagined solutions to the world's problems.

Jerusalem is Blake's greatest achievement in the illuminated epic, but his career in the arts did not end with its completion. By 1810 he had begun a tempera of *The Last Judgment* "containing upwards of one thousand figures" (J. T. Smith, quoted in Butlin 648). This large painting, the summation of Blake's long involvement with its subject, remained unsold at Blake's death and is untraced. Among several other late paintings, *The Sea of Time and Space*, dated 1821, is the most intriguing (Butlin 803). The presence of the Fates and an Apollo-like sun god in this complex composition indicate Blake's deep involvement in classical art and mythology during his final years. Yet, his written references to classicism are harshly critical. For all its detailed beauty, *The Sea of Time and Space* would also seem to indicate a rejection of Greek and Roman civilization by the male (possibly Isaiah) at the center of the design.[12]

Soon after their first meeting in June 1818, John Linnell's patronage and the influence of his engraving techniques had a major impact on Blake's life as an artist. Blake returned to some of his most important separate intaglio plates first executed years earlier, including *Joseph of Arimathea Among the Rocks of Albion*, *Albion Rose*, and *The Accusers of Theft Adultery Murder*, to revise their graphic style and add new inscriptions that substantially reinterpret

Figure 34 Four designs illustrating R. J. Thornton's edition of *The Pastorals of Virgil*, 1821.
Relief etching, 14.3 × 8.5 cm.

the images. *For Children: The Gates of Paradise* was transformed into *For the Sexes: The Gates of Paradise*. These revisionary activities offer graphic analogues for the themes of transformation and conversion in *Jerusalem* and other late writings.

In 1819, Linnell introduced Blake to the landscape artist John Varley, for whom Blake drew over 100 "Visionary Heads" (Butlin 692–768 plus a notebook rediscovered in 1988). Blake would call before his mind's eye characters both historical and imaginary and sketch their physiognomic portraits during séance-like sessions. Varley apparently believed in these characters' literal presence; for Blake, they embodied the reality of the imagination. Linnell was also instrumental in acquiring for Blake a commission to produce illustrations for R. J. Thornton's edition of Virgil's Pastorals (1821). Blake's first trial efforts were relief etchings (Fig. 34). As with his earlier attempt to integrate innovative graphics into a commercial project, the illustrations to Blair's *Grave*, these were rejected. But this time the consequences were happier, for Blake produced seventeen small wood engravings to illustrate Ambrose Philips' *Imitation of Eclogue I* which are now considered among the finest work in that medium ever produced by an English artist. Samuel Palmer, one of the young artists who gathered worshipfully around Blake in his final years, described the Virgil wood engravings as "visions of little dells, and nooks, and corners of Paradise" (*BR* 271). But this is a troubled paradise, for the primitive and brooding intensity of the designs and their images of sorrow and threat recall Blake's own disrupted pastoral interlude in Felpham under Hayley's burdensome patronage.

In 1823, Linnell commissioned Blake to engrave a series of illustrations to the Book of Job based on watercolors he first executed for Butts c. 1805–6 (Butlin 550). The twenty-one designs closely follow the biblical story, but also incorporate motifs representing Blake's personal interpretation. At the beginning, Job and his family attend only to the letter, rather than the spirit, of God's laws. He thereby falls under a false conception of God and into the hands of Satan. Job's sufferings climax in the eleventh plate (Fig. 35). Lying on his death-bed, Job sees below the hellish world of fire, mind-forged manacles, and devils his vision has created. Above, the consequences of his false conception of God are revealed through the cloven hoof of the threatening deity and his accompanying serpent. This devil-god points downward with one hand and with the other toward the stony decalogue. The laws of good and evil are the origin of hellish vengeance. Job's spiritual education and material restoration are pictured in the second half of the series. The Job engravings are the culmination of Blake's work as a traditional line engraver and have been interpreted as a commentary on Blake's own tribulations and the spiritual peace he found late in life.

Figure 35 *Illustrations of The Book of Job*, plate 11. Engraving, 19.5 × 15 cm.

Blake began in 1824 to prepare for Linnell a series of 102 watercolors illustrating Dante's *Divine Comedy* (Butlin 812). Many of the watercolors, and all seven of the Dante engravings, were left unfinished at Blake's death, as were his watercolors illustrating Bunyan's *Pilgrim's Progress* (Butlin 829) and an illustrated manuscript of Genesis (Butlin 828). In spite of these many pictorial projects and declining health, Blake did not completely abandon writing and the production of brief illuminated texts. All three of these works were probably meant for distribution to friends rather than for general sale.

Figure 36 *Laocoön*. Copy B. Engraving, 26.2 × 21.6 cm.

On Homers Poetry [and] *On Virgil*, a two-part tract etched in relief on a single plate (c. 1822), boldly proclaims Blake's anti-classicism. In the first part, his critique centers on a concept of general and abstract unity which others have associated with Homer's poetry and which Blake associates with similarly abstract moral principles. He proposes instead that "a Work has Unity...as much in a Part as in the Whole" (E 269) – a view that may be helpful in understanding Blake's own epic ventures. *On Virgil* excoriates "Greece & Rome" as cultures of war and dominion and "destroyers of all Art" (E 270).

In *The Ghost of Abel*, a brief drama etched in relief on two plates and addressed to Lord Byron (whose *Cain, a Mystery* appeared in 1821), Blake again considers the relationship between violence and the origins of religion. Adam and Eve lament over the body of Abel, whose "Ghost" cries out for vengeance, while Jehovah calls the pair to mercy and offers "a Lamb for an Atonement instead / Of the Transgres[s]or" (E 272). Byron, like Cain an outcast "in the Wilderness" (E 270), also deserves "Forgiveness of Sins" (E 272).

The *Laocoön* engraving (Fig. 36), datable to 1826–27, displays Blake's skill at using traditional graphic techniques to lend a sense of volume to a two-dimensional representation of sculpture. As in the Job engravings, Blake surrounds picture with text, but here the words are his own (rather than quotations from the Bible) and are unrestrained by framing lines and motifs. The inscription beneath the plinth reinterprets the famous Hellenistic statue as a copy of an Hebraic original showing Jehovah and his two sons, Satan and Adam, struggling with the serpentine dualities of good and evil. With aphoristic energy reminiscent of the "Proverbs of Hell," Blake juxtaposes nature, war, money, and empire to Jesus, art, and imagination, "The Eternal Body of Man" (E 273). "The Old & New Testaments" are proclaimed to be "the Great Code of Art" (E 274) in Blake's final testament as an artist and poet, one that offers on a single plate a summary of issues and attitudes he had explored at greater length in *Jerusalem*.

Notes

1. Joseph Viscomi, *Blake and the Idea of the Book* (Princeton: Princeton University Press, 1993), p. 316. For the production history of *Jerusalem* and bibliographic details, see pp. 338–60.
2. Northrop Frye, *Fearful Symmetry* (Princeton: Princeton University Press, 1947), p. 357. For a more detailed but equally skeptical overview of fourfold interpretations, see Stuart Curran, "The Structures of *Jerusalem*," in *Blake's Sublime Allegory*, ed. Curran and Joseph Anthony Wittreich, Jr. (Madison: University of Wisconsin Press, 1973), pp. 329–46.
3. For the metaphoric significances of the thread/cloth images throughout Blake's poetry, see Nelson Hilton, *Literal Imagination* (Berkeley: University of California Press, 1983), pp. 79–146.
4. "A Defence of Poetry" in *Shelley's Poetry and Prose*, ed. Donald H. Reiman and Sharon B. Powers (New York: W. W. Norton, 1977), p. 482.
5. Paley, *The Continuing City: William Blake's* Jerusalem (Oxford: Clarendon Press, 1983), pp. 283–94 (my source for quotations of seventeenth-century commentators). B. Dombart, ed., *Sancti Aurelii Augustini Episcopi De Civitate Dei*, vol. II (Leipzig: B. G. Teubner, 1863), p. 387 (bk. 20, ch. 17), author's translation.
6. Daniel Boyarin, *Intertextuality and the Reading of Midrash* (Bloomington: Indiana University Press, 1990), p. 110.

7. For the relationship between oral-formulaic poetry and Blake's, see Robert N. Essick, *William Blake and the Language of Adam* (Oxford: Clarendon Press, 1989), pp. 174–78.

8. These characters are also described in the Glossary to this volume. A straightforward summary of speeches and events in the poem can also be useful, for which see William Blake, *Jerusalem: Selected Poems and Prose*, ed. Hazard Adams (New York: Holt, Rinehart and Winston, 1970), pp. 728–42; Minna Doskow, *William Blake's* Jerusalem: *Structure and Meaning in Poetry and Picture* (Rutherford, NJ: Fairleigh Dickinson University Press, 1982), *passim*; "Event Catalogues" in Fred Dortort, *The Dialectic of Vision: A Contrary Reading of Blake's* Jerusalem (Barrytown, NY: Station Hill Arts, 1998), pp. 85–90, 155–62, 257–70, 385–400.

9. Paley, *Continuing City*, p. 234.

10. See the ground plan in S. Foster Damon, *A Blake Dictionary*, ed. Morris Eaves (Hanover and London: University Press of New England, 1988), p. 163.

11. David Bindman, "William Blake and Popular Religious Imagery," *Burlington Magazine* 128 (1986), pp. 712–18.

12. For a detailed interpretation, see Christopher Heppner, *Reading Blake's Designs* (Cambridge: Cambridge University Press, 1995), pp. 237–77.

Further reading

Blake, William. *Jerusalem*. Ed. Morton D. Paley. London: William Blake Trust/Tate Gallery, 1991.

Milton a Poem and the Final Illuminated Works. Ed. Robert N. Essick and Joseph Viscomi. London: William Blake Trust/Tate Gallery, 1993.

Curran, Stuart, and Joseph Anthony Wittreich, Jr., eds. *Blake's Sublime Allegory*. Madison: University of Wisconsin Press, 1973.

Dortort, Fred. *The Dialectic of Vision: A Contrary Reading of Blake's* Jerusalem. Barrytown, NY: Station Hill Arts, 1998.

Doskow, Minna. *William Blake's* Jerusalem: *Structure and Meaning in Poetry and Picture*. Rutherford, NJ: Fairleigh Dickinson University Press, 1982.

Essick, Robert N. *William Blake, Printmaker*. Princeton: Princeton University Press, 1980.

Lindberg, Bo. *William Blake's Illustrations to The Book of Job*. Åbo: Åbo Akademi, 1973.

Norvig, Gerda S. *Dark Figures in the Desired Country: Blake's Illustrations to* The Pilgrim's Progress. Berkeley: University of California Press, 1993.

Paley, Morton D. *The Continuing City: William Blake's* Jerusalem. Oxford: Clarendon Press, 1983.

Roe, Albert S. *Blake's Illustrations to the Divine Comedy*. Princeton: Princeton University Press, 1953.

A GLOSSARY OF TERMS, NAMES, AND CONCEPTS IN BLAKE

ALEXANDER GOURLAY

Adona	The name evokes Adonis, associated in classical mythology with anemones, early death, and mourning; see Ovid, *Metamorphoses* 10. See also **names**.
Ahania	An **emanation of Urizen**. Her name evokes both Urania, the muse associated with astronomy and the heavens (and an epithet of celestial Venus), and also the surprised laughter of discovery: "Aha!" She is associated with pleasure (Urizen calls her "sin"), and her twelve sons correspond to the signs of the zodiac. See also **names**.
Albion	A traditional name for England, and the name of a mythical giant inhabitant of the island. In Blake, the giant Albion represents the country and its inhabitants but also the fallen personification of all humankind, the Eternal Man. **Jerusalem** is his **emanation**. The Daughters of Albion are the women of England.
Albion's Angel	Blake's designation for the King's primary messenger/henchman (Bute?), who debated the thirteen colonial angels, especially Boston's angel (Samuel Adams?).
ark	Noah's ark symbolizes all that preserves the holy in the tribulations of this world, and is typologically related to the vessel in which Moses was found among the bulrushes. The Ark of the Covenant (an elaborate chest) held Moses' broken tablets of the Law and was kept in the innermost sanctuary of a tabernacle (see

veil). Blake employed arks in a wide variety of metaphorical ways reflecting several interpretive traditions.

augury
Roman augurs based prophecies on bird flight; an augury can be any kind of divination, usually based upon signs in nature.

ball
See **globe.**

Bard
Bards were prophets/poets of ancient Britain, often associated with the **Druids** and with native opposition to the Romans or Normans, as in Thomas Gray's *The Bard* (1757), which by Blake's day had subversive overtones. The Bard of *Songs of Experience* is Blake's presiding poetic persona in that book, a role parallel to that of the **Shepherd** in *Innocence.*

Behmen [Boehme], Jacob
The works of this mystical philosopher (1575–1624) profoundly influenced Blake's thinking throughout his career. Like **Swedenborg,** Boehme offered Blake a model for radical allegorical reading of the Bible.

Beulah
The happy land called "married" in Isaiah 62 is in Blake the best version of fallen existence, a dreamy paradise in which the sexes, though divided, blissfully interact in shameless selflessness. Beulah communicates in dreams and visions with **Ulro,** the least redeemed version of the fallen world.

Boston's Angel
See **Albion's Angel.**

Bromion
The name evokes "Bromius," an epithet for Dionysus meaning "roarer." As a reactionary bully in *Visions* and elsewhere he sometimes acts like another roarer, Boreas, the North Wind, who raped Oreithyia; see Ovid, *Metamorphoses* 6. See also **names, Palamabron.**

butterfly/moth
Moths and butterflies are treated very similarly in Blake, though the distinction between them should not be forgotten; either could be a "fly." Blake followed the classical tradition of associating moths and butterflies with the soul. See also **worm.**

cart	The cart that accompanies the **plow** is a dungcart.
classes	In Milton's theology, the Elect are saints predestined to salvation no matter what they do, the Redeemed are saved by Jesus, and the Reprobates or Transgressors are damned. In *Milton* Blake turned this scheme on its ear, making Jesus a Transgressor and representing the Elect as self-righteous Pharisees. See also **states**.
contrary	Contraries are alternatives that are both true and/or important, essential to each other, and yet apparently in opposition, such as justice and mercy, innocence and experience. See also **negation**.
converse/conversation	The word "conversation" historically includes various interactions between individuals, especially intimate ones, and in Blake's day "criminal conversation" was the usual legal term for adultery. Blake used the word broadly and with a strongly positive connotation.
covering cherub	Blake's designation for all the most dangerous false images or ideas of the divine, especially those demanding human sacrifice.
Devil	In *Marriage*, Blake's Devil offers antidotes to conventional heavenly thinking. This satirical creation should be distinguished from **Satan**, who is, at best, error personified.
divided man	The four aspects of the divided or fallen man are the humanity, the **emanation**, the **shadow**, and the **spectre**.
Druids	Druidism was the religion of the pre-Christian Britons, associated with the **Bards**, but also with human sacrifice.
Eden	Like most of Blake's places, Eden is a state of mind as well as a location.
Edom	The advent of the "dominion of Edom" in *Marriage* suggests that hairy, primitive Esau (a.k.a. Edom) will reclaim his birthright, of which he was defrauded by his younger and

	smoother twin Jacob (a.k.a. Israel); see Genesis 27.
elect	See classes.
emanation	When Eve was created out of Adam's rib, she became his emanation, a separated feminine counterpart with a will of her own. This separation is itself a stage or an aspect of a fall, giving rise to conflict and misunderstanding between the emanation and the diminished masculine entity that remains. Many of Blake's female characters are identified as emanations of male characters, and in most cases the relationship between character and emanation is somewhat like that between Milton's Adam and Eve (or Satan and Sin) at various points in their stories. A character may be an emanation (aspect) of one character but the child (consequence) of others. In *Jerusalem* the concept of emanations is developed most fully; both male and female emanations exist even within the integrated beings in eternity, but in that circumstance the emanations do not have a will or a voice of their own. See also **divided man, shadow, spectre.**
Enion	The **emanation** of **Tharmas,** the body, Enion personifies bodily impulses, especially maternal ones. See also **Enitharmon, names.**
Enitharmon	The beautiful **emanation** of **Los,** the Poet. Her name suggests "harmony" and is either a combination of **Tharmas** and **Enion,** or (more likely) these names were extracted from it. In *Europe* Enitharmon presides over the 1,800-year reign of a religion of chastity, guilt, and retribution. See also **names.**
Eno	Eno, an anagram of "eon," is an "ancient mother," representing the 7,000 years of human history in the fallen world.
Eternal Great Humanity Divine	The **imagination** perceives Jesus as all humanity in one man.
Eternals	See **Four Zoas.**

eternity	Eternity for Blake was not simply an infinite amount of time but rather the absence of the illusion of linear time and its sequentiality. From a truly eternal perspective, all events happen simultaneously and all space is the same infinite place. Much of the vertigo that attends reading Blake's prophecies diminishes when one recognizes that they are in part intended to make something like an eternal perspective available to us.
Experience	See **Innocence**.
female will	See **will**.
flowers	Flowers in Blake are associated with both transient beauty and femininity, especially the female genitalia, but one must also investigate the characteristics of each flower he mentions or depicts; most of his floral images draw upon myths, poetic conventions, and botanical peculiarities of particular species.
fly	See **butterfly**.
four/fourfold	Blake developed his own version of the mystical habit of thinking in terms of sets of four such as the four compass points, seasons, humors, and bodily organs.
Four Zoas	Revelation 4 describes four *zoa*, living creatures or beasts; Blake appropriated this plural term for his fourfold division of the aspects of all humanity, represented by **Albion**. The four are **Los/Urthona** (imagination), **Luvah/Orc** (passion), **Tharmas** (body/instinct), and **Urizen** (intellect/law). See also **Divided Man**.
generation	The cycle of birth and death through which life persists in the fallen world.
genius	Blake usually uses the word "genius" in its older sense, meaning a personifying or epitomizing spirit rather than a brilliant person. See also **Poetic Genius**.
globe	When seen from fallen perspectives, objects such as the earth or one's own heart appear to be globes folded in on themselves rather than infinite. See also **vortex**.

Golgonooza	The city of Golgonooza is the human body seen from a visionary perspective.
Har	In the unpublished poem *Tiriel* and in *The Song of Los*, Har and Heva are an aged Adam and Eve in a (neo)classical garden world; in *Thel*, the vales of Har seem to be a special version of Arcadia, traditionally a region of Greece once populated by amorous idle **shepherds**. See also **names**.
harrow	In agriculture, the harrow, tool of **Palamabron**, breaks up the earth turned over by the **plow**; in Blake both are also used in the **harvest**.
harvest	The culmination of Blake's agricultural master-metaphor, the harvest un-creates the created world at the end of time, and includes the **Last Judgment**.
Hayley, William	A famous writer (1745–1820) who patronized Blake (in both senses of the word), setting him up in a cottage near Hayley's house at Felpham. Blake recorded the resulting intellectual and spiritual struggle in *Milton*, in which **Satan** partly corresponds to Hayley.
Heva	See **Har**.
imagination	Blake's ultimate human faculty, the imagination not only perceives the divine, but is the divine. See also **Eternal Great Humanity Divine, Los**.
Innocence and Experience	Innocence and Experience are **contrary states**, different ways of seeing and dwelling in the world. Individuals in a state of Innocence are generally neither ignorant nor unaware of the darker aspects of life, but are sustained by confidence in the redemptive presence of the divine, perceived as both sympathetically human (often like a loving parent) and somehow nearby. Those in Experience are often acutely conscious of the limitations of fallen life and its sorrows, often cripplingly so, and for them the divine may seem inhuman, inscrutable, impossibly distant, and cruel, though experienced visionaries, like the **Bard**, may be bitterly, indignantly, or

	transcendently aware of infinite and eternal potentialities.
jealousy	Jealousy in love is a fearful projection of the **selfhood**; Blake rejected the "jealous God" of Exodus 20 as a false deity.
Jerusalem	The woman called Jerusalem is the **emanation** of the giant **Albion**, though she is also the city and has an assortment of symbolic attributes and associations, such as Blake's true church, the "Divine Vision," and Liberty itself.
Joseph of Arimathea	In legends Joseph buried Jesus in a tomb of his own making and later founded the first Christian church in England (at Glastonbury); for Blake he was an archetypal Christian artist.
lark/skylark	The lark responds ecstatically to the morning, and unlike most birds it sings while flying.
Last Judgment	A last judgment definitively separating truth from error is scheduled for the end of time, but is also possible whenever one achieves an eternal perspective. See **eternity**.
Leutha	In *Visions* "Leutha's vale" seems to be Oothoon's designation for the female genitals; in *Milton* Leutha plays a part corresponding to that of Sin in Milton's *Paradise Lost*, Book 2. In *The Four Zoas* she is the **emanation** of **Bromion**, and as sin or sexual guilt she is associated with several other characters. See also **names**.
limits	The idea of limitation in Blake often indicates impediments to reaching the eternal and infinite, but the word usually refers to merciful limits upon falling in various ways, as in the Limits of Opacity (blindness) and Contraction.
Los	One of the **Eternals** or **Four Zoas**, Los is the **imagination**, and his work as a blacksmith is to create poetry. He is the temporal manifestation of **Urthona**, his **emanation** is **Enitharmon**, and as the spirit of revolution he is the father of **Luvah/Orc** – passion and revolutionary energy respectively. See also **names**.

Luvah	The name suggests "lover," and in *Thel* and elsewhere in Blake he is an amorous Christ-like figure, sometimes associated with the sun. His passionate nature is also reflected in his alternative identity as **Orc**. He is the third of the **Four Zoas**. See also **Los, names**.
Lyca	The name suggests "wolf-girl," perhaps reflecting her sojourn among wild animals. See also **names**.
marygold	An emblem of renewable virginity, the marigold grows new flowers when old ones are plucked.
Memory	See **Mnemosyne**.
mill/Miller	The inferior adjunct to the **plow** and other agricultural implements; a grinding mill is also a complex but dead mechanism, and became Blake's figure for **Newton's** materialist model of the universe. The Miller not only grinds but also buys and sells the produce of the **Plowman**.
Milton, John	As the author of Christian epics in English, Milton (1608–74) was more important to Blake than any other predecessor, though Blake had significant objections to Milton's theological and social thinking – the satirical *Marriage of Heaven and Hell* and the epic *Milton* suggest the extent of Blake's admiration and of his reservations. Blake's several series of illustrations of *Paradise Lost, Paradise Regained, Comus, On the Morning of Christ's Nativity*, and *L'Allegro* and *Il Penseroso* constitute both homage and further critique.
Mne Seraphim	This obscure name vaguely suggests a hybrid connection with both **Mnemosyne** and the angelic **Seraphim**, but it is probably more important that Thel's older sisters, the other Daughters of Mne Seraphim, are busy shepherdesses like the Heliades of classical myth, who tend the flocks of Helios, the sun. See also **Mnetha, names**.
Mnemosyne	Mnemosyne or Memory was the mother of the Greek Muses, which Blake associated with

	inspiration inferior to that of **prophecy** or **vision** and imaginative poetry.
Mnetha	This name evokes both **Mnemosyne** and a scrambled Athena, the Greek goddess of learning associated with warfare. She sustains the degenerate **Har** and **Heva**. See also **names**.
moth	See **butterfly**.
mundane egg/shell	The mundane egg is the material world and its universe, the mundane shell the sky. See **globe**, **vortex**.
Nameless Shadowy Female	She is a daughter of **Urthona** and consort of **Orc**; she is a fallen Mother Nature, rather like **Vala**.
names	When Blake created characters he invited us to think about them as people, and to imagine their words and deeds as those of human beings somewhat like ourselves. He provided no glossaries to explain their names or tell us what they "really" represent, even though he must have expected that readers would find the names confusing, alarming, amusing, or sublime. Many of his characters correspond roughly to more familiar beings from various mythologies, but renaming them suggests that Blake hoped we would start afresh with them as characters, before someone has told us who they are and what they mean. At the same time, most of his characters are multivalent allegorical beings corresponding simultaneously to such things as mental faculties, emotions, psychological categories, political figures or positions, geographical entities, body parts, and so forth. Consider the various polyglot etymologies that have been proposed for their names, though many of them appear to be puns in English with echoes of familiar names from other mythologies. But one should also savor the human dramas in which Blake's characters interact before allegorizing them away. One more caveat: Blake's characters may change in radical fashion, especially when separated from

their **emanations**, and characters from one context may be presented from a very different perspective elsewhere, even in the same work, and may be known by several different names; this glossary greatly oversimplifies such complexities.

nature
: For Blake, the material world of external nature is an illusory projection of the fallen senses; the **imagination** allows individuals to perceive the connection of nature with themselves and the divine.

negation
: Unlike a **contrary**, a negation is the absence of a positive principle, as cruelty is the negation of mercy; justice, by contrast, is the contrary of mercy. See also **shadow**.

Newton, Isaac
: Blake consistently associated the mathematician, scientist, and philosopher (1642–1727) with narrowminded mechanistic materialism.

Nobodaddy
: This comical name suggests an imaginary, abstract, paternal sky-god on the model of Zeus, Jupiter and/or any other punitive God the Father. See also **names**.

of
: This slippery word, which occurs in many of Blake's titles and other critical phrases, should be scrutinized carefully. Does it mean "pertaining to," "composed by," "derived from," "owned by," "based on," "characterized by," a combination of these, or something else?

Ololon
: The collective name, suggesting "all alone," "ululation," or "alleluia," for **Milton**'s neglected "Sixfold **Emanation**" (his three wives and three daughters), as well as a river, those who dwell along it, a mountain range, and a solitary twelve-year-old virgin who speaks for them all.

Oothoon
: The name evokes James Macpherson's Ossianic heroine, Oithona, who fought back after being raped. In *Visions* she is "the soft soul of America," and in later works she plays various

roles as a woman frustrated in love. See also
names.

orc   An orc is a killer whale but also a terrestrial
humanoid monster: Blake's Orc represents
revolutionary energy, a manifestation of **Luvah**,
passion. The so-called "Orc Cycle" in which
rebels and tyrants endlessly supplant each other
is a non-Blakean invention. See also **names**.

Palamabron   In *Europe*, Palamabron is the son of
Enitharmon and **Los** and brother of **Rintrah**.
Like Rintrah he emerges in response to
oppression, but he is "mild & piteous" rather
than angry, and is distinguished as well from
Bromion and **Theotormon**. In *Milton*,
Palamabron struggles with the **Miller/Satan**.
His tool is the **harrow**. See also **names**.

piper   Traditionally a homemade panpipe is the
instrument of the languid shepherd-poet of
Arcadia and related pastoral worlds; piping
and composing songs (mostly about love, loss,
and the natural world) are treated as
interchangeable activities in pastoral poetry.

plow/plowman   A plowman performs the essential masculine
work of the fallen world, as defined in Genesis
3; the feminine work is **weaving** or spinning.
Blake thought of engraving as a kind of
plowing and represented himself as Chaucer's
Plowman, but in his poetry plowing can also be
a metaphor for the disruptive aspects of
revolution or even the processes of mutability.
Various characters use plows, including **Los**,
Rintrah, **Urizen**, and others. In Isaiah 2:4, the
destructive alternative to the plow is the sword;
see also **harrow** and **mill/Miller**.

Poetic Genius   Blake's ultimate imaginative being, at once God
and the "true Man," is the Poetic Genius. See
also **genius**.

polypus   A polypus is a cuttlefish or octopus or, in
medicine, an octopus-like tumor (polyp);
Blake's aquatic invertebrate, with additional
characteristics suggesting a jellyfish or sponge,

	incorporates all these senses, usually representing slow-growing institutions of the fallen world such as religions and governments.
prophecy	Not a prediction but a visionary account of reality, future, past, and present.
questions	Readers of Blake should examine his characters' questions carefully: not all seek answers.
Rahab	A harlot and monster in the Bible, Rahab represents militaristic religion.
ratio	Blake regularly punned on the modern sense of "ratio," fraction or proportion, and the older meaning of the word, reason, which apprehends only a fraction of reality.
Redeemed/Reprobate	See classes.
Rintrah	Rintrah first appears in *Marriage*, as a spirit of revolutionary wrath-to-come. Later books represent him as the son of Los and Enitharmon and group him with Bromion, Palamabron, and Theotormon; each manifests a different response to oppression/repression. See also names.
Satan	Not the Devil, but Error, the accuser of sin, who blinds the mind to the divine. See also Hayley.
self annihilation	Abandonment of the selfhood, which may seem like suicide from some perspectives.
selfhood	A term derived from the writings of Boehme (Behmen) that refers to the perception of oneself as being essentially separate from the divine and from other beings, leading to self-centeredness and selfishness. See spectre.
Seraphim	The Hebrew plural of Seraph, an order of angels, sometimes associated with inspiring prophecy. See also Mne Seraphim.
sexes	Division into the sexes is a major aspect of the fall. See also Beulah, emanation.
shadow	The aspect of the divided man representing repressed desire.
shepherd	Golden Age shepherds lived with as few as possible of the comforts and commodities (and attendant compromises) of civilization; Blake's

good shepherds are often typologically related to Jesus. See also **Piper.**

spectre/spectrous   The spectre is that aspect of the **divided man** generated by the **selfhood,** a parody of intellect consisting of self-defensive rationalization, especially in opposition to an **emanation.**

spinning   See **weaving.**

state/states   Each individual passes through states, stages of error, or fractional consciousness characteristic of given times in one's life, such as **Innocence** and **Experience.** States endure but apply only temporarily to any given individual. See also **classes.**

Swedenborg, Emanuel   Swedish scientist, engineer, and mystical philosopher (1688–1772) whose followers founded a church in London that Blake briefly joined and then repudiated. Blake's thought and writings were strongly influenced by Swedenborg's writings even after he left the Swedenborgian New Church. In the *Marriage* Blake satirically appropriated Swedenborg's announcement of the advent of a new age and parodied his visionary narratives.

Tharmas   One of the **Four Zoas,** Tharmas is the instinctual self. See also **names.**

Thel   Often glossed as "**will**" or "wish," this name more likely reflects the title of a controversial book by Martin Madan, *Thelyphthora* (1780), which means "destruction of the female," in which case the name means "female." See also **names.**

Theotormon   The name suggests "god-tormented." His character in *Visions* may have been in part a response to the autobiographical *Narrative of a Five Years' Expedition against the Revolted Negroes of Surinam* (1796) by J. G. Stedman. In later books Theotormon is grouped with **Rintrah, Palamabron,** and **Bromion.** See also **names.**

Tiriel	The son of **Har** and **Heva** in Blake's first abortive attempt at a prophetic book, *Tiriel*. See also **names**.
Tirzah	The "mother of my Mortal part" who is addressed in a late addition to *Songs* is more closely related to the sexual torturer Tirzah in *The Four Zoas, Milton*, and *Jerusalem* than to a woman and a city of the same name in the Bible. Blake may have been attracted to the name because it sounds like "tears." See also **weaving/woven**.
Transgressors	See **classes**.
Tyburn	The traditional site for public executions in London throughout most of the eighteenth century was the gallows at Tyburn. Blake saw the "Tyburn Procession" of doomed men and women as a vestige of **Druid** ceremonies of human sacrifice. Tyburn was little used after 1780, but executions continued elsewhere.
tyger	In Blake's day tigers were regarded as prodigiously and relentlessly bloodthirsty.
Ulro	The material world at its most fallen, from which the happiness of **Beulah** can only be glimpsed in dreams and visions. See also **names**.
Urizen	The name resembles Uranus, god of the heavens, and suggests a double-barreled pun on "Your Reason" and "Horizon," the limit on perception imposed by Your Reason. He is one of the **Eternals** or **Four Zoas**, associated with intellect and with various forms of rationalism, literalism, and materialism. He is usually tyrannical or at least wants to be so, but he is often weak and pathetic, and occasionally heroic. Readers should resist identifying all bearded old men as Urizen, or automatically assuming that Urizen is the bad guy in any narrative in which he appears. See also **names**.
Urthona	The proto-identity of **Los**, one of the **Four Zoas**. The name suggests "earth-owner," and

like Los (and Hephaestus/Vulcan) he is a blacksmith, associated with the **imagination**; he forges the **plow**. See also **names**.

Vala
The **emanation** of **Luvah**, Vala is Nature. The name may be based upon that of a Scandinavian earth-spirit, but in English it suggests both "vale" and "**veil**," associating her with both the natural world and seductively coy beauty. See also **names**.

vegetable/vegetative
The vegetable world is the world of ordinary material being, slow of growth and merely temporal and temporary. See also **Polypus**.

veil
Most veils in Blake are typologically related to the temple veil that separated the holy of holies from the worshippers and was rent at the moment of Jesus' death on the cross. Veils are also associated with coyness, blindness, selfishness, self-enclosure, the body, and the hymen. See also **ark, Vala.**

vision
Blake distinguishes ordinary "single vision," mere optical reality, from higher forms of vision that perceive things metaphorically, imaginatively and eternally.

vortex
In the physics of René Descartes (1596–1650), a vortex is a whirling object appearing as a sun or star in space, throwing off light centrifugally as it spins. The word "vortex" applies also to whirlpools and whirlwinds, so a vortex can suck things into itself and into another dimension. For Blake, the vortex was a way of explaining how a "Wild Flower" can open up to be "a Heaven" (E 490). Everything has its own vortex and appearance as one approaches it; as one passes through, it unfolds progressively on the other side like a globe or a sky or a man. In *The Four Zoas* **Urizen** constructs a mechanistic heaven of Cartesian vortices.

war
In this world human energies are perversely consumed in physical warfare, but in **Eternity** warfare is intellectual and creative.

weaving/woven	The traditional work of Eve in the fallen world is spinning or weaving, as opposed to Adam's work, plowing or digging (see **plow/plowman**). Blake often represents the material body as having been woven; *Auguries of Innocence* says it is woven of joy and woe.
wheels	Most of the many wheels in Blake are associated at some level with the gears of a clockwork, suggesting a mechanism like an orrery, but some, such as the eyed wheels associated with the creatures Blake called the **Four Zoas**, or the spinning wheels of **Enitharmon** (see **weaving**), are charged with other kinds of significance.
will	The will is the impulse of the **selfhood**. The female will is the impulse to self-protection and resistance to reintegration of the emanated feminine aspect. See **emanation**.
worm	Anything from a caterpillar to a maggot, a cankerworm, or an earthworm; some of Blake's characters refer to Man as a worm of sixty winters or of seventy inches.
Zoa	See **Four Zoas**.

GUIDE TO FURTHER READING

ALEXANDER GOURLAY

Important works by authors and artists other than Blake

Those wishing to understand Blake will benefit at least as much from studying the
texts that he knew well as from reading critical literature. Blake was a profound and
careful reader, though of course he read things in his own way. Bentley's *Blake Books*
(see "Bibliographies") lists some books that Blake owned, though he might not have
read them all or studied those particular editions, and many of his books (such as
a copy of Bunyan's *Pilgrim's Progress*) must have been thumbed into inky tatters –
and have not survived. All Blake readers should keep a King James edition of the
Bible handy (preferably one that shows alternative glosses), as well as a concordance
and a commentary that reflects eighteenth-century commonplaces. Blake apparently
read most poets whose works were available in English, even some who seem rather
uncongenial, but his readers must study Milton's poetry and prose, especially *Paradise
Lost*, as well as Spenser's *Faerie Queen*, Edward Young's *Night Thoughts*, and Ovid's
Metamorphoses. Blake's works seem less strange to those who know the poetic tales
attributed to Ossian and the writings of Emanuel Swedenborg; it is most edifying to
study the latter in conjunction with Blake's annotations, available in most editions
of Blake. Other sorts of writers who inspired Blake include Mary Wollstonecraft and
Thomas Paine, whom he admired, and Joshua Reynolds and Edmund Burke, whom
he despised.

One should also learn as much as possible about the iconographic and semiotic
traditions in which Blake was steeped, not only the high iconography of the European
art tradition, which Blake studied mostly in prints (especially Dürer, Raphael,
Michelangelo), but also vernacular imagery: Hogarth prints; children's books; satirical caricatures by Gillray and others; books of emblems and "street criers"; political
broadsides and posters; designs on fabrics, ceramics, and coins; scientific, botanical,
and technical illustrations; and a vast ocean of unpretentious commercial illustrations of the Bible, historical subjects, and literature, at the margins of which Blake
spent his whole career as a professional artist.

Editions of Blake's writings

The most widely cited scholarly edition of Blake's writings is Erdman's (usually called
"E"), which includes a quirky commentary by Harold Bloom. The 1977 edition of
Blake's writings by G. E. Bentley, Jr., includes judicious editorial punctuation, is

thoughtfully and extensively annotated, and contains many monochrome images of Blake's illuminations. For most purposes these two have supplanted the great edition by Geoffrey Keynes, called "K," which, however, remains useful because Erdman's *Concordance* (see "Concordances and dictionaries" on p. 291 below) is keyed to it. The selective editions of Blake's writings listed contain some helpful editorial apparatus. In addition, see "Catalogues, reproductions and facsimiles" on pp. 292–93 below, for reliable texts of Blake's *Notebook* and *Blake's Illuminated Books*. See "Internet resources" on p. 293 below, for some sophisticated electronic texts.

Bentley, G. E., Jr., ed. *William Blake's Writings*. 2 vols. Oxford: Clarendon Press, 1977.

Erdman, David V., ed., with commentary by Harold Bloom. *The Complete Poetry and Prose of William Blake*. (1965) Rev. edn. Berkeley and Los Angeles: University of California Press, 1988.

Johnson, Mary Lynn, and John E. Grant, eds. *Blake's Poetry and Designs*. New York: Norton, 1979.

Keynes, Geoffrey, ed. *Blake: Complete Writings with Variant Readings*. 1966. 3rd edn. Oxford: Oxford University Press, 1979.

Ostriker, Alicia, ed. *William Blake: The Complete Poems*. Harmondsworth, Middlesex: Penguin, 1977.

Stevens, David, ed. *William Blake: Selected Works*. Cambridge: Cambridge University Press, 1996.

Stevenson, W. H., ed. *Blake: The Complete Poems*. 1971. 2nd edn. London and New York: Longman, 1989.

Basic critical introductions

Michael Ferber's little book is an excellent beginner's guide to Blake's early works; Summerfield's much larger volume is not proportionately more helpful, although it covers more. Paley and Klonsky address Blake's visual art broadly.

Ferber, Michael. *The Poetry of William Blake*. London: Penguin; New York: Viking, 1991.

Klonsky, Milton. *William Blake: The Seer and His Visions*. New York: Harmony Books; London: Orbis, 1977.

Paley, Morton D. *William Blake*. New York: Dutton; Oxford: Phaidon Press, 1978.

Summerfield, Henry. *A Guide to the Books of William Blake for Innocent and Experienced Readers*. Gerrards Cross, Bucks: Colin Smythe, 1998.

A few major works of criticism

Bindman, David. *Blake as an Artist*. Oxford: Phaidon; New York: Dutton, 1977.

Damrosch, Leopold, Jr. *Symbol and Truth in Blake's Myth*. Princeton: Princeton University Press, 1980.

Davies, Mark. *Blake's Milton Designs: The Dynamics of Meaning*. West Cornwall, CT: Locust Hill, 1993.

De Luca, Vincent Arthur. *Words of Eternity: Blake and the Poetics of the Sublime*. Princeton: Princeton University Press, 1991.

Eaves, Morris. *William Blake's Theory of Art*. Princeton: Princeton University Press, 1982.

Erdman, David V. *Blake: Prophet against Empire: A Poet's Interpretation of the History of His Own Times*. 1954. Reprint of 3rd edn, 1977. New York: Dover, 1991.

Erdman, David V., and John E. Grant, eds. *Blake's Visionary Forms Dramatic*. Princeton: Princeton University Press, 1970.

Essick, Robert N. *William Blake, Printmaker*. Princeton: Princeton University Press, 1980.

Ferber, Michael. *The Social Vision of William Blake*. Princeton: Princeton University Press, 1985.

Frye, Northrop. *Fearful Symmetry: A Study of William Blake*. Princeton: Princeton University Press, 1947.

Heppner, Christopher. *Reading Blake's Designs*. Cambridge: Cambridge University Press, 1995.

Hilton, Nelson, ed. *Essential Articles for the Study of William Blake, 1970–1984*. Hamden, CT: Archon Books, 1986.

Mee, Jon. *Dangerous Enthusiasm: William Blake and the Culture of Radicalism in the 1790s*. Oxford: Clarendon Press, 1992.

Mitchell, W. J. T. *Blake's Composite Art*. Princeton: Princeton University Press, 1978.

Tannenbaum, Leslie. *Biblical Tradition in Blake's Early Prophecies: The Great Code of Art*. Princeton: Princeton University Press, 1982.

Tayler, Irene. *Blake's Illustrations to the Poems of Gray*. Princeton: Princeton University Press, 1971.

Thompson, E. P. *Witness Against the Beast: William Blake and the Moral Law*. Cambridge: Cambridge University Press; New York: New Press, 1993.

Viscomi, Joseph. *Blake and the Idea of the Book*. Princeton: Princeton University Press, 1993.

Warner, Janet. *Blake and the Language of Art*. Kingston and Montreal: McGill-Queen's University Press, 1984.

Wilkie, Brian, and Mary Lynn Johnson. *Blake's Four Zoas: The Design of a Dream*. Cambridge, MA: Harvard University Press, 1978.

Periodicals

Blake/An Illustrated Quarterly offers well-informed articles and reviews of recent books, an annual bibliography, and a review of sales of Blake-oriented items. *Studies in Romanticism* regularly publishes articles on Blake, as do *The Wordsworth Circle* and *Huntington Library Quarterly*. Many other journals publish articles on Blake occasionally.

Bibliographies

The indispensable bibliographies of Blake materials are Bentley's *Blake Books* and *Blake Books Supplement*, which catalogue in detail original copies of Blake's texts in print and in manuscript, all editions of his writings, illustrations in conventionally printed books, books he is known to have owned, and Blake criticism in all languages up to early 1993 with brief, occasionally acerbic comments on most entries.

Up-to-date bibliographical information (including book reviews) can be found in the annual "Blake and His Circle: A Checklist of Recent Scholarship," in *Blake/An Illustrated Quarterly* (see "Periodicals," above). Mary Lynn Johnson's chapter in *The English Romantic Poets* reviews the most important work up to 1985 and provides an incisive guide to Blake study organized by topic. See p. 293 below, "Internet resources," for additional bibliographical tools.

Bentley, G. E., Jr. *Blake Books: Annotated Catalogues of William Blake's Writings in Illuminated Printing, in Conventional Typography and in Manuscript.* Oxford: Clarendon Press, 1977.
  Blake Books Supplement. Oxford: Clarendon Press, 1995.
Johnson, Mary Lynn. "William Blake." *The English Romantic Poets: A Review of Research and Criticism.* Ed. Frank Jordan. 4th edn. New York: Modern Language Association, 1985. 113–252.

Biographies

All subsequent biographies are but incremental improvements upon Gilchrist, yet Ackroyd's recent book is often insightful, and Bentley's painstaking compilations of biographical materials, as well as the recent biography, are reliable and very complete. Several new biographical studies of Blake are soon to be published.

Ackroyd, Peter. *Blake.* London: Sinclair-Stevenson, 1995; New York: Knopf, 1996.
Bentley, G. E., Jr. *Blake Records.* Oxford: Clarendon Press, 1969.
  Blake Records Supplement. Oxford: Clarendon Press, 1988.
  The Stranger from Paradise: A Biography of William Blake. New Haven and London: Yale University Press, 2001.
Gilchrist, Alexander. *The Life of William Blake, Pictor Ignotus.* 1863. Reprint edn. New York: Dover, 1998.
Wilson, Mona. *The Life of William Blake.* 1927. 3rd edn. Oxford: Oxford University Press, 1971.

Concordances and dictionaries

Damon's dictionary is an essential tool for Blake scholars at all levels, but beginners should use it with care; Damon is always illuminating, but doesn't consistently explain how he arrived at his insights. Erdman's *Concordance* is keyed to the page numbers of the Keynes edition of Blake's writings (see "Editions" on pp. 288–89 above). A glossary of Blakean terms and concepts will eventually be included among the tools available in *The William Blake Archive*, and a powerful concordance feature tied to the Erdman edition (E) is available online at *The Blake Digital Text Project* (see "Internet resources" on p. 293 below).

Damon, S. Foster, with an introduction and index by Morris Eaves. *A Blake Dictionary: The Ideas and Symbols of William Blake.* 1965. 3rd edn. Hanover, NH: University Press of New England, 1988.
Erdman, David V. *A Concordance to the Writings of William Blake.* 2 vols. Ithaca, NY: Cornell University Press, 1967.

Catalogues, reproductions, and facsimiles

Bentley's *Blake Books* and its supplement (see "Bibliographies" on pp. 290–91 above) also catalogue individual copies of the illuminated books and many of Blake's illustrations and engravings associated with books. The standard *catalogue raisonné* of Blake's non-graphic visual art is Butlin's *Paintings and Drawings*, which includes terse critical comments in most entries, bibliographies on individual works, and useful color or monochrome reproductions of most of Blake's visual art except for prints; it catalogues but does not reproduce several large groups of works that are available in other books listed here: the *Tiriel* designs; the designs to Young, Dante, and Gray; the *Notebook* drawings; the *Blake-Varley Sketchbook*, and the illustrated pages of *The Four Zoas*. Examples of most prints, including illuminated books, are reproduced in Bindman's *Complete Graphic Works*, but the best catalogues of Blake's prints are those by Essick. Erdman's *Illuminated Blake* includes fuzzy monochrome images of one copy of each page of each illuminated book, describes variants, and offers detailed interpretations. The six-volume Blake Trust edition of *Blake's Illuminated Books* offers excellent color images of at least one copy of each page of all the books, careful transcriptions of the texts, and learned and thoughtful editorial apparatus. These are not as glorious as the earlier Blake Trust facsimiles produced at the Trianon Press, but they are even more useful for scholarly purposes. Dover Publications has issued inexpensive editions reprinted from the Trianon Press/Blake Trust facsimiles of the *Songs*, *Marriage*, and *America* and *Europe* (together). The images of illuminated pages and other Blake works at *The William Blake Archive* (see "Internet resources" on p. 293 below) presently rival or even surpass all printed reproductions in scholarly usefulness.

Bentley, G. E., Jr., ed. Vala *or* The Four Zoas: *A Facsimile of the Manuscript, and Transcript of the Poem and a Study of its Growth and Significance.* Oxford: Clarendon Press, 1963.
William Blake: Tiriel. Oxford: Clarendon Press, 1967.
Bindman, David, gen. ed. *Blake's Illuminated Books.* 6 vols. Princeton: The William Blake Trust and Princeton University Press; London: The William Blake Trust and Tate Gallery Publications, 1991–95. (The individual volumes are: *Jerusalem: The Emanation of the Giant Albion*, ed. Morton D. Paley; *Songs of Innocence and of Experience*, ed. Andrew Lincoln; *The Early Illuminated Books*, eds. Morris Eaves, Robert N. Essick, Joseph Viscomi; *The Continental Prophecies*, ed. Detlef W. Dörrbecker; *Milton a Poem and the Final Illuminated Works*, eds. Robert N. Essick and Joseph Viscomi; and *The Urizen Books*, ed. David Worrall. The plates from all the illuminated books, plus transcriptions of the texts in small type, have been reprinted in a single volume [Bindman, ed., London: Thames and Hudson, 2000] but it omits all the other useful scholarly and critical material from the individual volumes.)
The Complete Graphic Works of William Blake. London: Thames and Hudson; New York: Putnam, 1978.
The Divine Comedy: William Blake. Paris: Bibliothèque de l'Image, 2000.
Blake, William. *Blake's Water-Colours for the Poems of Thomas Gray: With Complete Texts.* New York: Dover, 2000.
Butlin, Martin. *The Blake-Varley Sketchbook.* London: Heinemann, 1969.

Butlin, Martin, ed. *The Paintings and Drawings of William Blake*. 2 vols. New Haven and London: Yale University Press, 1981.

Erdman, David V., ed. *The Illuminated Blake*. 1974. Reprint edn. New York: Dover, 1992.

The Notebook of William Blake: A Photographic and Typographic Facsimile. Oxford: Clarendon Press, 1973.

Essick, Robert N. *The Separate Plates of William Blake: A Catalogue*. Princeton: Princeton University Press, 1983.

William Blake's Commercial Book Illustrations: A Catalogue and Study of the Plates Engraved by Blake after Designs by Other Artists. Oxford: Clarendon Press, 1991.

Grant, John E., Edward Rose, and Michael J. Tolley, eds. *William Blake's Designs for Edward Young's* Night Thoughts. 2 vols. Oxford: Clarendon Press, 1980.

Keynes, Geoffrey ed. *The Marriage of Heaven and Hell*. London and New York: Oxford University Press, 1975.

Songs of Innocence and of Experience. London and New York: Oxford University Press, 1977.

Magno, Cettina Tramontano, and David V. Erdman, eds. The Four Zoas *by William Blake: a Photographic Facsimile of the Manuscript with Commentary on the Illuminations*. Lewisburg, PA: Bucknell University Press; London: Associated University Presses, 1987.

*Internet resources**

At any given time there are dozens of websites, most of them ephemeral, devoted to one aspect or another of Blake's work. The most important by far is *The William Blake Archive* (http://www.blakearchive.org), edited by Morris Eaves, Robert N. Essick, and Joseph Viscomi, which presently includes "electronic editions" of one or more copies of all Blake's illuminated books; these are especially useful, not only because the quality of the images rivals the best facsimiles, but because some images are unavailable anywhere else. At present the *Archive* includes an assortment of increasingly useful study tools, including an unannotated bibliography and a searchable electronic version of the complete text of Erdman's standard edition of Blake's poetry and prose, as well as links to several other sites. The most notable of these is Nelson Hilton's *Blake Digital Text Project* (http://www.english.uga.edu/wblake); it also offers Erdman's text together with a handy search engine that serves as a concordance.

* The publisher has used its best endeavors to ensure that the URLs for external websites referred to in this book are correct and active at the time of going to press. However, the publisher has no responsibility for the websites and can make no guarantee that a site will remain live or that the content is or will remain appropriate.

SEEING BLAKE'S ART IN PERSON

ALEXANDER GOURLAY

Much of Blake's visual art is both difficult to present and so fragile that handling and exhibition must be minimized, so few can study these works as he expected them to be seen. Museums and sometimes private galleries mount large and small exhibitions of Blake's pictures, prints, and books, but these are usually brief and entail such compromises as showing a single opening (one or two pages) of an illuminated book. Although some institutions such as Tate Britain in London almost always have a few important Blake pictures on display, those wishing to see particular Blakes must be willing to travel the world and seek special permission to study them individually.

Rules vary, but most major Blake collections will permit scholars, students, and some others to make appointments to study their holdings. If you want to see a particular picture or book, locate it by consulting Butlin's *Paintings and Drawings of William Blake*, or Bentley's *Blake Books* and *Blake Books Supplement* (for illuminated books and manuscripts and prints associated with particular books), or Essick's *The Separate Plates of William Blake* (for most other prints). Write to the appropriate administrator explaining why you are interested in seeing the piece (including if possible the shelf mark or acquisition number), summarize your project, suggest convenient times and dates for a visit, and describe your scholarly credentials; if you don't have any, include a letter of reference from an established researcher who can attest to your trustworthiness and seriousness about Blake study. You will have to make an appointment days or weeks in advance in some cases.

Bring a mechanical pencil or two (no pens) and a notebook – some collections allow portable computers and lightweight magnifying glasses, but you should check first. Few institutions permit private photography, but for a fee most will photograph works for you – you will need to seek separate permission if you wish to publish a photograph.

Selected collections with Blake holdings

(Asterisk* indicates a specialized catalogue of Blake materials)

Australia
　Melbourne: National Gallery of Victoria*

Austria
　Vienna: Albertina Museum

Germany
    Munich: Bayerische Staatsbibliothek (Bavarian State Library)
United Kingdom
    Cambridge: Fitzwilliam Museum,* King's College
    Glasgow: Pollok House, Glasgow University Library
    London: British Library, British Museum, Tate Gallery,* Victoria and Albert
        Museum
    Oxford: Ashmolean Museum, Bodleian Library
United States
    Austin: University of Texas
    Boston Area: Boston Museum of Fine Arts, Harvard University Libraries and Fogg
        Art Museum, Wellesley College
    Chicago: Newberry Library
    Cincinnati: Cincinnati Art Museum
    Hartford: Trinity College
    Los Angeles Area: Huntington Library and Art Galleries,* J. Paul Getty Museum
    New Haven: Yale Center for British Art, Yale University Libraries
    New York: Metropolitan Museum of Art, New York Public Library, Pierpont
        Morgan Library
    Philadelphia: Philadelphia Museum of Art, Rosenbach Museum and Library
    Princeton: Princeton University Library and Art Gallery
    Washington, DC: Library of Congress, National Gallery

INDEX

Abrams, M. H. 177, 181
Accusers 220, 265
Ackroyd, Peter 182
Aders, Charles 33
Adoration of the Kings 161
Ahania 221, 223
Albion 4, 30, 31–32, 105, 146–147, 165, 211,
224, 233, 246, 259, 260, 263
Albion Rose 91, 93, 220, 265
Albion's Angel 65
All Religions are One 3, 10, 88, 162, 191,
195–196, 198
Allegory of the Spiritual Condition of Man
104
America a Prophecy 9, 25, 42, 49, 58, 59–60,
64–65, 112, 114–115, 117–126, 129,
139, 157, 158, 210–212, 213
American Revolution 22, 37, 91, 120, 137,
158, 210, 213
Analytical Review 138
Ancient Britons 102, 236
Ancient of Days 156
Apuleius 173
Armitage, Thomas 20
Arnold, Matthew 170
Approach of Doom 41
Auden, W. H. 241
Augustan ideas 179
Augustine, St. 258
Austen, Jane 169

Babbage, Charles 115–116
Bacon, Francis 147, 213, 246
Barrell, John 182
Barry, James 22, 25, 86, 87, 88–90, 102, 135,
195
Basire, James 21, 23
Benevolence 220

Benjamin, Walter 177
Bentham, Jeremy 169
Berkeley, George 69, 173
Blake's annotations to 144
Beulah 146, 147, 151, 236, 242
Bible 24, 105, 110, 141–143, 153, 176, 234,
256, 258, 270
Blake's illustrations of 3, 27, 29, 31, 39,
40, 85, 88–90, 95–97, 108, 220–221,
236
Blake's view of 21, 144, 151, 165, 224,
234, 258
as Great Code of Art 11
of Hell 204
radical view of 141–143, 202
and state tricksters 110
Bion 231
Birmingham riot 137, 151
Blair, Robert 29
Blake's illustrations of 29, 40, 100–101,
121–126, 236, 253, 267
Blake, Catherine Armitage *mother* 20, 24,
53, 54
Blake, Catherine Boucher *wife* 7, 22, 28, 32,
34, 55, 57, 60, 235
Blake, James 20, 21
Blake, Robert 4, 20, 23–24, 41, 236
Blake, William 4, 8, 34–35
education and apprenticeship of 21
exhibitions of 21, 31, 40, 59, 101–103,
236, 253
insanity of 6, 257
letters of 19, 20, 133, 145, 220, 235, 257;
quoted 1, 9, 28, 35, 38–39, 58, 97, 131
as mythmaker 3–4, 8, 12, 13, 24, 25, 26,
143, 145, 155, 174, 215, 224–225, 251,
256, 258, 260
oral formulas of 258

CAMBRIDGE COMPANIONS TO LITERATURE